EXPLORER RACE
Creators and Friends
Mechanics of Creation

Creator, Friends and Mechanics,
with Zoosh through Robert Shapiro

Light Technology Publishing

ISBN 0-929385-97-7

Published by
Light Technology Publishing
P.O. Box 1526
Sedona, AZ 86339
1-800-450-0985

Printed by
MI**ION
PO**IBLE
COMMERCIAL
PRINTING
P.O. Box 1495
Sedona, AZ 86339

Other Books by Robert Shapiro

The Explorer Race Series
The Explorer Race
ETs and the Explorer Race
Explorer Race: Origins and the Next 50 Years
Explorer Race: Creators and Friends—Mechanics of Creation
Explorer Race: Particle Personalities
Explorer Race and Beyond

The Sedona Vortex Guidebook
(with other channels)

Shining the Light Series
(co-channeled with Arthur Fanning)
Shining the Light
Shining the Light II: The Battle Continues
Shining the Light III: Humanity Gets a Second Chance
Shining the Light IV: Humanity's Greatest Challenge

Contents

Introduction by Zoosh

September 10, 1997

Now that you have a greater understanding of who you are in the larger sense, it is necessary to remind you of where you came from, the true magnificence of your being, to have some of your true peers talk to you. You must understand that you are creators in training, and yet you were once a portion of Creator. One could certainly say, without being magnanimous, that you are still a portion of Creator, yet you are training for the individual responsibility of being a creator, to give your Creator a coffee break.

This book will give you peer consultation. It will allow you to understand the vaster qualities and help you remember the nature of the desires that drive any creator, the responsibilities to which that creator must answer, the reaction any creator must have to consequences and the ultimate reward of any creator. This book will help you appreciate all of the above and more. I hope you will enjoy it and understand that maybe more will follow.

Could you give a simple definition of your use of the term "creator"?

God. How much simpler can I get? You can understand creativity and you are not at all uncomfortable with that idea. "Creator" is perhaps a root of the word "creative." Yet if I were to say, "You can understand being godlike," most people would not be able to identify with that. Therefore I'd rather use the term "creator" instead of "God" because "God" is so much more distant to the average person's perception. I think people can accept being creative and even feel good about it, but the average reader of these Explorer Race books is less likely to be able to identify with being godlike.

Introduction by Progenitor of Zoosh

July 11, 1996

This is Progenitor. There is an awakening amongst human beings on this planet that is equal to the *total consciousness* throughout and beyond this universe! This is quite a fact if you think about it. This planet, like a tree's taproot, is the receiver of the sum total of all life. This means that *the conscious beings on this planet*—plants, animals, stone, the planet herself and people—*are focusing the sum total of all consciousness at this time.* This is going to last for about two and a half to three years, and it will have certain effects. First I will speak of the physiological effects so you will not be concerned.

You will from time to time feel the impact of an unknown and untraceable electrical field that will seem to stimulate you beyond the level you might normally experience. This means that you will sometimes have trouble sleeping.

You will have moments when you feel you are present in more than one place. This will be experienced as inspirations or visions of other places while your physical body is somewhere else. It might also be experienced (this is important) as sudden shared feelings associated with a loved one, whether they are with you or not. You might also have feelings from a counterpart, if you have another version of your soul on the planet.

More likely you will begin to share physiological feelings with other portions of your created soul line on other galaxies, even other universes. This is a very delicate effort. This could mean that a tree on this planet might suddenly feel the physical feelings of itself on another planet where it is a bush or a grass plant or a water plant or a member of a species that grows in liquid ice (not as cold as ice here, but cool and viscous).

Animals, including domestic animals and pets, might experience themselves in one of their many forms. This might cause them to behave oddly sometimes. When you don't expect it, they might sit down and seem to be meditating or sleeping more than usual—and *deeply*. This can also happen to farm animals. Do not be alarmed; these will be brief moments, and they will be up and around again soon.

But for human beings we have a phenomenon you can look into. You might find yourself experiencing actual physical feelings associated with one of your incarnated selves on some other planet. It will be at least a humanoid being, but it might well be a being who is obviously not human. This is purposely happening for you now. You might have moments when you are "phasing" (when you are sitting down or doing something relaxing so you don't have any responsibilities in the moment) and feel you are someone or something else. It will not have a lasting psychological influence; it will be a feeling that comes and goes.

This is being done now because it is vitally important (and the universe and beyond is cooperating in this effort) that you have the feelings of other beings (yes, spiritual beings) who are in those moments meditating. They know not why, by the way. They will suddenly feel the need to sit down and meditate (as you would call it) or relax (as some of them might say). They will feel themselves expanding.

And you will feel that. You might feel yourself expanding, but more likely you will feel these curious physiological symptoms. You might have the feeling or vision of your arm being very long and thin and perhaps yellow or brown or purple or greenish fading into white. Or your foot might feel odd, as if there is a claw where your heel is and a very high arch, like the foot of an ostrich. (There *are* beings who have clawlike feet, or at least something that has a bony appearance.) Or you might be sitting down and suddenly feel as if you were looking down on your surroundings from a great height, as if you were suddenly twelve or fifteen feet tall.

You might feel inordinately thin. Many beings on other planets are spare, as you call it, carrying no extra poundage. You might feel curiously lighter in frame, which might connect with a portion of yourself at a lighter, less dense dimension. You might feel as if you could bounce across the floor and leap very high, not unlike your astronauts on the Moon.

These and many other phenomena will phase in and out for you in moments when it is safe. There might be other feelings: occasional moments (nothing serious) of something like a nausea that will come and go, as if you are slightly nauseous but not quite. Or you might suddenly feel very hot, even in the winter. You might be wearing your parka out in the snow, relaxing for a moment, then suddenly get very hot and sweaty. (That's all right; unzip your parka for a moment and it will pass.) Don't assume that it's permanent or that you have a fever; it will probably pass within a few minutes.

The thing to remember here is that these beings are also feeling *you*. Remember that your role as the Explorer Race will bring you into contact with many beings, and they must have their own visions. They must know who is coming. Some of them will become very excited and pleased at the prospect of feeling you coming. It will be very much like an inspiration, a vision, "feeling a part of myself coming here," they might say (wherever "here" might be). Others might feel concerned and immediately consult their leaders or teachers. Either way, it will put them on notice that something is changing, and that is a good thing.

I speak to you of this now because as we begin this new book, we will be hearing from many, many beings all over the universe and sometimes even beyond. The energy of some of them will be so unusual and strange that individuals in this room might feel odd for a moment. It is also even possible that those of you reading this book might feel unusual. You might suddenly feel sleepy and have to lie down and take a nap. (Therefore this is a good book to read when you're going to bed at night, perfect for your nighttime reading.) You might also suddenly feel very stimulated for no particular reason, so keep a tablet and a pencil handy for making notes. You might get visions of pictures or places. You might even have a sensation of fragrances.

All these things and more are possible as we begin this new level of the project to introduce everyone to everyone else. This is the leading edge of greetings, the connection between all beings. This is your introduction to the universe and all who live within it.

What is your experience? Progenitor of Zoosh—Zoosh says you're the root, the basic core of who he is.

Yes.

And yet he has a separate existence from you?

No, not separate. Like a flower that might grow from a root. I like to think of Zoosh as the flower.

[Laughs.] I know, but what do you do?

I support the flower. The flower grows, but it does not live on light alone, though it does get supported by the light. The root goes into the earth and brings in water and nutrients from the soil. So I bring in nutrients of light, energy and a composite made up of compressed cosmic energy (which is the stuff of life) and a form of what I call *liquid love*, which is an eternal substance that will give Zoosh a leg up (this is not the proper metaphor) even if something is difficult for him. [Laughs.]

All right. If he's a friend of the Creator, you have your roots in what? How far beyond this creation? How far can you see?

The best way I can explain it to you is that I, as some others, have existed before the idea of creators dawned on anyone to try—existence for its own sake, *being*. If you had the opportunity to personally exist in the miasma of cosmic energy and liquid love, it would be quite sufficient, I assure you. Yet when one of our number says, "Why don't we do something with this?" we say, "Oh well, let's appoint some personalities to do something." Thence come creators.

Are you a creator?

I have not done that, no; I have observed it being done.

Do we each have a progenitor if we could get to the level of Zoosh? Do we have someone beyond that is different but still connected?

If we trace the leaves back to the twigs back to the branches and so on down to the root, I must say that everyone does have that at some point. Sometimes a person will have a life that is designed for some arcane purpose, perhaps not necessarily serving the overall needs or expectations of the soul group. In this case one might not feel particularly connected at any time with its progenitor. Yet when that life is over one *will* connect in deep sleep, perhaps, or deep states of consciousness and is often given that sustenance of liquid love and cosmic energy to keep going.

You might ask yourself (and I think you have at times) when you see or hear about someone who has experienced great tragedy, more than any one person ought to be called on to bear, "How can they go on? I never could have done this." But very often they go on because at some stage of deep sleep they will have been fed that liquid love and cosmic energy. And they go on and complete their cycle.

In this search here, like everyone, you're one of the roots of one of the friends of the Creator of the system. But almost everyone in this system was created by this Creator, so all their roots would lead back to Him, whereas yours do not.

Well, you might say that that is true, but certainly you might also say that the Creator's roots lead back also. So everyone is one; I have never seen any exception to this. I have no reason to believe there is an exception.

How can we here best be given more of that liquid love you spoke of?

It's not that you need to be given it so much. When you have the need, when your heart aches or when, as is the case sometimes, you are very lonely and go to sleep feeling that loneliness, in the deepest levels of your sleep (not always, but sometimes) you are given liquid love and cosmic energy. You wake up and feel like, "Well, this is another day," and go on, really forgetting that lonely feeling. It is because you are loved that you are nourished. Your Creator knows how difficult life is here for most people. Even those considered the privileged class still have great difficulties and sufferings, often unrecognized by others because they seem to be wealthy. They also are given this bounty that feeds, nourishes and sustains them when they need it.

How is this different from that percentage of love, originally 90%, that has been preserved for us and that is now being dribbled to us little by little?

It is different because just the tiniest, most infinitesimal particle of this liquid love would, were you to experience it consciously, change your life forever. You would feel nothing but unconditional love for all beings, and you would essentially become a loving, cosmic being on Earth, which . . .

. . . is useless for the Explorer Race?

Yes, and while this might be your natural state of being elsewhere, we do not wish to interfere with you. At the deepest levels of your sleep when you are connected to other places, and when this is allowed and you remember who you are, then it can be given to you. It remains in your body to nourish you, but at what you would call the unconscious level.

You said the expansion of consciousness on this planet was equal to the rest of the consciousness of creation?

Yes, and beyond.

What is the Explorer Race—one-tenth of one percent of the rest of the creation?

Certainly not that much—significantly smaller. The main thing to know is that many people's growth cycle is quite dependent upon what you show them that you can do here. This is a total experiment; it is the suspension of all normal (politically speaking) checks and balances, and life is allowed to run wild. Sometimes wonderful things happen, sometimes terrible things. To the extent that wonderful things happen, they are ofttimes utilized by those advocates on other planets who say, "Look, we must grow. Look, they did it without any support from anyone!" You see, those advocates who want their cultures to grow need support, too. On their planets there are no strident politicians and advocates, but usually philosophers—spiritual beings—not unlike a college professor or even an elementary teacher who might bring out the best in a student through encouragement and sometimes even a challenge.

So those of us who came here ultimately had a deep, deep faith that in the end it would work out well. Was that what we saw? Or was it just for fun that we came, just for the adventure?

I think some of you might have come for the adventure, but I think most of you came as spiritual beings (core spiritual beings, at least). I think you knew that it was worth the effort. However, some of you made a statement, a feeling that needed to be revamped (and it has been recently): that you felt it was worth the effort *no matter what the cost*. We had to change that because there have been some extreme costs lately. So now it's moderated a bit: "It's worth the effort, period." It is worth the effort, but we have had to take away that other element.

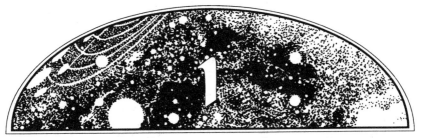

Andastinn, Prototype of Insect Beings

July 11, 1996

I am an elder of the race of beings living on the planet Destinteh (des´tin-tay). My name is Andastinn (an-das´tin). Our species are the prototype, the original beings of many of what you would call the insect beings. In our philosophy and intelligence we could most identify with those creatures on your planet that you call ants. While our sense of teamwork is perhaps not as obvious as theirs, we are not as small. [Chuckles.] (Don't try and step on *us*—you would be surprised!)

We are uprights like you. We do not have many legs like the many-legged creatures that we approve of on your planet. We have, like you, two appendages in the upper part of our body and two in the lower. We can walk on all fours [chuckles] or stand upright. We exist primarily at this time to provide philosophical encouragement for beings such as ants.

Many Earth species Leaving

Many of the creatures that you have taken for granted (they were here when you got here and they'll be here when you leave, is how you feel) are returning to their original planets. Some will do so as if by magic; others will suddenly die for no reason. Your scientists will come up with a reason, but there will be many of them that suddenly *pouf!*—go into spirit. So we consult with them, we support them, we provide them with the philosophical nurturing they need to reorient themselves to being respected beings.

On your planet they are like "unidentified walking objects." [Chuckles.] It is so ironic, is it not? Many of you wait for the ETs to come, yet they're all around you! So we help them make their spiritual changes. We even send emissaries to tell them, "This is how it might be."

The Ant Beings

Down below the ground many ants gather. When they know they are alone they act differently. [Chuckles.] When children know they are alone they act differently, don't they? (So do adults, I might add.) When they are gathered in one of their large rooms, like a meeting hall, one of us will project there as a white-light version of one of them. It is always essential for the teacher to appear to be one of your own kind, as some of your mystical teachers have done; they are recognized as being like you but different. When we appear in white light as one of them, we communicate telepathically with feelings and with visions we give them, images to remind them of who they are.

They have been living here for so long that they have come to think they have been forgotten. They have ancient stories that tell them they came from somewhere, but until we started coming to visit them recently, they forgot where. They have been here for so long that generations have been lost due to trauma (which might have been a flood, a volcano, an earthquake or, in more modern times, construction projects); whole lineages were lost forever that way, along with their stories and philosophy. We must bring it back to them.

We remind them of their lineage, where they are from. Because they are very ceremonial in their nature, they do things because it is how they've always been done. In that sense they are traditionalists. [Laughs.] We remind them why they do what they do, what it has to do with their home planet and when they can go home. We have been doing this lately with ants, with honeybees, with wasps and with (you'll be happy to hear this) the fleas!

Many of these beings look very different in their form at home. Here they must be very small so that they can go about their business relatively unnoticed by human beings and thus be protected. Because they're small they can go underground and usually be safe. On their home planet they are proportionately much bigger. And because they are safe there, they don't have to hide or go underground. Some of them live in very large underground cavelike structures simply because it is traditional, but also because it preserves the surface of the planet for future generations and does not destroy it. They find underground caves or dig a little bit where they feel welcome.

I speak to you about these beings tonight because they offer so much to you by example, and there have been those among long-lived peoples on this planet who have studied them and imitated them in ways that are known to travelers' mythology and somewhat even to anthropologists, so this is not a complete surprise to all of you.

So I say greetings to you tonight. I come by invitation of the Progenitor of Zoosh because he says you are now ready to hear this. Progenitor of Zoosh—he-she-it—you figure that out. Do you have questions?

Is your planet in the Milky Way system?

If you could draw a 45-degree angle to the Moon and then bounce off it like a ball at a 60-degree angle for about 400 million light-years, you would come to our planet. We are not likely in the near future to be seeing you, in terms of your visiting us [chuckles], but it is certainly possible, if we are called upon, that in your visions or dreams you might see one of our white-light beings talking to some of the creatures on Earth who are really extraterrestrials.

Komodo Dragons and Crocodiles

Sometimes we might be seen as one of these big Komodo dragon lizards. We know those beings because they are very misunderstood, and we're planning to talk to them even though they're not insects. We have a little flexibility.

We might also talk to crocodiles, because we've been asked to. It seems that the reptilian beings are having some difficulty communicating to their cousins here. I think there is some kind of radiated energy coming from your planet. Perhaps it's in the form of fear of reptilian beings, which has been fostered and encouraged yet is based on nothing associated with the beings themselves. Of course, as they manifest on your planet they are not all pleasant to human beings, but some of them are harmless, you know. (You know what they say: If there's a big animal you're afraid of, walk the other way.) So we've been requested to do some extra projects that are not exactly in our line.

Was it the Tenth Planet beings who are having problems connecting with the crocodiles?

No, we were not asked by people from here [this solar system]. We were asked by other beings who sometimes travel to see us; they are more of what I call a kind of loose-knit network of philosophers. When encouragement is needed, when one needs to know about one's lineage, whether it be a personal lineage (a family) or a species lineage, often we are called upon because this is what we do. If we are needed to speak to some type of being that we can stretch to speak to, such as this large lizard, we will try. If we can do it, we will. We would probably not be able to stretch to speak to a rock or a tree, and it would not be necessary for us to communicate to human beings because you *have* beings who can do that. However, we experimented with it, and after we discovered we could do this, we arrived in the diamond portal. (I mention the diamond portal because it is always associated with spirit beings; I believe some of your people know about this.)

Where is it?

There isn't just one. The diamond portal is flexible. It is usually utilized only by beings of reasonably evolved consciousness.

Can you tell us about both your consciousness and the social life of your planet—some things that might interest us?

How We Live and Travel

Well, it is in our nature to have an experience not unlike your inspiration. It is not what I'd call a universal mind, as discussed theoretically by some individuals, but more as an *access* to inspiration. If we need inspiration (especially if we have to stretch to communicate with some species of being not directly associated with us), we can ask for inspiration and receive it right away, immediately [snaps fingers]. (We don't actually have fingers—this is new to me, the experience of fingers.) Our people have the ability to work together to call for inspiration.

Now, this might interest you: Sometimes, if inspiration is needed and it comes through but is not enough (maybe the project is very big or requires a significant commitment on our part), we will gather at least ten of our beings together to form a circle, touching each other with our upper appendages (I think you do this sometimes). We will create a tone. Now, it's not exactly a tone that you would associate with a musical note, but I will try to reproduce it. One moment. [Makes long vibrating tone.]

It is an effect not dissimilar to musical instruments that use reedlike devices, so it is a vibrating sound. This sound helps us totally unite, so when we ask for inspiration as a larger group, it comes more powerfully to all members of the group, who receive it at the same time but in their own way (see, we are individuals). After this meditation or even a prayer (because we are certainly asking for something), we relax and speak to each other of what we had received, then we compare. Sometimes we receive pictures, sometimes thoughts, other times feelings and other times the sensation of a substance. We compare and put all this together at the end to give us a better picture of what we can and might do, you understand.

We do not have families as you do. We have incarnations not so terribly often. I realize that your population does not have a fixed number; it grows and expands, then shrinks for various reasons and grows again. Our population for our whole planet (we have other beings on the planet, but not that many) is probably no more than 50,000. I believe this might be because we need to have a relatively uncomplicated existence so we can serve the sometimes complex needs of others. Having a complex civilization would perhaps create a distraction.

You go all over the universe, not just to the Earth?

Oh, yes. When we are called upon to go to other universes, we travel there in light; it is the simplest, fastest and most comfortable way.

We have not been called often, but several times. If great numbers of us are called, sometimes we travel in something that would look like a compressed light wave. (I think a few of you have even seen pictures like this.) Occasionally we pass through here in one of our compressed light waves. As an individual traveling, we might be seen as a small dot of light. But with many of us it would be like a line, and perhaps the line would be like white light. Sometimes it would be almost squared off at the corners; other times it might be sort of rounded.

This is not light in the speed that we know it, I understand, because you would not take 400 million years to travel to here . . .

No, no, no . . .

So can you explain what light you're speaking about?

This would be something that is seen as light if you were sensitive and could see us. If you had an instrument that could pick us up, it would register as white light, but it is more akin to an instantaneous capacity. And we travel—it's hard to put this in your words now.

Do you fold space-time?

That's time travel; our travel is a little different from time travel. Even time travel is slow compared to this. We never simply go out and travel; we're always asked. And when we are asked to go somewhere, we are given descriptions of the beings and the planet so we can prepare. We focus on that. Because we know where it is and who we're going to help, we travel instantaneously, in significantly less time than it would take to travel in time. If we traveled in time to one of our normal destinations (anywhere from 100 to 800 million light-years distant), say 700 million light-years away, it might take us (by your calculation of time and by our older method of time travel) 7.5 seconds to get there.

The principle of attraction is the best way I can describe it in your understanding: It takes us about 1/10,000th of a second to get there. The advantage of this quicker travel is that there is less dispersion of our energy along the way. The longer you maintain the state of traveling in time, a certain consumption of energy is required. Using this other means, there is no consumption of energy whatsoever that we have been able to measure.

What kind of history do you have? How far back do you remember? What is your lineage? Where did you come from? What other earlier life forms have you inhabited in spirit? Can you tell us some of the things that would interest us?

Me personally?

You personally and your people.

Our History and Yours

I would have to go back to before where I am now. I believe that in your universe I have always been what I am now. I didn't mention it before, but we are basically immortal.

You existed when this creation was created?

We were created with this creation. Often beings who might have a role like ours would be needed immediately, so Creator said, "I need help."

So you've been conscious since the beginning.

Yes. Before that we were elsewhere as a species. It's hard to measure it in time, is it not? But I would have to say that for three generations before our service in this universe, we were in a universe that is beyond this one (I believe it is about two expansions beyond this one), and we lived, I believe, about three generations (I'm calling it generations, but as immortal beings we're not reproducing) and in a service role similar to that of teachers who appear as light but teach what those who are in service need to know. Before that I believe I was a portion of a creator, so there's no point in going before that.

You have watched as this entire creation unfolded?

Oh yes.

Earth's Arcturan Soul

Can you tell us from your perspective what the role of this planet is?

As near as I can tell, my understanding is that this planet is designed to stimulate change. As discussed by others, this planet was borrowed from the galaxy Sirius. This planet's purpose is to stimulate change in all those who incarnate here, but when you go out beyond the boundaries of your planet into your travels in your universe, you are intended to stimulate change there also.

One might ask, "Is that not similar to what happens on Arcturus?" And I would reply, "Oh yes, very similar." That is because the light existed within the Arcturus system before this planet existed. When this planet was evolving, creating itself on Sirius, it was asking for a higher purpose than simply its own life cycle and being a host for others. So it was granted an Arcturan soul. Thus all that occurs here is affected by Sirius (because it is obviously a Sirius planet, a water being, even though it is in your system, having water, ice and so on) and also by Arcturus. Change is a function of your life because the very soul of this planet is Arcturan in nature. Our perception of you is that change is what you are and what you bring to others. It is an opportunity, you know, that you offer to others. They are not required to partake in this opportunity, but it is available to them, is it not?

Our Enjoyment and Our Service

What is your greatest enjoyment?

Ah, thank you. I believe our greatest pleasure comes when we are speaking with various races (such as those I have mentioned on your planet and others, speaking to a great assemblage or a single individual) and there comes that moment of recognition when an individual we are communicating with suddenly realizes who they are and why they do what they do, and that their ways of being are not random acts of necessary survival but a sacred and holy dance from the source of their true selves. When that moment of enlightenment happens for them, oh, that is a wonderful thing for us! That is truly fulfillment. We see beings who are lost and confused suddenly become aware of who they are, and they are never the same again. They are happy with who they are; they feel good about themselves. As you might say, it improves their self-image and they grow. It's not unlike a child of your own being praised for something it knew it had done well and felt good about by people it felt good about, in that way learning who it and its people are. That kind of feeling—it is wondrous!

On this planet you're bringing the lineages of who they are to these beings, but on other planets, beings haven't forgotten. Why do you go to other systems and planets? What calls you to them?

When we go to other planets where everybody knows who they are, it is ofttimes to prepare the beings on those planets to go through some major change. Perhaps the planet is falling apart; if everyone can move and be evacuated, we are not called in. But if something sudden is happening—perhaps they are caught in a storm of particles—many spirit beings including ourselves will go there and guide them to their next level. Sometimes (this will interest you more) these beings might be going en masse to some other place, such as here on this planet at a time of tremendous change, and we help them. We prepare them for this change and we will put deep into their consciousness the memory of who they are that will come out in their lifetimes—in their dreams and in their visions, if they are a sacred people—and they will accept this happily. If they are simply imaginative, they will enjoy it.

So sometimes we are called upon to go to places where the people are evolved, yes, but where major change is happening. Occasionally we will be called upon to go see a specific individual who might be called to a higher spiritual purpose in which he will serve a wide variety of potentials. We will go and speak with him. We take whatever form is pleasing to beings and speak of all we know that interests them. We will not just talk to them about whatever we know, but we will prepare them.

Our Appearance

Are you on a dimensional level, or are you in a life form?

Oh, I suppose you could say both. If I had to state a dimension, it would be perhaps eleven.

So you don't have what we would call physical bodies?

We feel as if we have physical bodies, but if you could see us you would perceive us as having lightbodies. Yet we can, like you, touch ourselves, although we also have the capacity to reach inside ourselves if that should be necessary (which, I might add, never has been for me).

If you were to look in a mirror, what would you see? How tall, how . . .

I understand; you want some description. If I were looking in a mirror and using your measurements, and if I were standing on my appendages upright as you do, I would be perhaps seven-and-a-half feet tall. I would have a body that in my native form has sort of a large head that comes to a narrow point here. I have like a shell around me—I think you have beings like that here on this planet—and the rest of me is on the inside. [Laughs.] Where else? We have something that is very much like a tail, but if upright would not reach to the ground. It's hard to describe.

You don't have opposable digits. You don't really use your hands.

No, because we do not need to build or re-create things in order to survive. We do not need to cut down trees to build houses.

You just manifest them?

Yes. I might add that we do not eat and we have no waste matter. When one does not eat and has no waste matter and does not have to fear the environment, one can leave the environment rather as it is, you know.

Leisure Activity: Accessing New Knowledge

When you're not being called to help, what is your normal life situation?

Oh, we've always been called to help, but do you mean when for some reason I as an individual or another one of my people isn't involved in some project? We examine other universes. We might recline, as you would, and ask to see and feel places we have not been that would be appropriate and useful for us to know about. We might not have been called there, but perhaps someday we would. This can be added to the body knowledge. For instance, if we are called there, then whoever has meditated on this wisdom will immediately provide it to the body knowledge.

If one of you knows it, then everybody knows it?

No, no, it's not like that, because we do not choose to distract others if they are working on something. It is more that if one of us knows it, then any others who *need* to know it would essentially access the individual who knows it through a particular tone or harmonic that would suddenly stimulate that memory within us.

When the memory comes up for no reason, we know that someone is accessing it. Then we just experience what we experienced before. The more we experience it—visualize it, see it, smell it, taste it, whatever—the easier and quicker and more efficient we make it for whoever is calling up those knowledges and wisdoms within us. So we cooperate until it feels that there is no further call, and in that way it is added to the body knowledge. Perhaps four or five individuals are needed at the same time—or one. But it is still referred to as the body knowledge, because it is available at any time for anyone.

It is not that if one knows it, they all know it. I know the beings you're talking about there [Zetas], but we do not function that way. When beings function in that way they usually have a very slowly evolving mental consciousness.

Is yours evolving, or is it always existent? Do you look forward to some change as consciousness expands now?

No, I understand you. People look forward to a change if they are not satisfied with their present. But you can find people amongst your own races of beings here who are so happy in what they are doing that the idea of a change is not something they would look forward to at all. So we are happy in what we are doing, and we have always been fulfilled in this work. We do not feel desirous of going on to some unknown when we are happy in what we are doing here. If that should happen, then we will go.

But you don't see it as part of your process?

No, no, no. What we are *doing* is our function.

What Brings Teachers and Assistants to Earth

About your coming here: Did each one of the species ask, or was there some intermediary who asked on behalf of all the species here?

That's a good question. Most times there is an intermediary. When people (human beings, for example) ask for something, they often don't know who to ask. You know, they might pray or entreat or even look up to the stars and beg for assistance or even say, "I must know something and I do not know how to know this; please let me know this," or use many other ways.

When this happens, usually an intermediary (perhaps someone who's being prayed to, perhaps a cosmic teacher of this individual or even a whole group of individuals) will put out the call. Unlike picking up a phone and calling somebody else, they put out the call energetically, and it expands to all reaches of the universe at an increasing rate. It goes out slowly, then faster and faster and faster until it comes to those who can serve this need. We will go if we are the ones who can serve this need and if there are apparently no other individuals who will be answering the call. Sometimes there might be more than one group of individuals who answers it; in that case the cosmic teacher will request: "You, not you" or "You, then you," something like that, do you understand? A prior progression of some sort. Or it might be, "All of you at once, please." Then we will go.

In the case of Earth, can you tell us who asked you as an intermediary to come and assist here with different species?

Oh, you mean as we're doing now. I see. This was Enjenofjitzeketzen. This is an angelic being who looks after beings who are basically unknown for their best qualities by human beings. The angelics take a great interest in your evolution, your coming of age, and they know that all beings are here not only for their own purposes, but also to enlighten you. When you have not yet been enlightened by beings (bees, wasps, ants, whatever), then this particular angelic being will call us because they want to increase the strength of these beings. They want to increase their endurance so that they will remain here on this planet and that someday you might have the inspiration of who they are and what they have to offer, even creating a myth around them. And some myths *have* been created, much to the benefit and honoring of them. So this was an angelic.

Is there anything else the readers would be interested in knowing about you or your group?

Perhaps the most important thing for you to know is how meaningful what you are doing on this planet of yours is for the rest of the universe. I know it is very difficult sometimes—some of you live in really challenging circumstances—to remain alive. You just want to say, "I want it to be over with." Please know that however long your lives last, you are loved and cherished by all beings that I know of, and your service here as a human being on this planet will not go unnoticed. Everything you do here will be considered when you leave, not only for your own personal growth but for the evolution of the species as a whole.

This is a wonderful project that is happening here, and it is a worthy project of your souls. I know it is very challenging to be in these bodies that are not always very comfortable and sometimes seem restrictive. Perhaps the hardest part is having to forget who you are in your more immortal souls. So we salute you for making that sacrifice and assure you that you are appreciated. For now I will say, "Good life."

Kazant, a Timekeeper

July 18, 1996

am Kazant (I suppose K-a-z-a-n-t). I am from planet in distant past. We are unique in that we have perhaps, we would think, no more than five personalities on this planet. From those five personalities have been cloned enough individuals to maintain the planet's technology, but no more than perhaps 1400. The planet, however, is at least three times the size of your planet, and it had been used before we got to it, apparently by a highly technological society who took everything with them when they left. I don't think they had anything to do with you, but *we* have a little something to do with you. We are so far from your galaxy that if we had your strongest telescopes here (let's include the strongest telescopes on the drawing table, not even the ones out in space), we would need ten of them to come even close to seeing your sun.

The Crystal in Our Planet; the Boundaries of Time

We have perhaps a unique technology. We are situated in the center of the planet. There is a faceted crystal here that is free-floating at the exact center. It has at least 675 facets, and it is about three miles across.

We are a little different from you. We do not walk about, but we have the capacity to float about. We do not require to eat, drink or anything like that, but we do have a humanoid countenance, though I do not think our legs could sustain us if we were in your gravity zone.

It is our job to program, coordinate and synchronize time. Some places in your galaxy utilize time. Yours is one. Perhaps you might say that all places utilize time, but that is not so. In some places where civilizations are underground, time is not so much a factor because there is no need to divide day and night. It is experience, so we do not regulate them. Other places are also out of the boundaries of time. One gets out of the boundaries of time around the seventh dimension because at that point there is no need for time, only experience. But [in] third, fourth, fifth and to some extent sixth dimension (sometimes second dimension) we regulate time—it is our job. We do not interfere, but we know about all that happens at places where there is time. [We] draw a chart and even extrapolate such time.

We feel that it might be necessary now for your civilization to begin to take over some of what we do. We think that perhaps you will have the capacity to do this soon. We are going to invest your readers with time coefficient for fourth dimension. Time coefficient will not be given as a formula because there are those on your planet who would like to slow it down. But we will give it experientially.

An Exercise to Draw Fourth Dimension to You

Now, in order to draw fourth dimension to you, I recommend this: Those of you who can look at surface of a natural river, lake, stream, do that—most preferable. Those of you who do not have this available to you, try to collect rainwater. Look at surface of that in vessel. [It] will not work with water that has been treated or is captured water. Water [is] necessary requirement. Is possible to pollute water, is possible to change chemical formula, but water has *spirit* that cannot be corrupted.

Water is very much like lens focusing light. Because it has so much water, your planet cannot be stopped from going to fourth dimension. If water were to disappear overnight (of course, all life would disappear too), then planet would stay where you are. I feel safe in saying that, because those who would try to stop you from going to fourth dimension wouldn't want to do *that*.

So look at water, okay? Take preferably left hand, touch surface of water very slightly. Make certain [your] palm touches the water. Bend back fingers if you can naturally. So we want the palm on the water (there is energy spot there in the palm); touch the surface of the water very lightly. While you are touching water, hold picture in your mind's eye—or if you are unimaginative visually (not to worry), say words that remind you of fourth-dimensional experience: beauty, love, peace, calm, whatever—like that. Move palm up to third eye, pulling back on the fingers, and hold for about 30 seconds (no need to time it—you will know), all the while maintaining picture or chant associated with your vision of fourth dimension.

Next, repeat same procedure, touching heart area or heart chakra (either one) 30 seconds, then back again to touch the surface of the water. Then go to second chakra, touch 30 seconds (best to touch skin, so summertime most likely). All the while we want palm on body, but better not to have fingers touching body. (I will explain in a moment.) After 30 seconds (35 seconds okay, 40 seconds too, but at least 30 seconds and less than one minute) touch surface of water. Thank water in whatever way you choose. Pull hand up; thank hand. Then you are done.

Now, why not fingers? Fingers represent free will, because human being without fingers necessarily dependent somewhat on others for assistance. Granted, can become very independent with much training. But symbol of fingers and thumb—yes, means free will. But cannot will planet to go to a higher dimension with you alive on it, so must use faith, request, this meditation, also known as prayer.

We recommend this because it is associated with the history of your planetary cycle. Your planet is from galaxy of Sirius originally, and this is part of prayer meditation on Sirius done to preserve beauty. Done with both hands there, but you are not in Sirius now, so must use hand of request, hand of prayer, which is left hand. If cannot use left hand for some reason, use back of your right hand—next best thing. Just do the best you can; not easy to turn hand over, but do the best you can.

Now, our job is to coordinate time for every individual place, utilizing the position of all the stars not only in your galaxy but reference points to other galaxies. Full-time job, I assure you! That's why we don't sleep, eat, can't take time off. Takes five of us and our clones. Granted, we direct clones, but it's easy to direct clones that are essentially you because what I think, I can easily have assimilated by my equals. (Clones are not servants; they are my equals.)

Green Blood and Reptilian Cousins

In this situation I speak to you, send greetings, let you know that those who would interfere will be stopped by the true nature of life. I will say this also: There is an element of your body that cannot be stopped from moving to the fourth dimension. For starters, the natural color of your blood is green (but this does not mean you are chlorophyll-based, so skip over that one) because natural atmosphere [is] associated more with nitrogen, carbon dioxide, a few other things. It is a strain for your physical bodies and soul bodies to incorporate and utilize oxygen and so on—struggle. So liquid blood is first cousin of water. Not an accident churches often use this as a symbol.

Blood is natural gravitation to higher dimension. Blood wants to be green; hard to hold red, and is like magnet—naturally pulled. Is unnatural for blood to be red. When blood no longer exposed to oxygen in living being (of course, living being cease to be living for long! [chuckles]), in natural system blood is green. Skin, I might say, is green also. Oh, don't be afraid. You are afraid: "Oh! Reptilians! Run and hide!" say you. (I talk like you a little bit.) But that [green skin] is because [you are] cousins, but more about that later.

Now, the true reality: Who are reptilians, eh? I'll give you an example, describe pertinent first-cousin reptilian to you Earth people, yes. Scare you a little bit, but you can take it. Now describe perfectly for you: Here is reptilian—has either (little variety, not much) wavy or fairly straight light brown or light blond hair (light blond meaning not quite platinum, but close); blue eyes—oh yes!—typified by Pleiadians, but guess again.

True reptilian first cousins [are] blue-eyed blondes, eh? Reptilian, though. Light green skin, no scales. Scales—this is silly; reptilian human beings don't need scales. Only need scales if they live underwater, okay? They don't. They have fingers, even fingernails like you. Look very much like you, but light green skin. First cousins. On Sirius some of your cousins look like this, although the ones that used to live on Earth did not look like that—were brown, tall, long arms, long legs. I think your Zoosh has spoken of them.

Now, these people—these reptilian beings—you would find very beautiful to look at. Like I say, light green skin (well, you get used to it, you know) and not much body hair, okay? But on the surface everything else almost the same. Minor differences, but since this is a G-rated book I won't go into them, huh? (I could make a joke. It's a stretch, but I'm learning.)

Now, they're mostly the same [as you], okay? Things work pretty much the same too, but birth has to be with external egg, no pain of birth, just hunker down—squat down, that's the word—drop egg and then kind of gather around egg for a while. Gestation period outside the body twelve days Earth time. Painless birth, plenty of time to nurture young. Young hatches out, but does not peck its way out like bird. No beak, eh? When young is ready, parents know, break eggshell. Young pretty small when born, smaller than human baby. A full-grown adult is maybe 5'2", so egg long way is not humongous ("humongous"—I like that word), maybe about 4" long.

Now, these individuals have slightly different lifestyle: can give birth to egg maybe three, four times a year, but since birth painless for all concerned and since mother does not have uncomfortable memories of birth, more time for romantic interludes. (The more I do this, the more I am using your slang—no, colloquial language.)

Okay, I must talk to you about this because there [are] so much lies and even imagination about so-called monster reptilians that are capricious, that are harmful, especially to your children. This is all foolishness—made-up monsters that go *boo!* and scare you in the night. Foolishness, really. I can assure you, people on other planets much less scary than, well, some of your own kind, eh? Some of your own kind are pretty scary. Even just by being funny you can be scary, but that's another story maybe. I don't judge you, I just observe you, you know.

We can see all that you do inside the crystal if we look through the right facet. You must look through proper facet, not unlike TV screen, you know? [If you] want to see what's going on on Earth, float around and look through that facet. Selectivity comes from thoughts, then the rest of the way. Not so easy for us to check in with specific individual because what we do is general tasks. So can focus on certain people, certain places, but is very difficult to follow along with any individual, so we don't.

I think somebody is thinking, "Where are these first-cousin reptilians living?" Some of them live near galaxy Sirius, not too many of them yet because they are one of the first people you are intended to encounter. So they are kept a little bit away from you so they do not form prejudgments of what you are like. Wouldn't do for them to see scary movies. [They] might see somebody who looks vaguely familiar and say, "Why are they saying that about us? Not true." So remember, these so-called reptilians have warm hearts, okay? Not like your crocodiles.

I have to tell you something about crocodiles and other animal reptilians: They are not human beings from other planets in Earth disguise. They are what they are, and on their own planets they look different. Might even walk around and talk, but on your planet must be under cover. [Chuckles.] [They] take the form of animals so they [can] go unseen as ETs. If crocodile had antennas and spoke into a microphone, you might say, "This is not average crocodile. Maybe looks like crocodile, but isn't." But since they don't have antennas waving over their head and don't get in and out of flying saucers and don't speak into microphones to some unknown person in space, [they] can pass for animal. Good cover, eh? I talk to you a little bit about that tonight because I need to have you get past limited concepts of those who live on other planets. Any questions?

My Past and Future

Have you always done this? Do you have memories of doing something before you regulated time?

I do not have memory of doing anything before this. I think I and my friends were born to the task. Near as I can tell, have been doing this (let me see if I can get this in your years—not easy) for about 3.25 trillion years—long time. [I] think before this time there was machine regulation. But about 3.25 trillion years ago subtle types of life forms began to form, and it was believed advantageous to begin to keep better records. Even the most advanced machine crystal technology does not keep subtle records [that are] good about people—only more about trends.

Do you look forward to something after we move beyond time, when there is no need for it?

[To be] perfectly honest with you, the term "after" does not fit in our sequence, but I think maybe in another 1²/₃ trillion years of your time we take a couple weeks off, maybe go to Mars for a holiday, sit down in the sand and drink a cold root beer.

You're very familiar with the culture on Earth. Are you familiar with our history and our future?

Yes, familiar with your future because we have had to pay a little more attention to you because of your unique future. [In] most places where we set the time [it] is one setting, and we check in every hundred years or so. You are not just moving through time, but you are propelling and pulling through time. You are resetting the time, so we have to check with you every quarter second or so by your time. We check on you *all* the time!

How does that work?

Future selves pull you, plus now, Zoosh says, your lightbodies pull you. But also you are pushed by enlightened beings who lived in your past. Certain enlightened societies saw where you were going, and they are pushing you a little bit. Very, very few individuals try to slow you down for purposes of maintaining their own authority, but this is like an ant trying to stop a big rock rolling. Ant too smart, gets out of the way; these individuals trying to stop it maybe not quite as smart. Big rock win.

Our Cartoon Appearance and Our Planet

Can you describe yourself a little bit more in our terminology? If we looked at you, what would we see?

If you were to see me as I look now, I would be very . . . not two-dimensional, but very thin. If I turned to the side you would see me, but would be very much like wavy line. An artist could draw a wavy line—very much like that. We do not have a great deal of strength. As floaters (we float about), do not need the greatest aerodynamics; could be a strange shape and still float. Because we are working with you and other humanoids, ofttimes look [as if we have] two arms, two legs, body, head—okay, no reproductive. [Laughs.] Sorry, no need.

But I think you would find that if you looked at us from frontal view we would look almost like cartoon character. Cartoon character is cartoon not only to get a laugh, but to typify something that you can identify easily. We do not have highly defined features. You can look at your hand, and the closer you bring it, the more defined the lines become; then take magnifying glass and see lines that make up the lines and so on. We are not like that. We appear simple (simple on the surface) and do not have mustaches, beards and so on.

But we have the capacity to move throughout all dimensions that I am aware of, which is, [as] close as I can utilize in your measurements, from position of about one-eighth (which would be one-eighth of one dimension) to 33. Have not ever been beyond thirty-third dimension. I have heard there might be something there [laughs], but I've never been beyond there. Is a place where the personality of anyone (if I can use myself as analogy to any personality) is everywhere at once, but seems small and big at the same time—unlimited feeling, and yet precise knowledge of everywhere you are. No secrets at all, and yet because there is a great deal of creation going on there, there are constant surprises. So the joy of surprise is available, but there are no secrets, so is fun thing. I think perhaps it is number of Creator.

Do you travel to these places, or do you look into the facet of the crystal? How do you know they're there? Or does your planet have 33 dimensions?

No, [travel] out of necessity. Because it is our job to be time masters, we have been given the privilege to experience this (not my clones go—they will stay). The last time I did this I went up through central axis from core where we are to surface of planet at what you would call northern axis point on surface. Have similar gradient lights there (you call northern lights, yes?), and from light refraction—particles of light—move up in dimensions that way. But we do not move up in dimensions inside core where crystal is—possible to unintentionally affect time elsewhere doing this.

Regulating Time

So something comes out of the crystal that forms time? How does it work? How do you regulate it? Using the crystal?

I do not think we have actually formed time, but we regulate time by . . . our crystal is in very slow motion, moving on its own axis, which not visible, of course. Crystal is in touch with future and past—total future, total past of all potentials of given place, okay? So crystal is regulated to bend light to appropriate time sequence (I know I am defining the word by itself, not good, but doing best I can) and also light sequence. Crystal then for most places picks most benevolent future (in terms of time forward from this point). But you are intended to pick your own future, so [there is] less regulation in that context, but more precise regulation in terms of light focus. Light in future is brighter; light in distant past also bright. Light in very recent past is dimmer. So you are in loop of time, slightly unnatural loop, to correct error, I believe, explained in previous book by Uncle Zoosh. (I like that—more affectionate, eh?)

Time for you is regulated by potential uncertainty, otherwise known as what?—P.U.! [Everyone laughs.] Okay, little joke, very little. So because potential uncertainty figured in (meaning we don't choose your future, we don't choose anybody's future, we don't encourage given future), best we can do is to create brighter light, creating light path that you can choose to follow or not, okay?

Dying Takes You Two Million Years into the Future

This might be experienced, for example, by someone passing over through the veils, yes, to what is called death but is in fact life. They often will follow the light. When they follow the light, they actually go forward in sequence of time, moving through dimensions, moving toward light, which is your potential, okay? When one moves through the veil one not only moves through dimensions, but goes into more typical future. So one might say that as one departs the body, moves through veils, about the time one gets into the light near what you call city of light—where is unconditional love, angel voices and so on, possibly talking to lightbeings by then—one is in sixth dimension (from your perspective), roughly two million years into the future.

Everybody who dies does this, as far as I know—even people who have done things in physical life that they wished they didn't do. Where they go from there depends on many things, but they do this so they can have full experience of what they did in life, plus create enough time distance between what they did and what followed so they can see what followed. People choose to change a given life pattern and live another incarnation. If they feel uncomfortable about what they have done, they can look back in time and see consequences of their acts. So might choose to go back and incarnate after, to live in their creation; if they affected things in big way or small way, live close to potential outlet for consequences of what they have done. Or in some cases [they] might even choose, if is offered, to go back and live *before* that life—attempt to undo what they're going to do in the next life. Is possible. Is complicated, but can be done.

Is it always this warm on your planet?

No, the air conditioner is broken.

Oh. Where we live, heat, cold—unknown. Experiencing heat for the first time . . . different.

About Ourselves and Our Crystal

Have you ever channeled through anyone before?

No, first time. One of my clones spoke through Robert once before, presented itself as Time Master—little lie, but it was for a story, a time master story. It didn't count—not channeling to be published. Little lie. I let him get away with it.

As time masters, there are five of you, but do you have a social life? Do you have a mental life? Describe what makes your life fascinating. It's not all work and no play, is it?

All work is play. At level of service that we function, work is play. We do this because we find it very fascinating—no dull, very fascinating. And because fascinating, we are here. Creator would not have assigned this to us if we were "serving time," you know. [Everyone laughs.] We like this. Yes, we like this, so not sentence.

Okay, so there are 675 facets in your crystal. Can you see more than one place in each facet? You must.

Yeah, good question. Depending on color, tone (tone produces color) that can be made on total scale of music. Total scale of music for you might be, for instance, not only sounds you can make out loud, but sounds you can imagine up above and down below sounds you can make. So allowing for flat and sharp tones and all of this, total tones that can be made—close to 3000. So 3000 times 675 (math is not my strong subject) is [2,025,000].

Do you make this tone or does an instrument? Or do you visualize it or feel it?

We make it. Individual can make this tone. Clones can make the tone, too, but is not their job. If something happened to me, clone would step in, take care of it.

What could happen to you?

Nothing has ever happened to me. I said that for your benefit. Nothing has ever happened to any of us, but allowing for unknown potential (what is that? U.P.—unknown potential, U.P.!), maybe something could happen. That's another reason we have clone.

What dimension are you in? Do you have a plasma body? Does it feel physical?

As I say, depending upon who we are working with (we work a lot with humanoids now), we tend to appear that way. To each other, though, we would be . . . I look at my friend—he is a ball of light floating about. If you saw a ball of light floating about, you would think nothing of it. But if you saw something that looked kind of human floating about, it would catch your eye, you know. You see a ball of light in sky called Sun floating about, you don't think anything of it.

You said you were working a lot with humanoids now. What does that mean?

No, no. We work with many humanoids now, because what *you* are doing—not only at your dimension but the project you are working on—affects the whole universe. So, first to be affected are cousins, meaning those who would look like you in wide range, meaning basically humanoids.

How? Why?

Because [of] interrelationship of form. Forms have tones, okay? Humanoid tone, nine tones. No xylophone here, can't make one. But possibly with xylophone or vibraphone might be able to make humanoid tone; would have to strike nine tones, then tell you which ones are sharp and which ones are flat. In any event, because what you are doing is pivotal and because you are (unconsciously, you cannot help it) broadcasting this tone, all other beings in universe who respond in any way to that tone are all affected first, allowing even for eight and ten, utilizing digits here, allowing for *almost* humanoid and a little *more* than humanoid. That creates bulge in universe and then, very much like rubber band, first humanoids—bloop! ("bloop," meaning bulge), then everyone else comes along after you like ripple when you accomplish project goal.

Which is reaching the fourth dimension?

No. Project goal is cocreating with Creator.

Oh, that goal.

"Oh, yeah, that one, yeah, oh, yeah—I forgot about that one, right, oh yeah."

So you know everything Zoosh tells us. You're familiar with all of our thoughts now?

Uncle Zoosh

Yeah, we hear from Zoosh, too—Uncle Zoosh. He comes to entertain us, sing us a song now and then about your project. No accompaniment, but he is learning. Maybe a banjo someday or a tambourine—we'll see. But for now he sings us his song, and sometimes in the song, individual stories about individuals. A song might go on, in terms of your time, maybe hour and a half all the while we are working, but is very amusing. That's why we know sometimes Zoosh refers to himself as Grandpa Zoosh or Uncle Zoosh. We call him Uncle Zoosh for fun. He finds it *very* amusing.

We never heard of the Grandpa. He never told us about that.

Grandpa Zoosh. Sometimes it's Grandpa Zoosh when he talks nicely, lovingly, encouragingly. He has not had to talk that way to us because we are motivated. But Uncle Zoosh tells stories, laughs, sings songs. [Laughs.]

Our Future

So what motivates you, then? The lust or desire to . . . what?

Think about if you were doing what you always wanted to [do]. Nothing to hold you back, always wanted to do this. Think about if you wake up in the morning and a smile on your face. You rush to work because you always wanted to do that. (We don't really wake up in the morning—but smiles, yes.) We are doing what we like.

But you've always done this, so how do you know what else there is to do? This is the only thing you remember, right?

Troublemaker, eh? [Everyone laughs.] No, this is what I like. I don't know anything else to do. You talk to me more about this, and Uncle Zoosh [will] come and shake finger in your face pretty soon and say, "No meddling!"

So this is the first time you've come down to channel through a human?

Yes, never speak before. As I say, clone before, pretending to be time master.

Evidently there must be a sense of urgency or at least . . .

No, no, this is fun, is also opportunity, eh? You were casting about universe, asked for volunteers: "Who wants to talk tonight?" You know, my friends, they say, "Take a little time off, put your feet up, smoke a cigar." [Laughter.] Tell story, sing song. Pretend to be Uncle Zoosh for a while. [Laughter.]

You said something about dealing with humanoids. When we send that bulge, that ripple out, what does that do to you? Do you have to compensate? What consequence does that have for you?

No, when you have bulge, when you accomplish goal and bulge takes place, then we'll do *less!* Then we have coffee break, eh? When bulge takes place, when you start to take over for Creator and ripple effect goes out, we do less, see? Because then you'll no longer need . . . we don't have to worry about time on Earth anymore.

So then we're doing it?

Yes, exactly. You'll take over, see? Then we have time off. Find out what we're going to do next. Then I tell you what we're going to do next; *then* I will. Maybe you don't look quite the same then.

Making Tones

These 3000 tones you talked about: Do you actually make these tones out loud, or do you think them?

You can think them, but often make them out loud—very quietly out loud, no more than a measurement on your scale of seven decibels, but out loud.

And you project the color at the same time?

No, color naturally projects. If *you* make tones now, if you sing, color is there. You just don't see it. That's why some music affects people so strongly. If you make the tone yourself or even if you blow on the instrument, color is there. But play recording, no color. That's why music for healing must be done on the spot. Sorry, people who [are] creating music for healing tapes: It's okay; good psychological suggestions maybe help, but for true music for healing, make tones out loud or blow through something that make tones or [play] stringed instrument, but *physical* vibrating the air, making the color. Color is what stimulates the healing, but vibration also helpful. Vibration gives the color impetus, motion, direction.

You've got a great tenderness.

Getting better, listening to Uncle Zoosh prompting me in the background, whispering in my shell-like ear. [Laughter.]

Our Clones and Visitors to Our Planet

I have a question about the 1400 clones: Did you do just a few at a time until you got the whole thing laid out and you knew exactly that was how many were needed?

Yeah, few at a time. Started with just one each, and then we thought of other things to do, especially to maintain the integrity of the space we are in. There is so much space inside this planet—a big, big, big planet, but very hollow inside. But is planet, okay, not ship—we checked that out. There is sometimes necessity . . . in outer shell of planet (we are inside) thinner spots might be 65 miles deep, so clones spend a lot of time checking the surface and the inside integrity, not unlike an engineer might do to make sure there is no leak-through or leak-down, exchange of pressure and so on.

Are there beings on the surface of this planet?

No; no beings, but it's possible occasional ship might land, people get out. We have made it comfortable, what you would call parklike—fruit trees, you know, palm trees, coconuts, but no dancing girls.

Do they know you're there?

No, usually don't know we're here. I don't think anybody has ever landed and knew *we* were here. I think one ship landed and knew someone was here, but felt good. These particular individuals travel as compressed light, though they are lightbeings when you see them normally. And they knew we were in here, but also knew they were not supposed to interfere. Could have flown down and seen us, flown through surface down to inside, but evolved lightbeing knows they are not supposed to interfere—you understand. They're the only ones as far as I know who were aware we were here. Most everybody else stops, maybe has a little R&R . . .

Like one of our rest stops.

Yeah, they rest maybe for a little while and enjoy surface pleasures, then go on.

Time Upheaval and Time Travel

In the total course of this creation, humanity has been here just a very tiny part of a percentage point, so has time existed only during the Explorer Race experiment, or has time always been in creation?

That's a good question. There has always been some version of time, because time has been in most upheaval in dimension a little denser than three. Most upheaval in time is around 2.5 to 3. Right now is 2.5 to 2.7, roughly. Lot of upheaval in time sequences there very often, because [the] move from second dimension to third dimension has always been traumatic for beings and very often evolutionary on soul level. So in this sense have spent a lot of experience in that area. Did not really have to pay too much attention to you as Explorer Race body of souls until past 2.5 to 5 million years or so. Then we start paying a little attention, because then you started getting into sequence. Before then it was more existence than sequence.

Were we in the second dimension?

No, I do not believe your body of souls passed through second dimension as incarnated beings. I think perhaps a few of you might have time-traveled there. Nobody in this room, probably nobody reading the book, [lived there]. Time travel done even now with your soul group is rare. [You are] in infancy, though, getting started—plenty mischief to come. We will have to be alert because is possible [you might have] time-traveling with instruments instead of sense of energy balance, which is most accurate (proper what to do, where to go according to how it feels to love self). By putting faith in instruments and technology, is very easy to accidentally knock holes in time and make big mess. This [was] happening for a little while; been happening now for maybe 40, 50 years in your time, occasionally individuals doing this. We have to sweep up after them.

That's our secret government's explorers?

Yeah.

But as we get a little more technological, we're going to be playing too, just for the fun of it, and you'll have to sweep up after us?

A little bit, yeah, because in the beginning you will think, "Oh, crystals can do everything—*wonderful crystals!*"

How far in the future is this?

I think initial time travel utilizing crystal technology for growth spurt [will occur] for probably next 100, 150, maybe 170 years. After that, then time travel becomes a spiritual, heart-centered experience, no longer utilizing external mechanisms of any kind.

What advice can you give us from your perspective for the next few years as we move up the dimensional scale from where we are now [3.47]?

Utilize Love Instinct, Creation Tools; Don't Be a Follower

The most important thing is to become aware of body feelings. Utilize loving feelings to attain all accomplishments, because sense of warmth, sense of love (you all recognize this feeling) is best weathervane to know that you are doing right thing. Even [though you might get] what seems to be most wonderful advice from beloved and respected leaders (and there are a few of those to come), [it] is still best to utilize your own loving persona. You have discussed instinctual love before in publication, I think Zoosh and others. This is the best method. Please guard against following in general; rule out following leader and [do] not step on poison ivy on trail!

Following philosophically in near future [will be] very hazardous because might be . . . oh, no danger, but more likely you not utilizing your own love systems to create—re-create, as it were—love instinct (L.I., okay?). Then you [might] miss many creations, many of the old spiritual and even new spiritual techniques for where to go, how to get there, who with, when to get there, what to do to get there. Basically those groups, those technologies, are going to be rediscovered and invented in the next twenty years or so. So try to follow loving heart instinct to do what is right for you, because maybe—even if you follow charismatic leader and be safe and so on—you'll miss something you can do to create. So much of creation tools that Creator uses in benevolent, loving way will be dropping into your tool bag in the next few years. Use them.

If we learn how to travel in a few years the way I want to, can we come and say hello?

You can say hello now.

In the future, can we come down and see you?

Maybe, but knock first. We have place to receive visitors on inside where we are, but no one has knocked yet; only knocking [will] get [you] there, okay? Three long knocks, one short.

[Laughs.] Got it! You're a sweetheart.

Thank you. I think that's all for now. More later maybe.

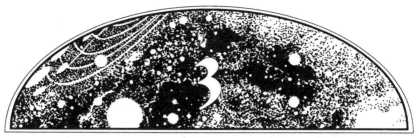

founders of Sirius, Creators of Humanoid forms

July 25, 1996

We are the founders of the galaxy Sirius, although we do not exist in that galaxy [system]. We have been attuned to the creation of different forms of humanoid beings. It is our responsibility to create these forms in the most appropriate way or to guide those (especially on Sirius) who have adapted our guidance to fit the needs of various beings in the various worlds.

Some time ago we were informed that the humanoid shape would be necessary to enable souls to explore physical life through a greater interaction with it. Physical life as you have known it to be on your world is primarily of your own kind and that of the animals and the plants, if you recognize them that way. Because it was our job to provide a being in many forms that would be less able to be omnipresent, it was our considered ideal to produce a being that would have to fend for itself.

Now, as you know, there are lightbeings who are in the shape of humanoids or who are often seen in that shape. The higher you go in the light spectrum, the less that beings have to take this shape; they take it only to seem less godlike to you. Many of you have done meditations where you have seen gold or white lightbeings who look humanoid, but they are obviously made of light. Yet even a sight like that, as pleasant and perhaps exalted as it is, does not necessarily cause you to feel it is a god or even a guide, but possibly just a form of life like your own in some ways. If they were to see a glowing ball of light, certainly the more primitive humans or humanoids might think it was a deity. Thus when you see a lightbeing that is humanoid in your meditations and visions, sometimes it is just showing itself to you this way.

Our world is located about 600,000 light-years from Sirius, still in your universe. Your universe stretches much farther than you realize. Your universe, as we see it, is not circular, by the way; it is more like a stretched-out oval, and we are at one end. This existence of ours, in this particular location at the outer boundaries of the universe, gives a perspective that allows us to see it all. [Chuckles.] And this suits us well.

Our interactions, then, are not with you directly, but since we have consulted significantly with the Sirian elders who designed the female human being in the form you now experience on Earth and who also supported and sustained modifications to the male human being, we are associated with you indirectly. There is also a third sex that does not interact with you directly. They have the capacity to reproduce themselves, but rarely use it. A human or humanoid body of the third sex is more inclined to be, if not immortal, at least long-lived because it is so much in balance. Actually, our favorite version of the human-being body is this combined, third-sex form, because by its nature it transforms discomforting energy in small quantities and actually has the capacity, in some cultures where this type of being lives, to transform so-called negative energy and transmit so-called positive energy, thus doing two good deeds at once. So of course we are inclined to favor this version of the human-being prototype.

Our Understanding of the Explorer Race

We feel that your race shows a great deal of promise, because not only do we understand that you are exploring consequences in your attempt to cocreate with Creator, but that you are doing it in the hardest possible way to maximize the consequences. After all, if one lives a highly spiritual life in a very balanced way, consequences are less of a factor, so we admire your courage. Sometimes we have to joke about it a little bit because we see beings making the same mistakes over and over. At first we thought that this was some kind of lesson the individual was learning. When sometimes we saw the same mistakes over and over one life after another, we thought, This is a lesson this being is not getting. But then we came to realize in the larger picture what this was really about.

When any one individual in your race experiences something repetitive (a lesson over and over again) even through different lives, very often this has to do with consequences to be known and understood by *many* individuals, sometimes even a whole race—especially during times when communication on your planet is gradually improving so that errors get broadcast about. When we realized that you not only learn as individuals but also en masse, we began to understand some of the more esoteric functions of the organs in your body.

For example, we were advised by Creator's instructors to include certain organs and certain portions of organs and body parts in the human that are not actually required, that you could live without. It was *firmly* suggested to us that we include these organs even though we thought of them at the time as extraneous. Now we understand that as you evolve not only spiritually but socially (social evolution for you has been very difficult) and as you improve your social skills, learning how to get along with one another out of necessity, you are beginning to activate as a unit certain body parts in their apparently primary functions. We always thought that body organs had a function, and that was that. Oh, we recognized a spiritual connotation, but we did not understand they could perform their function, have their spiritual connotation and still perform an entirely different function as well. This was quite startling. I will give you an example or two.

Surprising Functions of Some Body Parts

One of the curious functions we did not understand too clearly was the insistence on a very thorough bone marrow, because it would have been so much easier to create a bone in the physical self that would grow into solidity rather than be hollow. We argued that hollow bone would not be as strong as solid bone, and that solid bone, especially of a certain density, would be very much less prone to breakage. Yet the Creator's instructors advised us that breakage, however uncomfortable and painful that would be, would have to do also with your world of consequences, so we should not go too far in the creation of invulnerability, because vulnerability had a certain amount of life lessons for you as individuals as well as a race. So we said, "All right, bones will grow outward from bone marrow," and shook our heads [chuckles].

Now we understand. As you are beginning to learn that socialization skills are essential for your survival, we are beginning to see that the light you must encompass (the gold light) is now being produced by the bone marrow, especially in the larger long bones. It is being stirred up inside the bones, and when certain social celebrations or sometimes spiritual functions take place, the gold light is released. Apparently this light will not be released for an individual alone, but only in association with some group or mass activity. In this way apparently an individual's own gold light is not sufficient, but when combined with the gold light of many individuals has the capacity to support and sustain worthy goals. That was quite a surprise to us.

Nor did we understand why body hair is so important. We certainly understand eyebrows—these are essential!—and some hair on the head, most certainly—very essential, especially with a sun as close as yours.

But we did not understand why some individuals would have hair on their backs, and we certainly did not understand why there is hair under the arms and other such things that did not seem to make sense. And yet as you are beginning to learn more spiritual activities, what will apparently happen is that you need to have certain proofs presented to you, things that happen suddenly where everybody says, "Look at this!" We have been informed that for many of you, during certain high spiritual and potentially even social experiences, your hair might change color—possibly white, possibly very pale blond. So this other function of the hair is primarily to create physical evidence that will point to something having happened—to get your attention, as it were. Another surprise for us.

There are other things discussed before that have to do with the internal organs. I will not go into it, since apparently that has been explored in previous channelings. We have had to conclude, then, that even our part in guiding the Sirius elders toward their creation and modification for the betterment of the human bodies has had a wider, more significant purpose than even we realized.

Creator's teachers informed us initially that an entire race of beings needed to be created to learn these lessons, as I said. You might ask, "What exists other than humans?" But you know, it is possible to be quite physical without being a human being. You have many animals to demonstrate that to you, yet such a surprising variety of animals has not caused great recognition on your part that the lessons of physicality are not so very difficult. They are simple. Perhaps we created your brain just a little bit too complex, because it tends to seek out the complicated answer and discard the simple one. Well, that is an *oops!* on our part.

The third sex does not have such a complex brain; their thought mechanism is activated primarily through intuition, so no internal memory functions are required. Thus the brain is much smaller. Memory functions use a significant amount of your brain; so in our attempt to help you to achieve wisdom, we have apparently overaccentuated the brain. It appears, according to Creator's teachers and the evolutionary therapists I have discussed this with, that even now you do not need fully 40% of your brain. And as you evolve as a species, you will eventually tend to have smaller brains. This is because the human being, which you are (not just the humanoid, but the human being), lives and functions much more easily on instinct, also associated with inspiration. This creates a situation where your memory, which is external to your physical self (much more convenient than memory function can be), will be much, much more massive when your memory function is working this way in everyone. Probably over several thousand years the human-being brain will shrink. Well, I guess we must have goofed there! [Chuckles.] (I like little words of humor.)

Our Origin

So you probably want to know the name of our planet and what we are called, maybe even how I am referred to. Our planet is Chefah (chay´fah). We are not actually within a solar system, even a galaxy; I don't think we would be considered part of the galaxy nearby. We are a planet that does not spin on an axis, so, being lightbeings (little balls of light, if you could look at us), we do not require a great deal from the planet. We do not eat as you do or such things as that, so the planet is primarily a place for us to gather.

What would you call my people? I think I will have to find a translation here in your language. I think maybe "speaks with light" seems to be the closest translation I can get, or maybe "demonstrates with light," but that is perhaps too specific, too narrow a definition. Let's see if I have another option here—Wayshowers of Light. Perhaps that is the best.

My name? Well, I must say we don't go by names here or even tones or colors. We have the capacity to recognize personalities from person to person, if I might use that word, so I'm sorry I can't give you a name.

The Initial Request for Our Assistance

Who were the beings who came from the Creator to ask you to do this?

The beings who came? Apparently Creator's teachers do this often. These beings came looking rather like us. Apparently when Creator's teachers come to visit a race of beings, they will adopt their form so they will be received comfortably. They indicated names . . . no, I think they indicated forms. One indicated itself as a spiral and the other as a circle. Of course, being somewhat spherical ourselves, we recognized that one, but we were not at all certain what the spiral was about, so it was demonstrated through intonation, which is our manner of communication. Intonation has to do with a feeling tone incorporating cycles of wisdom that start in the middle of our people, and as it radiates outward tends to become denser, not because the people are denser, but to compensate for the dissipation.

When we were informed by the spiral that it meant the unfolding of new life forms, then we understood we were going to be involved in a life-form project. This is what we do, yet it was quite wonderful to be instructed. The instruction took, in terms of your time, perhaps a thousand days. The instructions were very detailed, and if you consider the incredible detail of your physical selves you will understand why it took so long for us to integrate such instructions.

What was your experience before you created the humanoids? What had you created before that? Why did they come to you?

I believe they came to us because we were sufficiently detached from our creations that we did not need to follow them. Apparently they have worked with other body engineers who have become very much attached to how their creations would turn out and have interfered with the natural evolution of these creations. The way we create something has a lot to do with why we can remain detached. We do not create something directly. We intonate the prototype and then, since we are the teachers of the Sirius elders, we guide them and *they* do the creation. Because it is also not a creation of their thought, they too become less attached, though compared to us they are more interested in the outcome of you as a people than we are. We are not disinterested; we simply know that you live on no matter what, and we look upon this as a way of learning, not the last thing you will learn and certainly not the last thing you will do. It is just something you do for a time in order to learn.

What life forms have you created before?

The Living Diamond Portal

I expect the most familiar one you might identify with is the living diamond portal. Most portals that I know of are alive, but the diamond-shaped portal can be utilized almost like a vehicle. One can step into it on one's home planet, for example, and direct it. Most portals go where they go, but this one can be directed and does not fly to some specific place. You step into the portal on one side of the universe to get to the other side of the universe, and you are momentarily in something not unlike a void. Then you image where you want to go, which is most easily done by picturing someone you know and perhaps care about. In this way you travel instantaneously in the portal to that place, because the portal will serve loving spiritual beings. If a person who could not hold loving spirituality were able to access the diamond-shaped living portal, when he stepped out of the portal he would be where he started out. You must prove to the portal that the journey is a loving, worthy one by holding that energy. The portal is fed in this way. The portal lives on love. We felt that was a worthy contribution.

Do we have one on this planet?

They come and go. They have been seen by some of your people. Living diamond-shaped portals do not live somewhere—they travel.

Were any of them photographed when we were publishing the cosmic photographs?

I think maybe one at a distance.

The History of Humanoid Bodies

What planet were the first humanoid bodies used on?

First *human* bodies?

Yes, the ones you created.

We created humanoids, including humans.

I see. Where were the first humanoid bodies?

The first humanoid bodies we created were, I believe, inaugurated on Zeta Reticuli. They are a *very* old species. That is where we were able to discover what could be done and what to change. They are truly experimental beings. For example, on their own planet they do not walk about; they glide. They have legs and can walk, but they choose not to. They can move somewhat elevated over the surface; that is what they as souls wished to do. They did not wish to be overly physical. [Chuckles.] But we felt that in order to truly interact with your physical reality, walking would be a particularly human thing to do (or even, I might say, particularly humanoid). So we left them as they wished to be and continued to evolve the humanoid shape. Of course, in the case of human beings, we were required to make you quite vulnerable to maximize consequences. [Chuckles.]

Where were the first human bodies?

I think the first human bodies might have been on Draconia. Draconia was a particular planet in the galaxy [system] of Draconia. I think this planet has moved to another galaxy now, but the closest I can get in your language is Mats-ts-ta. This planet had the first human beings. There were not man, then woman [laughs] (nice story, but strictly a story, though), but man, woman and third sex all at once.

This might amuse some of your people: Oftentimes you will feel like you are missing something, and the assumption of some of you is that this is your soulmate; others, perhaps more spiritually aware, might feel it is your masculine or your feminine side, depending upon what sex you are. But in point of fact, that's not so. What you're really missing is a third sex, because that is the being that causes ultimate balance. Without the third sex, consequences become overwhelming. I don't want to question Creator, but perhaps Creator took the third sex away from you so you would accelerate your growth. With the third sex, life is much more benign; however, growth is slower, so perhaps this was Creator's intent.

Can you tell us the flow of the human beings? Draconia, then to where? Do they still exist in that form there now?

Not in Draconia. Let's see.

You said the planet was now in another galaxy. They have evolved up the dimensions then?

No, no, evolution is not up. Evolution does not exist at all. One simply does different things, okay? There is no evolution that I have ever observed. One either has all knowledge, or chooses to have less in order to learn something. I am not aware of any being ever having existed who started out in their beginning with a small amount of knowledge and then grew more, no. Always they start out with all, then choose to eliminate part of that to learn something. So evolution is not a true fact.

So after Draconia, then where?

One moment . . . Zentah, on a significantly different plane of existence. I do not believe a Zentah galaxy has ever been manifested below seventh dimension, so a great many humanoid beings exist on Zentah in the seventh through ninth dimensions. There are lots of experiments in forms, functions and activities there. I believe it was perfected there, the seventh- through ninth-dimensional humanoid beings, especially human beings.

Can you tell us the flow? Would they create in a place, or were they exploring?

No, not created. Creation in Sirius with our guidance, then out to various places to try them out, usually places where they would be undisturbed, often places where they would not contact any other form of life so that dilution of racial characteristics was kept to a minimum.

After that what was the flow?

Let's see . . . I think maybe then the first version of the Pleiades star system. This is not the Pleiades you have with you now. The first version of Pleiades was allowed to evolve to higher dimensional status not only because of spiritual experiments, but because of their fantastic success in those experiments. Then people, teachers, guides, everyone, said, "We would prefer to continue to do this at higher dimensions," so they were granted a move to higher dimensions—about the eleventh dimension up through nineteen. At this time the Pleiades was eight major stars (from your perspective) in a slightly different constellation—a little more round. Now things are a little different. It's not so round, but dimensions exist on the level of—let's see, I think they do not really have a third dimension anymore, not where people live— from about 4.25 to 4.50 to ninth dimension.

An interesting fact is that the tenth dimension is not usually a place so much as a feeling, so the tenth dimension would not be described in any way physically, but as emotional. Pure, unconditional love and other joyous emotions is my knowledge of tenth-dimensional experience.

After the Pleiades, then where?

Pleiades, then to Sirius—where, I believe, was the first opportunity for humans to experience water and other liquids. Liquids were relatively new at that time on Sirius, and water was very popular with Sirian denizens. But a form of liquid clouds was also popular then and now; it felt, not like water, but in some cases like syrup and in other cases like very heavy mist. For example, lying down in liquid clouds heightens and amplifies imagination, so if one is imagining something wonderful, it would become something fantastically wonderful, without your doing anything; it just happens.

Other liquids also became very popular—liquid nitrogen and sulphur were popular for a time. Liquids associated with atmospheres became very popular because people could become saturated with something they had been breathing beforehand. They could suddenly lie in it, not unlike your having a physiological capacity to lie in a pool of liquid oxygen (which, of course, would kill you now). If you *could* do this it would cure many, many diseases, so it is very therapeutic.

So that was the beginning of your interaction with substances you had not truly experienced before ("you" meaning human-type beings). I believe it was the first time human beings became exposed to the planet you are on now, but at that time it was in Sirius. I believe that the first humans in *this* part of the universe started out in the interior of Saturn, moved to the exterior of Mars, then to the interior of Mars. By that time we are more up to date in terms of your understanding of the time line, as you call it.

Then they went to Maldek before they came to Earth?

Correct.

The Founders and the Reshaping of the Universe

Are you what Zoosh has called the Founders?*

Oh, I suppose. We do have a few of our number living inside your planet. It used to be from the second to ninth dimension. I believe that now our people are in 2.9 (almost out of second dimension) to 9.3.

Were you described then as having beautiful, very soft, furry bodies?

No, no, those were not Founders. Founders are lightbeings. Those were Andazi.**

So how many of you are there, everywhere and then here?

Here inside Earth the numbers vary, perhaps anywhere from 100 to 1000, occasionally 10,000 if something needs to be done. But on our own planet I should think [there is] a variation in the numbers. Not all personalities need to be present at all times, and when they do not, they combine with their core personalities. Any core personality might be able to produce 100 to 200 fragments of personality, so the population probably ranges from one million to 400 million. I do not remember in my lifetime our people expressing as 400 million, although I have heard that once it was about 373 million for a great creative effort—I believe at

---

* See *The Explorer Race*, p. 96, p. 109, pp. 318-319 and *ETs and the Explorer Race*, p. 73, pp. 100-101.
**See *The Explorer Race*, p. 41, pp. 47-49, p. 61, p. 63, pp. 100-101 and *ETs and the Explorer Race*, p. 72.

that time it was the reshaping of the universe. (The universe was originally somewhat spherical in shape, but is now, as I say, ovoid.)

Why?

It was necessary, from Creator's perspective, to create sort of a stretched-out sphere, because a sphere tends to be in balance at all times no matter what, and anything that *needed* to be out of balance—such as your planet or other isolated places for the purpose of learning—could not remain out of balance. It would rapidly come back into balance because the shape of a sphere supports balance. So Creator said, "Let's stretch this out. It will create a distortion. Even though the underlying element of a sphere is present, if we pull it out it becomes like an oval. And if we twist it a little bit, the potential for distortion in some places is available."

Did this happen at the same time as the concept to create the Explorer Race?

I think before that, because there were a few species attempting to re-create their points of origin (where they came from), and in order to do that they needed to use about one-tenth of a percent of negative energy, which did not have the capacity to survive in a sphere. This took place before the Explorer Race was stimulated.

What does that mean, "to re-create their points of origin"? They came from beyond the creation?

Yes. Point of origin necessarily creates not only who you are, what you are, but ultimately what you will do. Sometimes races will achieve all they can achieve and wish to re-create their point of origin so they can start a new lesson or a new learning process. In order to do this, sometimes they need to instigate small amounts of energy that have the basic emotion of dissatisfaction, but in a very dilute way. So negative energy, allowed to assist in this way, was used then as a means of propulsion rather than an integrated force of being.

The Use of Negativity

Was this the first effort to use negativity in a creative way? They just couldn't use enough of it to really solve the problem.

Oh, yes, they *did* use enough. They were able to re-create their point of origin. We can't say that it was the first time negativity was used this way, because the negative energy did not have much chance to interact, since it was used like a spring—a propulsion based upon a repulsion. The negative energy was used as the repulsing force, and the point of origin was transferred this way. The whole race could move suddenly back to its point of origin, but it could not deflect from that position by even one-tenth of one degree. By utilizing the repulsion of negative energy, they could deflect slightly—I believe it was about one-thousandth of a degree—just enough to retain most of the qualities they liked in themselves, yet enough to assimilate new qualities that would allow them to re-create their society, their worlds, their people and so on. That planet and those people did not survive.

As interesting as that re-creation of origin might be, it was not a direct expression, not a means of integrating negativity for the purpose of finding a use for it. I think that was initially done a little before the Explorer Race left. Then I think negative energy went to Sirius (the Sirius planet that has been discussed) right around the same time that the Explorer Race was launched. It took the planet on Sirius a very, very long time to become totally negative.

You don't mention Orion in this . . .

No, because the negativity on Orion did not come until much, much after its inception as a place of life as you know it. I don't think negativity on Orion goes back much more than a few hundred thousand years.

Really?

Yeah, it was a relatively short-duration experiment on Orion. Short but not sweet, eh?

My Background

What about your lifetime? In birth years, how long have you been conscious in this incarnation?

This incarnation began during the beginning of the universe. You cannot measure it in your years. I'm sorry.

You've been conscious since this creation?

Yes, but not before.

So you were generated by this Creator, you were part of . . .

Yes, we were generated by this Creator.

What do you anticipate the consequences to be for you and your people by having participated in the creation of humanoids?

This is a very interesting question. I am not at all clear on that. We were told that as a result of our participation we would receive some form of enlightenment. We said, "Oh, very good," and we went on, you know. But we have not knowingly received this yet, so we think that perhaps whatever outcome we will benefit from has not occurred yet.

What was your motivation?

Oh, simply to do it—how often do you get the chance to create an entire type of being? We have had the chance to create *forms* of beings, but I think it was really one of the few times in which we had a chance to literally create an entire race from the beginning.

Who guides you? Who are your founders?

Usually, our guide comes in the form of that ball of light from Creator. Only with the inception of humanoid beings' creation did the spiral come, but normally our guide is a sphere of multicolored light. It shows itself, sounds tones, shows some liquid light within. Usually what you would call a fingerprint creates a certain color, sound and tone that we recognize as our guide.

Is it possible that one of the benefits that might accrue to you is going on with the Creator when He moves up to find out more?

It is certainly possible, but we have no reason to know that it would be true. We do not know this.

The Zeta Reticuli

Why do the Zeta Reticuli say they are our past lives when they were created long before the idea of the Explorer Race?

Oh, yes, certainly they say that, because the Zetas that you talk to are in the future, so they do not look back to the origin. If they looked back to the origin of their species, they certainly would say that others have been their past lives. You would say perhaps that a year ago was a portion of your past, and if you were concerned with that period, that would be the past you would care about. But if you were concerned with twenty millennia ago, then you would be concerned with *that.*

They are interested in you because they did not know that you were in their past at all, and when they discovered that, they realized that they, as they exist, will either become transformed to ninth-dimensional beings (as are their now teachers who look like them), or they will continue in the form they now occupy. They have chosen to be a ninth-dimensional gold-light version of themselves. They have been told that depending upon what *you* do—what you learn, how you choose to choose, what you choose, how you solve your differences, how you embrace each other—all of these things will affect whether they will be ninth-dimensional or maybe seventh or sixth. So of course you, as their past lives, are important to them. Certainly they have other past lives that go before you on the level of an ancestor. They, just like you, also have past lives that are other races, other beings. One is not always a Zeta.

So you as an engineer created a form that was then inhabited by souls.

Oh, yes. Certainly we did not create the souls. We created the form.

But the souls themselves create the bodies, so you created the matrix or the pattern or the original framework?

The souls do not actually create the bodies in terms of what we did. The bodies are now mostly fixed for the last significant time (granted, some changes are happening now), so the soul sprouts the individualistic aspects of the body. But the actual *form* of the body is something we created. The human being is not going to grow a leg out of his chest because he wants to be individualistic. [Laughs.]

But you created also the potential that we are going to move into? That was part of the original creation?

The Third Sex

Well, yes, because of optional evolution. I expect in time that the human being on Earth will evolve more into what I have referred to as the third sex. It's much more gentle on resources. You don't have to eat too much, you don't damage life around you and it's a much more spiritual, integrated life form. Maybe this will happen sooner, but probably later, I should think. The third sex will certainly reappear amongst you in numbers in at least five to ten thousand years, but I would be surprised if you did not evolve as human beings into that shape by 100,000 years. I would be very surprised indeed. [Laughs.]

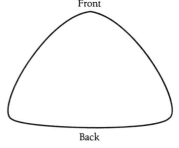

When you say "shape," is it a shape different from what we have now as human beings?

It's a little different, yes. If you were to look at the body shape [asks for pencil and paper]—from the top, you understand, a gradual curve like a circle would be the back. This is the shape of the trunk of the humanoid third-sex being. The front would be more the angular-shape aspect. This allows the radiations to move in specific directions. It is also a little more durable.

Earlier you said there was no evolution, and now you are continuing to use that word and talk of evolving. Can you explain that?

I'd rather say *social* evolution. There is no evolution in terms of consciousness, in my understanding, meaning that the totality of one's being is always this complete thing. Regardless of what form one might take to live a given life, whether it be humanoid or something entirely different, if that life is intended to learn anything at all, then something will have to be forgotten temporarily during that life in order that other, new things can be created. If on the other hand nothing new is intended to be learned, then all knowledge ought to be available. That is what I am saying.

When I say you will evolve into this, I do not mean that you will evolve physiologically into this shape. I think it will be a choice of the Earth-human prototype, because the third sex is so much more comfortable. Even though you think you are attached to your polarized bodies, in five or ten thousand years when there are at least a 100 or maybe 1000 third-sex beings amongst you, by that time you will have the ability to feel what other beings feel. While there are spiritual people amongst you now and even sensitives who can do this, by that time everybody will be able to do it. And when you feel how good it feels to be a third-sex individual, I think you will make this choice, although it is my opinion only.

Is your work completed in creating the humanoids?

We have not made any new forms of humanoids for many millennia, so unless something changes it seems we have done what we need to do.

What is the nature and purpose of your relationship to humanoids now?

No particular purpose. We are largely simply . . .

Detached?

Yes. Detached—yes, good word.

Interference in Your Humanoid Form

What about all of the experiments that have been done by all of these interferers?

With all of the interference that has gone on, I will give you the net cosmetic effect, okay? Cosmetically, the only real difference is that you no longer have webs in your fingers. Initially, your hand had a web closest to the knuckle. It allowed you to be more adaptable to water. Remember how you loved liquids so much? The web made it much easier to swim. Not webbed toes—oh, I suppose it depends, splitting a hair (that's a good one I like, "splitting a hair")—a teensy little web in the toes, but insignificant.

But other people meddling in your DNA: External is the only thing I can see, and no webs anymore. But I believe it's still a latent characteristic amongst some people, so occasionally it's seen and is considered a physical anomaly. Internal changes: Perhaps a major one to mention is the now existence of what is called the appendix. You originally had (and probably will again someday) an appendix that has a small opening at the surface so that if there is some particularly toxic substance in the body, it will be discharged through that opening, which has a one-way valve. Nothing goes in, but something can come out if it is particularly toxic. This alone will allow the physical human being to extend her lifetime three and a half times what it is now. Now toxic substances are simply processed. What you know as the aging process is largely caused by the absorption of toxic substances—the normal way for a human being to die, to cross over. The degeneration of physical form should take no more than five days, not a lengthy time of so-called aging.

What was the intention for the length of a life?

It was intended that you live at least 350 to 450 years. We believed that for what you had to learn you could accomplish so much more if you would have a more contiguous history. You don't know very much now about your history a few thousand years ago because you don't live long enough to accumulate the wisdom and stow it in places that are readily accessible. Short-lived people have a very hard time to accumulate wisdom on this planet.

Why was the life span shortened so much?

We didn't do it!

Who did?

We didn't do it! You brought it up originally when you said people interfered. Ask *them!*

You don't know why they did it?

Oh, I have my opinion. I believe it was done to maintain some control over you, slow you down, make you dependent on others—generally slow down the results of the whole purpose of your existence. Of course, you cannot stop it, but you can slow it down.

What is the function of your being now?

To *exist!* The function of any being at its core is to exist as pleasantly as possible.

Other Work We Do

What do you do in your existence now that you've completed your work creating humanoids?

We've completed our work with humanoids, but we have other things. Occasionally we are called on by Creator to support or sustain some other type of life. We have modeled or, as you say, engineered. This interests us; most of the time this is what we do. What's an average day like, you might ask. We do not sleep. We do not experience day and night; it is consistent light. We experience feelings, and our feelings are interpreted in motions.

If you were to see us and were to arrive on our planet in a vehicle, perhaps you would hover. You would see clusters of ourselves, light spheres, and we would move around, not unlike the way you might move if you allowed your hands to move around. Sometimes some of us will cluster together if we're having the same feeling, moving up and down, sideways, not unlike a water fountain. It is a dance of life, is the best I can express it to you. For someone such as yourself and your race of beings, it would be hard to conceive of doing this all of the time—eternally, from your perspective. Yet if one experiences life as a celebration, as totally untainted, unconditional love all of the time, in my experience it is not a feeling one grows tired of.

Thank you. What other sentient beings or forms that consciousness would inhabit have you created?

We were involved in the creation of the light disk. This is ofttimes made up of lightbeings sometimes like ourselves, sometimes like other lightbeings. As a means of travel, one unites in as many numbers as necessary to form flat, somewhat circular, occasionally two-dimensional light structures in which to go from place to place. This was an adaptation.

The Prototype Cat Being

Another example (let me see if I can come up with one relevant to you) . . . oh yes, this ought to be relevant: We were involved in a prototype of a being whose cousin you now recognize as the cat. The prototype cat being is actually an amphibian that lives in liquid! This liquid would not be as thick as water, not as thin as steam, but the being moves not unlike an amphibian through water. It does not actually look like a fish—it has no gills—but consumes liquid totally efficiently, no waste whatsoever. Its fixed population does not decimate the resources. Its distant cousin, which you experience as the cat, has similar consciousness in terms of its total spiritual depth, but the so-called cat body has quite significantly adapted to this planet.

Prototype Cat Being

What do they look like on their home planet of Caath [kahth]?

They look, yes, like amphibians, but not like fish as you know it. The form is very much like a disk, but not round like a flat disk. Do you want me to draw it?

Oh, that's the form you created for beings who live on this planet of Caath?

The prototype being of the cat. The general form only, the prototype being.

Have you ever talked through a channel before?

I believe once.

Through Robert, or someone else?

Through Robert in another aspect of my personality. I speak now through my core personality. The aspect spoke through Robert very early on in his channeling. I believe perhaps the first entity he channeled, Cretann, was a portion of my personality.

Meddlers and Contributors in Human Genetics

Once you created the prototype, you said it didn't change very much at all. We got all these stories of beings coming here and creating humans—but we had all been created already! What were they doing?

They were creating variations. Most of these variations do not exist anymore because the human variation can exist only if it is adapted to the environment. When they created their versions, most often they looked only at the biological functions of the physiology. They did not program (as you might say, computerwise) internal organs to have spiritual or even higher-purpose functions.

They were slaves, right?

They were strictly physiological and had no ready means then to be raised to higher elevation. No soul could stay in a life form like that for long.

So the bodies that we occupy now, were they reseeded over a certain time all over the planet?

Not reseeded. Most experimentation done in the early days rarely took place before the human prototype was encouraged or seeded here by Sirius elders. These individuals who came to experiment with the human prototype ofttimes visited Sirius first. They were made aware of the experiment, since it was not a secret, and were even given a certain amount of genetic material as long as they were reasonably light beings. They were allowed a certain amount of input, especially if they could put forth a reason, a justification for their own genetic material being included in your bodies.

Some of them justified it very well, such as Andromedans, who came down and produced a variation of human being that could not survive indefinitely, but they showed us that there was something that could be of value. For example, Andromedan basic genetics have the capacity to adapt the brain and nervous system over time to challenges that might overcome other species, such as profound changes in climate. So Andromedans proved that their genetics, to some slight extent, should be included. So it was added by Sirius elders.

So this whole taking of DNA, some here, some here, some there, from all over the galaxy—that was after you did the prototype. Then the Sirian elders basically contracted this original body suit?

We created a prototype in our consciousness and encouraged Sirian elders to create a physical prototype. The prototype initially stayed on Sirius. Then after other beings from other galaxies came and said, "How about this? How about that?" (the project was well known around the universe), some of their genetics were included if these races could prove that there was value in it. Most of the time the value was in the eye of the beholder, but sometimes, as in the case of Andromedans and a few others, the value was an actuality.

Were the prototypes called Adam and Eve? Where did that come from?

Oh, that is a story, a nice story, but a story nevertheless. We must stop now. Thank you for attending. It is only so long we can do this, you know.

Thank you very much.

The last message is: We have a belief in the value of this experiment and believe that the highest good will come from it. Good night.

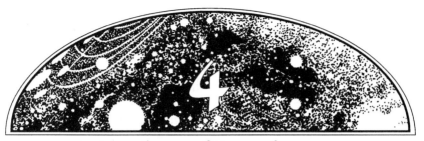

A Teacher of Buddha and Time Master's Assistant

August 1, 1996

I am one of the teachers of that one you call Buddha. It was my amusing manner, perhaps, that caught his attention to help him to find peace in chaos. [He speaks slowly and with gentle humor throughout.] He felt that this was something worthy to pass on to others, and so expanded on my original intention.

I felt that perhaps he could speak with the elders of the religions of the time, but he had a different idea. He thought maybe we could establish a manner and means of value and offer it to anyone concerned, so in this way he expanded my original purpose.

I'm sure you haven't heard of me. I was simply a minor monk in a quiet little temple. But when you are unknown, sometimes you can accomplish more because they don't expect too much of you. When you do something that is even slightly interesting, it is considered a sufficient contribution for your lifetime. In this way one can be relatively unfettered and grow the flowers, which is what I prefer to do, you know. I can speak a little about this person; I spent a little time with him.

Did you come deliberately to work with him, or did you just happen to be there?

I was there, you know. I was born to it, so there I was. He happened to pass through there at the time and stopped to admire an old man's flowers. We had our little talk then, and after that he would come by every so often—by your measurements maybe twice a week.

Was this before he attained his realization, or after?

I think while he was striving toward it. But you see, he lived in an area that was very unstable politically and he was always being distracted. I might have helped him to develop his concentration by showing him how I planted and worked with the flowers.

Flowers, in order to look most beautiful, need a great deal of love and attention. When you are working with them you must give them your complete attention, and sometimes a word here or there doesn't hurt. I allowed him to work with me sometimes, and I believe he understood the nature of the flower meditation as a result. This takes the meditation of focusing on one thing (as all learn on the pathway of true development) to the next step, where one focuses on many things at once and yet can give all those things total attention without distraction from any external source. There might be a battle raging, but it matters not. There might be people arguing; it matters not. There might be children playing; it makes no difference.

Buddha's Vision for the Many

I believe it was this expansion that allowed him to see and go beyond my encouragement of one thing to something that could be applied to the many. I never saw it as anything that could be applied (especially in your time) to so many people who work and are people of the world. I always felt it was meant for those strictly on the path of awareness. But he always had vision. He said, "No, no, I don't want it to be only for a few; I want it to be for the many." I even tried to tell him that the many had much to do—they had to work, they had to look after their children. There was so much; how could they find time to develop this concentration? But he said, "Oh, you will see. It can be done. It just requires devotion time every day."

In those days you were either in devotion all day (people like me) even if you were doing work, or you were not involved at all. But his vision was that one could be of the outer world and still have time for meditation. Oh, he was a visionary, yes.

Do you feel that what we have of his teachings now is what the Buddha really taught?

According to what I can see, most of what he said has been preserved quite well to this day. I believe that might have been because what he was doing in his day was regarded by many to be of value. He could so easily have been caught up in the political or even religious factional affairs, but he would not allow it. He would treat everyone the same, whether they be of common livelihood in the outer world or they be princely, whether they be established as an important religious figure or be just beginning. It was perhaps this method that allowed what he had accomplished to become so widely respected, because it was perceived by the many to be of value, not by the few. Things perceived to be of value by the few tend to be relegated to the few, but those perceived by the many are written and preserved and perpetuated.

Perhaps this was his greatest victory, because it has been preserved today very much the way he proposed it originally. It has never become elitist. As a matter of fact, the people who practice the things he supported are perhaps the least elitist of any pathway even in your time. He always encouraged great tolerance, reverence and interest in other people's sacred pathways, and even this has been written into what he believed.

So not only his methods but perhaps also his personality are still preserved today in what is called Buddhism. You know, that's the one thing that perhaps he would have been a little shy about. Nevertheless, it is acceptable.

Did his teaching have an effect on you and the rest of your life?

No. I felt good to see what he was doing, but I *had* a life. I had a life before I met him and I had a life when he went out to do his work. My life remained very constant, so I cannot say his teaching affected me, but certainly my friendship with him was most pleasant.

Do you work with him now?

In spirit, you mean? We are peers, but I cannot say I work with him directly. Nowadays I find that I'm still allowed to be able to work with the essences, or the individual spirits, of flowers. So my work goes on, but from the spirit world.

Are they essences of flowers of this planet or someplace else?

Living inside the Planet in 2500

I believe it is this planet, though somewhat in the future of your now time, because everything is very green and lush and beautiful. I don't think there are people living on the surface; I think they are inside the planet. Let me see if I can get a year for you of your calendar . . . I think it is right around 2500. The whole surface of the planet now is very much like a park.

And the humans live inside?

Yes, in spaces that have been there for a long time. I believe, from what I have come to understand, that spaces within the planet have been here for a very long time, just waiting for people to occupy them. These spaces might not be fully discovered until around 2270, when the dimensional doorway will be discovered by several spiritual individuals who will be exploring a particularly beautiful canyon. They will discover the dimensional doorway accidentally (as very often happens). They will be singing and telling jokes and laughing and having fun and lo, the doorway will open because of their mood and their song. This way they will discover that the door accommodates those of good humor and song and *only* those. Thus if you are too serious or upset, you are allowed to have that, but elsewhere.

So much of what is inside your planet now is protected because one must have a certain feeling around oneself to enter this world.

Can you give us an idea of what the population is in 2500 inside the planet?

Well, I think it is quite fixed. It ranges between 37 and 38 million.

And they come on the surface of the planet to enjoy it?

Not very much, because they have oceans and parks and sunshine inside the planet. Oh, I think that occasionally they might fly over the surface just to enjoy it, like you might take a ride in the country to enjoy the beauty. But I think the surface is mainly preserved for the plants and animals.

Did you have lives after that life with the Buddha on this planet?

No, it turned out to be my last life. I have had much time to consider the value of it and to be grateful to the monk in charge of my little temple, who allowed me in my old age to, as he said, "play with the flowers." A good person.

Buddha in the Present

Can you tell us what the Buddha does now?

He's very actively involved with you even in your time. The meditative state you call nirvana he achieved long ago, and from this state he is in connection with all dimensions of life that are attuned to beauty, something he always appreciated. From this position he projects through his self this beauty to those who might choose to meditate in his suggested fashion on Earth. He projects it to Earth to those living on Earth now.

So he doesn't have an active role in the government of the galaxy or a position where he interacts with other beings on that level?

Remember, he never sought that. To him, the average person, the common person, was just as important as the mightiest prince. Why would he change his point of view now? No, no, he does not seek anything that has to do with direction; even influence has never been of interest to him. Even when he was doing his work when he was a physical being, he did not promote what he was doing. It's just that because it was such a wonderful thing, people sought him out. He has never been interested in any form of influence other than the achievement of the state of beauty—of the mind, body, spirit and feeling that he has been in for many years now.

Okay, thank you. We had read a reference that he was in the Federation in some executive position.

Can you imagine him doing that, really, as much as you might know about him? My opinion, from my observation only, is that perhaps one of his teachers might be doing that. But we were not seeking influence in our time. We were available with what we had to offer to help make the lives of others more pleasant and perhaps help them align more clearly with the intention of spirit, but not to say, "This is the way."

Since your name didn't get in the record books then, can you give us the name you had at that time?

I'm afraid if I do you will simply just say, "What a wonderful being!" How about if I give you a translation? A moment . . . "he who embraces the spirit of flowers."

Is that your name now?

Close enough, but perhaps in a little different language. I don't think I can make that language with this physical self. Sounds are very incompatible with the human language-making mechanism.

Could we get you to assist us with our flowers here in this time? We're going to be doing a lot of work with some flowers.

I would recommend that you treat them each as individuals and sing to them. I always would chant to them in my little garden. [A rumble of thunder sounds.] The sky speaks!

Like the chants.

Chanting to the flowers—they always seem to like it very much, and they would be strong. I used to say (well, the person in charge used to say, but I repeated it) that the flowers respected spirit. So I recommend chanting and understanding that flowers are individuals just like people. Some need more attention; some don't want too much of it, just like children.

Thank you very much.

Good night.

Zoosh: Well, that was different.

The being who talked about regulating and calibrating time did not create time. Is there a time master who actually creates time?

I think that time is an after-effect of the exposure to the physics of planetary-body movement. It is more like that. One tends to quantify day and night, so that essence of time would perhaps simply be an observed factor. But I think it is also possible that we could ask, "Does a time master create time?" I'd say that Time Master, if we can call him that, would create . . . have you ever made pasta?

Yes.

If you've ever made pasta, you shove the dough through this little device and out come little bits of things. It's very much like that. He shoves the material (time) *through* something, and out come strands of potential time sequencing, which are then available.

Can someone talk more about that?

A ll right. I am Time Master's apprentice. He will not speak to you because he's always laughing, and he cannot get enough of his worded sequences in between laughter [spoken gently, with laughter bubbling between phrases]. He's very cheerful. I am quite serious, but I cannot live with him without getting a little cheerful myself.

Why does he laugh so much? Because of his own joke, this time thing?

He does consider it that. It is like spaghetti sauce! How many ways can you make it? After a while the spaghetti begins to taste like something else. That is his stock joke, I think.

So he's a very funny character, and you cannot be around him without being affected. But he is the master and I am the person who stirs the ingredients and shoves it through the pasta maker, as Zoosh would say.

So who is the Time Master? Does he have a name?

Time Master is a sufficient name. You know, at this place of existence people do not really use names. It is more like titles, jobs. I understand that many of you have names that have to do with jobs and so on—baker, tailor, yes?

Where is this place where you two are doing this thing?

He's making jokes in the background; I guess I have to pass them on. He says, "It's in the laugh zone." It is roughly between the nineteenth quadrant of the thirty-third level of the eighteenth dimension, and he's saying, "in the corner in the back."

Okay. The timekeeper we talked to the other night uses a huge crystal and its facets to do his regulating. Who created the crystal in the center of that planet?

It seems to me that this was something of Creator. My master says no, it was not his creation. He says, "Don't blame *me* for it!" (He is joking.) "No," he says, "Creator created the crystal."

Do you use it? How do you create time? Can you tell us about it, other than the spaghetti analogy?

It is a pretty good analogy, really, but let's see. It is much easier to create time backward, and that's how we do it. We take a look at Creator's scenarios for different beings and how Creator generally sets up the intention for their lives and accomplishments and goals and intrigues—everything. Then, having a scenario to look at, we apply. My master says, "We create a recipe." That's about it—we create a recipe for a time sequence that would bring this about in the fullest way possible. It is not our assignment to bring it about in the quickest way; really quite the opposite. Creator would prefer, if He has some intentions in mind for groups of souls, that those intentions be accomplished. So sometimes we create a very straight and flowing time. At other moments we will make it long and bending, though it would seem like tortuous time. For any group of souls to achieve what has been laid out in front of them, they must have the opportunity to do so. So we create time backward.

Creating This Loop of Time

How did you create this loop of time we are on now?

That was easy to do, my master says, because it was basically a joke. The idea was how to get here from there. You had to get to a place that was where you just came from. It would be as if you were going down a trail and walked through a door. Ten feet past that door you realized you forgot your car keys, but the door doesn't swing the other way. So you have to walk *waaaay* around the planet until you can come around the other side and pick up your car keys. It's very much like that.

So we created—okay, okay, *Time Master* created, I just shoved the ingredients in the blender. From the point of where you had to come back in, he just stretched the time and tied it into a bow tie, went zippity-zippity like this with his . . . well, he doesn't have hands, does he? But he pulled out a loop and stretched it in such a way that you would be able to experience the most you possibly could out of a few hours.

It is intended, I believe, that you come back about 26 hours before you left. So Time Master took that 26 hours and stretched that entire

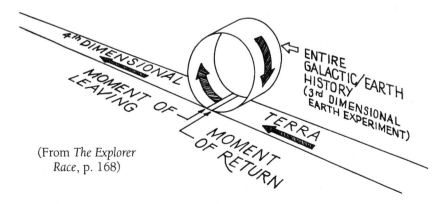

(From *The Explorer Race*, p. 168)

loop you've been on. All this time, for millions of years, is basically 26 hours stretched out to a mighty long, thin piece of time spaghetti. That's what it was—26 hours stretched out into thousands of lifetimes. [Chuckles.]

In our terms of time, can you give us a date when it started?

It's hard to do because it's interdimensional. It's easier to give an analogy. I'm picking somebody here in the room. This young woman over here has now lived on this sequence of lives about 43 lives so far, and her sequence started about three, four million years ago, times her sequence, times 0.38^2. *No, no, it's a joke!* [Laughter.] It's impossible to tell you because it's interdimensional. You started out at quite a high dimension, but then you had to descend to a lower dimension, because in order to stretch 26 hours into millions of years, it was necessary to immediately go interdimensional.

We mentioned that to the Creator. We said, "There is no way we can turn 26 hours into millions of years unless we immediately go to another dimension that's slower. Then we can make it as long as you want." Creator said, "That's fine" (in Creator talk), so we did that right away. If we hadn't done it right away, you might not have had enough time when you got back to that dimension to return to 26 hours before you left.

What dimension did we start on?

This looks like right around 5.25 to me. But because the universe is expanding in some way that you have something to do with (I don't know about all that, it's not my business), it looks to me like you're coming back at right around 4.7. So after you come back you're going to have the chance to complete that dimensional doorway to the fifth dimension fairly soon.

So the entire Explorer Race experiment was accomplished on this loop of time?

Yes, and that's why I'm saying millions of years, because you had lots of places to go, and the only way for you to get there in 26 hours total was to immediately descend to lower vibrations to stretch time. Let me give you an example (no joke now): If you had one second of time at the seventh dimension, and we brought that second of time as it exists on the seventh dimension to, say, the third dimension, you would then have about 10.5 billion years.

That's why when extraterrestrials tell you they live a thousand years (comparative to your time), sometimes they are speaking of their own dimension's years. You might have been told that someone lives ten thousand years or that they are immortal. When you are told that they are immortal, you have to understand that they might *appear* to be immortal to them at their dimension (and certainly at your dimension), but if they were to go up in dimensions, their time of life would be measured. I will say this: There is a lot of math on this job! To all you mathematicians and even the geometry people and physicists, you'd have a lot of fun here.

What's the significance of the 26 hours?

I believe someone had made a decision on your behalf that needed to be altered, and you had 26 hours in which you could remain in that place in that dimension. But after that 26 hours you would have gone in many different directions. Imagine floating outside a spaceship with your space suit on and throwing up a deck of cards. All the cards would go in 52 directions and you have only enough fuel to go get one of them. Well, you could spend a long time picking up that deck of cards. To keep you united as a group, it was believed necessary to grab you by the tails and send you on this journey. You must remember that Creator had a plan for you, and to fulfill this plan you had to stay together.

Is there some way we could visit you or the Time Master?

Following the sound of laughter is useful . . . let's see. I don't know if mathematics would be useful. If you have ever talked to a physicist well on in her art, you will notice that no matter how serious she or he might have been when she was learning and the more she knows about physics the more humorous she gets. If you can, be around these people who are often laughing at just about everything, because they realize the tremendous joke in the upper echelons of physics (by the time they get there they realize that fixed laws of physics do not exist). Have a few laughs with them and you might hear an echo. That will be my master.

Do you and he remember anything before this job? Do you have memories of previous jobs or previous lives or previous creations?

No, I do not. One moment. My master says he existed before this assignment as a portion of the spirit of humor. Now I understand why my master is such a funny fellow. But he was removed from the spirit of humor for this job. He says Creator has always thought of time as being rather amusing.

Is he a relation to the Jester? [See **Shining the Light II,** *chapter 17].*

No, because sometimes the Jester can make jokes at the expense of others.

So he has a purer, more loving . . .

He has never made a joke at my expense or at the expense of anybody that I am aware of, so maybe not the Jester.

Time Wheels

Are there any places on the planet where they have something like time wheels that keep time? I've seen what I call time wheels (I didn't know what they were) in various places—huge wheels in space, and some I've seen underground lying flat. Are these related to different areas that need to keep time for various reasons on the planet?

I know what you speak of; let me ask my master. Master says that these are clocks, but they are clocks that communicate in color and tone. They do not exactly keep time as you have experienced it, but they are set to the time of the future, like an alarm clock. As an alarm clock it is their bias to help to pull the planet and her occupants to this higher dimension that you are achieving. So I think it is more an alarm clock.

At Silbury Hill in England I saw two huge wheels, one on each side of the hill. Can you be specific about different information or different frequencies or whatever they're keeping?

Here we have one that is associated with direction, moving one way. You have seen this. Then there is another one moving the other way that is associated with future. The one that is associated with direction speaks in harmonics through stone. The other that is associated with the future speaks with the song of songbirds. Yes, songbirds have an important function. There are some songbirds that are bright orange and yellow, of whom there are few left on your plane of existence. Since the clock is of the future, future birds will come to give the clock messages. The clock must reset itself in order to move up the sequence of dimensional expansion or slow down the sequence if something has remained unaccomplished.

Do you calibrate that?

We do, yes. We do this like telegraphed tones or colors, and these messages will arrive in some way that is relatively unnoticed, though we have used rainbows in a pinch. Nowadays we often speak to the songbirds of the future because the present songbirds are too busy trying to preserve themselves. We speak to them of the future, and I think that if there are enough songbirds here, they are instructed from those future ones about what to do, where to fly, how to sing, when and how long— very complex. One would not think, looking at such a little innocent creature, that it has the capacity for such erudite physics. Never prejudge.

Back to the 26 hours: When we get there, what will have happened at the end of that 26 hours? What's going to happen now?

You will change your minds. You will have enough recollection of the experience that you will change your minds, and the sequence, albeit at a slightly denser dimension, will continue. I believe this denser dimension is Creator's safety mechanism.

Are you talking about the 3.0 and the ones who are coming behind us?

No. I am talking about when you return you're going to be at 4.7, not 5.25 where you started out. Being at 4.7 is a safety mechanism. This way, as you continue to move up in dimension, you will show Creator that you have truly accomplished what was intended. By the time you get to 5.25, mistakes will be ruled out. And you will move rather quickly to 5.25, probably within one generation, perhaps even no more than a score of years.

The Council's Mistake: Deciding to Control

What is the mistake that we're attempting to change?

As near as I can tell, it was basically a decision based on control. One must naturally release all control to exist at higher dimensions. You cannot have any control at all. The decision was made to control something, and that does not work at higher dimensions. But on the other hand, it made it much easier for us to stretch that 26 hours into lower dimensions, because in lower dimensions we were able to expand and lengthen that sequence because control does exist in the lower dimensions, and the consequences of that decision could easily be experienced.

Who or what is trying to control who or what?

I believe there was a decision to disregard the absolute benevolence of Creator and to pursue the idea of Creator's *will.* Creator does not have will, as much as I am aware. Creator is a mass of potentials and perhaps even blessings. But I am not aware that Creator has ever exercised will. Again, will is truly an aspect of control, is it not?

Were there names or personalities?

Someone to blame, yes?

Something we would recognize in myth or in story? Is this Lucifer's rebellion?

No. I believe it was a council of the most wise beings. They simply chose the idea—it was such a simple thing, you know, at the time . . . they are saying (I am sequencing into their time frame; here's what they are saying): Their speaker says (no, I cannot speak the speaker's words) that the intention was to discover whether there was something else besides Creator's love. The intention was to see whether Creator had a design for life. A design for life falls neatly into the category of Creator's will. But Creator does not have a design for life that Creator imposes. Creator might encourage or give you opportunities, but Creator does not impose anything upon any of Creator's offspring (which you call souls).

It was that seemingly innocent desire to include, to seek, to ask for, to be directed toward Creator's design for life that created the potential for Creator's will, then man's will, then woman's will, then willful children—everything. It also created the potential for being right and wrong. In other words, it unintentionally created the separation. Because it was separation, it was infinitely easier to separate you from that dimension and bring you into the world of polarity, where separation is a given. There you could experience the fullest possible understandings, a complete examination of separation—experiencing its benefits and, most important, its consequences—as Time Master says, to find out what you did and how to get out of it.

But wasn't this a setup? Because there was, after all, the intent to create the Explorer Race, which would use negativity in a positive way?

Oh, I think Creator might have had this as an idea also, but I do not speak for Creator. I can only give you my point of view. Certainly that is possible.

Ask the Time Master. Is that his understanding? Was this the beginning of the experiment, or was this something that happened, after which they said, "Well, let's use this for this experiment?"

I think the latter. Time Master indicates that it was a choice that allowed the Creator to exercise the option to create Explorer Race. Creator has told Time Master that you would have become Explorer Race inevitably, but probably much, much later in time sequence had you not made that particular decision. When I say "you," these nine souls were apparently those after whom the branch of souls was patterned. Creator chose to pattern your soul images after these beings. Time Master says they were a little taller than most of you on Earth, averaging around eight feet, but occasionally you have a few throwbacks, people who are eight feet tall. There hasn't been one lately.

Did the council have a name, like the Council of Nine?

No, I do not think this was the Nine. *They* would never have made a mistake like that. I have never heard of them *ever* making a mistake, but I have not lived as long as my master.

So there were nine souls on this council. They're part of us, they're involved in this, right?

Yes, they have to do that or they would not understand the consequences of their apparently benevolent decision. To them it seemed very benevolent.

Are they incarnated now?

No.

Are they guides and masters, or what?

They are energy around the planet; they follow you in energy. They experience. They have been given the gift to have feelings such as you have, but in spirit form—most unusual.

They've not incarnated ever?

Well, they are incarnated in the sense that they are still themselves, but if you were to see them they would not look like human beings; they would look like energy. Sometimes they take different forms, but they have feelings like you. This was granted to them as a means and as a gift to understand. Most spirits do *not* have feelings like you. Feelings like you have allow you to learn.

Do they have any type of identity that we could use if we ever need them to talk to or interact with?

I think they most often appear as blue light. They have interacted extensively with the citizens of the Pleiades. This is perhaps because the citizens of the Pleiades did not choose polarity as you did, so they have been allowed to interact with them to support and sustain (as Time Master says) their *oops!* Citizens of the Pleiades would seem to not have chosen polarity at all, though I can see many of them as men and women, and that certainly looks like polarity to me. Time Master says they have in some cases chosen benevolent polarity. I see.

In this time loop we're in, when do we come up for that twenty-sixth hour? What hour are we on now?

The Fifteenth Hour

What an interesting question! Let me see. Time Master says you're in the fifteenth hour, but you will make the last amount of time very quickly. As you come back into the loop, you will experience it quite quickly. But you are in the fifteenth hour. (Time Master shows me on a graph.)

So we'll accelerate, and that gets us into the other dimension—the fourth as we come down the loop? Like gravity accelerates a car?

You are now coming up the loop, but I think it is not acceleration; it is pull. You are being pulled from the other side. You can be in your automobile and have acceleration, and this is something you control for the most part. But when you are pulled, sometimes you do not notice. It is surprising and can disorient you for a time. You have been getting pulled a lot lately; that is why so many of you are disoriented. Not only is time changing, but also your physical parameters are changing. One cannot remain oriented when the ground moves underneath you.

How many years will it take to get from 15 to 26?

How can I say that? Time Master says, "Huh-uh."

Is everyone on this planet going at the same speed? Will they all come out of the loop together?

Interestingly enough, yes. One might think that people who seem to exhibit dense manners of behavior would be moving slower and spiritual people faster, but it is not so. They are all moving at exactly the same sequence. An interesting question, that.

I'd like to get a little bit into the strands of spaghetti. There are alternate realities, possible realities, probable realities: Do they all exist on separate strands? Are they all coming together now? How does that work?

You are now all on a similar strand. If there are groups of souls on an adventure such as your own, you will exist basically in the same strand. But what happens if one being should choose to experience some unique strand of time? For example, to experience time in reverse (which can be done), one could conceivably start out as an older, wiser individual with accumulated wisdom and then gradually move backward to the point of your inception. This is oftentimes done by those examining a cyclical life after they have lived one on Earth. They will resequence time from back to front or front to back (whatever you want to call it) from where they are. Time Master says, "Just tell them to figure out how they got here from there, and in order to do that, you go back." That is one way an individual soul might experience time. So there are many choices.

The President's Return; the End of Separation

I was thinking particularly of the President whose time line was moved to another reality. Are there other realities—close, parallel, coexisting, but faster? How does that work?

This President you are referring to is not the President you now have?

No. This is the President that Zoosh went with when the secret government moved his time line to another reality.

I see. This President, I believe, is simply existing in an alternate reality, a reality very close now to your own. I think that when this president returns, he will most likely be a premier or president of the united nations of the world.

Are he and that alternate reality coming back together to be totally in one space? Is that what's happening?

Merging at some point? Yes, I think they will merge right around 25 years from now, and then this being by that time will become president or (I think they will have a different title) director, perhaps, of the United Nations of the World.

Do all human beings born have their own time line?

A question for Time Master, surely. Time Master says that everyone has his own variables, potentials, offshoots. Time Master says this has to do with choices you might make, but basically you are born to the time line that exists so you will have the opportunity to experience the lessons of what Zoosh calls Explorer Race.

I'd still like to find out all about these different realities. At some point are they all going to merge into one?

No. Time Master says choices must always be available for many to learn many different things. All times, all sequences, all souls are *now* one. If you change your perspective as you do when you move through the veils after life (and sometimes, Time Master says, at the deepest levels of sleep), then you can literally feel yourself being a part of all beings and having all knowledge, all wisdom and so on (Time Master says, "all humor"). So separation is part of a temporary option that we are involved in providing, but it is very temporary.

Until the fourth dimension? Until when?

Until you move through the veil, until you move to the deepest levels of sleep, until you are perhaps more accomplished spiritually—I would guess around 4.7 dimension. I think when you are in 4.0 (as

Zoosh says, 4.1 and so on), all of you are still not that accomplished spiritually yet, but you will have released some of your self-destructive patterns. The *basis* of self-destruction, of course, is the desire to return to the One. You cannot destroy your immortal personality, can you? So sometimes these self-destructive attitudes are very short-sighted. But as near as I can tell, the true spiritual accomplishments and the feeling, even in states beyond meditation—the feeling that you come and go and exist in life to feel connected with the One—is more of a fifth-dimensional thing. By the time you are in 4.7 you will be feeling that.

How do these realities work? What is the barrier? Is it a level of frequency? What keeps them apart?

Ah, here we come to math. I would say it is easier to express in terms of tone. If you can obtain or simply stand in front of a xylophone, each tone that is clear, true (a good instrument has clear true tones) would be a mechanism. The mechanism is tone, not exactly frequency as you measure it now because that is missing two or three very important structures, one of which has to do with the feeling of total love (unconditional, as you say). It is a physical feeling and tends to radiate or emanate a certain energy. Another factor that frequency instruments miss now has to do with the inclusion of the betterment of all beings. (Time Master doesn't want me to give you the other one.)

The main thing is that the dimensions, the options, the choices, have very much to do with tone in harmony with feeling and attitude. (What I just said encompasses the thing Time Master does not want me to tell you.)

So we choose a particular time stream and particular reality that to us is the only reality. But is there a part of us in a parallel reality who thinks that it's experiencing the only reality?

No, no, because while that might exist in some other dimensions and some other places, in order to learn the lessons of this place, one must be able to devote one's total attention here. That is why you do not remember who you are here. If you remembered who you are, you would easily move past all of the lessons here, plus you would have much distraction. Here one must be totally caught up in life and forget who one truly is in order to learn. No, this type of distraction does not exist for the average person, though there are some spiritual people, some shamanic people and some identified as schizophrenic who can do this. Granted, they must be able to maintain this in a way that is of comfort to themselves and others around them. Occasionally these people do exist. In your society (which is perhaps less tolerant of people who are different) they are not always treated so well. But by being able to be aware of other potential existences and even true personalities at other optional levels, one can call on a great deal of wisdom one has not actually earned in this current focus.

In this present focus, then, we can call on those other parts of the soul that are inhabiting these other realities. Is that what you're saying?

No, I'm saying that some people do that, but it is not intended that you do that too much, because it will take you *out* of the lessons that are here. And if you do not learn your lessons in this life, you will surely come back into this time sequence. Those who think that they can be picked up by a ship and go to the Pleiades and just let go of this whole Explorer Race thing—guess again!

Probable Realities

Is it possible for a soul to have a way of making its own kind of loop to have an experience of different possibilities or choices?

You mean a choice you have made, and you would like to make a different choice?

Through dream life or astral activities, is it possible to explore several things? I'm trying to understand how Seth's probable realities fit into tonight's understanding.

I cannot say through dream life. Perhaps the best way to do it would be through meditation, because that is something you can focus or aim. But the "probable realities" of that particular being—I believe we have already discussed this. It is *options.* If, on the other hand, you are referring to the idea of a choice that one has made, and it has its consequences—if one would prefer to make another choice, this is not allowed here because it interferes with your lessons. Certainly at other levels you can do this anytime you wish. But you do not have those lessons there. If consequences are *not* the lesson, you do not have to experience them.

No, I think that probable realities exist in theory, and in some cases in practical application as one is moving through dimensions. Time Master says to give you an example: Many of you do not have the same personality that you had in 3.0 dimension; your personality has altered. Partly this has to do with an expanded spirit, but also with your experience and who you are in other dimensions. This is an example, I believe.

No, I think that it is not intended that you escape from the lesson of consequence. After this life you can change it—between lives, you know, when you examine it and go back and say, "Where did this decision come from?" This is a precursor to the examination—to find out exactly where it came from. This happens very often between lives beyond the veil.

After Rediscovering Who You Are, You Resequence

Let's go back to where we joyfully come out of this great experience. What sort of adventure lies ahead of us at that point?

I think you spend quite a bit of time (Time Master has built this in) discovering who you are, individually and collectively. Collectively would mean, of course, two by two, four by four, exponentially all the way up, even including, Time Master says, all beings everywhere. This takes a certain amount of experience. Although it can be experienced beyond the veil in that moment of total oneness, of being a portion of all beings, it is intended that you have the opportunity to experience this perhaps for 25 to 35 experiential-time years.

As you move through this experience it will be almost like going through the veil, only not completely, of course, because you will remain physical. But I think it is like a reward; Time Master says that rediscovering oneself is like a reward *while* you're rediscovering it. Once you are locked into who you are and know who you are, the reward is over. Even though you enjoy it, and that is pleasant and wonderful, the moment of the joy of discovery is over. Time Master believes you deserve this, so, as Time Master says, why rush?

Okay, then what? Do we have a lot of choices? Do we have a commitment? Do we have an agenda? What happens after that?

Life! Nothing in writing—whatever you want. There is no limit, according to what I know. You mean, where do you all go from here? asks Time Master. You go all different places once you have resequenced. You go where you want to go. Some of you go to the highest dimensions, some of you to the lowest, if you wish. Some of you to this side of the universe, some to the other side—wherever you wish.

So we're going to stay in this loop until we resequence, until we repeat that?

Yes, when you resequence—when you get back to 4.7 and then move up to 5.25 and make the other decision—then you can do whatever you want. Of course, it is during that time you will probably explore space, come into contact with people to fulfill your potential as the Explorer Race, as stated by friend Zoosh. But I think that at some point in time you intend to cocreate with Creator, so I expect it will happen after 5.25. I feel quite certain of that.

Do you have a name we can use or relate to besides Time Master's Assistant?

Time Master calls me Assistant, and I've never known any other name, so I guess that is my name. My name is Assistant.

If we looked at you what would we see?

If you were to look at me you would see star fields. I am not encapsulated as you are. One cannot work on time and be encapsulated *in* time. Even you who are spiritually attuned and who visit other times do this outside of your encapsulation in the immortal you that has no boundaries. So I cannot be physicalized like you because there are boundaries that . . . well, look at this—these [physical surroundings] are boundaries, you know, all of this.

What does Time Master look like?

He likes to say "like many suns," but he also looks like star fields.

So how does what you do relate to the Timekeeper, who talked about regulating time? What is your interaction with that crystal in the center of that planet? Do they consult with you?

Time Master says that occasionally they do consult with him. (Time Master indicates also that he is not a "him," but this is just how we are referring to. . . "her." [Chuckles.] Okay, I can make a joke too, yes?) So yes, Time Master does consult with these individuals on some occasions. Time Master says, "Do not use the word to define itself."

After we get to 5.25, how does time work then, and what is your interaction with us then? There is sequencing and there's experience, but not time as we know it?

I think that time is not measured in days. It tends to be measured more in accumulation of wisdom. One's body might grow from childhood to old age, yes, but time is measured more by how much wisdom you acquire that is of value to yourself and others. So it is slanted, in a sense. One does not accumulate wisdom for its own sake, but for the sake of its application. So when high-dimensional beings or extraterrestrials tell you how old they are, they are using their accumulation of wisdom converted to years, which to them means simply how long it would take you to accumulate the wisdom they have if you were to go on living in this body but exposed to circumstances similar to theirs. Mathematics!

You're a wonderful speaker. I wonder if Time Master could just say a few words, or can he keep a straight face long enough to . . .

At the end of our conversation Time Master will make a brief statement.

All right. Tell him his assistant has been great.

Well, he says he's not going to give me a raise—but that is acceptable.

Is there anything else we haven't asked about that would be helpful to put in this book about time and that is not advanced mathematics?

Maybe to just know that even though you seem to be living in sequence of time now, you are actually living very much like extraterrestrials in terms of acquiring wisdom. Except that you have chosen to acquire wisdom en masse as the Explorer Race rather than as individuals. Time Master says you do acquire wisdom for your individual personality, but because it is intended that you apply so much of what you have learned as an Explorer Race way of being, even within this context you are living in the time of acquired wisdom. Thus what seems to be sequenced by days, weeks, months, years, is in fact actually sequenced by wisdom.

So we're getting wisdom whether we like it or not?

Yes, we all do that.

All of the Explorer Race is getting wisdom?

Oh yes, I do not know of *any* being who does not acquire wisdom wherever they might be. For any being the acquisition of wisdom is a given, Time Master says.

What happens when the Creator moves on up to explore His own potential? Do you stay here and maintain time, or are you going to have some assistants who do that and you get to move up?

Time Master says that is when I am promoted and Time Master goes with the Boss.

All right!

So I will say good evening, and Time Master has a brief statement to make.

[Time Master gives a big and very long laugh.]

Now, Zoosh speaking. As you can see, other beings have humor besides myself and yourselves. We do not bring through only extraterrestrials for this book, but beings from all over. It's going to be a marvelous collection of adventurers.

Absolutely. Do you think you can make an appointment with the Buddha? I'd love to talk to him.

I will ask him to aim some of his nirvanic energy toward your deepest dream state tonight. I will even ask him to do that for anyone who is reading this. Reread this just before you go to sleep and ask for that, and perhaps you will remember when you wake up the many colors of reality that Buddha has acquired.

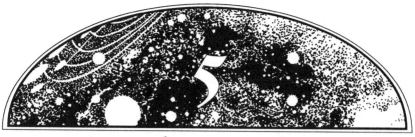

Designers of Human Physiology

August 8, 1996

reetings. We are the individuals from the organization planetoid. It is our job to set up, sustain and maintain, modify and even mitigate organisms, microorganisms and their components. We exist and consult with those who have established the form and format for your corporeal selves to provide a system by which your corporeal selves can be kept from getting too strong and long-lasting. [Laughs.] I'm sure that sounds strange and ruthless, but the soul's experience in your physical bodies was designed to complete all of its core lessons, mitigating lessons, even lessons you might opt for during a lifetime of no more than 95 Earth years.

Physical forms, when they are amplified by light waves such as your own, and evolved beings such as you are tend to coordinate themselves with those light waves and become more long-lasting. On the surface you might find it to be ruthless to program your physical selves to age (or disintegrate, as we would call it), but in our experience it is so easy for your lightbodies to become actively engaged in perpetuating the length of one's physical corporeal personality that without the restrictions that we might impose, the tendency is to live in the physical self for 350 to 550 years. Your physiological body certainly has that capacity and might in some circumstances survive for 750 years.

In days gone by the physical self was able to sustain itself for great lengths of time when there were fewer individuals on Earth and there was a desire for a human presence. At those times we did not interfere at all and did nothing to create an oxidization process by which break-downs would occur in your cell walls. But in recent years we have been informed by Creator's assistants that your souls needed a faster turn-over. With this need for the soul to experience its lessons and come and go more quickly, we have cooperated to shorten the time available for an individual in the physical self.

To some extent this has to do with how many of you are here. If you lived to be even 350 years old, the population crush would become impossible to deal with and the accumulation of wisdom would tend to alter the intention of the Explorer Race scenario, which, to the extent I understand it, is that you evolve as a group rather than as individuals. My understanding is that your evolution has been significant even *before* you are allowed to manifest here, because any individual soul is consid-ered inexperienced if they have not had some form of spiritual mastery before incarnating here.

Glandular Dysfunction (Old Age) and
Genetic Dispersion (Change)

So we have been requested over the years (since it is our job to work with cells and biologicals in general) to create glandular func-tions (not diseases) that would excuse the soul from the physical self for cause—otherwise known as old age or the deterioration of the physical self. Our job, then, has been to create a vast web of genetic dispersion so complex that it would be self-reproducing and also change on its own. Each individual portion of DNA itself will tend to evolve along its own line of evolution. This makes it like a code that is very hard to crack because it is never stable, remaining in constant motion and thus very difficult to predict even by the greatest mathe-matical computers.

The purpose is not to harm you, but your immortal selves come here to have a brief moment to learn and grow, not to stay. Your immortal powers are restricted here, but they are needed elsewhere. Why do you think that so often these days you must suddenly sleep in the middle of the day? When you fall into these deep sleeps, it is always because you, your specific self, are needed elsewhere; your immortal powers, your innate gifts beyond the veil of this physical life, are needed elsewhere and you perform deeds in some part of the universe, perhaps not even on Earth. Then you return from this very deep sleep perhaps in twenty or forty minutes and go on with your lives.

That is an example. These immortal powers are needed, but these moments of using them in your sleep are not always enough. That is why you cannot be spared to come to this place for too long even for such a worthy cause. So we do not feel at all sad at our job. We also know that as a result of your coming to this place and forgetting who you are, it is natural to want to perpetuate your lives, being caught up in the myth that this is all there is.

No, I feel it is very important for you to not overly linger. This does not mean that you should jump off a cliff, but rather at the end of your natural cycle know that you will go on and be involved for a time with whatever gifts and abilities you have before you incarnate elsewhere.

So much is going on now that you are needed even in sleep. You might ask, "Why do we sleep? Does the body need to rest?" Oh, I have been involved a great deal in the process of the creation of the form of the physical body of the Earth human. I can assure you, the body itself does not need much more than two, maybe three hours of sleep a day—deep sleep, reasonably restful sleep or even a meditative state. But very often you sleep six, eight, some of you ten hours a night. This is because you are required elsewhere to do things that only you can do, and sometimes with other souls who are currently residing here. If you understand that, then you will know our purpose.

Our Location and Numbers

If I were to say what our planetoid is called . . . I'm calling it a plane-toid because it is not a naturally created planet. We had a natural planet once, but it did not survive the several trillion years that we needed it, so we created (biologics being our specialty) a form of second cousin (not a clone), a modified version of our planet that is basically a living being that we live inside. This living being is about one-quarter, maybe one-sixth the size of your moon. One might call it an asteroid if there were not living beings within it. We prefer to call it a planetoid because it is our home.

Do we have a name for it? I don't think so. At times we refer to it as (let's see if I can get this) Mitan-tch-tas-tda. Sometimes we call it that. You might ask if I have a name. I don't think I have a name I can trans-late. There aren't so many of us here, you know. In terms of individual personalities, at any given moment there are no more than 700 of us. We have individual jobs, yet we have a capacity to communicate tele-pathically at any moment with each other. In some ways you might say we are facets of a larger personality; yet, not being restricted by the lim-its of an oxidizing physiological self, we've chosen to maintain ourselves in this job because of its value and benefit to you, as we see it.

Is your planet nearby?

Oh no; I would have to say it is fairly close to the point of the unfold-ing of the galaxy Sirius, physiologically speaking. We remain close to that even though material spews out to form planets, stars and so on. These materials go their way; our planetoid is not so much affected by physics as by our need for it to be where it is.

Why does it need to be where it is?

Because it is so close to the source of creation of this galaxy, which has a great deal to do with the design, maintenance and culturalization of the human-being physical form. -

Is that like a black hole in space?

No.

Okay, so you created the pieces that the Founders needed for the creation of our bodies?

Cellular Degeneration and Structural Instability

Yes, we designed into the system an ability to produce and reproduce itself, but with a given life span, cellularly speaking, so that when cellular tissue breaks down at the point it chooses to reproduce itself in some form, it tends to pass itself on in a slightly degenerated form. This allows for what you call the aging or degenerative process; that is something built in. I realize that cellular tissue does not seem to reproduce itself, but be replaced. Nevertheless, it reproduces itself by intent.

So the DNA is degrading, then. Is that what you mean?

The coding of the DNA does not degrade. It remains quite the same throughout your lifetime. But the ability of the cellular structure to maintain its once youthful and vigorous state is lost, because at the point where it begins to give the message to be reproduced in some way, it has already achieved a degree of old age, so it tends to degrade. This is intended; that is how an aging process was created for you.

When did you learn this? Before the Explorer Race?

We learned this long before this universe. We were requested by your Creator to come to this part of creation as it was beginning to unfold and create cellular structure such as we have as well as create and perpetuate a slightly unstable atomic and subatomic structure so that your DNA would be subject to a great deal of changing forces. In other words, Creator wanted variety in a constantly shifting form.

Did you create all cellular structures on this planet, including plants, animals—and humans?

No, we are just involved in the human experiment. That is why I am speaking for this book, because that is what you are interested in, yes?

Our Previous Work

What civilizations or universes or schemes did you practice on before you came here?

Oh, not practice, just continuing. We were involved in the original creation of the composition of light on the subatomic level. We were also involved in the wave-form code that can be most easily expressed as a pulse harmonic of sound. We were also involved in the application of that last technology (if we can call it that) in the creation of the colors white and yellow, but we were not involved in the other colors; that was somebody else's job.

Did somebody assign you to the colors and that mission?

We have always done this. I do not remember a time when we did not. Is it egocentric to say it must be us? [Chuckles.] Then I'll say it, because we have always done this, and I do not remember anybody assigning us.

What created your movement to be involved with white and yellow light? Did some energy spur you?

Oh, you mean who asks us to do these things? Various creators have asked us to perform these various tasks, and if it falls into our purview—what we can actually do—and if we are not over encumbered with other projects, we will take it on. But in terms of the beginning of ourselves, I would have to say there is no beginning; it has been a continuum.

Are you engendered by this Creator, or are you from outside this creation?

We were in existence long before this Creator asked us to participate in Its bold experiment.

So you came in with Creator? Are you one of the friends of Creator?

Oh, I don't know if we are qualified for that inner circle, but we did not come in initially. I believe your Creator did not initially plan to create this Explorer Race project, but when It did . . .

Then He went out and got experts, and that included you?

How's the joke: "If we do say so ourselves"?

What form do you have, or do you have one?

If you were able to see us, we would look like white or gold lights with a cord going back to a central white-gold light. We number 700 in all, with the center being our infinite cortex.

Is that established in this creation, or is that out of the creation?

We are able to take it from one creation to another. I do not know if "established" applies.

But you came here as a unit; you're not connected to something beyond this creation. You came here as a being.

Yes, we came here as a group in our planetoid.

Do you have a name as a group, a logos identification?

I don't think we have a name.

A sound?

I don't think so. Let's see if I can come up with some recognizable pattern. [Pause.] No, our response comes as a result of a feeling identifiable as a need from sources we would identify as creators. And these creators would have to be qualified. This means they would have to be involved in a creation. We do not come to talk or to theorize, only to apply.

How is your ability to create cellular units used in other universes and creations?

What We Can Do for a Soul

Sometimes we have been called upon to create a tremendous diversity for an individual soul. Occasionally, a soul (what you would call an immortal personality) decides that it wants to experience a given lesson or set of lessons in very subtle but similar forms. Occasionally an individual is involved in an effort that I would call becoming a junior creator, meaning that this kind of life series *always* precedes becoming a creator. If this is something we have not done before (it's happened four or five times) and if they have a need, we will come and design related, but slightly altered, genomes and patterns of genes (or patterns of particles, if you choose) that will form some image of light or mass that, by its very slight alteration, will be able to play out variations of a given lesson or set of lessons.

For example, this might be a human being who would take on a given lesson, and in a series of lives experience that same lesson as one sex or another, and different races or different nationalities or subgroups. This allows an individual soul to scrutinize a lesson from all available points of view within that particular genetic body type.

Being handicapped and all that?

Certainly, or even gifted.

It's a belief system that they needed to play through?

If they wish to play through. We have responded to this only four or five times before, and these individuals were always getting ready to become creators. This is a typical thing a creator will do before it chooses to establish itself with the responsibility of creation and megacreation. One might say, in the larger sense, that you as the Explorer Race taken en masse are all here on Earth doing that right now—examining a set of lessons from every possible position through the variety you have available here in races, cultures and so on.

What you're saying is that you provide the cells for the human body that have all the bacteria, viruses, hormones and a kind of clock to slow down and stop at a certain time . . .

No bacteria or viruses. Bacteria and viruses are associated with Mother Earth. Mother Earth joins in our project in the sense that she does not care to loan you her material mass for too long. She says, "Yes, take my body if you wish, but bring it back soon."

So how can we get a body that is perfectly functioning and useful and still not keep it too long? What can we do to rejuvenate the body while we're using it? We could leave it in good health. Let's say we have a body for eighty-five years—we don't have to let it degrade. What can we do to make it useful for those years and then leave it?

Why would you want to do that?

Who wants an old, degraded body?

Oh, you do not understand your mortality. You learn nothing, nothing at all, being in a perfect healthy, disease-free body. You learn from being challenged! This is a place of learning here now, and you cannot be a member of the Explorer Race and *not* learn—no, no. This is necessary variety. To even *desire* to remain young and vigorous your whole life, and then supposedly . . . at the snap of your fingers or the wave of a wand you are going to throw the body into the sea and somehow go on?

No, the intention is for the body to change, to go through youth in its vigor and middle age and old age—to change. Remember, one of the aspects of variety is to go through youth, ages of responsibility and old age. This is built in; it is intended. Why would you even *want* to remain young and vigorous your whole life? It isn't as if you die. The body is reclaimed by Earth and you go on as young and vigorous as you have always been. This experiment—this moment of feeling old and tired and even diseased and injured—is so fleeting in the totality of your complete existence as to be faster than the blink of an eye. When taken in the totality of your existence it is nothing. So you would throw the body away?

We've done it an awful lot of times.

Degeneration: Acquiring Wisdom

I think you learn sometimes more *between* lives, eh? No, there is too much to be learned and gained by change to let it go. We support change; we see its value. Each one of us in our planetoid represents a different facet. We do not claim to have the experience you are having, but we do understand the value of many different points of view. One cannot acquire that knowledge of the value of different points of view if one has not personally experienced different points of view about the same thing.

A human child will have a unique point of view about something and perhaps say, "I will always believe this." As the child gets a little older she changes her point of view because of who she is as she evolves, as she becomes more, as she has more experience, as she grows older, as she degenerates. She might change her point of view about that one thing a thousand times. This is largely because of her ability to evolve and acquire physical wisdom. The cells do not simply degenerate; *they acquire wisdom.*

The wisdom, you might say, is there already because Mother Earth has all this wisdom. And yet the wisdom is activated within the cellular structures by your actions, your beliefs, your knowledge, your experience, what you find out is true for you and what you find out is not true for you. The knowledge and wisdom is there in the cells, *activated only by your physical experience.* Yet when you join together in a group you are able to combine your experience and be more as a result. That is only natural, since you are different faces of the same being.

All right, if there are 700 of you beings and you're all a different facet of the one being, do you learn from each other telepathically, or do you actually change duties and look out from different facets of this being?

We are assigned to different duties that we desire, that we like to do, that we enjoy. There's no need to learn from another because we have shared experience in our central core—our central cortex, to use an analogy of the brain.

You have implied that you're here right now because some people are becoming able to use light waves to live longer lives. So what are you doing that's going to be a little different?

I did not imply this, no. I am saying, why do you want to live so long? It is not as if you die—you change. "Death" is a word to explain this change, but there is absolute continuity. Why do you hold your limits to you so tightly? It is, of course (I answer my own question), because you are not allowed to remember who you are—because the moment you remember who you are it would not only defeat the experiment, but you would go join that total you and abandon the experiment.

I understand why you embrace your limits. And yet Creator, at the moment of death and sometimes even before death when you have the chance to prepare for it, lovingly helps you to recognize the continuity, and the moment of death then is not the enemy at all. It is the friend that brings the doorway to your continuum.

Okay, but what you're talking about is coming to an end now. It's changing. We're going up the dimensions, so a lot of what you're talking about is almost history.

Yes.

What are we looking forward to now as we go? We're almost at 3.5, so as we move up the ladder, how is this going to change? How is your work going to change? How are our bodies going to change?

Current Work on Human Genetics

We're very active now on your behalf, greatly altering your genetics (unseen by you, yes) to work more directly with light. The genetic structure itself is beginning its existence as light; if one traces a genetic particle back to its point of origin, it is light. We are working to allow the full being to encompass the transformation of light such that the self can coordinate the experience in a more joyful way.

Right now you are not consciously aware of the induction of light. You are aware sometimes of your lightbody going out, but you are not aware of the lightbody coming in to create and re-create you. You will become more aware of that through various meditation techniques and other means, both taught and inspired, and then you will be able to literally request that the waves (that can be measured) of your human physiological self become longer. You will do this not to extend your physical life, but to be able to see farther, feel farther, know more, have greater senses so that you are able to access your future intelligence, your future feelings, your future magic—all of these things.

Specifically how are you doing this?

We sing. It is a form of tone color, vibration. It is a harmonic pulse. I cannot measure it in terms of your cycles, so I'm sorry I cannot give you that. If one could hear a recording of it, one would say it resembles music. But it is not exactly that. It does not sound like a chant or even a monotone, but like a musical chord. Utilizing this form of resonant remagnification, we are able to sound the invitation to bring your physiological structure to move up the genetic scale.

It is intended that as you move up the genetic scale you have less physiological matter from your seeming point of origin and more light. Yet light is matter in its own right; it is matter attuned to a significant frequency, but matter nonetheless. Within that context it is our job as well as our joy to "pro-form" (not "pre-form" so much) a given wave feeling of energy that will speak to your genetic particles, and through the reproductive cycle invite children through every generation to be born who are of a slightly higher dimension. In time this supports, sustains and allows the change to a higher-dimensional experience.

You might ask, "How could that affect an already living being?" Yet if the living being itself, through the change of its cellular structure, ceases to degenerate mentally but continues to be excited with life, then regardless of what happens to the body, the mental process continues and is stimulated. A single thought might be carried through the entire process of death and on to the continuum of life through that doorway. Not that that is so desirable, but that's an example. In this case I do not state that thought is the ultimate, but rather that thought is the *link*—that which keeps your interest in this project, because so much of this project has to do with acquired wisdom, and acquired wisdom has a great deal to do with thought and feeling.

Does the harmonic pulse affect the lightbody, which then rays out and changes the DNA, or does your pulse affect the DNA?

Neither one. It is before that takes place. It is as if you could draw a picture of your dimension expanding, and as it expands (you with it) . . . let's say the dimension is expanding spherically and at some point you meet not this barrier, but this *light greeter,* who then excites, with light and a harmonic, your cycle of perpetuation (otherwise known as your genetics). It's as if you run into it; it is there waiting for you. In this way we do not interfere, you see. You come to it rather than our imposing it upon you.

Now, because of the way I speak and its effect on this voice box, we will have to end. But I will say for now that it is our great privilege to work with your Creator and you, as portions of your Creator, on this most valuable and worthy project. I must say that I believe that even after the project is over, we will remember it fondly. A good experience.

All right, Zoosh speaking. That particular being did not have a name such as Frank or even Jesse or even James.

I think the being, in referring to your dimension as expanding, meant the Sirius galaxy only. The center of the Sirius galaxy was where they chose to be because it is a convenient location to stay in touch with you. There are a great many individuals on Sirius who stay in touch with what's going on here—quite a few. So I think they stay close as a way of being in touch. I don't think it was more complicated than that. It was a white hole, though—you were right about that.

Were they really seventh- or eighth-dimensional in our understanding?

I think they are not at all restricted by dimensions. As far as I can tell, they have access well beyond your Creator's access. As a matter of fact, I think they know where Creator is going. [Laughs.]

I didn't get a chance to ask if they were going with the Creator or if they were going to stay, but they said they were going to leave when the Explorer Race was over.

I think that they will be in demand elsewhere.

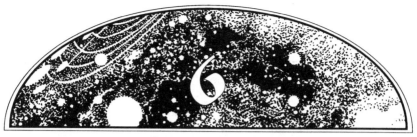

Avatar of Sea Creatures; and Quatsika, Messenger for the Dimension Makers

August 15, 1996

ou have asked for a wisdom keeper associated with something other than what you know about. I came to your planet about a million years ago. I came here to work with and instruct the sea creatures. I didn't come for the people, but what I have been involved with has indirectly helped you.

When the beings came from other planets they were told what you would look like, but not much more than that. They were told that it would be their job to help human beings adapt to the world of the sacred, having been artificially cut off from that world. The rough parameters of your experience of an unconscious mind were explained to them. Most of the sea creatures have what amounts to your unconscious mind as a *conscious* mind, so they needed to know how they could relate to you, since there would be no intermediate language. The language between beings with an unconscious mind that is conscious would be some form of telepathy. But since your unconscious mind would be in large part cut off from your experience (I think it's starting to come back in just about now), you would be unable or unwilling to communicate as an equal.

I came as a warm current so that I could travel anywhere I was needed. That was my form—a warm current. In this way I could pass through certain sea creatures that did not readily absorb thoughts but could absorb feelings. I could also pass around those sea creatures who are very wise and can communicate with any form of life that is reasonably sentient, such as whales, dolphins and some sea turtles. (They can communicate with just about anybody as long as they are even basically sentient.)

It was my job to prepare them to behave like animals. [Chuckles.] You see, they did not know what animals were when they came here! That was not a concept they were familiar with. In all of the worlds they came from, everyone was an equal, regardless of what they looked like, and the communication system worked equally between all beings. They were informed that they would be a class of being known as an animal (that which is not human), so they needed training to know how to act like an animal. One of the things they had to learn was not to look you in the eye very much, because when a human being looks another human being in the eye, it means there's supposed to be some kind of connection or contact. So we had to train them to look you in the eye sparingly, only looking each other in the eye. This was very foreign for them, something they really did not understand.

It took almost 100,000 years to train everybody in the sea; it was not my job to work with people on the land. (I don't know who took care of them—it wasn't my work.) I would sometimes also interact with creatures who were around the sea (and occasionally in it), such as winged creatures. Through them I would get the story of what was happening on the land.

Thus I worked with many different beings, all of what you call the fishes and everybody else in the ocean, including some creatures who live at such great depths that their chance of seeing a human being were extremely limited. Nevertheless, because your radiated energy would at some point become pervasive, they needed to know what they would be feeling then.

What was your experience before that?

Before that time I existed in a condensed light matrix that is still present on ninth-dimensional Earth. This matrix, if you could see it, looks very much like liquid, only it can fly in the air as well as remain in pools on the ground.

What do you do now?

Creatures Leaving the Earth

I still visit the sea creatures from time to time. I spend most of my visiting time now helping the sea creatures who are leaving Earth, attending their needs as they make a soul journey back home to their native planets. Many, many are leaving now. For the most part their work with you is done. They have been told that if they wish to go home, they can go home in spirit form and leave their bodies here. This is why sometimes you will have many whales or even porpoises wash up on the beach and no one knows what happened. Sometimes they have succumbed to a disease, but more often than not they decided, "Well, if we can go home, let's do it!"

Then several of us will come and form a liquid-light ship because they are so used to liquid now, and most of them come from planets where there is some kind of liquefied atmosphere, or at least water in some form. After we form a liquid ship we slowly (for there is no rush) pilot them back to their home planets, where they are greeted as long-lost astronauts and are expected to tell many tales about their adventures here, which they do after they have enjoyed their welcome home.

Are all of the animals going to leave before the pole shift?

I don't know if there's going to be any greater pole shift than you're experiencing now. There will be an experience of change of *attitudes*, and the magnetics might change. I don't know if all of them will leave. I will be available if they do.

My Experiences

What are your earliest memories? When did you become conscious?

I don't remember ever being anything *but* conscious, and I've almost always been liquid light. But it was a unique experience for me to be liquid water—that was new. Also, I had not experienced warm or cold temperatures much, just an even temperature where one does not really notice the experience of warm or cold. So I cannot tell you how long I have been in existence, because as far as I know it is forever.

Why were you given the task of working with the animals? What were your experiences before you did that?

I think it was because I am so at ease in liquid and because I am what you might call a clear channel. I have the capacity to pass on any wisdom that any sea creature might need. [Chuckles.] Granted, it might not work with you too much, not being of the sea.

Pass it on from where? What kind of wisdom?

All of these beings in the sea are from somewhere.

You can communicate with them from their home planets, then?

If that is the direction of the knowledge that is needed. But sometimes it would come from an emissary from the Creator here in this creation. I would always see the emissary as a waving light like this [makes motion].

So you are not from this creation?

You mean, am I from around here?

Generated by this Creator?

I'm not from around here, no. I am not from this Creator, no; but I have seen this Creator grow up and I appreciate being involved in Its creation.

So were you brought in as an outside consultant later for the Explorer Race?

[Laughs.] I like that—an outside consultant. Yes, yes, I'm an outside consultant, but I did not present a bill to the Creator.

Is there anything else you'd like to tell us that we don't know to ask about?

I think the most important thing is to realize that not all avatars come for the human being. Because the life of the human being is so intense, one does not often look beyond one's own experience. Occasionally one might look beyond to include other human beings, but not necessarily other life forms. It's important to know that other life forms also have their guides and teachers.

That's why I came to say hello for this book and perhaps talk to you about other things someday. I wanted to remind you that wisdom comes not only to those who seek it, but also to those who need it, and it must come from a source that they can hear. So universal teachers—yes, they exist. But *specific* teachers—we also exist.

What are your specialties, or what would be most meaningful to talk about with such a wisdom keeper?

Anything to do with sea creatures—anything.

You're like the avatar of the sea creatures?

They might consider me that.

Did you learn at this point about the experiment that this Creator had going here, even though you were working with sea animals? Are you familiar with it now?

Oh, Creator took time to painstakingly explain the experiment before I came. It is like receiving a telegram, in a sense (though it is vibration), in which the Creator laid out Its plans and objectives. Creator asked if I would come in a supporting role during the time of your engagement here to advise the sea creatures how to pretend to be animals.

How did He know you existed? How did He meet you?

As far as I know, He knows everyone. He's a member of the key club—He's got an executive key that says, "I know everyone." But I don't think He's been everywhere.

Do you have any idea how many beings like you He has involved in this experiment?

That's a better question for Him, but I would say many, not few. I have run across at least 50 or 60 myself. Of course, I have not been everywhere on Earth, but wherever seawater is, I have been there. So good night.

Thank you.

Zoosh: All right, something a little different. Let's see if we can get the attention of the dimension makers. I think they might be too erudite for you, but we'll see.

One of them came once when they had to patch some holes in the dimensions. [See Shining the Light II, chapter 6.] Was it the dimensional overlord?

Oh yes, that's right.

There were nineteen anomalies that he answered questions about. It was very interesting.

That's right. Let's see what else or who else . . .

I am Quatsika, and it is my job to act as a messenger for the dimension makers. The dimension makers felt that they would be too dry (dusty, as it were) to speak to you, I think, because they do not think or communicate in words. They perhaps felt that as an emissary or a runner, I could do this better. So perhaps I will act as a go-between and translate for them.

Great. What would they like to say?

They want to know what *you* want to know. They do not have anything they want to say; it is up to you.

Okay, you take the stuff of the Creator and you build dimensions. How do you do that?

First comes the concept of creation—what this Creator or any other wants to do. *Then* comes the creation of the dimension. So first is the concept: maybe who will people the dimension, what is desired or expected of them, and what might be their ultimate intention or purpose. Once this has been laid out in significant detail (much more than you can imagine), then comes the creation of the dimension. Of course, in your case the dimension had to be thick—it had to slow you down. It had to have gravity built into it and at the same time *no* gravity. That was a bit of a riddle.

That is why atmospheric envelopes were created. Before this dimension you have, I think there were no atmospheric envelopes the way you have them now around planets. There wasn't the need for so many gases to hold an atmosphere in. Thus this dimension represented quite a challenge. Also, it had to have something that other dimensions do not have to such a degree—doorways to other dimensions. This dimension is riddled with them!

In my measly experience (which numbers no more than 400^{10} trillion years of interacting with dimensional overlords) I have never seen a dimension with so many holes in it that manages to stay together. This is entirely new to me. You've seen Swiss cheese—that's nothing! You've seen foam rubber—no! Even in this room right now I can easily see three dimensional doorways. And they're in motion, so they come, they go, all the time, everywhere. I think it's because spirits and other life forms come all the time to see what's going on in your dimension—and not just in this place. One might not expect (and I understand why) there would be so many from other dimensions who would want to come here to the Earth (known as "the odd place" in other circles). But even from other places in your own dimension, people, spirits, beings want to see what it's all about. And they're particularly interested now that your universe is going through this dimensional shift. It's a *circus!* It's amazing, it's . . .

The hottest play in town?

It is a good show, yes. Even in this room as we sit now, beings are coming and going. Since I've begun to talk, 50 or 60 have come and gone, and there are at least 20 or 30 sitting around watching you, wondering what you'll do next. And that is not an anomaly; as near as I can tell, that is normal.

Exponential Expansion between Earth Dimensions

I have watched a dimensional overlord create the nineteenth dimension of this planet. (I'm trying to be relevant, okay?) That was an interesting experience, because one might think that the expansion is singular from one dimension to another (meaning that there is the same number of expansions between each dimension), but that's not true. One might expand, say, two to three times between the second and the third dimension. One might expand, say 40 to 50 times between the sixth and the seventh dimension. But the expansion between the eighteenth and the nineteenth dimension is at least 760 times! I was quite surprised. I had no idea that this was the case here, because it isn't the case in other places.

The dimensional overlord explained to me that this planet—right where you are—requires at least 32 dimensions of itself to be available, because it needs to be in every place that your Creator has established in this creation, even if that place is only a potential. (I think that most of the dimensions, once you get past 25 or 26, are basically potentials that might be used someday.) Your planet has the capacity to be in all of these places—and is. And you know, once you get past the twenty-fifth or twenty-sixth dimension, there aren't a whole lot of planets out there to be seen, because most of them don't need that potential. Question?

Let's start with you before we do the dimensions. Are you from this creation?

Oh, you know, *much* before that. I knew your Creator one hundred times before It was created, meaning, I can trace your Creator back to when It came out of Its stem, until It split. Creators are not like other beings. Creators do not have many branches and many different lives. Creators simply create to the maximum of their capacity and split in two. So when I "go back a hundred," that means I knew your Creator when It was part of something else. When I first met the portion of a creator being that would later become your Creator, it never occurred to me that It would ever evolve to this lofty position. I say "lofty" because so much is done here—such an unusual creation. It just goes to show (as you like to say) that you just never know about people!

Every creator splits in two every so often, and then each of those split—that's the mitosis of creators, how they divide and multiply?

As far as I've seen, that's how they become more. This is a process I have noticed many times. When they split off, you might ask, "Where do they go? Do they go off to some other space?" Understand that space is an abstract, that infinity is truly infinite. I have been around, and I have never been anyplace from which I could not measure infinity in all directions from the center of my being. I've covered some miles, as you like to say, and everywhere I've been, that's what creators do. But you know, your Creator wants to do something different. Your Creator wants to go *up*, as it were. He wants to leave and have you take over. He doesn't want to split; He wants to see if there isn't something beyond this that's new. I didn't think He had it in Him, but who knew, you know? Who knew? You can't tell. When you see a man, when they basically look like light amoebas, who can tell? They all look the same.

What dimension, from your perspective, would be the dimension that we manifest from?

"We" meaning you?

The human being. Would we have to consciously go to, say, the twenty-first dimension to be able to be here in third and manifest physically?

What would be the point? I mean, really, this is a milk bottle you're living in, you know; it's something you return. Why would you even *want* to limit yourself? You come here as a lightbeing (that's what you are), and as a lightbeing you are completely unlimited. I understand that you are asking how far it is possible to take the human physical being. Is that what you're asking? To what dimension?

Reaching through a Doorway to Manifest

How far do we have to go up until we can pull something down and manifest it in our hands? Do we have to go the twenty-first dimension, or can we go to the fifth or seventh? Do we grab something in the seventh but still stay conscious to manifest it in our physical, third-dimensional hands?

Oh, I wouldn't think you'd have to go much beyond the fourth or fifth dimension. You wouldn't want to grab too much, anyway, because for one thing, it wouldn't *want* to be grabbed.

But is it a dimensional activity? Is it related to dimensions as we understand it?

You mean to create something in your hand?

Yes, benevolent vibrations . . .

Is that what you're saying? To create something in your hand, such as Sai Baba does, hmmm? It is not exactly a dimensional activity; it is more of a doorway activity.

You find a doorway and reach in, you mean?

You ask the doorway to come *to* your hand.

And then?

It is true magic.

Dimensions in Other Creations

Okay, so you created dimensions. Can you give us an overview of what dimensions are like in some other creations, then explain how this one works?

Allowing for your terminology, it will be a struggle, but I will do what I can. Imagine, if you can, a dimension whereby time and space are not valid, where you could be in any point of infinity as long as you were in that dimension and you could be anywhere in that dimension's infinity. Dimensions are not created with boundaries. They are created for a specific purpose and they go on to infinity.

Now, imagine a dimension in which you are so spread out that you are limitless, yes? That would be a dimension only slightly different from your own, because here there is only a slight temporal limit to your awareness of the fact that you are limitless. You are given that temporal limit so you will discover every possible ramification of creation for the time when you become responsible for creating human beings who will be in the temporal world. But it is your nature to be infinite. The distance on the soul level between the dimension of being infinitely everywhere and the dimension where you are now is only one-tenth of a degree of light refraction (see, it doesn't translate directly), otherwise known as the sixteenth dimension.

One might say, "Wow, we're awfully far from the sixteenth dimension!" But that is not true at all, because there's only a thin veil that allows your souls to remain in these bodies, a very thin veil. And when you pass through that veil you can easily be in the infinite. As a matter of fact, the first feeling you have when you pass through the veil *is* the infinite, because that is your natural place to be. You don't have to take many years and lifetimes to work your way up the dimensional scale—you *are* that. You have to struggle, I think, to qualify to be temporarily dense. It is hard to describe a dimension that is so foreign to the linear mind. The overlord is using "the infinite" to describe it because it is actually so close to what you are.

Could a dimension be better described as the vibratory rate of the soul?

Not really, because a dimension is not a place or a thing. It is not even a feeling. (That's where it's complicated, because a soul could be described as a feeling.) A dimension is really an abstract word meaning *a focus of personality.* That's the best I can do, because when you are asleep you travel dimensionally. Your personality goes out of your body and travels to another dimension, not necessarily in space, but in focus.

Could dimensions be characterized by color or vibration?

Only if one were trying to create a filing system, but not if one were actually seeking to go somewhere. If one were seeking to go to, say, the sixteenth dimension from here (if one had been to the sixteenth dimension, which all of you have), one would recall what the sixteenth dimension felt like and then you would be drawn to the doorway that would take you there—but only if you remained within a consistent personality.

But if you were to disperse your personality or join with other personalities, it could be quicker or slower depending on their experience. If they had been there before, you might get there quicker. If at least one member of the group had *not* been there, it might take longer to get to the dimensional doorway because one of your group has no ability to be drawn there, not knowing what it feels like. That member of the group would essentially be baggage.

As we get more evolved, does our personality that remembers third dimension, or wants to come back to it actively, have to remember this third-dimensional personality so that it will get us here?

No, no, you as a personality simply have to remember the *feeling* of having been here. You don't have to remember the personality that you have now, because this personality is at its core the personality you've *always* had (as far as I know), but without some of the compromises you've had to make (if I can speak in front of the world) in order to get along here. The basic personality by which most friends and others would know you would be easily recognizable. So I would say that you don't have to recall this personality to come here; you only have to recall from your experience what it *felt* like to be here, and then you would be drawn to the doorway that would bring you back.

There are some beings of dimensional mastery, such as dimensional overlords, who don't need doorways. They simply travel for cause to any dimension at any moment. They don't travel for pleasure per se, because their work is their pleasure. They will be drawn to a dimension at any moment through a need by that dimension or a need by the Creator. They are drawn to any other dimension based on a need from someone who can broadcast a need to them. (It would have to be someone who knows their telephone number.)

Overlord Creation: No-Gravity

A few minutes ago you mentioned no-gravity and gravity, and that this was the first time you had to create them together. Can you explain what you mean by no-gravity?

The dimensional overlord here has never, before the creation of this third dimension that you are in, had to create in such close proximity the potential for a spinning body (such as a planet) to have some form of gravity so close to a spatial point that didn't have gravity. In many of the other dimensions the veil around a given planet is kept there by the planet *and* all of the beings on the planet functioning together to attract specific needs. But here on this planet most of the human beings are unconscious, so the planet on her own (plus whatever assistance the other forms of higher life can provide, also known as the animals) must invite the atmosphere to remain.

So it was necessary for Overlord to create an atmospheric envelope that would be drawn to the planet (and to the many other planets in your solar system) without needing the beings peopling the Earth to do so even unconsciously. It was absolutely necessary, you understand, to cut off the recollection of who you are from even your unconscious minds until recently, because the unconscious has such a broad power to communicate to the subconscious—and the subconscious is kind of gossipy. Whatever the subconscious knows, it wants everybody to know and will broadcast that message by whatever means available. So I think it was a challenge for Overlord; Overlord had to stretch.

So there's gravity on the planet and then there's no-gravity—where, just beyond the atmospheric envelope?

Yes. Even no-gravity can be created within a gravitational situation here on the planet, given certain physical circumstances. That wasn't easy, either. That was, as Overlord likes to say, a neat trick.

How did he do it?

Well, you know, a plane diving in certain circumstances can create artificial negative-gravity circumstances. But I can't explain to you how Overlord did it, because the mathematics alone is well beyond your present level of physics. I will just say that it involves reversing, duplicating and turning inside out many of your equations. Although your physicists can understand reversing an equation, turning an equation inside out is a little more complex. I don't know how to put that in your words.

If you have been doing this for 400^{10} trillion years, how do overlords know so much more than you do? Have they been studying in universities, or what?

They *need* to know more. And this is my job. Oh, I think I know a few things they don't know, but when it comes to creating dimensions—well, I'm just the messenger.

Personal Information about Quatsika

You're an apprentice, right?

Oh, no, *this* is what I do.

What you do is carry messages for them?

Yes.

Who do you talk to besides us?

Well, I have not spoken to any Earth humans before this time; there was no need, really. No one said, "Hey!"

No one called.

That's right. I have an unlisted number. Generally it is my job to communicate, to bring messages from the dimensional overlords to other creators elsewhere. That's what I do, because creators are so busy all the time. If someone doesn't actually come to them and sing them a message, then they just haven't got the time.

Are there many like you, or are you unique?

Oh, I think I'm not alone. I must admit I have heard of other messengers, but I haven't actually met any. It might be fun to meet one, swap stories . . .

Do you have a form of sorts?

Oh, you mean, do I have a physical body? No.

A lightbody?

No. I have a consciousness that spreads to the infinity of all the creations I've ever been in, so . . . I'm here, I'm there, I'm everywhere.

So once you communicate with a creation, you can maintain that piece of you there, that thread or connection. Is that what you're saying?

As far as I can explain it, I would have to say I understand infinity because I am it.

Who are your peers, then? Who do you talk to? You carry messages, but what do you do for fun?

You understand, I don't actually go anywhere because I *am* everywhere; the message travels along my being. So who do I talk to? Who do I hang out with? Where do I go on a Saturday night? [Laughter.]

How do you learn concepts like that?

Oh, I've been listening. I have lots of time to listen, you know, because messages might come every year or two in your time. Sometimes a hundred years go by without a message. I have *lots* of free time.

So you look in on planets and people and . . .

Oh, certainly. I listen, so I don't feel lonely. That's why I know some of you pretty well.

Oh, really. That's good news, right?

Yes; that's why I could talk to you about your personality. I know you pretty well.

Do you want to say more about that? How can you look in on each of us?

You have to understand that as an infinite being, I *am* you. Wherever you go I am there, so when you are infinity (as you are, by the way, and that's why I think you're being exposed to me tonight) it's not possible for you to *not* be somewhere.

Except here, when we're playing the game of pretending that we're only here.

Yes—for you, yes. But for me, I cannot do that, so I have been aware of some of you for a *looong time*. And I do not forget; I do not have the luxury of forgetting, although sometimes that's good. I think maybe I'm the logical messenger because I don't forget. And I also know my way; I know how to be everywhere.

It sounds like you could give us a book about the other creators.

Well, I could, perhaps, talk about some. I've seen some extraordinary creations, including the creation of the smallest to the largest. Your Creator has not created the largest; I have seen much bigger. Because your Creator had a very specific purpose, it wasn't necessary to create anything larger than this, and this is pretty large. But I have seen much larger. Usually you'll see creations that are much larger when their creators do not have such a specific purpose. Since your Creator's purpose was very specific, it didn't have to be much larger.

Tearing the Veil with Its Null Charge

What is the veil made of? You said a degree of frequency or a degree of light?

Which veil?

The thin veil of the third dimension.

Oh, the veil that keeps you from knowing everything, who you are, about the infinity?

The one we pass through at what we call death.

Well, I'll have to describe it. The closest I can get is that it is made of polarity, because here everything you experience has either a positive or minus charge. But the polarity of the veil does not have either one of these charges; it has no charge, as you understand it, so you cannot accidentally fall through the veil, because it would have to be charged one way or the other for you to pass through it. Having no charge whatsoever, it is incompatible with your world. This means it is compressed very thin and does not allow anyone or anything to pass through unless it can maintain a momentary null charge.

Which we do when we leave the body?

That's right, and which beings do when they come to visit here if they do not need to use a doorway. If they use a doorway, they get through it without having to create a difference in charges. But the veil is made from a null charge.

Are the overlords spending much time repairing patches and holes? Is that a problem right now as we're moving pretty quickly upward?

It's a *big* problem, because this hasn't been done before and your Creator said that It had every reason to believe there would be a tremendous amount of tears and rips. Oh, it's more than full-time. The dimensional overlords had to actually re-create themselves so there would be enough to go around. Yes, there are hundreds of new holes popping up every second. It requires a lot of work.

What causes the holes and tears?

It is normal to pass through from one dimension to another using the cycle of what you call death—the natural change. But to pass through as a living being as you are now, you are essentially ripping through the null-zone veil with your positive and negative charges, and the veil is meant to *stop* your passage. You are being forced through it, so naturally it tears. When you experience the fourth dimension you will have ripped through the veil, meaning that you would have had to add a null charge to your makeup, thus having then positive, negative and null charges. I believe the null charge is going to have everything to do with your change of mind and change of being. You don't *do* anything—it just happens.

As part of the accelerated evolution?

Well, you have to remember this: You must devolve quite a bit to come here, so you're just getting something back that you've always had, only you're doing it in a complex way. It's like "how hard can we make this?" But that is necessary in order to drag everybody else with you, because it isn't normal for a whole planetary system or whole creation to rip through the fabric of dimensions. Normally one goes through during a natural cyclic change, but your planet is ripping its way through the dimensions and is going to bring everybody with you. So when you go to the fourth, everybody else moves on up, too.

You mean as planet Earth's inhabitants go to the fourth dimension, then so do all the other beings in third dimension everywhere—is that what you're saying?

Yes, as far as I understand. That's the why the job is so big.

And that's why we get a lot of your attention, then, because you're carrying a lot of messages here from or to the Creator?

Well, I carry messages generally to the other creators. The dimensional overlords might send messages, yes, but when your Creator wants everybody else to know what He's up to, that's when I get activated. But I do carry some messages from the dimensional overlords;

and I hang out with them. (I do like your slang so much.)

Absorbing the Null Charge When Tearing Through

You talked about a null charge that we would need to incorporate. Do you have any idea of what the mechanism for that will be?

Oh, I think as you tear through the veil you will just take it on, because if the dimensional veil is eliminated, that energy must go somewhere, so you will absorb it. And after that, anytime any of you meet *any* veil with a null charge, you will be able to pass through it. This means either that you're going to have a very short trip through the fourth dimension (because the fourth- and fifth-dimensional veils have null charges), or they're going to have to change the charges on those veils. I don't know what they're going to do yet.

Now, you also mentioned another kind of veil that has to do with ignorance. Is that a completely different type of thing?

Completely different, yes. I would say sometime between 2000 and 2011 you will tend to remember things that are beyond this life experience as well.

I will simply say this in closing: The dimensional overlords are pleased to be involved with this project, and the other creators are *very* interested in your Creator's project. That's why they like to have messages so often (every hundred years or so in your time is very often). They are most interested to see what you are going to do, especially since you will be joining their club at some point in the future. So they are, well, watching.

Would you probe outward through your infinite tentacles and ask them if they would like to talk about their creations through you, perhaps a dozen of them? Or you could tell us what you know about them so we can get an idea of the incredible diversity and variety of what's out there.

I will ask; it is possible that they would speak directly and not through me, but I will put out the word.

You could share what you know, too; you might have a different perspective.

Well, I might be able to speak your lingo better than they do, so I might come in handy as an interpreter. Largely that's what messengers are, you know—interpreters.

I'd like to put that forth as a possibility.

All right, I'll put it to them.

Thank you very much.

Good night.

Zoosh: Well, all right, short night tonight, eh? I think that's about it.

Explanation of Dimensions

What is your perception of the dimensions? You speak our lingo even better than that fellow did. Explain it. To me they're like layers, one on top of each other. Or they're like one here and then one's wrapped around it or something. Tell us about dimensions.

It is only because you have to have a spatial linear reference that you would see that. Dimensions are not unlike music. A tone, even though it is distinct and clear unto itself, blends with other tones when a chord is made. Dimensions are very much like that.

Well, we've been inside this thing like a little piece of layer cake or something for so long that we don't know that—we've forgotten.

Well, that's all right; I am not chiding you. I am just suggesting that as an analogy.

So it's not like climbing up the ladder to the next dimension, is it? Is it like expanding from the center outward?

Oh, it's not even that.

Is it right here where we are?

Yes.

They all exist here at once. It's a change in focus, then; we don't actually travel anywhere.

Right!

So as we expand to encompass the eighth dimension, then we can simultaneously act in all of them at once?

Yes . . .

Or is it still a focus—we have to be in the eighth—or the seventh—or the sixth?

No, no, once you get past the seventh dimension, there's a lot more flexibility in dimensional experience. I'm not saying that it is progressive; I'm just saying that once you're past the seventh dimension for whatever reason, moving between dimensions is significantly easier because you (in the form you'd take *past* that dimension) do not disturb dimensions in any way.

Right now cats and some babies (if not all of them)—beings without veils to spirit—would notice another dimensional being floating through the room. But if that being were beyond the seventh dimension, the chances of the cat (for instance) noticing that being are less likely unless that being *wants* to be noticed by the cat—meaning that their tracks are lighter; there's less of a disturbance, less mass.

Right. When they came to create the third dimension here, it was evidently a really big deal; it had evidently never been done before. Can you say anything about that from your perspective, adding to what the messenger said?

I would not attempt to clarify what he said; I think he did fine.

Or add to it?

No, not really. I don't want to do that because whatever I say will tend to water down what he's already said.

What do you think of the project to have the other creators talk to us?

Interesting—I like it.

All right.

And I'll say good night.

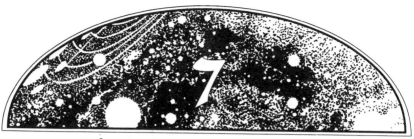

The Empath Creator of Seventeen Planets

August 22, 1996

will discuss an aspect of my creation, because many of the ancestors of your people have passed through my creation in distant time past. I will speak of one planet in particular that Zoosh felt was appropriate for you.

A Desert Planet for the Empath Race

Before I established this universe I felt to create something that could be beneficial to a race of beings with which I had had an association. These beings are evolved now, but at one time they were burdened with too much responsibility. These beings are empaths. It was a race of beings that existed before my creation, so I felt honor-bound to assist them to release some of this entrapped energy within them.

Now, I created a planet that your Creator studied extensively on Its journey toward Its destiny of the creation in which you now live. This particular planet was, as far as I know, the first prototype of an all-desert planet. Desert had been experimented with before by other creators, but not for a whole planet. This desert planet primarily functions to extract everything that does not fall under the heading of what is absolutely needed by an empath.

After creating this planet, I sent an emissary to the point of origin of the empathic race—which is hard to describe from where you are, but it's a long way. This emissary informed the guides of the empath race that a planet had been created on their behalf so that they might have a longer, more industrious and benevolent life.

You see, they were a race of beings (and still are in some places) that could live for 700 or 800 of your years, but because they would take in the discomforts of all forms of life they met, they would become so encumbered with discomforts after perhaps 70 or 80 years that they were unable to transform. They could transform some discomforts in an ideal society, but when going to places that were troubled or burdened—such as your world is now—they would become so overwhelmed that they could not process it all. Then, after only about one-tenth of their life span, they would have to return to their point of origin and simply go into a dormant state until the end of their lives. You can see that this is not right.

So I sent the emissary, and the emissary invited the empaths to bring some of their people who were in the dormant state as well as others who could care for them and create a colony on this planet, which they did. Because of the planet's effect, the individuals could spend (in terms of your time) from 12 to 18, perhaps 24 of your hours there and be significantly rejuvenated, and after three days be entirely rejuvenated. Then they could resume a life. Thus these beings, after becoming charged with discomforts, would come to this planet and release before they returned to their point of origin.

The Renewal Role of a Desert

I am bringing this up because it is my understanding, in communications with your Creator, that many of you souls who are inhabiting Earth could not (and some of you would not) manifest here without there being significant desert so that you could be renewed. I mention this because I have seen from a distance that you are beginning to spread your cities into the desert. It would be good to leave some of the desert as it is so that you can go there, especially those of you who are empathic and who take on the discomforts of other life. You can go to the desert, stay there for one, two or three days, bringing all the water you need and perhaps food and shelter.

I believe that if you are out there on your own you will probably release all those discomforts, because desert has the capacity to pull from you all that you do not actually require for your existence. This means, of course, anything extraneous that is in your body. As some individuals have discovered, it can also be healthy in other ways. But I want to remind you because so many of you have roots in the empathic race, and if you visit the desert at least two or three times a year or perhaps more often, you will feel much better.

What do you remember before your creation? What kind of experiences did you have before you became a creator?

I was a portion of the ensoulment of the empathic race; I have mentioned that. I was also connected to three other creators, some of whom you might hear on another day. As that, we traveled great distances. I believe you might say that our primary function was to move at a great velocity, form different sounds and shapes, and help to create a rhythmic resonance between the ninth and eleventh dimensions. There was a time way back when, in order to go from the ninth to the eleventh dimension for any reason, you had to go a very roundabout way. There is such a significant difference between the ninth and the eleventh that the passage could be accommodated only by a swirling combination of tones, shapes, forms and colors. For beings to get from the ninth to eleventh dimension it was necessary to leave a portion of ourselves there so that anybody who needed to have such transit would enter a portion of ourselves, be reduced to their transient shapes (meaning the natural forms of their essence as well as whatever physical apparatus they had adorned themselves with), then be toned from the ninth to the eleventh dimension.

There is so much high spiritual resonance in the eleventh dimension and beyond that it must be protected. The tenth dimension is a natural barrier. There are legitimate reasons to go from the ninth to the eleventh, so we set that up. That's one of the things we did.

So you knew several other creators before they created their creations?

Yes, and we all gradually became involved in our own individual focus, what we wanted to do. I'm still involved in that. Although the desert planet, I must admit, is not a major facet of what I am doing, it does relate to you because so many of you are empathic. I have studied your people from a distance and have calculated that at any given moment (though it is not always the same individuals) 90 to 97% of your people are empathic. I believe that this has a great deal to do with why you do not live very long.

I understand that your Creator does not want you to be in this school too long, so perhaps that is why He has not instructed you on the release of such cluttered lights that you are. Not all of you are empathic. Some individuals, I have noticed, never are, but this is very rare. Most have that quality so that you can learn. Apparently there are a few amongst you who are designed to be either outside of or an exception to society's rules and who do not need to be empathic—but as I say, it is uncommon.

Did our Creator also come from this empathic race or have a connection to it?

No, this is something that I believe your Creator is well-versed in, but there was not a direct connection. Your Creator was very interested in variety—how much, how many, what kind, where, when and so on. It is in your Creator's nature to gather. I believe that is why your Creator gathered up the empath experience for the intended outcome of Its Explorer Race, which you are. And since most of you are empaths, It obviously must have felt that empathy is a good learning tool. I have found it to be so.

Can you graduate from being an empath? It's really hard sometimes to exist and take in a lot of things. Can you go beyond that and be able to live more easily?

One graduates to *become* an empath, not the other way. By becoming an empath you *must* learn. You must qualify to be an empath. It takes many, many lifetimes and much interconnectedness with many different creators. Becoming an empath is very often the final, if not one of the final, steps to becoming a creator, because one is constantly assailed by problems that one must resolve. Empaths realize they are empathic at some point before the end of their lives here. No, the graduation for an empath is creatorship.

What happens if you spend more than three days in the desert letting go of things?

Aside from becoming dehydrated? (Bring enough water.) I think three days is enough. Bring what you need to protect you, but I think three days is sufficient.

But if you spend ten days or so, what happens? Does it reverse itself in some way?

I think there is a temporary reversal that is easily transposed when you return to society. The advantage of being in the desert is that there is not much life. When I say "desert" I don't mean high desert, where there are trees and plants and animals. I mean *sand*, understand? Sand is very often quartz, so it is very resonant.

If you stay there too long it is possible that instead of returning to being an empath when you come back, you will continue to project, but this will reverse itself naturally within three days. I do not think it is a problem, providing you have enough food and water and shelter.

Empathy: An Explorer Race Qualification

If you are familiar with Zoosh's story of the ancestors—the contributors to the Explorer Race—how would you weave the empath race into his story?

What a nice question! The empath has a racial consciousness and was very much involved in your evolution. In order for your souls to become aware beyond your own immediate boundaries (be it your light souls or be it a life such as you have), it is essential that you arrive on this planet having experienced some empath lifetime. It is my understanding that since mastering empathy has been accomplished by so many, all of you have had at least one lifetime either as a master empath or in training with a master empath so that you could come here and learn. If you cannot feel the subtle, you will miss your most profound lessons here. I think Zoosh has told you before that no one comes to Earth school without having at least one life of mastery; most often you have at least three or more.

Your group, your beingness, the source of who you are, has invariably passed through the empath source. To go to the empath source one does not go to a planet; one goes to a window in space. If you were to look at the empath source, you would see something akin to . . . have you ever seen heat waves rising in the distance? It would be a ripple in space. If you were to look at it, it would look like heat waves or like looking through water. This ripple is the existence, the source of the empath. As you approach it (only when you have had a master empath life would you be able to pass through), you would not go through a dimension. You would go into a world that exists to teach the ultimate mastery of feeling, both emanated and received. It is a small ripple in space; if you measured it by your measurements, perhaps it would be three miles long by a mile and a half wide. That is the empath source. If you went around to see it on the edge, you wouldn't see it. So in a sense it is two-dimensional. (Some of you will have to rethink your ideas of two-dimensional; it is not a place for the dull-witted.)

This existence, then, can train many billions of souls simultaneously. It encompasses all times; it is a timeless and an all-time place at the same moment. It is a place where one can contact any and every life form in one moment or in the same moment. It is a place of ultimate mastery training of the feeling self and spiritual self and where quantum mastery is studied.

Levels of Mastery

In spiritual mastery you understand the ways of the spirit in all form. In material mastery you understand your interaction as a spirit with all matter. In teaching mastery you understand the means, manners and mores by which you learn and teach all beings. In quantum mastery you go to the absolute core resonance of all beings, which you can understand everywhere so that you can *become* it at a moment's notice. Those who are quantum masters can form their souls into a planet or any kind of being from a dandelion to an elephant to a *phasod*. (You don't know what that is, so that is my little joke. A phasod is basically an atmosphere, a manner and means most important.) There are levels of mastery beyond that, but perhaps those are the most important ones for you to be aware of now.

You are all spiritual masters when you come to your planet. You learn levels of material mastery. Some of you even learn levels of teaching mastery. But most likely you will not learn quantum mastery for some time yet, although there will be a few of you who will play with it. I explain this to you so you will understand the infinite potential for becoming more.

Empath Source in Eleventh Dimension for Quantum Mastery

I'm not really clear. When you say this is a source, is it a source beyond this creation that we can tune to, step into or go to? It's not a part of the Creator that is empathic that we were created from and get energy from?

It is not a portion of this place. This ripple in space, as it were, is not in your creation. It was not created by your Creator. It was not even created by myself or my companions. It is something that exists in the creation at a very high dimension indeed. As a matter of fact, it is in the eleventh dimension. This is to protect it from any willful or unintentional intrusion or incursion, because the levels of mastery taught there—well, they go beyond my understanding. I have not gone past perhaps nine or ten levels of mastery, but in this place where the empath is trained, I believe they have at least 150 levels of mastery. Since I do not need to know most of those yet, I will do them in the future. It is something to look forward to.

But you can imagine it; you can go there in your imagination, because the imagination knows no boundaries and is not stifled by time or space. Imagine it; see if you can experiment with quantum mastery—something in your future.

In your creation are there similarities to this creation? Are there dimensions, solar systems, galaxies, planets, individual beings?

The Restorative Creation with Dense Space

In my creation, which is about three and one-half times as massive as your own, there are about seventeen planets.

In your whole creation?

Yes. The weight of the mass between the planets is three times denser than the planets themselves. In this way the planets cannot be interfered with by *any* outside influence and they are all as pristine as when they were created. They all perform unique and individual functions, and only those who are intended to go there are focused there (you would say, brought there), and they exit in the same way (such as the empathic race to the sand planet). This kind of creation allows a tremendous amount of observation to notice given effects, and the gravitational field does not exist as you experience it. The planet is floating in a space mass that suspends it, so it does not orbit or rotate; it is fixed.

What was the purpose of this region, this state?

It was my intention to create a pure, focused means by which it would be possible to add to or, in the case of the empath, subtract from given primary races a means and manner to restore them, to refocus them, to regenerate them without the slightest intentional or unintentional interference.

So it's a place of healing and regeneration. Are these beings generated from you, or are all the beings that you help from somebody else's creation?

They are not. Some are generated, but for the most part they are from other creations. In this way I am able to be of assistance with this creation, and to some extent this creation functions as a problem-solver.

Explosion of the Negative Sirian Planet

For example, in your creation there was recently an explosion (do you remember?) of a planet with much negative energy in a galaxy called Sirius that is all positive. You could say that yes, the beings who lived there have been transferred. But what about all the negative energy? What about the planetary residue? Where did that go? How could it be safe for Sirius?

Well, one of my planets can process, reconform and receive all energies that are incompatible with any place. So one of my emissaries went to a planet near there to await its destruction, and while the beings of the planet were being transferred, the planet, with all of its extraneous energy, was resonated to my creation, where it is now being refocused into its original tonal components. In this way the negative energy is transformed by disinterring that which has caused this natural energy to become self-destructive, bringing that out of the original particle matrix and allowing the condensation of that which you call negative. This distillation process leaves most of the planet and most of the physical matter intact, and it can then be used as energy and matter by anyone. It is sent from this creation I am in to anyone who requests it. Thus it might go anywhere to any creation.

The condensed negative energy itself is then gradually, lovingly transformed and allowed to become its higher self. When that takes place, it then has the love and ability to transform its dense residue. This is how masters are born.

You might ask, "How is it possible that negativity could spawn a master?" Yet all life has a higher vibration of itself and often, in an ultimate irony and benefit, that higher vibration of itself will have the manner and means to transform its degenerated self.

What you do is awesome. Is it the only one like it in the larger creation? Is this a new idea?

I don't know of anybody else doing it, but then I have only ten or eleven levels of mastery, so I could be ignorant. [Chuckles.]

Do any other creators do as you seem to have done—see a need and then fill it?

In my experience, yes. That is what makes creation such a desirable goal. To be a creator—this is something *you* are doing. Even in your daily life you often see things you wish you could change. How many of you have said in a given life, "If I were king or queen for a day, I would do this and that"? You are born and bred to be this so that you will see something that needs to be changed for the better. It is your nature and that of all those in creator school. Souls strive to become creators because they crave not only the ability but the responsibility and the ultimate authority. With authority goes responsibility, and it is perhaps the responsibility that ultimately drives a creator.

Are you alone in your creation, or did you bring in friends to add tones or levels of ability to help?

I am alone. I did not bring others in, but your Creator brought others because your Creator's intentions were complex. Mine were perhaps more simple.

Do you do what you're doing, learn everything you can from it, close up shop and then have another idea for another creation?

I do not think we will close up shop. If I have another idea and I have fulfilled all my responsibilities here, I will perhaps spawn an apprentice. [Chuckles.]

The Beings on the Seventeen Planets

What about the beings you created, the sentient beings you generated in your creation? What is their appearance, their form? Is there a generic, people-looking people, or do you have different-looking beings?

Most of them are quantum masters, so they can take any form and travel anywhere if necessary. As I said, the planets are all performing resonant work—you might say recycling! Very often the beings on the planets are not from my creation, so most of the beings I have spawned I would refer to as my emissaries. I must admit to having created, however, one being that is primarily a companion. I suppose you would describe it as a "dog," but it is the essential spirit of joy and rejuvenation. If you were to see it in the form it usually takes, it would be perhaps as big as . . . well, if you were to stand on top of an 8000- or 9000-foot mountain and look in all directions, as much sky as you could see would be as big as my dog. [Laughs.]

So you have a limited number of generated beings?

Yes, because my planets generally perform a service for others, and therefore my emissaries never need to number more than perhaps 200 to 220.

Did you create them as quantum masters, or have they evolved up through a series of experiences?

They were created as quantum masters so they could take the form that is appropriate when approaching other civilizations or even other life forms. They have the capacity to be a star, even a mass of stars. They could appear, I like to say, as a dandelion.

Are the planets themselves ensouled by sentient beings who have their own lives?

Oh, certainly, certainly they are sentient. They have their own personalities, yes.

Is there one soul that is with a planet forever, or . . .

No, no, they are all able to function for *any* of the planets. Yes, that is another function of quantum mastery. Actually, one learns the basic skills with material mastery, but with quantum mastery (which is perhaps more related to material mastery than to teaching mastery) one can understand and become, or at least become resonant with, any energy form in existence (which, as far as I know, covers it all).

So you created the planets and then any one of the 200 quantum masters can ensoul or enliven that planet, and in time they can change from one to another?

They could, but usually they don't. They don't really ensoul the planet; the planet is itself ensouled, just as this planet is ensouled (the one where you live). Beings do not ensoul the planet; the planet has its own soul. Granted, some personalities might wish to join in and ensoul the planet at any given moment, but the planets are usually their own souls. So my emissaries are usually on the go.

So they go out to other creations.

Yes.

And search out and see what needs to be done?

Exactly.

And bring beings back?

Yes, invite them back if they wish to come and if their creators give permission.

Were you involved when Maldek blew up in this solar system?

We were not involved in that. That explosion, I believe, was handled by others.

Why Seventeen?

When you created the seventeen planets, was that because there were seventeen major functions you realized you wanted to provide?

How wise you are, yes. Unfortunately, Zoosh feels that fully sixteen of these do not necessarily relate to you, and I must admit they don't relate to you in terms of what you are doing now. I will give you an example—this is allowed. There is one planet where nothing moves at all. It is the nature of life to be in motion, but this planet is suspended in time, so *nothing* moves. This is important for certain life forms that have been aggrieved in some way, that perhaps have had some great loss and become unable to transform that loss within their souls. They might be invited, generally one at a time, and they would become the whole planet—but in total, absolute stillness, where it is possible to examine without any interruption all that you are. In these moments one does not experience distraction in any form and immediately notices what needs to be done.

I see that some of you might feel this is relevant, for it is not something a human being would do. Your system is quite different. When you move into your natural essence at the end of your physical life, you easily shed all discomfort—yes.

This experience would most often occur in some highly complex being who has had some transformation, perhaps even creators who, because of their responsibility, cannot directly deal with their own grief and discomfort. Thus when their responsibility is alleviated or relieved by others, they might come to this planet and take time to let go of all responsibility for anyone other than themselves and become able to see and feel clearly what must be done to transform them. And they will do so there, after which they can either continue with their own creation, or perhaps (if they have been replaced) begin another—whatever they wish.

This does not relate to you directly, but I am telling you this so you will understand that there are places where one can go even at higher levels of mastery to resolve some conundrum.

I know you don't have a name, but if we ever want to talk to you again, is there any way we could refer to you, some symbol or name we can use?

Hmm, let me think. Why don't you just describe my creation and call me by that description? Or ask Zoosh to fetch me. [Laughs.]

Like "Creator of Seventeen Planets"? Is that what you mean?

Yes, "the creator of seventeen planets with more mass between the planets than the planets themselves" and so on—something like that.

Might you at any time create an eighteenth planet if you discover a new function that is needed?

In terms of your time I have not created anything beyond seventeen for approximately 20 trillion to the 450 billionth power years, all right? And the last one I created was . . . you'd think it would have been the first, but the last one I created was for the empaths.

Personal Information

What about your social life? Your creation is you, but can you interact with other creators—with your peers?

Certainly.

And come and go? How would that work?

Oh, any creator (once you are doing such things) can communicate with any other creator anywhere. Yes, I might say this is a pleasant social pastime, a way we keep in touch with one another and inform each other of what we have to offer each other. It's a networking group. It is Netscape for creators!

Have you ever talked to a human like this before?

I think I have spoken with a few humans, yes. Some who are in the human form have visited this place in their essential shape and color and tone, but not too many.

Do you have a special way that you travel? I'm curious about what I'm seeing. I almost see two rings around you, as if you are sitting within something that's open. Is that related to you at all? I don't see you, really; I see what's around you.

That's good; I'm glad to hear that. I do not "travel," as you would say. One travels to see something one has not seen, and when you are a creator . . . I can see everyone's creation from here quite well. You might say I have very good eyesight. What you see is part of my inner and outer resonant core, but I must admit that if we were face to face you would probably not see my face any better than you see it now.

That's an interesting statement: You can see everything in every other creation everywhere.

As far as I know, all creators can do this. And so we can not only discuss our creations with each other, but we can see them, feel them, examine them. That makes it much more fun and allows for infinite variety. There are always creators creating, and almost always they are creating something that the other creators would find to be new in some way, which is why we never really get bored. [Chuckles.] The wonderful thing about creation is that it is very creative!

Is there ever a time when a creator (I don't know if they're ever young or whatever) is not aware of others at first?

I think not; I'm not aware of anybody at creator level like that, but certainly students in creation school, such as yourselves, might have moments like that, but not at the creator level. That is why it is necessary to be motivated at the creator level, because you are so aware of what is going on elsewhere that you must be motivated to what *you* want to do, or you might just spend your time . . .

Watching everyone else?

Watching others, yes.

Like a great big cosmic soap opera. In a very condensed way would you explain your understanding of what our Creator is trying to do?

I believe your Creator is intending to prove the existence of dimensions as living beings. Your Creator is interested not only in variety, but in personal individuality. I believe that this is why your Creator wishes to expand to a higher level than even *It* is aware of. (And certainly many creators are not aware of all things—I am not. I am aware of many things, but I am aware that there are things I'm *not* aware of.)

I believe your Creator intends to define, observe and interact with the largest of the large on a personal level (such as a dimension) and the smallest of the small (meaning a cosmic particle) on a personal level. As I understand it, your Creator is very interested in intimacy, in personality and in how all intimate personalities fit together to form the grand existence.

I think for now we will say good night and perhaps another one of my fellow beings will speak next week, yes?

Absolutely. We're honored by your presence. Thank you so much.

❖ Robert's Comments on His Experience

Well, first I got really, really hot, when that Creator came through, and then I started getting numb—my hands went totally numb.

Why did he keep your fingers together?

Apparently it had something to do with being able to maintain the contact, and my hands could be apart for only a few moments and maintain the contact. I think in those moments Zoosh jumped between my hands to keep that contact going. It was some kind of circuit.

Did you see his creation?

I think I saw the desert planet—and I could see the mass between the planets. I could see that it was much thicker. It looked—not syrupy, but it looked substantial. I could see it, but I don't think I can describe it. It looked like it was holding the planets rather than the planets floating in it. Wow!

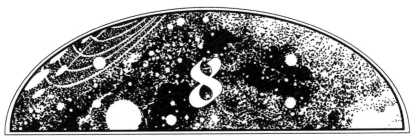

Shapemaker of Portals

August 27, 1996

oosh: As I've said before, different waves of people are waking up at different times, and as you know, everybody's waking up now. We're providing explanations, stories—granted, myths—yet these are all designed to guide you, not to lead you. I'd love to give you the answer you want, but I'd have to add a disclaimer that says, "Those are the facts *now*."

To other channels out there: Do not be intimidated because Uncle Zoosh says this is how it was at any given time and you're channeling something entirely different. These differences are valid. You speak to different segments of the population, and who's to say which is so and which is not so? You have to hang your star on the one that feels right for you.

I have someone here who functions in the world of specific shapes. Speaking of this individual, its primary job is to coordinate the right shape, color, vibration and harmonic to portal and doorway entrances in order to bring through the right folks to accomplish what is necessary in doorways and so on.

That sounds wonderful.

I am the shapemaker for different portal sequences. It is my job to precisely attune a portal's shape, color, tone (actual heard tone) as well as harmonic so that specific individuals from certain times can access the portal, and also, for everyone's safety, so that others who might be there cannot access them. Let me give some examples.

Round portals are ofttimes seen by sensitive individuals of your own people. They are a perfect circle. If you could use a compass or even measure them electronically, you would find that they are startlingly, perfectly circular. I mention this because it is by design. If the portal opening were to vary even slightly from a perfect circle, it would allow vast numbers of individuals, perhaps animals, sometimes even portions of planets, atmospheres—vast possibilities—to leak through to the other side. Naturally, this is not acceptable.

The Circular, Leakproof Portal

Let's talk about a perfect circle. If you were to go around to the side, even if you were very perceptive, you might not see it because the opening from one dimension to another utilizes the two-dimensional vibration—not because your second dimension is low, but because it makes it more discreet.

Say that you're standing in front of this portal. Besides the circle, you might see lines (I will give an example in the channel's experience)—darker colored lines and perhaps slate blue lines. This series of lines is not dissimilar to your universal bar code that is creating a common system of classification. It's startlingly similar in concept except that it has depth, unlike the codes seen on your products. Although it looks two-dimensional from the side, when you look at it from the front you can see that the color is moving. It appears in some way lifelike, as if it were alive, and that is because it has many layers. Even now the more complex codes utilized by your cryptographers have not only a surface code but deeper layers of code. This is how things are kept reasonably discreet.

As we look at this thing, it is floating. You see it (as a sensitive person) for only a short time because it is there for a purpose. Perhaps somebody is coming through; perhaps it is there as an option for *you* to go through. How would you know if it is for you to go through? For starters, if you see it and if others around you do not, it is potentially for you to approach. If you approach it and it moves back slightly, move slowly toward it. If it moves back slightly again, maybe it's not for you. But continue looking at it, because if you look away perhaps it will not be there when you look back.

Observe it and move forward. Don't rush it; if you do, pouf! it will be gone. It is like a shy creature; it is alive in its own way. Perhaps you take another cautious step or two and it moves back only slightly, so now you are getting very close. You are so close (perhaps three or four feet away) that you begin to feel the effect of the vibration. If you are a sensitive person, perhaps you automatically begin moving your arms or legs to accommodate the passageway. It is not so much a code to open the lock; it is more the greeting.

You move right in front of it and bend down, and even though you are moving very slowly and it is moving back slightly, you are moving forward faster than it is moving back. (I'm not recommending this, you understand; I'm saying, suppose.) What happens if the portal allows you, accommodates you? Do you step through it to another world on the other side? Possibly. But it is equally possible that you might find yourself in a passageway. Passageways sometimes move you back or forward in time, and since the portal was opened to you, it might have to do directly with your life.

Also, the passageway might have to do with allowing others to scrutinize you to see if it is safe for you to traverse the passageway and safe for others when you do so. Sometimes it is a means of checking you out a little further, though the portal itself has some capacity for this.

I mention this now so you will understand that the potential for seeing portals these days is greatly increased. Eight or ten years ago it was quite special even for a sensitive person to see one or two portals in a lifetime. But nowadays it is possible for sensitive people to see a portal or two every month. Even people who do not regard themselves as particularly sensitive might easily see a portal without knowing what it is or mistaking it for something else. I cannot tell you how many portals in the dark of night have been mistaken for a light in the neighbor's window (perhaps conveniently so, for the topography is taken into account when portals are accessed on a coming-and-going basis).

Another interesting thing about portals is that sometimes they are not meant for the passage of any being. Sometimes they are meant for the introduction or the reduction of something: something is passed into your system or something in your system is removed. (Perhaps nowadays the latter is more common.)

A Current Backup in Stuck Spirits

Right now your Earth is going through much upheaval. She is becoming much more adamant about using her electrical body and not allowing you to capture it so easily for your purposes. As a result, she needs to have some assistance. There are always a few spirits who are stuck. On Earth now (counting the land, not the sea) spirits of once-living beings (human beings, animals, occasionally ETs) who need assistance to be brought to where they need to go number perhaps 2.5 to 3 million. If we throw in the oceans, it is pretty close to 10 million.

These are not evil spirits or anything like that. They are very often people or animals who died so suddenly that they were not aware of having passed, and when their angelic beings came to take them through the veil to the next world, they did not understand. When these beings come, they do not drag you—they invite you. (It is an invitation but not a requirement.) These days I think it is a little more of an urgency. They are more inclined to say, "It would be good for you to come"—advocate a little bit, you know, because the Earth cannot accommodate such energies anymore.

Let's say there is a ship in heavy seas, a freight vessel perhaps not too new, and the crew is doing all it can to just hang on. Then suddenly a big wave washes over the top of the ship and takes them all down. (It happens especially in very heavy surf. People who travel on the sea lanes know about these things.) The people don't die instantly, but it is a radical change. Some of the people who were battling to keep the ship afloat do not realize that the battle is over, so they continue. Sometimes those of you who have sailed either commercially, militarily, industrially or even for pleasure might pass through a portion of the ocean or even a large lake and get an uncomfortable feeling. It happens so often that you don't want to go through that area after that. It's possible that some disaster happened there and the sailors, who still think they're alive, are trying to maintain the seaworthiness of their vessel.

That's where I come in, especially now. I work with their souls, their guides, teachers and angels, with Creator. Because they've been on Earth longer than they need to be, we work very often with their future lives. It is a big coordinated effort, and it could be for as many as ten, twenty, fifty, sometimes hundreds of people. You cannot take one out at a time; you must take them all out together.

It is vitally important to arrange the color, harmonic and vibration codes and, more important, the shape of the portal that would extract them. In my example here of the men at sea, the last time we did this a few days ago there were about 35 souls. Two or three people, by the way, survived, although it's hard to imagine how. The other 35 had to be taken at the same time

In this circumstance a circle would be inappropriate as a portal because we had to get them out very fast. Because they weren't all going the same place, it was tricky. We have to take them beyond the veils, but not all the way. We take them to what I'd call a staging area, and quickly.

The Diamond-Shaped Portal for Stuck Beings

The diamond shape works best for this, and it is often seen and appreciated by spiritual individuals because it allows very quick transit for many, regardless of their point of origin. It does not take individual beings huge distances in terms of dimension, and time is not the factor here. It might take a soul anywhere from one-quarter of a dimension to five-eighths of a dimension from where it was—far enough that it is no longer stuck, yet near enough for the individual teachers, guides and angels to reach. This whole process takes perhaps one-tenth of a second, but if you slowed it down, you might become aware of all these numerous functions going on.

Interestingly, some might go in triangular portals (some with the apex up, some with it down), some in the diamond, some in the circle and some in even a spiral portal. There's a portal shaped like a spiral [draws]. This is roughly the shape. Sometimes you might see something like that.

The Spiral Portal for Fractionating

The spiral portal very often will take beings (its usual use) who are going either from many to become one or (in the opposite direction) from one to become several. This happens sometimes when you have different incarnations of an individual or (coming the other way) perhaps a split in an individual when the individual is forming several chains of lives. Thus the spiral can be used for individual or mass purposes. It is often the shape used when a universe or a star system is created in multidimensional facets.

You might wonder how the different dimensions of a planet get created. How is it possible physically? Usually it doesn't happen right away. One particular model will come to a creator's consideration: "This is how I see this planet, this solar system, this universe, even this individual or even a plant."

You have species of plants or animals that are closely related. The creator might say, "I like this particular planet very much. I would like perhaps nine or ten dimensions on the variable rate that are versions of this planet. They will all be portions of the same being (planet) expressed in different dimensions." That's where I come in.

I take that individual creator's idea. Creator might say, "This is my idea of this soul. I think of this person as an explorer or an adventurer, and I want 26 dimensional versions of this soul." (It would be same for a planet.) I would have the model of that soul provided by that creator (I do not create souls), and we run that soul through one of those spiral portals, which creates a spin. I have drawn that portal as if you were looking at it straight. Now imagine looking at it from the side . . . I'm drawing for you, albeit somewhat poorly, what amounts to a side view. If we can imagine the portal in perspective it would be like a braid, and

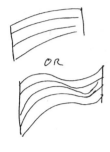

the soul flares into as many of these braids as necessary. The soul (or the planet, the solar system, the galaxy or the universe) is thereby launched into multiplicities of dimensions.

Your Creator has come quite a distance to accomplish this vast and wonderful creation of which you are a portion. Yet your Creator is watched over and loved by creators who have done more—evolved— and your Creator is loved by those beings.

Heart Council's Plan for a Universal Ripple

Once upon a time (I like that phrase) this group that I will call the Heart Council (for they are source love) said to me, "We would like very much for you to spin, with the use of one of your spiral portals, many levels of this particular creator's creation. And I "said" [chuckles] (we communicate in different ways, but I "said"), "Is this creator not going to create this for itself?" The Council said, "We are working with this creator from a distance. This creator has an idea and has spawned a portion of itself to become its own replacement creator. We think this idea is so good that we want to include this creator in its own objectives of creation. We want to provide another level by which it can achieve, but because it will not have created that level itself, it will have the pleasure of discovering it."

"So," they said, "can you create multiple levels of this creator's creation so that this creator can expand, going up into another level of its own creation and so that the creator in training"—*you*, the Explorer Race it is preparing—"can take over this creator's creation, looking forward to a similar manner of evolution, if not through the same level of creation, then through a new creation or re-creation it would create for its own expansion?"

I said, "Yes, it is not complex, but it will require the absolute cooperation from *all* souls, including the creator to whom you refer and all life forms within this creation."

The Heart Council said, "We can provide this, but it can last only (converted to your time) about 1/10,000 of a second." I said, "That's plenty of time." They informed me when the exact moment would occur and told me they would do something to stimulate the attention of all beings. They decided that at the moment you on Earth received all (100%) of your heart energy back, it would create such a ripple throughout this whole universe that everyone's attention would be lovingly drawn in that brief moment. The moment itself will last perhaps one to two seconds, but not everyone will feel it in the same moment.

There will be one moment, although only 1/10,000 of a second long, when everyone will feel that great surge of love (as if a rubber band had been released), a tremendous release of loving energy all at once. And in that exact moment will your Creator's creation (the creation of which you are a portion) spin through the spiral portal and create, according to the Heart Council's request, nineteen versions of Itself. This allows your Creator to pass through variations of its own creation expressed at higher amplitudes. (The word "amplitude" does not quite fit, but it is close enough.) And for that 1/10,000 of a second your Creator will feel the full love of the Heart Council from which It was originally born. In that moment your Creator will be embraced by Its own creator; then the totally loving energy of the Heart Council will embrace your Creator and flood your Creator with all the memories of who It has ever been.

Creator Chose to Forget Home

You see, when your Creator, who was perhaps the nucleus of the idea of the Explorer Race, went out on Its own, It chose to do something that proved to be a valuable experience. It decided to forget where It came from. It would not forget Its abilities, skills, potentials—none of that—only where It came from. It would forget home. Your Creator perhaps felt that even though this would be a personal sacrifice, the tremendous realization that would accompany Its remembering the full feeling of home might allow a greater catapult effect in Its desire to create something new. (Creators must at least be creative, but they also must utilize all the tools at hand.)

So your Creator donned, however minuscule, the veil of ignorance of Its home, and while It felt great love coming from somewhere for It, It did not quite know how to find Its way back home. Your Creator believed that by being unable to find Its way back home, It would be more inclined to create and to stay on the job. Even you as a people have these qualities. When you know you can't go home for a while, you are inclined to get to work and see if you can make something like a home for yourself and your family, even your friends. It is something you take for granted, but it is not an accident. It is literally a portion of your Creator's experience.

So your Creator knows there is more, and feels ongoing radiated love from this "more." When your Creator decides, *"This is the moment!"* you will have gotten all your heart energy back and have done all you must do, that catapulting effect will take place. Not only will you and the universe of your Creator benefit then, but your Creator Itself will benefit.

You see, in my experience I have discovered that the one universal absolute for all civilizations, from the most bizarre to the average, is that the component of love holds things together and also stimulates, supports and very tenderly nurtures the *new*. There is nothing that all creators celebrate and are thrilled more about than something entirely or even partially new. I have seen it happen. The thrill is an experience unlike any other. The thrilling moment of something new is unique, and everyone feels it. (Some don't know what they're feeling, but it sure feels good.)

I want you to understand that as magnificent and loving and profoundly creative as your own Creator is (of which you are a portion), there are others who are also nurturing and supporting as far as beyond can be. However small my role is, I have seen much.

I have to tell you, it is a wonderful thing you are doing here, and unique, as I understand it. Even when your Creator had the idea, a thrill of energy went out to other creators elsewhere. And they have been watching, because this is a wondrous new thing you are doing that your Creator conceived of. That is why so often here everybody is watching you and cheering you on. This is something new, and I can assure you that entirely new things are rare. And entirely new and wonderful things are so rare that creators everywhere are listening (on sort of the party line of creators). It is a wondrous experience.

Portals for Individuals

I wanted to explain the spiral portal because it has such a significance to you on a personal level. There are other different and unusual portals—certainly there are many different shapes. Sometimes they might be a singular portal, meaning a portal for a particular being who is perhaps functioning at a light level. This kind of a portal would be the exact shape, color, depth, harmonic and vibration associated with that being so that no other being can use that portal.

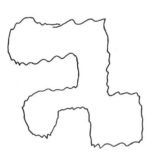

I will give you an example [draws]. This example is a very specific portal for an individual being. It would have specific colors, depth, harmonic and shape—very specific—so that only that being could use it. This is a wonderful safety mechanism, because you can leave the portal parked somewhere, and flocks of birds can fly right through and stay in their own dimension. The sea can roll all around it with no effect. Only that being accesses that portal, and when that being comes back and accesses it, the moment it passes through it, the portal closes and follows it. In that way the portal does not remain a moment longer than necessary.

Now, these portals do not punch holes in time (to anticipate a question). They actually do not affect time and space at all, because they are so precise that even the time and the space have been requested permission for the portals to be present. If the intended place for the portal is not quite right, it will be moved to where time and space feel it is safer, better, more appropriate. Time and space are not bent, nor are holes punched, because the portal does not harm anything.

I mention this to you because at any given moment (say, in this small town) there might be three or four of these portals floating about. When you consider the vastness of the universe and beyond, that's quite a few, because there are so many places to go. This small town has become a very attractive place to visit because of the tremendous experience and the pushes and pulls of the magnetic and electrical fields.

Sedona, a Birthing Point of Catapult Effect

There is in this place—Sedona—a tremendous mechanism taking place even now as we speak to generate its own time and space harmonic. There are a few other places where this is happening at the same moment. I will mention a couple of them: Ayers Rock in Australia, a very holy place; deep within the country now called Siberia (I'm afraid I cannot be exact where); about 90.32 kilometers due north of Helsinki, Finland; and about 200 kilometers east by southeast of Easter Island. There are several others, but those are the ones I can mention now where this same energy is taking place.

This is really the birthing point of the energy involved in the catapulting effect. The heart energy is coming in gradually, but toward the end it will come in quicker, sometimes in chunks, and when it is received in total, the generated energy will function very much like a catapult. The energy will hurtle to all points of the universe almost simultaneously, taking one to two seconds (which is almost simultaneous, considering the great distances), hurtling that shared experience of all human beings receiving their heart energy on Earth. Nothing will take it from you, but the wonderful feeling that you all have will be shared—broadcast, as one might broadcast a wonderful moment of an opera or even a rock concert to the universe all at the same moment.

The catapulting effect uses magnetism, electromagnetism, electricity and what I call inverse electricity (very important in the coding of portals and in lightning). All of that will come together and will literally *hurtle* that shared experience to all points of your universe. That is why beings are coming here and to Ayers Rock and near Easter Island and Helsinki and other places. They are coming to observe the dynamic energy effect that is building.

I mention this because some of you at this time are feeling extremes of energy. About 70% of the experience is what I have described. Occasionally some of the extremes of energy are associated with creations of human beings, but mostly it is this great cosmic catapult effect building up. I want you to understand that even though you are experiencing moments of discomfort, in the long run this effect is intended to broadcast something very comfortable indeed. And once it happens, it will be over. It won't need to be done again, and the energy in these places will become comfortable once more.

I want you to know that there are a great many beings watching over you, including those amongst you who are very spiritual beings and sometimes beings that you would not imagine were so spiritual who are on the other side, perhaps having passed over recently. They are watching with love and appreciation and understanding. This is a wonderful project; many beings are coming to watch you.

They won't get in your way too much, but those of you who are very sensitive (sometimes even those who do not consider yourselves sensitive) might feel something—perhaps a light touch to the skin, behind the ear or (if you are wearing shorts) on the leg. It will always be on a portion of bare skin. I'm not talking about the touch of a spirit. This touch often feels like the lightest touch of a feather upon just a hair on your skin—the lightest, most gentle touch. Often this is one of your other selves, a reincarnation, visiting you; perhaps a beloved being you have either lived with or know well; perhaps even an angelic touching you with a feather, as it were. This is something beings can do with great concentrated effort to let you know you are loved and appreciated and help you feel the great connection all life has now with this project. If you should be privileged to have those experiences, enjoy them. You are literally being touched by a loved one from across dimensional fields.

Are you creating the mechanisms here for the catapult effect?

No, that is what is so wonderful. I did not.

Who did?

You are creating it.

Humanity?

Yes, your collective souls with Earth Mother and all her and your electrical bodies and electromagnetism and all of this—*you* are creating it! It is not only passing the test—it is *past* the test. It is a marvelous thing. And of course it draws my interest because here you are doing something . . . I feel in a way that you are like an apprentice.

It's a gift to the Creator so that Creator can go up?

Yes. It is a way to send a kiss to the Creator, which the Creator will feel.

About Me and My Work

How did you learn how to do your work? Do you have apprentices? Were you born this way, or did you apprentice?

I believe "apprentice" is the appropriate term, but I was not conscious of my apprenticeship until I was almost doing it. I was a portion of a larger consciousness—not unlike yourselves, who were lovingly birthed from Creator to go on your great voyage. I noticed that I was being birthed from this massive being, which I have referred to in passing. This great being said, "We need simple and effective means of creating variety, and we think that because you have a great love for variety and mathematics (closer to geometry), you will love this job." And they were right! I'm very fond of the job; it is very fulfilling.

What massive being was it that you were birthed from? The Heart Council?

I believe this was (though the term might seem as if it doesn't apply) the higher self of the Heart Council.

When did you become conscious? You have watched creations birthed and birthed and birthed over eons.

It's hard to describe in terms of years, but I can best say that in the time it has taken your Creator to be birthed, to travel as much as It has, to create your creation—all of this time—if you multiplied that by $15,460,382^2$ it would come pretty close to being my point of origin, in terms of my being aware of myself as an individual.

So you get to go to all the creators, who all say, "I want this, I want that"?

Yes, this is very much fun. I have several apprentices, so I don't have to do everything at once.

Did you birth them, or attract them to you?

Actually, I did not birth them. They're all volunteers, and they approached me a long time ago and wanted to do this. I'm not exactly sure where they came from, but I could certainly give them a recommendation. They have done well, and it is fun to have someone to speak to that knows . . .

That understands what you're talking about?

Yes, we all need that, don't we?

So where do you hang your hat? Where do you get your messages?

I like to stay close enough to the Heart Council so I can hear all about the latest news. Although I am able to be everywhere at once, I'd say that I hang out close to the Heart Council.

We had another being talk to us a couple of weeks ago who was a messenger, and he said that he could connect with anything in infinity at any time. So you have that kind of outreach?

Yes.

What we're learning is that creators are great, but there are lot of other interesting job opportunities out there.

Well, that's what your friend Zoosh wants you to understand, that sometimes things you don't really think about . . .

Somebody has to do?

Somebody has to do—exactly. Just because you don't *see* the plumbing doesn't mean somebody isn't cleaning out the pipes.

So you love what you do and you're looking forward to more of the same. There isn't anything you aspire to?

Oh, no. You know, it's a funny thing, and you can identify with this: Very often people in a corporation or even a government agency will sometimes not seek or even accept a promotion because they like what they're doing. They know that if they get promoted they won't be able to do that anymore. It's possible that someday I'll be approached to go on, and I suppose that if I am I will have my apprentices take over, and that would be good. But I'll tell you, they'll have to make the offer pretty good.

You said you were birthed from a greater being doing the same thing, so there must be others out there doing what you're doing.

That would be suggested, wouldn't it?

Are you aware of them?

Not in the levels of creation in which I function, so perhaps they are functioning at other levels.

There's always a beyond, that's my line.

Yes, I have never found anyplace where that does not apply.

Do you have an identity, if we want to ask you something again?

Oh, I suppose you could say the Shapemaker of Portals.

Wormholes and Personal Portals

What about wormholes? Does this fit in anywhere?

No, these are more like anomalies. They are in your physical sciences at this time, but are only theoretical.

They're real, aren't they?

They are real, but they are rare. They are usually caused by something traveling too fast as it goes through dimensions without getting permission to pass through that space, time and matter. Since it is so rare at the higher levels of travel, it is usually something that has been struck by something else, such as a meteor striking something, perhaps one of your satellites, and a portion of it hurtles off somewhere. In space it would keep going infinitely as long as it doesn't hit something or run into friction. Things like this require an emergency team to come and repair it. That is basically how a wormhole effect takes place; it creates a temporary spatial distortion.

So we don't want to look for wormholes to travel in; it's something to fix.

No, don't ever do that, because even if you could travel through it (it is possible, but I would never do it, because the potential for winding up someplace that you cannot get back from is very high), the chances of traveling predictably to a place is very low.

As creators, should we be able to create our own portals?

I cannot say *should;* I would rather say might or could, if there were a reason. But the only reason I'm aware of is to observe, study and learn—

certainly not to escape or go elsewhere.

What would be a legitimate reason for creating a portal? Has that ever happened?

A personal portal?

Yes.

Oh, yes, there are several here now, as I indicated.

Are those individuals aware of these portals?

Certainly, because they've come from someplace else. For the most part I have never seen anybody do this who is not a lightbeing, because you cannot travel physically through space through one of these portals (obviously there is no air). It is always done by lightbeings, usually beings who have an interest historically or anthropologically, for example, or sometimes even a personal interest. Most often it is done for study, and it is only allowed if that study will result in some greater good for others. It is not allowed simply for curiosity.

Those portals are there for lightbodies to come here, not for humans to find them and go someplace?

Exactly.

That's the confusion.

Experiment with Shapes to Discover Your Own

If you can imagine, think about over the next week or two or three as you read this: What is the shape or combination of shapes that feels most comfortable to you? Keep the shapes simple—circle, square, triangle, diamond. The diamond might or might not be made up of two equal triangles. Draw the shapes; they don't have to be perfect.

Draw them on plain unlined paper. It doesn't have to be anything fancy; a paper bag will do nicely. Notice which shape causes you to feel more comfortable, then play with it, experiment. Try superimposing shapes over other shapes if none of the simple shapes seems to feel good to you. I am not giving you a portal design here; I am saying that the foundational element of my work is understanding which shapes apply to which beings.

You can discover your own personal shape. I am not concerned that you might create a portal from this that will cause you to tumble about in some universal place from which you will have to be rescued, but it might help you to know what shape you are and what resonates with you. By knowing this, ofttimes you could create that shape out of cardboard or, for the more artistic, wood or clay—any material—and carry it with you. It is about twice as effective (in its comfort to you) if you make it yourself rather than have someone else make it, because then you put your personal mark on it.

I'm going to recommend for those of you who want homework to do this. It is startlingly empowering, nurturing and encouraging. One would not think that holding or manipulating or touching a shape you have created could have that effect, yet something as simple as a simple shape—a circle or triangle, for example—can. And ofttimes when you combine them with other shapes it can work as a tool to prepare you for other lives and even help your communications with other beings elsewhere.

So become more aware of shapes around you, and know that all shapes that I am aware of exist for a very specific purpose. Nothing is random; it is all part of a grand plan. Good night.

All right, Zoosh here. How do you like my idea of a guest for the evening? What a sweetheart!

Yes, there are some very special individuals out there, and this being is one of my "faves."

It was such a heartwarming thing to hear about the moment when we get our love back. I was going to ask him for a date on it. Do you know it?

I don't think we have a specific date, but now that you're at 3.49 . . . you know, it alters things so much to move up even a decimal point, but going from 3.875 to 3.9, for instance, will profoundly change what is, what has been and what could be. In my experience this is not only rooted in your Creator's desire for variety, but it is very much a pleasurable effect, because one is never stuck. Even if you feel stuck, it won't last because everything is in motion; at some point something will move that might not have any direct connection to you (or so you might think), but it can get things moving. In my experience it is not an accident.

There are no accidents. Some things take longer and some things are shorter, but all things come together in their own moment. On that note I think I will say good night.

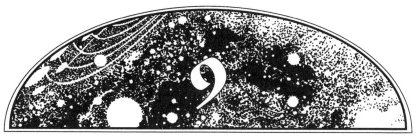

Creator of the Inverse Universe, Our Creator's Creator

August 29, 1996

oosh: I've got somebody interesting to introduce tonight. What about the creator of your Creator? Let's see if we can make contact.

Your Creator's Beginnings in My Inverse Universe

Greetings. I will speak a bit about my consideration toward the exponential launch of your Creator. When your Creator was placed upon the path of Its individuality, because It would choose to explore all avenues of variety, it was necessary to launch or birth this being exponentially to place multiple levels of the same being into personal individuality.

Before your Creator emerged It traveled through the universal experience of inverse reality. Your Creator came from what you can call the inverse universe. This vast array of dimensions, unlimited in scope, is involved in the before and after of everything, but it is not involved in any way in the present moment. Everything that *will exist* and everything that *has existed* is a portion of the inverse universe. In this way it is possible to create ideal moments for the birthing of new ideas or new realities, new concepts that might at some point grandly arrive to create avenues of expression for many.

The inverse function is not unlike something being inside out. If a sock is inside out, you turn it the right way and then it is useful to you. Ruling out current fashion trends, one does not normally use things inside out, but being inside out is a step before their usefulness. Since we are using laundry as an example, sometimes when you are done with that sock, it goes into the wash inside out.

When the soul is created, the material of the soul is inside out, for all intents and purposes, before it arrives to take life in the form of that child-to-be. It is involved in what could be, what has been or what might have been, but it is not involved at all in the moment. It discovers the present moment through physical reality. Physical reality is entirely associated with the moment. Even though you might ofttimes consider what might happen, what will happen and what has happened, the actual creation of your reality takes place in the present moment. This you know.

I want you to understand that the inverse universe is complementary to your universe—complementary but not the same. When the exponential creations of your Creator explored the inverse universe, it was clear to me that that which chose to become your Creator (and the creator of all that you know in your universe) could not stay and make your creation in the universe where I exist. That was my intent. Because of the nature of the inverse reality, it works much more completely with something complementary, and it was my intention to give birth to that complementary aspect by way of your Creator.

So your Creator traveled with Its exponential parts in this exploration of my world, my reality, for longer. . . you like numbers, don't you? If we take the combined total of the length of time of each and every soul that has manifested as a member of your Explorer Race and placed all those lifetimes, incarnations and reincarnations in a row, that's how long your Creator, in Its exponential parts, explored the inverse reality to see if Its intended creation of multiple physical and energetic dimensional realities could fit in the inverse world.

If you were to see your Creator traveling through the inverse world with vision similar to your own, It would look very much like multiple octaves of color superimposed one over the other, creating a mass of colored striations. The color would not be cloudy; it would not have the quality of individual expression, as one might see in a cloud in your sky in which shapes are not often repeated. No, it would be orderly: striations of color with many depths—layered, with all striations going one direction as seen from the three-dimensional visual perspective you utilize most often.

Inventing an Exit from the Inverse Reality

Your Creator realized that Its joy could not be found in the past or future but could only come about as a result of departing that reality, so with the help of a couple of Its friends It had to do something that all creators must do to prove they are worthy of being a creator and can accept the consequences of their own creation: Your Creator had to find Its way out of my world as well as an avenue by which It could come to the world It would create.

Your Creator realized that It would have to initiate an exit to leave the inverse world, so It asked for a guide. [Chuckles.] Your friend and mine—Zoosh—said, "Oh, I'll be happy to oblige," and brought a couple of companions. (We'll talk about them some other time.) Zoosh did not in any way interfere with your Creator's moving out of the inverse world, but he let your Creator know: "I'll be on the other side when you emerge into the pathway to what you will create."

This is not so much a conundrum as it appears, for very often even now, if you need an exit to another world, no matter where you are and what you are doing, you can easily stop and begin to daydream or fantasize. That truly is the creation of another world. All your Creator had to do was pick a time, a moment to do so. But since your Creator was birthed in the inverse world, picking a moment in the present to emerge in transit to Its own creation required that your Creator *invent the basis by which It would create.* So you see, the exit was not only your Creator's own making, but laid the foundation for your Creator's entire creation.

When your Creator realized that, It quickly focused Its entire accumulation of knowledge and, looking not unlike lightbeings passing through a lens and being focused, It drew on all of Its past and future, all of Its exponential parts, focused them through the lens of the present and emerged into the passageway that would bring your Creator at some point to the place and moment in which It would create your world. I will not describe the trip, for that was described quite extensively in the third Explorer Race book *[Explorer Race: Origins and the Next 50 Years].*

Birthing the Explorer Race

My intentions for your Creator have been fulfilled completely—not, however, on the basis of what your Creator has created by Itself, but by what your Creator has done in birthing you. As any parent can understand quite well, although one loves and appreciates one's own children, it is not until the grandchildren arrive that one fully enjoys being a parent. It is very much like that. When your Creator took responsibility for giving birth to something that would not only replace It and is intended to be better than It in some ways, this creation (which Zoosh calls the Explorer Race—you) was a portion of Itself that It had not fully explored. [Chuckles.]

That is a requirement. In order for a birth to work correctly and for the best to happen, a level of ignorance is essential. Ofttimes the less one understands of the soul of one's child, the more one can learn and enjoy that child because it is a pleasant surprise. When your Creator found Its most insatiably curious parts and launched those out to become the Explorer Race (yourselves), your Creator did not completely understand everything about that portion of Itself. When you have a portion of yourself that is insatiably curious, because it is constantly seeking it does not easily communicate who it is, being defined by its acquisitions. And because of the variety of its acquisitions, you do not necessarily completely understand or fully appreciate the nature of your offspring. You might define something from its outer appearance, its most obvious qualities—such as this fireplace here—yet there is so much more. Any stonemason knows that there is more—a framework and so on underneath. So it is with any birth; a degree of ignorance is essential.

When your Creator birthed you, I knew then that your Creator had discovered the true value of the present moment, because the present moment can never be controlled. It is ofttimes the platform or foundation for some new creation, because spontaneity and the unknown factor are always a portion of creation. Your Creator let go and said, "Here is a part of me I'm releasing that I would like to become the Explorer Race on the basis of its foundational qualities of curiosity and adventure. It will discover who it is on its own." When your Creator let go of you to do that, I then felt fulfilled, because that is what I did when I let go of your Creator.

What Your Creator Left Behind

You might ask, "What about all of those exponential parts of the Creator? Are they all condensed and focused through the lens?" Not all. When one creates something exponentially in the physical universe, it multiplies itself. But in the inverse world it creates varietal past and future, and those varieties will exponentially multiply in *their* unique variety, creating infinite potentials for past or future. Your Creator did not choose (nor was it necessary) to bring that level of infinity of the past and future with It to Its point of creation because there were only a few past scenarios and a few future scenarios that were desirable for you as the Explorer Race. (Certainly there were other pasts and futures for other beings in this creation, but since one's child is often the main focus of one's life, the focus is on *you*.)

So most of the varietal past and future was not necessary to bring along. All of this awaits your Creator. When your Creator is replaced by you and expands to rejoin all that It was before It came on this pathway to create this creation, It will pick up again all of that varietal past and future plus the tremendous variety and potential of the moment, which It has thoroughly explored in Its creation. It will have available to It the multiplicity that is exponential in its variety. One explores variety in the present moment entirely differently from the way one explores it in the past or future. Your Creator has become a little bored because Its capacity for something new has been severely limited by not having access to those multiple varietal pasts and futures. When It has that, It will not only be able to apply what It has learned in the present moment of creation, but It will have an infinite variety of applications once again available to It in exploring these other sequences.

Now, when your Creator expands to Its next level, It will pick this up, but I will be waiting there (and I think your Creator knows this) to embrace in my own way your Creator on Its return, to support and sustain It, perhaps with a little pride, and to gently and lovingly share Its joy in feeling complete once again. In order for this to happen, you will have to take your Creator's place, but I think you will do that.

This has been my introduction to help you understand a little bit who I am and a little more, perhaps, who your Creator is.

The Loop of Time to Explore Overemphasis on Thought

Did our Creator get the idea for doing this present loop of evolution [see both chapter 21 and the diagram on page 168 in The Explorer Race] *to redo that decision from your inverse reality?*

Yes, that is an example of inverse reality, where one can create what is basically a knot in time to explore something more thoroughly. One alters reality just enough to literally exist out of the present. This loop of time *is not in the present!* You are operating to some extent in inverse reality even now. This loop of time is separate from your present reality. You were going along, then you had to explore by going through this loop of time. You have stemmed from the beings who made the decision referred to in *The Explorer Race* [the Council of Nine, chapter 21] and you needed to utilize the inverse reality to explore *outside* time the consequences of that decision. You had to develop sufficient responsibility to realize how such a seemingly innocent decision could become wholly and unexpectedly corrupted. Yes, inverse reality was used here.

Could you express from your point of view what the decision was that we made, the one that we are changing?

These beings, who represented nine core functions of reality, blossomed to become all of you. Before that you had basically expanded to being nine, then you expanded to become many more. But you are still basically those nine. The apparently innocent decision was to allow the focus of your continuing reality (as it moved forward from where you were then) to become more involved in *thought* and less involved in *feeling*. That is my perspective. It was this decision that required an exploration of many potential pasts and futures to see what-if? It was, you might say, your Creator giving you a chance: "Okay, but before you do that, look and see what could happen."

So this loop in time was created which, in its closure, will necessarily be uncreated. The accumulated wisdom will remain, but not the accumulated knowledge. In this way souls will not be wounded. The wisdom and the justification for the wisdom will be present, but pain will not. Pain was designed to be a motivating tool, but not necessarily immortal.

That decision, as I understand it, necessitated a little boost by your Creator to say, "Okay, you can do that. Now look at *this*." Of course, as a result of looking at it over the past millions of years or so, you have had the opportunity to see how a creation more involved in thought and less involved in feeling would make it possible to become less aware of how others could be injured by seemingly innocent acts.

The Solution: Feminine Technology

Here is an example from your own time: the choice to pursue the machine age. You can list over and over again the wonderful benefits to human beings that have come about as a result of technology as you know it (the moving parts in machines). Yet you can list far more things that have harmed individuals as a result of technology. Does this mean that technology is bad? No, it just means that what is defined as technology needs to be redefined, needs to become what has been called *feminine* technology so that feeling is ever present and that no material used to make any tool or machine is in any way involved *without its permission*.

The moment something is involved without its permission, it will suffer, but if you are involved in thought you might not know it's suffering, because you do not have sufficient feeling to be aware of the suffering of another being. Though you might think a being is a rock, it is a liquid—everything is alive, yes? It was necessary to explore the consequences of the decision in a way that could be uncreated so that souls would not be scarred, yet you would know and would arrive back in that loop of time before you made that decision with the wisdom, not to control your decision, but to make it in a more enlightened manner.

That is the key, as any parent or grandparent knows: If you want your children to grow, become knowledgeable, learn and become more, you don't make the decision for them. You give them the facts as you know them and hope that they will modify their decision in some more benevolent way, yet remain creative and unique.

When you get back you will not make the opposite decision; you will simply make another creative decision that will, at the very least, equalize feeling with thought, perhaps even making feeling *more* than thought, including levels of thought you do not utilize now.

For example, you might use thought and feeling tied together that is past- and future-oriented as well as present-oriented so that when you think of something, have an inspiration or extrapolate how you might create something, you can *feel* that creation in the future. That would be very advantageous. Think of how many mistakes could be avoided doing it in this way. This is not a way to determine *what* to choose, but an example of how you might modify that decision.

Based on the experience and the wisdom of the beings in the loop of time?

Yes.

What about your reality? Were you born in an inverse universe, or did you choose it?

I created it.

You created it? You came from a regular universe before that?

No, I came from another creator, as all do.

But not from a creator in an inverse universe?

No.

You created the whole concept?

My Birth from the Void

I created the experience of it, because that was my choice. When I was in my creator (that which created me) I was in what you would call the Void, that which defines everything else. The Void is not nothingness, but that which defines other things, just like the dark of the sky defines the stars. The stars are all the more beautiful because of the dark sky; if there were no dark in the sky, the stars would not be seen.

My creator who birthed me was essentially the Void, and when I was there I wanted to have an avenue to explore that which had substance. I was interested in substance—that which could be sensed, that which could be defined. So when my creator birthed me, I naturally followed the same route that your Creator did: I explored the entire creation of my creator. When I could not find the type of substance I wanted, I created a pathway (as your Creator did) by way of my motivation for substance, then moved into a long and very wide tunnel. During my passage through this tunnel I had an opportunity to see the creations that had been created up to that moment outside the context of time—the creations currently being experienced that had anything to do with substance, from the least to the most visible. I had a chance to explore what others had done, and this took a significant amount of experience (time, as you would say).

I had an opportunity, then, to be educated. When I had had enough education and was beginning to pass through the tunnel for the second time, I decided I was prepared to begin my own creation. That is when I decided to seek my definition, not only in material matter but in the experience of time. I was fascinated by what had been done and what could be done, so I decided to focus on that. At that moment I did not realize that when I gave birth to your Creator It would explore the present, because to me, the Void had been the present—it was totally present, you understand? It did not occur to me that when giving birth to your Creator I would essentially give birth to a being who was interested in a variation of the present.

Yet if one looks at lineages at all, themes often tend to follow family lines. "Grandfather did this," skip a generation and then, "Granddaughter does that, too." This is not an accident. This represents a braid that runs through lineages so that worthy ideas (sometimes not so pleasant ones) are not lost but are explored in greater depth from different points of view according to who the creator is. You, as individual creators in training, qualify for that definition.

Does each creator birth only one offspring, or do you have many?

I can only speak for my creator, who "sprang me off," as you say, just as I "sprang off" yours. In what I have been exposed to, no, that is not a limit. It is possible to create as many as you wish, which is why I created exponential versions of your Creator, which I've already explained. Theoretically I could give birth to another, but there is no need, because there is a level of responsibility on my part for your Creator, to say nothing of my own creation. I want to be able to give sufficient focus to my own creation, pay attention to what your Creator is doing and still have time to think about where I came from (my creator). I think it is certainly possible to have more than one offspring, but my lineage did not do so, nor did I. Within the context of the creation in which you are living, I believe that your Creator will follow that lineage as well.

The Shapemaker of Portals said that our Creator had to forget where He came from. Is He just now remembering? Haven't you been able to communicate with Him all this time?

No, only indirectly. If I had been communicating with Him, He would have begun to remember the varieties of the past and future that He had left behind and it would have distracted Him. When one talks to one's parent (you can understand this) or even one's grandparent, you begin to remember things you had forgotten. In some cases that's good; in other cases it is mightily distracting. It was believed important to let your Creator pursue His own goals with a minimum of side chatter.

Did you forget your creator when you started your creation?

No, I did not have to do that, because I actually worked in significant concordance with my creator. My creator had created the Void, and since I was creating past and future potentials, possibilities and so on, I needed the Void in order to lay my creation out. So I literally built my creation upon my creator! Thus forgetting or leaving my creator was not a requirement.

Did he create a void or the concept of void?

My creator created Void. Before my creator, I am not aware of Void having existed. It is hard to believe, is it not? It is fascinating to consider that what appears so obvious, so eternal, is not in fact eternal; it was created by someone. Is it not a compliment to the success of that creation that it is considered eternal?

Yes, I thought it was the substrate of everything, like every creator had used the Void to get the potential of the stuff of creation.

Of course you would think that, and naturally my creator considers that as a success, one might say.

Did you have to go before the Council of Creators to explain your idea?

No, that is not often the case. One does not present something so much as experience a moment when one says, "Oh, *this* is what I want to do." If it is for any reason inappropriate, there will not be disapproval. Instead, not unlike a loop of time, that individual creator would have the opportunity to see consequences: "If you do this, then what about this?" This does not mean you can't do it, but that you must factor that in and resolve it. It is by way of a challenge. If you do not want to factor that consequence in and resolve it, then you might pick something else.

Sometimes one creates resolution through whomever one births. Your Creator did that. It was shown the potential of "what about this?" and decided to accept the challenge and have help (advisors, you might call them). It also understood that the "what about this?" would basically be resolved through your birth.

It is interesting, is it not, that even now in your civilization it is thrilling to discover that your own children or grandchildren are exploring what you have missed, have not felt fulfilled about or are curious about. You do not actually live through them, but you have the pleasure of feeling that somehow whatever you missed is being carried on by future generations. This is not accidental. [Chuckles.]

Our Creator brought in friends to help. Did you do that, too? Do other creators do that very often?

I did not, but it is not unknown. It is especially common when one is setting out to do something new and unique, because with the new and unique there is always the pitfall that you might unintentionally do something catastrophic. That is why advisors are very helpful, especially if they have had experience in avenues unrelated to your own, in which case they will perhaps help you to avoid catastrophic decisions. Since your Creator intended to do something unique, it was necessary—and I believe it was a good decision—to bring along advisors.

There were eight of them?

Yes.

They were all creators before they joined this Creator?

Yes.

Can you say a little about what each one brought to this creation?

The Eight Companions of Your Creator

One brought a total and complete understanding of all levels of physical reality [Synchronizer of Physical Reality and Dimensions]. Physical reality is defined as the first-, second-, third-, fourth- and fifth-dimensional physical realities. Another one brought in a thorough understanding of maybe. The Master of Maybe is basically involved in constant search, exploration, expression and creation of what might be. Having that varietal basis is tremendously helpful when one is involved in something essentially new.

Another friend brought in a very thorough understanding of frequencies and octaves [Master of Frequencies and Octaves]. Your Creator had a pretty thorough understanding of that, but was missing some knowledge relating to frequencies and octaves as expressed in the interactions of light frequencies. (Remember the lineage of your Creator: myself, and before me, the Void.)

There was also a being who had an overwhelming spirit of youthful enthusiasm [Spirit of Youthful Exuberance]. [Chuckles.] That was necessary because your Creator would be spending a lot of time creating different beings who would experience an evolutionary cycle in which they would be child, adult, senior—that kind of sequence. Your Creator was very interested in both variety and sequence. Youthful enthusiasm would be necessary so your Creator could understand how and why things might go astray even with the best of intentions. Thus this being was a necessary advisor.

It was also quite important to bring along a total master in the field of the imaginary [Master of Imagination]. Your Creator had focused a significant amount of experience in all aspects of reality, but had very little experience in what you would call fantasizing, imagination or realities built on threads, as it were. An advisor with expertise on imagination would not only be helpful and in alignment with the expert on maybe, but could also help your Creator to appreciate the potential involved in imagination. This is why you have a tremendous capacity for imagination. Your Creator believed that regardless of what extreme or even banal circumstance you might find yourself in, as long as you had an imagination you could either escape or apply something you had imagined. Your Creator believed sufficiently in this tool, as a result of

Its exposure to this being, that you now have this skill.

All right, let's see—there's also Zoosh. We know who Zoosh is.

How do you see him? How do creators see him? What quality did Zoosh bring in that was needed?

Zoosh is more than a single element. Zoosh is perhaps best known for the capacity to weave a story into reality, so you might say that Zoosh is a weaver—an honorable profession, I might add.

Now, who else? Oh yes, there was the Master of Feeling. Now, your Creator had significant experience of feeling, but It asked the polarized feminine Master of Feeling to attend your Creator's creation—not immediately, but during the latter portion having to do primarily with your launch (birth) and the sequences before you replace your Creator. The timeliness of this being's advice, guidance and energy was believed to be a valuable influence for you. This being was asked to come along to influence radionically more than to bring ideas or thoughts.

Last, there was the plasmic master. The Master of Plasmic Energy has the capacity and wisdom to understand how the life force functions between color, pulse, harmonic, matter, time and so on; and how this cosmic, breathing plasma literally unites all life through what you define as love. Love interacts with creative enthusiasm in all existence, meaning all existence everywhere as well as the creative enthusiasm in any being.

Lineages

Are they related to lineages?

These masters? I don't know that you could say they are specifically related to lineages, because they are made up of different . . . well, we'll look at one. No, it is not associated with singular lineages, but it might be associated more with what I would call an expanding awareness. If we loosely define lineages as that which comes from something to be something, then expands to be more, one can say that it is related to lineages.

How many different lineages are there?

How high can you count?

Okay. Why do lineages originate? Where do they originate?

They have to do with motivation, individuality and the foundation of creation, which is expression.

Then how are certain people selected to carry certain ones?

Oh, you are not selected; you are *associated* with that lineage, you come from it. There is no selection; it is, and you are a portion of that. A person who is a portion of any given lineage will inevitably recognize another being who is of that lineage. If it is a fellow human being, when you meet that person you will immediately feel a rapport. Or even in meeting some other form of life—a stone, or an element such as rain, lightning or a mountain; it is very possible that even a planet could be part of your lineage as well as another person. Sometimes your people go up on ships and various individuals are there. Most often there is someone present associated with your lineage who is either of the extraterrestrial race that brought you to the ship or from some other race. That being, who is either a past or future self or someone on your lineage, will be able to relate to you, calm you or speak with you most easily because you will feel that rapport.

What about marriages? There are people with different lineages who unite. Are they supposed to cross or reunite lineages? What happens?

In your society there are circumstances in which lineages are incompatible, especially nowadays in a time of such great ignorance. But there are cultures on your planet where lineages are understood, especially more ancient ones such as the Chinese. (Granted, the current government has suppressed certain knowledge, but it's still there.) These cultures could understand lineages, the rapport when two lineages come together; they also understand that two beings coming together create more than they might on their own. Nowadays if this type of union is intended to take place to create more, the beings will know in some way, if they are spiritual. If they do not know, then they will discover most likely in some philosophical way. Anything else?

Yes. The elements that are part of the eight beings you described seem so familiar that I'd like to ask, were they a part of the creation itself? And do we in this creation have part of those elements ourselves?

Good question. You might notice that they resonate somewhat, so these are advisors, not your direct Creator. Your Creator would not have asked for these advisors had It not felt that It wanted to have somewhat of a family of creation. Because they were unique and they colored your Creator with their advice, I would say that their influence is part of *your* creation. They are more like godparents than grandparents.

Is there communication between the Internet and the spaceships?

A moment . . . it is not direct. Let us understand that messages sent electronically are basically messages sent electrically. To send a message this way is a way of degrading (not in the sense of putting down). If one were to make spaghetti sauce and added too much water, the sauce would become thin and less flavorful. Sending a message telepathically is infinitely easier for them to pick up than sending it through the cacophony that results when the elements of the computer and the electrical body of Earth are not happy being used that way. It is a densification.

If you want extraterrestrials to get your messages, send them direct; don't use machines. Machines are made up of beings who are unhappy being used in that form. If extraterrestrials were to listen to those messages, they could not help but pick up the discomfort of the machines and the electricity itself, so generally they do not. But if one types in a message to a machine, one thinks of the message first, does one not? Or one can be inspired, and extraterrestrials might pick up the message from your inspiration if it is important to them. But not from the Internet, no.

I'd like to get back to the creation level. When you imagined your way out of the Void and our Creator imagined His way out of the inverse reality, each of you first traveled within the creation that birthed you, then went out and traveled through the other creations to see what was out there. Then did you simply get drawn to a place? How did you choose a space? Do you have levels, dimensions, planes, realities? How does your creation work?

My Creation

Finding a space has everything to do with being inspired. When you are inspired it very often comes unexpectedly. You might ask to be inspired, but it is rarely there when you ask for it. Sometimes you don't even know you need to be inspired, but suddenly the inspiration is there. It works the same for us. We are like you and you are like us. It is through sudden inspiration that we know *this is the space.* We feel it; suddenly it is there. It is a feeling, not a thought. Suddenly we know: *We are here—this is where we begin.*

Understanding more about my reality has to do with all of what might be. You might say that my reality has to do with potentials. I found the exploration and the expression of potentials to be the most fulfilling thing for me because I wanted to complement my creator, as your Creator has complemented me. But I also wanted to add something; I wanted to provide something, to bring forth a palette of many colors that others could paint with. It was my intention to broaden the available materials of creation not only for other creators but for individual beings so that they might have fewer limits to their imaginations.

Do you have individual beings in your creation?

I have some, yes. I discovered that the tool of imagination could be used by beings who would choose an experience primarily of imagination. When one is imagining the past or the future, something happening, you might say that the function of imagination is happening mechanically in the present, but what they are actually imagining (creating) is taking place in a time that is not their own. There are some beings who are very interested in this who, in the essence of their souls, would do this and nothing but. Therefore I have a race of beings involved in this, and they have managed to add depth to imagination. But by and large I am less involved in the creation of individual races than in potentials.

Do you have levels? I'm trying to find some way to understand it. You have spirits, souls, physical . . . do you have dimensions? How does it work?

I have to put it within the context of your reality, which is different from mine. You might ask the storyteller Zoosh for his perspective on that. I have really put it the best way I know how in your words.

You have a race of beings, but are there are exponential parts of you doing this imagining and creating and searching out possibilities and potentials?

No, not exponential parts of me. I am one being, complete; my explorations have entirely to do with the future and the past. These are the best terms I can come up with because of your function in linear time, but it is not exactly the future and the past.

You are functioning in your reality; your power is in the present moment. In my creation any individual's power is in the past or in the future—what might be, what might have been. That is where their power is to create or re-create past and future in all of its infinite possibilities. That is the best I can do, and I will have to say good night.

Thank you very much.

A ll right, Zoosh here now. Anything else?

Is there anything you can say in your words that can help us understand that this creator's creation has dimensions, or whatever he meant? Does this creation have physical beings, spirit beings, soul beings?

I can show you better as a picture. If your creation is this (picture me holding a sphere), then this creator's creation is that which supports and sustains *your* creation—a sphere around your sphere in which you float lovingly. Good night.

❖ **Robert's Comments on His Experience**

Boy, that was really a stretch.

Are you taller? Are you okay?

[Chuckles.] I feel I've got thin spots in my reality. I feel like in some parts of my realty I'm a tree and other parts I'm Saran wrap.

[Laughs.] Could you see the Creator's creation?

Yes. It was hard to describe it, but in the middle there was . . . I couldn't really see anything definitive, but on either side there was a tremendous variety of light. It defined strata of different realities, but right in the center there was the light of itself, but not specific material. It was more of the light of its own being, but to either side there was all this variety of creation.

He talked about the past and the future, but there was no present moment, no substance to the present.

Well, it exists in the present, so there was light in the middle, but there wasn't anything like going up and down. It went from the left side or the right side (for lack of a better explanation), but I didn't see anything coming up or down.

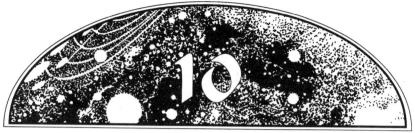

Creator of the Void, Preamble to Individuality

September 3, 1996

I am the Creator of the Void, that upon which all that is distinct light and matter is patterned. It is my intention to provide the foundational mass upon which all that is distinctly unique, specific and even individual can be strewn or mapped. Before I had considered the creation of what you can call space, or the Void, there was tremendous expression of light, color and sound. While it was beautiful and exciting and spectacular in many ways, there was not much peace, quiet, solitude. One could find these things at various dimensional levels, but one had to be very focused to maintain a separation from the celebration of life around one.

My Creator, a Tornado of Life-Creation

At the time of my considering this, I had not yet come from that which created me. That which spawned me would look like a tornado on its side, but in space; the place of emergence would be the wide end. It is a place of the creation of life through the mixing of various elements. Even on your own planet tornadoes do very much the same—they mix things together, not always pleasantly. Where I was it was pleasant, but it was exciting all the time. Although that can be very pleasurable, there are times (and you can all identify with this) when quiet was very desirable, yet unavailable.

Is the creator behind you what we call the Center of Creation—the total, the chaos, the beginning?

Slightly before that, because the one behind me . . . remember, it takes *from* the chaos, mixes the chaos up, whirling it around like a centrifuge. That which naturally goes together will come together; that which belongs with other things will go with other things. The centrifuge effect is happening for you even now where you are. If you're supposed to be with this person, then you are; if you're supposed to be with somebody else (or even someplace else), then you are. When your life is upset, you find that place. It is not a punishment, but a *function* of creatorship.

So I would have to say that the being who spawned me is not the chaos itself, but is just in front of the chaos and is that which creates just enough order so that creation and creatorship can be benevolently launched from it.

After I considered that I would like to participate in creating something upon which other things could be defined, my creator spawned me. Since I was a portion of that being, I busily spun out into space and dimension and looked for a place where I might create a zone of quiet and general spatial reference.

The Void: Connection and Definition

You might say the Void is a tool of communication, because wherever it exists it creates a connection as well as a definition. The stars in the sky have space between them, and though there is life in that space, there is also a void.

It was my dream, my vision, to create this vast area and to simply be in the quiet of it for quite a while. Once I felt satiated with the quiet and the calm, then I was able to invite other beings to quietly produce here and there a galaxy or a dimension where gentle life could be created— not too much cacophony, but a gentle quiet, more of a meditational lifestyle. I allowed and appreciated this, enjoying that level of life just as one might enjoy a spice in a favorite but somewhat plain meal. In this way I was able to create a bridge between excitement and definition.

Definition, to my understanding, is the preamble to individuality. It might be considered the preamble to separation, but I don't see it that way since I believe that the Void essentially *unites*, in a fabric that allows other things to be seen, felt and noticed.

Ofttimes people think that the Void swallows things up. But that is not so. The Void does not do this because it is expanding. And since it is expanding and goes wherever other creators might desire to utilize it, it cannot swallow things up because it is moving outward. I do understand the anomaly of what is called a black hole—which, I might add, is essentially a transformational portal—but that is not so much what I am.

Is it true that creators give birth by mitosis, by separating into two?

Not necessarily. Some creators do this. In my experience, my creator—that which spawned me—was really in the creator business, if I might use that term. I was not the first. No, I believe that my creator spawned many, many thousands of creators before I was encouraged to go out on my own. In my personal experience, then, I would have to say that this is not an exclusive thing. Perhaps creators who came after might have had one. But I do not think the term "mitosis" is appropriate for creator birthing.

If we try to visualize it, you are this great Void; then you spawned our Creator's creator, who has the pasts and futures, and it's cradled in your creation?

That was once a portion of me, yes, and I think that it was able to consider that possibility because it had the peace and quiet (I realize I am taking credit) to ponder for a long time what it would like to create that's new and also what it might like to enjoy. I think this creator had such time because of the peace and quiet.

You created the Void so you could get peace and quiet away from the cacophony. The creator you created wanted to initiate the activity of pasts and futures after experiencing the stillness of the Void. Then the next creator—ours—seemed to react to that, going to the center to create a present moment. It's almost like each one was . . . not in reaction to the creation they were in, but . . .

Ofttimes they build upon each other.

Lineages: Similarities Plus Something New

What's missing from the last one would be provided by the next one. Is it like that?

Yes. This is not unlike what happens with children and parents. After adolescents go through their rebellion in order to find their own individuality, they become similar to their parents—but something is added. Our lineages are similar: we are similar to our creator, but something is added. The foundational ethic is the same, the general persona might be the same, but the focus, the joy, the pleasure of creation is slightly different. One can see a progression. It is perhaps easier (as they say in reverse engineering) to see the progression going backward than going forward.

Many spiritual teachers on this planet think that the Void is the ultimate source of creation, but you say it's not. How did you get the idea for it?

Well, I'll tell you. You know, very often creators have their inspiration from that which is above them. For instance, inspiration might come through for you many times every day, but the inspiration that is actually heard and that you build upon is that which resonates with you or feels wonderful or answers a personal need in that moment. I was receiving inspiration all the time, yet suddenly this inspiration answered something undefined. It was a solution to something I had been desiring but could not define.

When you are living in a world where something has not been created yet, it is entirely unknown. To give a mundane example, think about the world before the paper clip or the staple.

Or the fax machine.

That's right. In this world you do not think about it because it's not a part of that world. And yet suddenly it comes to you from higher sources and you have available to you, entirely unexpectedly, this wonderful inspiration that you want to participate in and build and focus on. When that moment happens (not unlike for a human being), that's where you want to put all your energy.

When a creator in training (as I was) has such a focus, it is just about then that the creator of which you are a portion begins to let go of you, because it can feel that inspiration. It is a celebration, it is a birth, it is a great joy to your creator. It lets you go because you are about to do something that, from its perspective, is unique and wonderful, and that is *new* for a creator, which is most important.

And needed.

Well, if it appeals to a creator, it is assumed it is needed. My creator did not see any need for a void where *it* existed. But when *I* became interested, then my creator knew "it must be needed somewhere, or my offspring would not be so enamored of it." So it is really the parent trusting the child. In that case I was the child.

How the Void Functions

What about your creation? How does the Void work? You said there are some planets and galaxies. Are there any people? Are there dimensions? Are they individual?

But these are not of my creation. The interesting thing about my creation is that it is one thing only. It is not the galaxies that I have invited others to come and create—if they were quiet!. [Chuckles.] If you were to look out into space and see the quiet dark of space between the stars, the energy that makes up that quiet dark really is the Void. So where I am there is only the quiet dark. But because your Creator was interested in having some aspect of the Void in Its creation (because my creation is constantly expanding), your Creator said, "Oh, I'd like some of that; I'll put it between the galaxies and the stars."

I provide that for your Creator and your Creator modifies it for Its creation. Now, if you were to come to where I am (the Void), you would be very calm and rested; everything you had ever been worried or concerned about would fall away. It would be the ultimate place of complete and total rest and relaxation. You would not even be bothered by dreams. While dreams are good, you would not have the distraction. There would be no spatial imagery; although there would be spatiality, it would be *quiet* spatiality.

At first you'd go through a period of adjustment during which all your cares and struggles and worries would fall away, then you would just rest for a time and enjoy it. After that you would begin to expand, not because I am expanding, but because you would feel totally and completely safe to expand. You see, the Void really represents absolute safety without anything to distract you from total safety.

You would begin to expand and before long you would be everywhere that I am and beyond. Because you would be in me, you would feel safe to go places that even as a soul you had never felt safe to go. You would go because the route of safety and security and total unconditional love (which spawned this Void) would be felt at all times but without imagery. So it would ultimately be a feeling of complete and utter relaxation. It would allow you to observe. As the Void I am able to go anywhere to observe all your Creator's creations, and you also would be able to do this.

Your Creator has modeled something in its creation upon that. Sometimes people die suddenly, unexpectedly. I bring up this example because of a recent happening here in your neighborhood. People are physical and full of life, and the next moment their physical bodies are damaged or destroyed. But their personalities and their lightbodies are still alive; they look at the scene, saying, "What happened?"

If their lives had been relatively safe, comfortable or fulfilling, the angels (lightbeings, I call them) come and take them to their next place beyond the veil. But sometimes, if their lives were upsetting, full of strife and struggle and confusion (not necessarily these individuals) . . .

Did somebody just die in this accident down the hill? [We had heard sirens and activity after the channeling began.]

A moment. If it had been something extreme or the person had suffered terribly in his/her life or had had a lingering illness with great suffering, ofttimes your Creator will have a special place for them. Yes, the angels come to get the lightbeings and very tenderly take them to this place, where they will float in a version of the Void, and all of their struggles and cares and griefs will fall away. The Void has the capacity to discharge all of these great travails as one might discharge a battery, and soon the soul is floating comfortably.

[About 20 or 30 minutes earlier two people on a motorcycle were killed instantly—although we didn't know that then—in a collision on a curve down the hill from this gathering.]

Sometimes a being might do this for 30 or 40 experiential years in your creation. Your Creator modeled this after my creation because It felt that this was something a soul could do when it had been terribly traumatized and was not ready to go on through the veils to the City of Light because it was not yet done with its earthly life.

In the case of one of these individuals in this accident, as well other individuals from your neighborhood and thousands of individuals from your planet, where suffering was involved and anxiety and struggle is left behind, these beings do not wander the Earth or go to some astral plane to suffer—*never!* They are taken to this place, where all of these terrible sufferings are gradually released from them, and they relax and float in a version of the Void. When they are comforted, then their light spirits, teachers or angels come and take them to the City of Light, where they're nourished and prepared for their next life.

The Makeup and Extent of the Void

Are there other creations inside the boundaries of your creation besides our Creator's creation and your son's [Creator of the Inverse Universe] creation?

Well, if one allows for the few galaxies that I have in my creation, which is really small compared to your Creator's . . . [chuckles] your Creator is an exciting fellow, likes many different things, but I have just a few galaxies. I did not create these; I have lent this space to another individual who, interestingly enough, is still having physical lives like yours but is beginning to practice creatorship. You might say it is a student creator who is involved in this creation and is willing to go by my guidelines. It is creating light galaxies similar to what your creation might have in your seventh through ninth dimensions that have beings involved in service and in other creations.

These beings are very quiet and gentle, sometimes sending emanations from their people, sometimes simply involved in re-creation and restructures for other creations. Having them in my creation allows me to experience slightly the excitement of life from which I came. It's in what you might call the outer boundaries of my creation, but when I get lonely for where I came from but do not want to go back to the "almost chaos," then I focus my attention in my young friend's creation.

If your creation, your Void is here, is there a demarcation between it and the creation you came from where you'd experience much light and activity? Are they far away from each other?

It's not really a place. A place would be where you are living here in this small town, yet it would be more like a *thing* that is available to other creators. It's hard to describe. It is some *thing*. It's not really far away, because wherever versions of the Void exist, I am there. Therefore I am here; I am easily able to speak here tonight because your Creator has utilized some of my creation. I know what you're asking: At what reference point did my creation begin, and was it someplace far away from here?

Yes. It began *very* far away from here. It's hard to describe; I cannot say miles, but very, very far away from here. But since it is constantly expanding, it has already expanded through your Creator's creation and beyond. When this was developed by me through the inspiration I received, other creators saw its value at once. Even if they did not wish to use a great portion of it, they immediately requested that I expand to their areas so they could adapt it or use it to their benefit. Not unlike the creators who have created the past and the future, other creators said, "Oh, I would like some of that, too."

So it is a creator's job not only to create something of its own—an expression of itself—but to make its creation available to other creators at a moment's notice to blend it in the whole of all creation.

So that's how you expand—because they ask, and then you expand to where they are?

Yes.

It keeps going because it's such a good idea.

Yes. And if a creator does not have a use for it, I'm not insulted; I simply do not expand to that creation. I might even go around that creation to get to others, but I honor that creator's creation. To answer your previous question, I honor a general demarcation line which, if I had to give a spatial reference, would be perhaps 25 to 30 light-years of space at a given moment. This would allow that creator to continue its expanded creation and give me enough warning to get out of the way should that creator suddenly expand. [Laughs.]

My Interactions with Others

So are you all alone? Because of this transforming power that removes stress and trauma, do you invite beings or creators or people in?

Not exactly. Do I invite consciousness, individuals? I'm available for them to come in, but what often happens is that creators (or even allies of creators or guides associated with them) will observe what I am doing and request a portion of it. For example, a given angel or guide could ask for only as much of what I am doing as would fit into the palm of your hand. In the case of a spirit teacher, this happened recently, so I will describe it. A spirit teacher said, "I need to be able to show one of my pupils the Void, but because this pupil is sleeping" (this was a being on Earth), "I think it would not be reasonable to expect us to come to the center of your being. Could you give me some of your being, enough to be about the size of a baseball, that I might show to this being?"

I said, "Yes, certainly." So a baseball-sized portion of me, which might reasonably be held or floated above somebody's cupped palm, was shown to this individual. The student had a tremendous fascination with light and all of its varieties but had not stopped to consider what defines the light. So the spirit teacher said to the student, "Come into the Void briefly," holding that portion of me. The student and the teacher went into the Void and the student was able to experience the matrix (I might also be referred to as the matrix) that defines, supports, embraces and, I believe, nurtures the light and any mass within it. In this way the student was able to advance his understanding of creation. One might build a house, but one builds it on the ground and something defines it; one builds it within space. So in this and other ways I am available to spirit teachers so that they might help others. People do not always have to come to me; sometimes I can send a portion of me.

So all the creations before yours were created out of immense light. They were great creations of beings, but there was no darkness, no void, no—would you say definition?

That is my understanding: I am not aware of anything that existed before that. The wonderful thing about this is . . . the greatest compliment for a creator (it might be the opposite of what you'd expect) is that beings who live in its creation *take that creation for granted* because it seems to have always been so. In other words, they trust that it is natural. Although they might be thankful to the universe for all being (which thanks come to me and others), they believe it is so because it is natural. It is a great compliment for any creator that its creation be accepted as part of natural life. That means you've established your creation! [Laughs.]

So the basis of the creation is your consciousness, which is peaceful, quiet, nurturing, sustained. Would you say that?

Yes.

How were you able to expand it so far when others have more of a fixed piece of real estate? It's the ability that you have to expand when . . .

Needs As Magnets

Ah, that is an interesting question. Do you know, it is not my ability; it is the *need* of others that pulls it. That works very much in your own creation. When you have a need—whether it be for some spiritual lesson or sometimes even a simple object, and have no idea where it would come from; you just have the need, feel it, long for it, wish for it—that need is usually fulfilled in some way. It acts like a magnet; it goes out into reality saying, "I need this." And wherever reality exists and is available to fulfill that need, it rushes toward it. So I am not responsible for the tremendous expansion of the Void. It is the *need of others*—other creators, other beings within the creatorship, all other beings who need and benefit from the Void—that has allowed me to expand and to continue to do so.

If it were possible to see a picture of the Center of Creation as throbbing light . . . I realize it probably doesn't work this way, but have you expanded around it, have you come out this way?

I cannot describe it. I have expanded through it.

Through it to the other side?

Yes, and if there is a desire for the Void anywhere within that space, it is available there also. But if it is not desired, it is not required. Ofttimes creations, since they are spherical in nature (starting at a point and moving out in all directions), will go right through some other creation—giving that creation the availability of whatever they have created out of the loving gift of it—and on past it.

So there's an overlap.

Yes. That is why ofttimes your Creator (or Zoosh or someone) will tell you that other worlds are right here. Even other creations are right here available not only to your Creator but to you as well, since you are creators in training. That is very unusual for individual beings such as yourselves.

How do we get there?

You don't. It comes to you.

Give me an example.

Practical Uses of the Void

That's why I gave the example of going to the Void. For instance, let's say your readers have had a tough day and they come home and it's like, "I can't watch TV or read; I don't even feel like playing with my dog. I just have to lie down." While you're lying down, ask that the Void be present around you, that it discharge all of your discomforts and that it allow you to be refreshed, floating, in a pure state of being. Then just relax into that energy. Since it is available for you it might be able to happen. The fewer distractions you have, the better, so no noise, no ringing telephones, no doorbells. If there is noise around you, plug your ears. If your dog is nearby and wants to jump up on the bed with you, no problem; once you get into the energy, the dog will rest and relax and enjoy it, too. But try to do this in as quiet a time as possible. It can be done.

What a gift! What else would you like to tell us about your creation that I don't even know enough to ask?

Your scientists are now heavily exploring genetics and the building blocks of life. Sometimes they discover these building blocks when they're looking for something else. Perhaps the greatest joy to a scientist is to discover something entirely unexpected and pleasurable. Yet as scientists view life in its smaller and smaller infinitesimal representations, they are becoming fascinated with the space between the atoms and even the protons and the neutrons. I can assure you that a variation (your Creator has adapted it) of the Void exists there. I want to confirm something that your scientists suspect: *the unlimited energy you are looking for to power everything is the Void.* When you can tap into the Void energy, it has the capacity to be everywhere.

The Void As a Connection to Unlimited Energy

The Void is, in a sense, an open circuit, meaning that it flows past your sun and past billions and billions of suns too high to count. When you tap into the places where there is more energy than they know what to do with—suns millions of times the size of your own that would love to share with you what they have—you will then have unlimited energy, which you can even use to create an electrical highway to the planets, not unlike what many flying ships from other planets use. They travel on time, yes, but how do they get through space when they travel on time? They travel through this unlimited energy path that has to do with their personal need, their personal focus and a shared benevolent and benign love between the motivating force and that which wants or needs to be motivated (meaning a traveling vehicle).

Scientists, you are on the right track, and you will be able to do it. In the process you will discover that to work with this energy and have it work with you, you must do so in a respectful and loving way. You cannot use it in any purposefully destructive way. I'm using the term "purposefully" because it is possible to unintentionally usurp some other life form when you are beginning your experiments. You must make it clear that if it is at all possible, you would like all life forms to be free to express themselves and be uninjured by your actions. This must be spoken out loud. Your intentions at this level of science are *everything!*

Is it like what happens when we draw energy from Mother Earth? The energy we draw from you or the space modeled after you does not deplete you, does it?

No, it does not deplete anyone. It is a shared thing, just as your sun has much, much more energy to give you than you can use right now. Uncounted suns, some of which do not even have solar systems around them but want to have planets, are fulfilled by energizing other things. These suns would be thrilled to provide energy for your creations, especially if they are loving, benevolent and goodhearted. Adventure that does not cause harm to anyone is goodhearted. A desire to explore space and all its beings is goodhearted. Feel free to use it for your traveling vehicles in space.

So because you surround us, we live within you and you know everything about us?

Yes.

What about this "going up" that our Creator wants to do? Is that something that you perceive? Do you know what's up there? Have you been there, or do you see what is there?

I don't think that is my desire; I think that is something your Creator desires to do. But I know where I came from, and your Creator will rediscover that soon. Your Creator has felt that ignorance can be used to create a heightened sense of the joy of discovery, which It chooses to experience and pass on to you to experience. Yet this is not a portion of me. You know, creatorship is truly a wonderful thing.

Let me close with this thought. When one has established one's intention to be a creator, as you all have, it is truly the beginning of a magnificent voyage. One discovers what works and what doesn't work in creator school here. In the process you sometimes discover that something that doesn't work for one thing seems to work very well for something else, though you hadn't considered that at the time. This wonderful voyage invariably leads to more expansion.

Don't feel that because you'll all be creators someday, you will be losing something on Earth. Nothing you have gained or valued by being a physical person will be lost; you can always reexperience it. You know, even if it is the embrace of a loved one or the nuzzling of a favorite animal, the sweetness of a favorite candy—whatever it is—you can always experience and reexperience it at the creatorship level, on all levels and with many more senses than the ones you have now. Nothing of value will be lost. Know that it is the beginning for you. You have come from a creator; you will replace your Creator; and you will go on and on and on beyond even the concept of infinity.

I can assure you that creatorship is a wonderful, joyous experience. Even though it might sometimes seem challenging, know that the creator school you are in now will serve you very well as you go on in the life of creation. Good night.

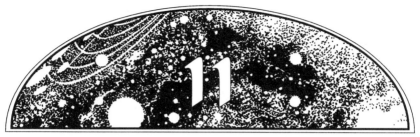

The Tornado-Shaped Creator of Creators

September 5, 1996

am the Creator of Creators. Up to now you have heard from creators who were comfortable reproducing themselves singly, at least so far in their cycles. But it has been my opportunity in my "lifetime" [chuckles] to be connected to what has been termed the chaos before creation. I draw that into me in what is like a centrifugal effect, where it spins not only at physical speed but also within itself. In this way the matter that is not purely of itself is extracted, and that which is intended to be with it comes to it as it moves through me. Thus by the time it is "launched" in the usual flash of light, it is then prepared with the true, pure essence of itself and any and all assistance that it might desire for its creation.

You perhaps wonder if I have ever created any other type of place. No, I simply operate as a portal, but a portal with intent, a functioning portal, if you would, spinning (always in a very exciting fashion, I think) and launching creators. They come when they are ready, of course, as any child does, but generally I find that in terms of your time measurement one will emerge (occasionally two or three at the same time, but usually one) every 3 to 127 years. Sometimes the process is very quick, at other times slow and multileveled.

I have found that this exercise of creatorship has been very rewarding. I do not, however, tend to observe the creations of those I have created. I truly let them go, because the process of creation on my part is so involved and so precise that all of my attention is paid to what is happening with me, within me and that which enters and exits me. I am not self-centered, obviously, but I must pay attention to what I am doing. That is my introduction.

Relationship to the Center of Creation

So how did it start? You came from the Center of Creation and then became conscious?

I am never aware of being unconscious. I am never aware of coming from anyplace other than where I am. I believe I have always been doing this. I am truly unaware of anything before—or after, for that matter. I am truly functioning in this moment only, and even looking at myself from a distance, I don't think I have ever come from anywhere. I might have been smaller at one time (I can see that I was once smaller), but I've always been where I am.

Very close to the Center of Creation, but not in it?

The Center of Creation, having everything in it at once (easily referred to as chaos, in the most benevolent sense), is just a membrane away from where I pull things in. You could picture me almost like a tube that goes into the center and draws out that which wishes to come, never anything that wishes to go elsewhere or remain where it is. It is on a volunteer basis only.

Are you a tube that the creators go through and are birthed from? Does that have something to do with you, or is that after you create them?

I can only say this: I believe that all the creators I am aware of, including your own, have all passed through me. It is a process. You can imagine when you drink water that it passes through you, always taking the same route. Granted, the responsibility level is a little different, but it is all right to perceive this as a mechanical function, though there is more to it, of course. As far as I know, I am that tube, although it is possible that there is another. In terms of what *you* have experienced in your infinite selves, I think you have always come through this way. I believe there might be another tube that cycles things back into the Center of Creation, but I think I am that which you could call the exit. [Chuckles.]

Ah, so you're "it"! I mean, there are not many like you; you are basically the one.

I think I am it, yes.

So would you say the Center of Creation is part of some larger creator?

This I am really not sure of, because my position is such a responsible one. I cannot ever take time off to go seek elsewhere. I could not say because I am so active all the time, but from what I can see from here, I would guess that there must be more.

Are you aware of a couple of groups we've heard about—the Heart Council and the Council of Creators?

I am aware of those. I believe they stemmed from beings who passed through me. You must remember that when one is spawning creators, such as I am, by their nature they would be creative and might be involved in the creation of other creators. So, as your relatives might say, I think I might have known their grandfathers. [Chuckles.]

Oh, that's incredible! I didn't realize there was only one. Talk to us a little more about what you do, how you focus. We really don't have enough information to probe as much as I'd like.

Beings Refined to Their Essence, Then Spun with Companions

I understand. Picture a point of light that is very bright—too bright to look at with your eyes, but you could look at it obliquely. This is the Center of Creation, as you have called it. I am very close to this. There is what I would call a boundary whereby that which emerges from this point of creation is allowed to mingle with all else, perhaps understanding for the first time its unique individuality, perhaps even experiencing the idea of community of individuals, yet so exposed to and confronted with so many other beings that there's never a moment of pure self.

When one of these ideas or beings or even things (personas, if you would) approaches my entrance, the communication is felt by both of us. My communication is, "This is where to go if you are prepared for the responsibility of creation." (They would not emerge from the point of creation into me if they were not prepared.) When they come in, they immediately begin the spinning process, quickly becoming their pure selves. Although this might seem disorienting to you as physical beings, it really isn't. The whole purpose is actually to orient the being to the essence of themselves so that they can feel their true and total essence as a thought, an idea, an inspiration, whatever. In this way they have the opportunity to know what they would create from.

It is so easy as a creator to become overwhelmed by the responsibility and the variety of what you might be creating that it is possible even at the creator level to forget who you are and become totally consumed with your responsibility. This does not harm what you have created, but you can sometimes as a creator lose your way, because you can forget your original purpose. This is theoretically possible. My job is to start off these creators with a total and complete saturation of themselves so that they can never lose this. They have time, you see, moments whereby they become totally and completely familiar with their absolute essence. This is something that becomes so familiar after a time that no matter what the variety of one's creations, a person, an individual, a creator, will not lose that feeling and can always return to it. So I realize what I am doing is responsible to them and to all those down the road that they might affect.

As they move through me (let's say they are halfway through, for the sake of spatial reference), after a time they might have become familiar with themselves. If they are ready to be launched, they will quickly go ahead. But if they want to pick up other influences (perhaps they wish to have company or essences of creation that are not their specialty; they might wish to have friends within me), they can locate these friends and be centrifuged with them and these influences. During this spin the proper places, the proper tonality, the harmonic of where everybody is located within this individual creator (within this single being, if you would) become comfortable. They choose, not unlike the way material in a centrifuge "chooses," to separate out into its equal parts of being. When everyone is reasonably comfortable, then they are launched.

Where they go and what they do is usually motivated by themselves. They might go on a journey to explore other creations before they begin their own creation; that is not at all unusual. However, just as commonly they might immediately go to where and when or what is the place of their creation and begin—and everything in between and more. Sometimes they travel great distances to find the exact space for their creation. Sometimes their creation is to be massive and unlimited in its scope; at other times it is astonishingly small—such as the creator who decided to develop the particle structure.

The Creation of Particles

Once upon a time everything was made of light and there were no particles. If you as a scientist were to examine smaller aspects of things, you would be looking basically at a form of compressed or liquefied light. But there once was (this is an example) a creator who decided to create something infinitesimal rather than something massive. That infinitesimal creation became highly influential, went many different places and seeded the infinitesimal in other places.

This Creator of Particles (as you might describe molecules, atoms, neutrons, protons and so on) passed through me quite some time ago, and I was intrigued by its intention for its creation. I knew immediately that this had not been done. I thought it was a wonderful idea, especially in places where highly philosophical or scientific achievements would take place whereby they would join in some capacity, sometimes becoming the religious, other times simply becoming something unique. When I heard of this I must admit I became excited and enthusiastic, though that is my normal state of being. Although I cannot really take the time (as you would say) to look in on that creation, I have heard from others who pass by me (sometimes my creators send a messenger to me to tell me how they are doing) that this creation of the infinitesimal particle world has been highly successful and widely adapted by other creators. This is an example of the beings who might pass through me.

My Tube and a Second Tube

That's exciting. Can we visualize a long tube where they come in and then go out the other end when they're ready? Only the one closest to the front can come out, right?

The tube is narrower at the point where it enters the Center of Creation and broader at the point where creators emerge to go where they choose, so I look like a tornado on its side. If you were to see me from a distance, I might have that appearance, though I would not have the debris, however [laughs]! I would be many different colors—very beautiful.

It is apparent from what you said that the creators do not recycle themselves through your tube again, but their creations apparently do, or portions of them. Is that what it looks like to you?

You know, I had not thought about this before now, but my impression is that . . . the other tube, I can see, is taking in matter and putting it into the point of creation. My understanding is that this is not necessarily that which has used itself up or is ready to be recycled. I believe it is actually material (including everything from thought and feeling to mass—harmonics, colors, everything) that volunteers for this process. Perhaps this material has done everything it wishes to do, since it has been created and is now ready to move on to something uniquely different. I do not believe this is something where old creations go to die, as it were. I think it is on a volunteer basis.

But it's not through you? It's another tube, which goes back . . .

Yes, another tube.

As these creators and volunteers pass through you, you get to feel what each is thinking about and planning as their thought becomes purer.

Yes, first I feel the essence of who they are, then what they request (who they wish to be with) is available within me, even though a portion of that being, harmonic or creative energy might be very active in other places. At all times *all* benevolent influences of creation are within me, so this wide range of ingredients is available to these creators.

First, I feel who they are, and the moment I feel this I have a pretty good feeling for what they want to create. Then, as they move through me in the process, I can feel how that inspiration or idea is modified as a result of those they wish to create it with or as a result of the experience of purification and passage through me, for one tends to consider and reconsider one's creation. So even though there might be thousands going through me at once, there is always an opportunity for me to check in with each one individually.

Let's say a creator wants to do a creation. There are tones, feelings, experiences or levels of skill that he doesn't have, so does he call them forth from you?

It is like this: When a creator or a creator candidate emerges from the point of creation into me, it has already qualified. No one comes into me who is not qualified. There is some kind of filtering process within that emergence point that allows only those beings who have the capacity and the quality. One could ask, "How is this known?" I believe that as those beings emerge from the Center of Creation (and this would support your theory), they might have been someplace else to have proved themselves, or else this inner creation simply knows what they are about. I believe that they qualify *before* they reach me.

So it might be fair to visualize this chaos totally filled with ungodly numbers of conscious, sentient, experienced beings?

Yes, but I would have to say that they are "godly" [laughs], though I understand your euphemism. It is interesting to consider that they are not all creators and that some of them go elsewhere to do other things.

And all of the creators come through you, like a purification or qualification or creation chamber?

It is not a qualification; they have already qualified. They purify, because when they are in this other space before they come to me, they are exposed to total chaos—benevolent chaos, granted—but everything is there at all times. It is very easy for them to be part of the whole there, but less easy for them to be uniquely individual. The only way one can experience a sense of calm, peace and self-assurance in that chaotic situation is to be part of the whole; then everybody doing everything is natural. Trying to maintain individuality in a circumstance like that is not possible. So when they come into me, they have not only the right but the responsibility to reattain their individuality. That is when I begin my process.

Your Creator and Friends

You don't have a chance to look at the creations very much, but if you look at our creation—of the Creator and His friends—He might have met them in the chaos.

No, I have heard about your creation. Your Creator has sent me a messenger, and I know the creation you are in. Yes, your Creator's friends who came with Him were all centrifuged (if I can use that word) within me, and they and your Creator still have portions of themselves in me. All creators who have passed through me always leave portions of themselves in case other creators wish to use them. This means that I am not only having all of these beings available within me, but that I am constantly having more beings available within me as creators emerge. In this way my life is not of sameness; it is exciting because there is always something new being added.

And connections made. So tell me about our Creator, then. How did He and His friends come into this creation? Who went through you?

Your Creator was spawned by someone else, but the *potential* for that which spawned your Creator can be traced back to me. All of these potentials were induced into the being who passed through me and eventually spawned various generations. You must remember that creators who have created other beings have also re-created—that is how it works. But your Creator and all of the beings It was associated with were a portion of other creators who created them. Then going back . . .

To the Void . . .

That's right, the Creator of the Void did come through me, plus other creators. The Creator of the Void had within it all that could spawn your Creator. All of these ingredients are mixed in so that when the Creator of the Void wished to reproduce itself, it could do so, then continue to reproduce. When your Creator eventually came out, It would still have all that It wished within It because that had been placed within the Creator of the Void.

This allows creators to create. It is within the nature of creation that creators have connections to that point of light from which *all* creation blooms and also have within them connections to all other creations so that they can utilize what they do not necessarily think about or are not directly involved in. Therefore they do not have to come home to me to be influenced by beings they wish to have with them. They would simply look within themselves and find those beings. Even in your own philosophy (as I have heard) very often philosophers tell you to look within yourself. That is the origin of that idea.

Something you said about science and philosophy are words that are used in our creation. But is this a constant in all creation—that there's science and philosophy?

No. I am trying to use your words and philosophy as much as possible so that you are reasonably able to assimilate what I am saying.

Don't you ever get a vacation? I mean, can't you stop and go out and sightsee?

Oh, I *am* on vacation; my work is my vacation. This is what I want to do. However, using your idea, if I ever wished to go someplace else to be something else, then a creator would emerge, go through the process within me and replace me. Then I would go elsewhere. But you see, *I* would not create that creator; it would come externally. The creators who go through me tend to create their creators directly.

But it would be someone coming from the Center of Creation who had the idea and wanted to do that?

Yes, although I do not think there is any point in queuing up at this time. [Laughs.]

Visualizing/Feeling the Infinite

All right, so how can we visualize the infinite? There's a Center of Creation. If there's a center, then there must be creations all around it . . .

No, please understand that if you wish to see things in the infinite, the sphere is the best way to visualize it. However, the infinite can be felt much more easily than it can be visualized. For example, begin by being in a room you are happy to be in or by being out in nature; then allow your personal self (ego) to become a portion of all things where you are. Just that would give you a very good idea (though in a small way) of the infinite.

If you allowed yourself to feel the existence in this room tonight of all the stones, the wood, the metal, the beings, the cats, the people—if you could actually feel your tail wagging as a cat or feel the water molecules moving in the fountain or feel the calm and peace of the stone crystals not only as an emotion but a physical feeling *all at the same time*—you would get a fairly good idea of what the infinite feels like. So start small! [Laughs.]

We have messengers who say that they are connected to the infinite and that they can go anywhere and give messages. You are obviously connected to the infinite, right?

Yes.

Although you're too busy, you could feel any of your creators anytime you choose?

If I chose to do that, yes; but in order to do that more than just occasionally, I would need to have an assistant. I would need somebody who could spell me, because what I am doing requires constant vigilance.

Say more about that. What is your focus, your thought, your intent, your action?

My intention is to help these creators purify and keep the rate of their internal and external spin at the exact rate that is correct for them, even though next to them might be another creator spinning at an entirely different rate. Multiply this times several thousand going through me at once. This requires extreme vigilance. I must also hold the intent of being very nurturing and lighthearted so that they do not become too serious—which is very easy to do for a creator, believe me. I must also be enthusiastic so they will become excited and look forward to emerging, not unlike the way a mother might encourage a baby bird to fly out of the nest for the thrill and the fun of becoming part of its living world. I must be this so that they will not become so attached to me that they'll want to stay [laughs]—what kind of responsibility would I have then?

But they are in a sequence, like one, two, three? You said it's wider at one end, so does the first one in go out, or is there some other order?

No, it is wider at the point of emergence in case more than one happens to be exiting at the same time. This is not common, but it does happen. And because they emerge in a flash of light, I need to be wider at the point of emergence.

The Spinning Process

If you are purifying them, what happens to what is taken out of them?

Of course, there is nothing negative about what is taken out of them. As a matter of fact, very often it is simply the influences of all they have come from. If these influences are potential and benevolent for a creator, then they will remain within me. If, on the other hand, these influences might be involved in something else—perhaps to be an individual soul or even a potential etheric planet planning to become physical and where I am is inappropriate for it—then it will move on. If you can picture the inner cycle, it will move to the outside of me. The inner spin moves material away from that point of creation and the outer spin moves it back toward where it came from.

So it just goes back into the Center of Creation?

Yes, and then it simply finds its way to where it needs to go. I have found, though, that beings who go back where they came from are the better for their experience in me. They have seen much more of creation; sometimes they've experienced a significant amount of creation-level energy. In my experience, I believe this will sometimes give them a broader perspective of whatever they wish to do.

I don't understand how beings go through who go back. Could you clarify that? Where do they come through?

Can I have a paper and pen? Thank you. [Draws.] This is not the best drawing, but it gives you an idea.

Center of Creation
(point of creation)

Creator of Creators

The small circle is the Center of Creation and the tornadic effect (without the lines that would help you see it spinning) is me. Picture an inner boundary and an outer boundary. When something comes off of one of these spinning creators inside me, it goes into my inner wall (it's not a wall, but that's a good enough description) and stays there for a time. It does not spin, however, because it is not part of the creator going through the creator process. It stays there. Although it is involved in the spinning of the entire portion of myself, it does not spin on its own, so it has the opportunity to retain all of itself—an idea, a soul, perhaps even an ensoulment for a planet. In this way it is itself.

If it is unique and wishes to become an influence in a creator, it has the option to stay within me. If, on the other hand, it has places to go, it has the equal option to move slowly and gently through my inner being to my outer being, which spins in a different direction. One spin brings things out from the inside; the outside spin brings things back into that creation.

You could ask, "How did it get caught up in that creator in the first place?" That creator, in order to maintain itself, must be a portion of *all* of the beings inside the point of creation, and sometimes as they come into me they are enjoying that. If they enjoy it they are likely to have more beings with them, not fewer. This is a filtration system that gives all beings the opportunity to do what they want and to do more if they want to, though they are not required to.

I understand now. The beings going back in are sentient beings, not just the sloughed-off part of something else.

Correct.

And if it gains from the process of being in the tube, it goes back and is enriched even if it doesn't become a creator.

Yes; I might be biased, but I believe they do gain.

My History

You began this with all its incredible complexity, springing from something without a memory of anything before, having the thrill and the focus and concentration. Someone or something had to have created you, right?

Oh, certainly. I agree with you. Nevertheless I am not aware of having come from anywhere to where I am. The Void was well aware of having passed through me, but I am not aware of having had that process myself. As far as I know, I have always been here with the Center of Creation. Now, it is possible that the Center of Creation and myself might have come from somewhere else, but I have no memory of it. So I'd have to say that I have always been here, but I am allowing for the possibility that there could have been something before that I don't remember.

Is there anything in you that says there's another part of you that lives on another level into which you could expand?

I am not aware of that motivation or possibility about me.

There is always something beyond, isn't there?

Well, I believe that that is a very important motivation for you and other human beings right now, but when you find out exactly what you want to be doing in life and you are doing it, why do anything else?

The last creator I said that to told me I was a troublemaker. [Laughs.]

Well, I wouldn't go that far.

What you're doing is so incredible! But is there any other way out? There's this throbbing, scintillating Center of Creation where everything is happening all at once with all this light and activity. Can the beings in there go someplace else? Only the ones who want to become creators go through you. The others come and go and can come back and do whatever they want?

Oh, yes, there are a great many exits from that point. My exit has only to do with those who would become creators. Yes, they emanate like the light from a light bulb. But those who wish to become creators come through me. The best way I can describe it is what I have done. It is a constant radiation. I do not think that there are exits like me. I believe that I am like this so that if a being wishes to become a creator, it is drawn to me or motivates itself toward me. It must to some extent prove its capacity and responsibility by finding its way to me, opening itself up to be attracted and at the same time ducking in the right door at the right moment. I cannot speak so much for other things, only what do.

We have been told by Zoosh that we are like apprentice creators. We will go through you when we replace Creator?

Your Creator

No, because you are being offsprung by your Creator. The process you are using is much different. Normally a creator simply gives birth to another creator, who will start its own creation and that is that. But your Creator wished you to be greater than Itself, to have the capacities It had plus more, not based upon what It arrived with but on what you yourself could generate. So you are involved in a different process. I could say, yes, you came through me; yet at the same time, as you take the next step to creation that you are taking now, you are not coming through me in that way.

You're very, very familiar. Is it because you've looked into our creation, or because you've used what's in Robert's consciousness?

No, I am not using Robert's consciousness; I am using the information brought to me by the messenger that your Creator sent.

Aha!

As far as I know, your Creator sent a messenger to all other creators. It came to me because your Creator wanted other creators to know what It was doing, not only for our advice and energy (should we choose to offer it), but also so this unique process would not be perceived by any creator as . . . for example, some creators are involved primarily in repairing other creations. Your Creator wanted to make certain that everybody knew that nothing was wrong in Its creation and to not interfere in the process. Your Creator has been sending messengers to other creators for a very long time, so we are kept well-informed about your creation.

Our Creator, I understand, did what we're doing down here. He separated Himself exponentially; He's not all here in this creation but has higher parts of Himself that He will join when He leaves this creation. Is that done very often?

No, very rarely. I cannot recall its having being done before. I believe that your Creator did this because It wanted to have a common bond with you, Its creation. It did not want to put you through something that It would not put Itself through.

So where is that part of It? Where is the rest of Him? Is it just parts of Himself that He pretends don't exist?

No, it's parts of Himself that He has actually isolated from His own being so that He cannot access them and so He can be involved in His creation. If He were suddenly to be replaced by someone else (such as yourselves), He would no longer have responsibility for His creation. Then He could devote His whole focus on the other parts of Himself and find them. But He cannot find them while He is occupied in this creation. That is a safety mechanism He established so that He would never say, "Oh well, I'm tired of this now. I don't want to wait anymore." [Chuckles.]

But these other parts, in an analogy to ourselves, are totally conscious and out there functioning and doing something, right?

As far as I know, yes. I believe that they are primarily giving your Creator energy and encouragement, perhaps a little enticement. But I do not think that they are involved in another creation such as your Creator's creation right now. In this way, I might add, they can remain pure. And by remaining purely a portion of the essence of your Creator, your Creator can find them much more easily when He is done with His responsibility for this creation.

Might that set a trend? I mean, might other creators . . . well, maybe not.

Oh, you mean do as your Creator has done? Once something unique has been done (usually one waits to see if it has been done successfully), then it is certainly possible that others might do it. But we'll wait and see. [Laughs.]

Other Creators

Okay, somebody said that most of the other creators do not create creations with individuals in them the way this Creator did. Can you help us understand what the other creators create?

Ofttimes creators will have unique ideas, such as the Creator of the Void, the Creator of Past and Future and the Creator of Particles, and as such their focus is very specific and they do not need individuals or variety. Your Creator was interested in something specific, but it just so happens that the specific thing your Creator was interested in was something that allowed for the expression of a great many individuals. Your Creator is interested not only in individuality, but in variety, and it is the natural expression of such an inspiration to have many, many beings.

As I say, most creators do not do that. Most creators are involved with some foundational element of creation, such as the Creator of Particles. Just think about it—all of the particles having personalities different and unique unto their own being. It's true; particles have personalities, even portions of particles that make up atomic structures. Just because they're small doesn't mean that they don't have a sense of self. Yours is quite a special creation, I believe.

But particles had to have been created before this Creator could create individuals with all the little particles in them?

Oh, yes.

What are some other examples? One creator explained how he created the seventeen planets to help other creators. What are some other types of creations that we can gain something from?

Well, let's see. I'll have to pick ones that are relevant. Some of them I have to skip over because they sound so rudimentary that you'd have a hard time believing that they didn't exist before their creation. I think I've mentioned the main ones, actually. I will briefly say, though, that the creator (I alluded to this before) of up and down and side to side (the Creator of Directions) was, I thought, an interesting creation, because before that, creations tended to be a unified field. Everything was everything and everywhere, not unlike chaos, only more uniquely focused. But when the Creator of Directions established that, it was really the foundation for individuality in a lot of ways, because that creator was actually responsible for the creation of spatial reference—of being here, not there; of being there, not here. Now, *that* did not exist before that creator created it.

Before that, everything was everywhere?

That's right, everywhere. This was truly revolutionary, and it was a necessary creation before your Creator could express individuality through Its individual souls. That was another interesting one. I wasn't going to mention it, but I see that it does have relevance to you.

It does. What about the idea of dimensions and levels of evolution within the creation? Did someone create that?

Yes, I think so, but let's see. That, I believe, was created by a creator I did not spawn directly (it was spawned by a creator I spawned). I believe the dimensions were created from the broadest to the simplest, or what you would call from the top down. I must admit that at the time of that creation (I have not received a messenger from that creator, but I have received one from *its* creator) a lot of creators did not perceive any great value for the lower dimensions. But that was before *your* Creator came along and said, "Watch this!" [Laughs.]

What about time? Was time utilized before?

Time? I believe that the Creator of Directions (and spatial reference) birthed the Creator of Time Sequences, but time sequence and spatial reference are so close that I don't think that the latter creator left. It was birthed, but it stayed in the same place and expressed itself *within* the creation of spatial reference.

The one who created the seventeen planets alluded to the fact that one of the planets was for someone who had such great trauma that he might need this isolation to reconsider—like a creator who had been replaced. Is this something that happens very often?

No, very rarely. If a creator is ever replaced because of some harm to it (I do not know of that happening), then I believe that it would immediately move back to the Center of Creation. That might be a contingency plan, because I don't think this has happened. But on the other hand, it could possibly happen to an individual soul, even something that is ensouled (a planet or galaxy, for instance), in which case that being might go there and be able to come to peace.

Will the portion of Creator's curiosity that became the Explorer Race form back into one being or into a group?

Moving through the Veils and Leaving Your Patterns in Them

I believe that you will become a total sentient consciousness; this is what I believe your Creator has established. Right now as you move individually through the veils at the end of your soul cycles (even if millions come through at once, but that is not usually the case), I believe that if you could see that individual membrane as you come through it, it is flat. Since the membrane itself is a living being, anytime any soul goes through it, that soul is patterned, understood and re-creatable by the membrane itself, not unlike the way computer programs work, at least the basic program. (Not to give a plug to any company—that was a pun, wasn't it? I like that.) [Chuckles.] But the membrane knows.

I believe your Creator intends to cause the membrane to become somewhat conical at some point. For souls who have left the Explorer Race experience and do not choose to be involved in becoming your Creator's replacement (which, I might add, is possible), that original energy will have been encoded within the membrane. And when the membrane forms a conical shape like a teardrop and re-creates the origins of your soul energies, it will invite all souls who wish to participate, but will not require it, for it is possible that some might wish to be or to incarnate someplace else. All portions of your soul light will not be required to be there at the same time, though they will be required to leave their soul-encoded signature in the membrane.

So that's how we become one being; then we turn back to the one being that was in the center?

Replacing Creator

Yes, and still have the possibility to do more. I believe most of you will want to be the Creator, but there will certainly be some who will wish to pursue individual lives and lifetimes. That will be possible through this means.

When the Explorer Race becomes a creator to replace our Creator, we're basically baby-sitting somebody else's creation, right?

Yes, but they are intended to run it differently.

Ah, so they will put their own stamp on it.

Yes, it is intended that the Explorer Race do that; that is why your Creator has put you through this long process. Your Creator can then prove not only that denying portions of self necessarily re-creates those portions, but re-creates a greater sense of self and more variety, more capacity, thus exponentially expanding the potential for what a given creator can do. Mathematically speaking, that's what your Creator is trying to do by creating the Explorer Race to become a creator. I believe that this is how it functions. If you come to the point where you are done with your Creator's creation, then you will simply *birth from yourself* a creator to carry on with that creation, the portion of you that wishes to carry on with it. Then you will go on to do whatever you wish on your own elsewhere. After being the Explorer Race, that will be your natural intention, anyway.

You're so busy, so focused, so intent—do you ever miss communicating with a peer? You don't really have one.

Oh, you must understand that peers are going through me all the time—the beings who are creators. I am a creator, they are creators. I am constantly in conference, so I am able to communicate with them (as you would understand communication to be) and they with me. So I am never lonely.

Ah, I understand. I was thinking of someone who did what you do, but you're the only one who does what you do.

Oh, I see. No, I am uniquely doing that, yet most creators are uniquely doing *their* specific creations.

Shutting Down a Creation; the Number of Creators

Do creations last forever, or can they shut them down, take a vacation and do another one?

Yes, that is also possible. After you have completed something, it is possible that instead of shutting it down, you will make it available for as long as other creators might wish to access it. This might mean that you have to birth a replacement to basically wait until no one has any further interest in it or is doing it for themselves on the creation level. Or you might simply wait until that interest is no longer there. When it is gone for a significant time, then you can let it come to a natural end and go on and do something else. This has been done a few times, but not many.

And the few times it was done, they went off and created something else?

Yes. Usually it would be something that grew out of what they were doing. I am aware of one occasion when it was something entirely different, but in that case this creator created a replacement.

. . . for himself that would take over the original creation?

Yes.

The numbers don't mean anything, but there are thousands of creators? Millions? Billions? Is there a way we could comprehend it?

Just know that every soul, every personality (even particles have personalities), has the capacity to be a creator—not simply the potential but the actual capacity. How high can you count? In terms of those who are actually creating something massive like your Creator is, for instance, I suppose there would be several billion, but no more than that, at least that I am aware of. Because of my work, of course, I might not be aware of many things.

Well, I don't know who we're going to ask to talk to someone is more aware than you are. Is there anyone else we don't know about that we can ask who would have as much information as you do or more?

Oh, I cannot say how much they have, but it is possible that the Center of Creation might talk and that you would be able to get more direct information. Perhaps that would be something to do next time. On that note I will say good evening.

❖ Robert's Comments on His Experience

I had a pretty good picture of that creator. Sometimes I'd see it from the point of emergence of creators and other times I would see it obliquely, not directly from the side. I never saw it directly from the side, but always obliquely. It was always in motion; even though it might have been spinning, it was always flexing about and moving, which sort of reminds me of a tornado. Like a dance.

The Center of Creation

September 12, 1996

Zoosh: Now we're going to hear from the Center of Creation. I don't know whether it will be possible to have a lengthy session because this energy is so strong I can screen it only up to a point for Robert. We'll do it as long as we can and maybe not take questions. Normally, when one channels an energy this strong, one has to build up to it, but we'll see how long we can do it—"we" meaning the team here. [Chuckles].

I am that which creates. It is my expression to release and cycle all matter that might be involved in any form of substantive creation. If something can be seen, sensed, felt, quantified, measured and so on, it is my job to condense, focus and express that matter. I am not bringing this matter from someplace to here. What I am doing is largely inverting through light columnation and projecting matter, including the matter of energy and that which is between all things you call space.

I have always been doing this (to anticipate your question). I cannot even imagine what it would be like to recall anything before this. Before the advent of time and space I was doing this. I will admit that the intention of creation, the specifics—how things would be used—were not laid out then, but the plan was.

Creating the First Past to Provide Momentum

I have on occasion spoken of the plan. The plan is basically a reverse-engineering concept, which has to do with how we should structure the past to allow for the present. Almost everything that you can remember, as well as that which other species might remember, have been created because of the plan. Even in your creation much is focused slightly in the future, and much of that focus requires the momentum of growth, which is often seen as a progression of ideas and expressions. Therefore, the creation of the past has been vitally important in order that the plan, which involves the expansion of all creation (including myself), might be carried out.

It was believed by those of us who discussed the plan that the only way for all of creation to expand was that there be some tension that would attract us toward some potential for expansion. Hard as we tried (this was before the plan), we had been unable to expand strictly on the basis of our desires. It was then that several creators who were beginning to express themselves suggested that if an occurrence, a progression (even variables of progression) or a past could be created, it might give us the amplification we needed—the drive, you might say—to support and sustain an expansion based on momentum.

At this point in creation momentum was created and applied. It did not exist before then. And it has proved to be very effective, providing a most satisfactory result. Now we all are on the brink of expanding, and all creators I know of—as well as their offspring, who will be or are now creators—are very excited, and rightly so. It is a wondrous thing. I think you do not fully grasp that this seemingly little thing that you are involved in to re-create time, space, life—all things—will pass up the line, as you might say. The expansion that propels you into creatorship and propels your Creator to Its next level will increase in its magnitude as it moves out in its expansion wave. So by the time I feel it, the expansion will be at least 500,000 times more powerful than what your Creator will feel when it gives your Creator a boost. This is most helpful.

I can see the potential futures, and I must admit I am also excited because there are things I have felt. Before the plan I would have said that I felt all things. But now that the plan appears to be fruitful, I will soon feel something I have not felt before: this magnificent expansion, which I believe will allow me to produce more material with greater variety. There will be more beings who require variety, substance and that which exists before substance, which is basically attraction. This will allow me to do more, which any creator longs for. Question?

Other Creators; Supplying Substance and Space and Recycling Inspiration

We talked to the tornado creator [Creator of Creators]. Are there other creators around your periphery or someplace else who create creators?

Oh, many more creators, yes. You have not covered all of them. Some of them work in combination, such as the Heart Council, as you have mentioned—many creators together, perhaps serving different aspects of some central theme.

Are there others who use a mechanism like the tornado to create creators?

I think that what you are alluding to visually as the tornado is sufficient to create creators. It is certainly possible that other creators could create them. But it is as if one would say, "Well, I like what you're doing so much I think I'll start doing it, so you'll have to find something else to do." [Chuckles.] You know, that wouldn't be very nice.

Up to this time I can visualize the Center of Creation. Do you create all space that all the other creators create within?

Space, matter, attraction, motion, propulsion—yes, all things that have any expression in what would be felt as substance by a being within that space, but also including what is *between* substance (you might refer to it as space, but it is actually attraction).

So those of you who created the plan inspired our Creator?

Yes. It's as if a tool were invented before its full application was apparent. We invented it to be able to expand, but as a result, other creators applied it to their creations if it fit (such as your Creator) and not only amplified our original vision, but made it better.

So your peers are other creators? Is there only one center?

I believe this is the center.

Who created you?

I cannot even conceive of that concept because I have always been here. That question could only be answered if I had been at one time someplace else or something else. But I have always been here.

So we have finally found the ultimate creation, then? The ultimate creator?

Well, I can only say that I cannot step back for a broader view. [Chuckles.]

Okay, so you create and it flows out, but there's a flow back that recycles. Is there another source of whatever comes into you that you create from? Is there, from some higher or lower . . .

Unused or unapplied inspiration, when it is no longer of need or use to any being, flows back into me for recharging and recycling. Many individuals are inspired; sometimes they act on it, most often they do not. This energy of inspiration is a unique energy of its own; it holds its own octave. If the inspiration is not used very quickly after it takes place, that energy will return speedily to me.

The center of all creation is all light, all energy, and within that position you've created individual beings, individual personas, lightbeings? How would you say that?

No, I could not say that I have created anything individual within my zone of space. I *am* it. But I create certain beings for other creations. If other creations do not have access to something I can access, I might then create beings or thoughts or portions of either one of those, for example, which then will find its way to whoever can use that piece of the puzzle to complete its creation.

Could you give us an example?

An Echo to Deliver a Tone

Yes. There was a creator, one I have not heard from for some time. I think this being might have evolved, because when evolution takes place (evolution is expansion), ofttimes a creator cannot communicate for a time. I feel that's what has happened. This being had a need to produce a single-tone echo. The purpose of the echo was manifold, but it was intended that this tone be able to travel throughout all universes. The tone is like that which would begin something. This creator realized, however, that due to the influences of all existence, it would be changed, distorted and ultimately combined with other tones, and it did not know how to get this tone unchanged to all creations.

I suggested that the tone be bounced off various places, times and spaces, and that the bouncing of it would basically create an echo whose reverberation would more likely be able to communicate the true tone than simply sending it on its own. That tone would be like any life—curious, interested and involved. With that piece of the puzzle, this creator was able to utilize the echo effect to deliver that tone. It hadn't even thought of using an echo, possibly because it hadn't ever heard of it.

My Appearance; Souls Returning for Something New

If we visualize a circular place full of light, incredible activity and billions and billions of beings . . . there are beings there. Where did they come from? That's where the creators come from, right?

If you can, visualize something not dissimilar to your sun, but collecting as well as radiating, so that light and energy flow in as well as out and the beings flow in as well as out (should it be necessary for them to rejoin me, which is frequently the case). If you can picture that, then you will have a pretty fair idea of how I would appear were you to see me.

Except that you would be gargantuan, bigger than our sun, right?

Larger, yes, but I do not need to be so large. I am, compared to your sun, perhaps 1000 diameters bigger. While that is large, it is not the largest. No, I am as big as I need to be, but no bigger.

Why would beings need to be called back to you?

Sometimes beings have fulfilled their souls' or senses' desires and they feel that they are worthy of perhaps a new project, a new direction. You yourselves might have a soul self that develops many lives along a certain theme. At some point those lives are fully expressed and developed and lived, and the soul feels so happy with what it has created that there is no need to create anything else to fulfill that intention. It might come to me to be given either other levels of intention whereby it might create along similar lines, or a different intention altogether. Souls do not have to do this; obviously they can simply go on. When they wish to go on in a familiar or similar persona, I am available for such encouragement.

Would that be souls on the level of a soul incarnated on this planet now, or the level of a creator assistant, or could it be anybody at any level?

Any level, but most likely it would be a unified soul who might have forty or fifty lives running around the galaxies at a given moment—the main soul for that series of lives. It would not likely be an individual soul for an individual being or an individual incarnation.

In our creation what we would call the monad is what the Creator created as a spark of life from the Source. Would it be more like a monad than a soul, which in our terminology is a little further down in the creation?

No, it could be an individual soul, not likely individually expressed as a single being, but an individual soul producing a chain of lives and then anything beyond that.

Is there any way to give a number? Are there billions of beings churning around in the Center of Creation?

At any given moment probably no more than 500,000 trillion.

So beings come together there who want to be creators. They meet there and then go through the Creator of Creators' tunnel or tube, right?

Why Creators Might Choose Individual Lives

Yes, or they might simply want to be inspired in the direction of their creation. They might be on their way to being creators, or they might already have been creators and are choosing to be more simplified in terms of their creation, like a soul with its many lives. Sometimes creators will say, "Well, that's that! I did what I came to do and I'm done." If they wish to go on (and this has happened before), sometimes they will say, "Well, maybe I will start creating a chain of lives and be an individual."

After they've been a creator of an entire creation.

Yes, sometimes they will because—it is really such a simple reason—it is fun. The level of responsibility is minuscule by comparison; it is like taking a vacation.

Has that happened here in this creation of the Explorer Race? Have any such beings gotten involved in playing with it?

I do not think any creator has chosen to become individualized where you are in your creation, no.

As we have had described to us, a creator is created full-blown and then begins an adventure of doing what its essence is about. It looks like that's the only way creators are created, except that now we're told that we're going to become creators. Is this the first time that this has ever happened?

No. Creators can become creators in any progression they wish. If their creation is going to have infinite variety, they might choose some smaller (in terms of simplicity) creation, such as a soul with many lives. On the other hand, they might not; they might simply travel about like your Creator did to get ideas and encouragement before beginning. There is no fixed method.

One must always remember that when extrapolated back to the beginning, you are all creators. The joy of creation is so profound that to forget who one is for a time in order to experience the great pleasure of creation at a more simple level is something worthy of doing. A creator is not goofing off to do that; it is perfectly viable. Ofttimes when a creator has created a massive creation and decides to have a series of individual lives, it will do that series. And during those lives, as a result of that simpler, less complex interaction, it will get some idea or inspiration for a new creation. It must finish that chain of lives; otherwise it will not understand how to go about its creation. This is because all things are balanced within any chain of lives so that a being can feel the value or lack of value of a given creative idea. Once it has finished, it might go back to being a creator (they almost always do)—or should I say go forward?—and create something new and different. Thus having a string of individual lives is often a way to garner inspiration.

We understood that there were very few creations that fostered or created or allowed individual lives. What choices do these creators have? What creations can they go to for individual lives?

Oh, it is not my understanding that individual lives are so rare. Perhaps when considered in the mass of all creation, you could say individual lives are rare, yet it is a relative term, you know. If I were to say that one out of every 100 creations had individual lives, that is still a massive number when taken in its full impact. A creator might have a chain of lives in many places.

I understand. Zoosh had said that when our Creator went on His travels, noplace He looked had individual lives. He apparently didn't go very far.

About Your Creator

That's true. If He could have traveled for a significantly longer time, He would have found some. But it was to your Creator's advantage to not see too much variety, because He was somewhat preordained to express Himself in a varietal fashion. This level of expression for your

Creator allowed Her to be almost driven (if not obsessed) to express every level of individualism that might be available. For instance, no two cells or even atoms are exactly alike even if they are from the same material—certainly leaves and fingerprints and so on are not exactly alike. Your Creator created in minutiae the idea of variety, but there's also a broader view. Your Creator decided to take more of the infinitesimal view. Your Creator felt that in stimulating and acquiring re-creation, She would give herself as much opportunity as possible.

But how does this work now? When He/She rejoins the higher parts of Itself, it's only because He separated from those parts when He began this creation, right?

Yes.

The Creator has a unity, and He chose only parts of that unity to express in this creation. But you see all of Him.

Yes, and when your Creator rejoins all of those parts of Itself, It will then be able to reassess the potential for Its own future based upon the vast experience acquired here in this creation.

And then It will probably create another creation?

Most likely It will, but, being more whole and more complete, It will be able to do it differently.

But the mission will be complete here, fulfilled?

Oh yes, your Creator's mission will be complete.

What about the plan? Is there more to your plan than this Creator's mission?

Oh yes, because it was intended that *all* creation expand. It wasn't intended only for your creation.

Okay, but I thought we were the trigger that would make it expand.

You *are* the trigger. But the trigger is the lever, not the effect; pulling it begins the effect. So yes, your destiny is self-serving, but it also serves others, intentionally or unintentionally. Yet what happens to so many others results from the plan's effects—expansion in all ways.

Even, for example, something as simple as an inspiration for a new product. The product will have depth and a vaster application after the expansion. It will seem to be some little simple thing in the beginning—a thumbtack or a paper clip, that kind of idea. After the expansion the thumbtack will have vast possibilities, much more than the original inspiration for its application. This simple example will be magnified much more for other, more complex inspirations.

How many beings were involved in the plan?

Not too many. I think there were only about three creators. I must admit it wasn't my idea [chuckles] to create the plan for the momentum and so on; it was another creator's idea. That creator "discussed" that inspiration (creators get inspiration, too) with its friend and then they "discussed" it with me.

Can you say who they are—or would we know them?

Well, I don't think they have any direct or even indirect effect upon *your* creation. I could say something about them, but it is not really applicable. One of them is the Creator of Conceptual Effects, meaning that which could happen; even what *should* happen (I'll use the word "should") is within this creator's purview. I can't say they are involved with cause and effect, but they are involved with effect. If something happens anywhere, it is that creator's job to deliver the variety or even the singularity to allow the multilevel effects of that action or creation. Although that might be interesting, it does not directly apply to you because your Creator provides that for Itself.

Then how would you say He is inspired? Where would the inspiration come from if there is no level involved?

That's a good question. It is not unlike yourselves, who have a conscious, an unconscious and a subconscious and have parts of your body you don't think about—an autonomic system that keeps your heart beating and so on. Vast amounts of myself are automatic because they are repetitive. Setting them up to be automatic is of value. Inspiration is automatic, but because of my responsibilities, I do not always pay attention to every individual inspiration for every being.

So when this creator was inspired with the idea of momentum (you can see how a creator interested in effects might get that inspiration), I did not give that inspiration any more attention than any other. That creator speculated about the potential for momentum. It was, in the beginning (as most inspirations are), the best guess. [Chuckles.] Looking at it on paper, so to speak, it didn't look all that promising. It just goes to show that when there's a good idea and many individual beings like it, they'll take it to heart and then it can truly express itself.

That's what happened. Many creators, as well as individuals within their creations, felt it was a wonderful idea. And because there was so much excitement about the idea, it was able to become more than if it had been just an average daily inspiration.

About the Center of Creation

If parts of yourself are automatic, you must be part of something larger. Your perception is that you are everything . . .

No, no, I do agree with you. It's suggestive that there is *something else.* I have always been here and I have always been doing this. If that is so, where might I have been before this?

Well, our Creator was created out of His creator, so maybe you were a potential?

I have always been here. It is a conundrum, yes, but I have always been here. Certainly I think it is fine to believe that there might be more.

But you have no peers, nobody above you or before you, so there's really no one you can point us to to ask who might know?

No.

How will you expand? You have to expand to make this thing work, right?

It is my pleasure to expand.

What are you doing to expand into if you are all that is?

I'll find out! [Laughs.] You see, it is one of the joys of creation that you can give yourself a little ignorance. I decided I would do that so I could have the pleasure of discovering what I become. Many, many other creators have done the same thing, because the great joy of discovery is . . . ah, it is wondrous! Especially if one does not normally experience that.

You said that you had to focus attention on certain things, which didn't allow you to always pay attention to everything else. What is your focus? What is your job? How do you do it?

I have explained this. I create all that is experiencing itself in any way as substantive. At the nineteenth dimension, for example, you could not see beings there, but they are there and they experience themselves as substantive. I am responsible for creating the energy that forms into those beings. I might not take responsibility for the form, but for the matter, yes.

What do you focus on? How do you perceive what you have to do? Do you visualize it to create it?

Again, this is automatic; it is not something I have to think about. It is not something I have to try. Since I have always been here, I have always been able to do this; it is simply something I do. When your heart pumps your blood around in your veins, it is something you do, but not something you *try* to do.

Do you see or feel a need?

I might very well feel a need from somewhere. Ofttimes this is a reaction to an inspiration, but not always; sometimes it is simply a need. If that need cannot be fulfilled by anyone else, I fill it. But I am very careful not to fulfill a need that some other creator can fulfill. If I do that, it is as if I would be telling that creator that it is not good enough. It is like a parent relationship; I want that creator to fulfill the need if it is capable of doing so. If it *can* fulfill the need, I will wait until it does. If that creator requires inspiration to fulfill it, I will be happy to oblige. If, however, the need is pressing and it cannot fulfill it, I will give that creator some piece that is missing from its awareness about how to resolve it. But I won't butt in. [Chuckles.]

Okay, so are you aware of all the creators and all the creations by tuning in to the desire, or do they send messages?

Oh, I'm always aware.

You're aware of everything because it's all within your being?

Yes. That is how I am able to be quickly responsive, not unlike a computer with unlimited memory.

But you can channel or feed inspiration toward them if you feel they need it.

Yes. The delicate part of my work is *not* interfering, and that relates to the smallest expression of creation. One must always encourage those who can do these things. Yet if it is pressing, you might help them, but not do it *for* them. If you did, they would come to believe that it might not be their responsibility. And if they believe that, their growth will be stifled. Responsibility is a very important factor of creation.

What are all those 500,000 trillion beings doing in the Center of Creation?

Oh, they're not here all the time. That's why I said "at any given time." They're coming and going.

Where are they coming and going from?

They're coming from everywhere and they're going to everywhere. That's why I say that at any given time they might be there, but they don't stay.

But what do they do? They come for inspiration? They come to meet people? They come to interact? Do they come to get something?

They come to get something. They might meet other creations—other bits and pieces—but that's not why they're there. They're there to receive something that being within me helps them to receive. An inspiration, which might be delivered far away and not within my body, would be useful, but it might not charge them with the pleasure and excitement of a creation. I am, if nothing else, love, joy, inspiration, excitement, pleasure—and, yes, responsibility. [Chuckles.] By being within me they are charged with this energy like a battery, so they go to their creation, however big or small it is, with this energy to begin.

So what we're calling the Center of Creation is this light, this frothing, bubbling . . . everything would be your body, and what we call space would be your energy field?

Yes, that's close enough, although I am not bubbling and frothing; I am just basically radiating outwardly and inwardly. As your own scientists have discovered, if a particle can radiate out and in at the same time, the source of available energy is infinite.

And on this little planet we will soon discover that.

Yes; your theoretical physicists are there already.

They will make it practical, and the obstacles, in the sense of control, will be gone?

Well, the original idea of the fusion reactor was based upon that concept, but even though in small experiments it did not work out, it was a good baby step toward tapping infinite energy.

So you are intimately aware of everything on this planet?

If I pay attention, yes.

What else would you like to say?

I will simply close by saying that creation is not so much an end in itself, but it is always a beginning. Infinity can be described as a beginning. It is intended that this beginning be nonstop, for in that beginning lies the ultimate fulfillment of all existence for everyone, even an individual's heart/love energy. As such, know that your beginnings are infinite also.

Thank you very much.

Good night.

All right. Zoosh speaking. I think maybe we'll stop there for the night if that's all right.

May I ask you one question?

Yes, yes.

You have been to the Center of Creation. What did you go for, and what do you feel you got?

Oh, I needed to go to be informed, to perhaps glimpse beyond. What I have seen beyond the Center of Creation is very much a reflection of my own being. This leads me to believe that there is something beyond the Center of Creation, but ultimately it is ourselves.

There's no one to probe further? We've gone as far as we can go for now?

Yes, I think that's as far as we can go, although we can still hear from other creators—the Heart Council perhaps next week.

Well, tell him/her/it thank you very, very, very much.

I think that being heard that, but I will compound the salutation.

Thank you.

Good night.

❖ Robert's Comments on His Experience

Oh, I could—when that being was talking I could see rays of light going in and out at the same time.

That's what I'm sitting here thinking about. I never heard of radiating inward and outward at the same time before he said that.

And it felt much more complete. When I've looked at light bulbs or saw light radiating from the sun, it always felt like there was something missing. And now, after being exposed to that being, I see what was missing. Light has to go in as well as come out, and then it's complete.

You don't feel overdone or cooked?

Well, I feel ready to come out of the oven, but I don't think I feel overdone. It's hard to say at this stage of the game.

Well, Zoosh is getting pretty good. You feel the love and the wisdom and the joy, but he keeps you from harm.

Yeah, I think so. These beings are so powerful, though, I can't really hold the energy as long as I might be able to channel Zoosh or something. You know, in the beginning when I was first doing this kind of work I would experiment with various beings and I could maybe channel them for five minutes. Now I feel pretty good about being able to channel these powerful beings for the first time and be there with the process for this long.

When Zoosh was talking about looking beyond the Center of Creation, he said all he saw was himself.

Yes, I could see that. I could see a reflection of what he was seeing. It's not clear now as it was then, but it was like looking beyond something that was all black and seeing himself. He was definitely seeing himself.

The Heart Council

September 17, 1996

We are the members of Heart Council. It is our job to oversee the applications of the love energy as focused through the heart center of all beings. We do not regulate so much as support. Perhaps the most challenging level of support is from your planet at this time when so many individuals, in order to learn and become educated and responsible creators, have been artificially cut off from the continuity of the felt loving energy.

It is not our job to assist in the conceptualization of heart energy, but to monitor its level insofar as it is a feeling. Right now, including the whole of the universe and even universes beyond, we are directing fully 58% of our total energy toward your planet. As a matter of fact, we have had to call for support from beings who do not normally perform this function to carry on in our stead on other planets, especially with the young. As you know, in the first two years of a being's life it decides whether to retain that form or not, so nurturing young ones is acutely necessary—and there are many young ones all over the universe and in universes beyond. So we have asked for help from another council that oversees all feelings. And because they are related to what we do, they can actually fill in for us a little bit.

In our focusing on your planet perhaps the most challenging time we have had to deal with was in the late forties, when many of your societies were radically changing socioeconomically as a result of the world war; then again later in the early seventies, when there was a sudden expansion of awareness that has taken practically 30 years to integrate itself.

The Stepped-Up Transfer of Heart Energy,
Feeling the Feelings of Others

Since your year 1995 we have reached the highest level of our focus in transferring energy to you. Some of this is because you will be receiving (and I believe are receiving now in a trickling form) your own true heart energy, which has been kept safe for you inside Earth. This is part of the reason many of you have such strong feelings now and why when they come up they cannot be ignored. As you attain more of your true heart energy, messages that were once confusing to your physical body will become immediately understood because of the ability of your hearts to message your bodies. Also, as you begin to acquire the knowledge to tell the difference between what you *think* would work and a truthful assessment of what is *actually* working, you will begin to become consciously aware of what must be done.

Many philosophies have abounded with Earth people for some time that state if one individual is in pain, then all suffer. Yet in the age of technology much of this has been forgotten in the enchantment with the movable machine. As the feminine energy of Mother Earth is being released all throughout herself, coinciding with the release of your true heart energy, this heart energy is becoming more prevalent (though not yet predominant) in your societies. As it becomes more predominant, you will find that you have almost no tolerance to allow *any* being, be it human, animal or plant, to suffer within your immediate proximity. You will be able to feel both their physical and their emotional pain. For your own good, if for no other reason, you *must* help them to feel better, to be clothed or fed or sheltered, to have water, to be nurtured, perhaps even radiate love toward them so they feel that someone cares about them.

This natural condition for you is gradually returning. It is in your nature to feel the feelings of all beings. That is an element of a creator, but it is also an element of that which has sprung from a creator, which is you. Of course, one cannot grow by having this condition, so I believe that in the experiment of the Explorer Race the rules were perhaps understandable. But as a spokesperson for the Heart Council, I would have to say that we were not in agreement with the method. We were told that all the suffering would later be eliminated, but that does not eliminate the suffering as it happens in the moment. We felt it would have been much better to have kept the discomfort level to no more than 10%. And we do not approve of allowing the discomfort level to have reached such an extreme here.

We would not criticize your Creator, because we understand that your Creator was also learning and felt that the only way you could move beyond suffering was to understand it only too well. That is why your Creator granted you the tool of pain, which in its insistence demands attention. We see now how pain is a powerful tool, yet being who we are, we cannot support the suffering of beings even for learning purposes.

We love your Creator and we support that being, but we have yet to be convinced of the method used. We can see the future rewards, yet we feel (as the feminine polarization of your Creator feels) that the method was perhaps subject to improvement. I speak to you of this because I understand that your Creator will be replaced by you at some point. I hope that you will not be so broad in the allowance of discomfort. Your Creator did not so much shove discomfort at you as allow it. We believe that was perhaps too "magnanimous."

We hope that you will countenance a replacement for yourself someday through some other creative means, and we believe you have it within you to do this. Your Creator quite clearly wanted you to be able to understand every ramification of the effect of suffering. It is my understanding that your Creator did not want suffering to happen again, that It felt strongly that minor discomfort is the best growth tool, but was truly adamant in Its insistence that suffering must be eliminated. If one can grasp this about your Creator, then perhaps one can understand Its methods in allowing discomfort when you create it and in not interfering with it so that you might learn and grow.

So I do not judge your Creator, but [chuckles] it would not be *our* way. Perhaps we are biased. Question?

About the Heart Council

Can you say how many members are on the Council?

It varies, you know, because in most senses we are one, yet sometimes individual personalities are called for, such as now. I would suppose, in terms of the greatest number of individuals, we have never had more than 473, and most of the time we never have less than 3. But the energy level and the total confluence of our being remains the same.

Did you wake up and find yourself doing this, or did you have a job before this? Have you always been doing this?

We had a job before this. I think that perhaps you could say we graduated to this. Before this we were the energy of love, but we did not monitor it; someone else did that. As the energy of love, we were, I believe, promoted to our current position and other energies replaced us. We did not replace ourselves, nor were we birthed by that which we replaced. It seems to be some kind of a hierarchical progress. We have not been here long.

We are aware of many creations. We saw this one being created; we watched your Creator come. But in terms of eternity or the infinite, it is not that long. We will probably be here for quite some time yet because we have not even begun to have a glimmer of interest in doing anything else. If we should, I expect we will move on like that which preceded us, and that which is now the energy of love will perhaps be in our position. Who can say?

Where did your predecessor get promoted to?

You know, I don't think I've ever looked. This is one of those jobs where, [chuckles] when you get promoted to it, you have so much to do you do not have time for extraneous thoughts. But let me see . . . they seem to be at a confluence, a coming together of white and gold light. I think they are involved in the job of creating the energy that precedes light. Light itself is made up of something. There is an energy which, if you were to look at it, would be transparent. Occasionally in its denser capacity it might look a little less transparent, but it is a transparency that precedes light. They seem to be involved in the manufacture of this energy.

Were you created in the Center of Creation, or as one of the creators? Or do you have any connection? Can you look down from where you are and see the Center of Creation?

Well, it is not "down," but I will see if I can.

Up or out? I'm trying to get a reference.

There is not a spatial reference; it is a feeling reference. But a moment . . . I cannot trace us back to the Center of Creation, though it is logical to assume we came from there. But I have found that in our profession what is logical is not necessarily so. I seem to be able to trace us back to that energy which precedes light but no further.

Since all the creators in this system and the Center of Creation use light, then it would seem that possibly you come from that which created the Center of Creation, because light must come from beyond that.

Well, that sounds rather grand and maybe it is so, but I think I shall not brag of this.

I'm really fishing. I'm trying to find somebody who can go beyond the Center of Creation when telling us where it is from.

Perhaps next time we can hear from our predecessors, who are now creating the energy that creates light.

The Means of Inspiration

Good work! Do you inspire creators? We were told by Zoosh that sometimes you send inspiration to creators about what to do before they become creators.

Sometimes even *after* they become creators. If they're involved in some major consciousness- or life-changing project such as your own, we will sometimes send an energy stream to these beings if they have a space for it, which means that they have a question that has been answered, but that answer feels incomplete. When there is a feeling in any being—be it creator, human being, spirit, even a temporary being that exists as the result of imagination—of something that it needs, we can send the feeling energy that supports and inspires a foundation for the concept. But we do not send messages that would be readily interpretable mentally.

As you receive an inspiration, there is often a wonderful feeling that goes with it. We would perhaps (not for everyone) be involved in the feeling. It is as if you were sending something down a river; we would be the river, but what is sent is sent by someone else. We are the means, yes.

So who would send that inspiration, then? A creator?

That would depend. In the case of a creator, it might be its own creator, it might be the Center of Creation, or it might be any other creator or even that which exists before and beyond a creator in order to provide the stimulation and the support for resolution. When working with a creator or anyone who will become or has been a creator, it is different. One does not provide answers; one provides support and sustenance to achieve the answer. In the case of a being who has not been a creator, will not be one in that life and is not working on a plan to become one in the future, then a more practical message might come. For instance, an animal or perhaps a fly would need water urgently, and the inspiration might come in the form of a smell. (Water does have a smell, especially when one is desperately seeking it and lives by one's instincts, such as a fly.) We would perhaps provide an aroma or a feeling within the fly ("fly this way, not that way"). This would be slightly more than an inspiration; it would be a direction.

But you can aim that feeling specifically at the exact timing of the being?

We can aim it at a neutron or a particle of a neutron. Do you know that some of the most profound, insightful beings I have ever had the opportunity to communicate with are at the atomic and subatomic level? It would really be wise to include particles in this book, because some of them have very inspiring things to say.

You're wonderful! Not only are you saying wonderful things, but you're giving good leads.

[Chuckles.] It is not an accident that particles look like universes and solar systems; it is not an accident.

Ah, we have much to learn. So you're supporting the Earth people. Do you aim at the oversoul, or at each human specifically? How do you do that?

It is more of a blanket energy. It is a beam aimed at Earth, yes? And it is aimed spherically from the outside in so that all beings on the surface (and, for that matter, under the surface) have this energy available to them. So it is not like sunlight. It is more of a full-time experience. Since this energy is omnipresent at any given moment, if the need is there it will be fulfilled. The being, especially if it is involved in a highly creator-oriented string of lives, will not often be provided with the answer, but will be supported toward the answer. Ofttimes people will pray because their circumstances are so difficult, and they will ask to be relieved or to be inspired to know something so they can understand why they are suffering. The message they get will ofttimes be a feeling. I will give you an example.

The Man Who Prayed for Understanding

In a recent situation a young man was in prison. His experience there was not simply of isolation but of foreignness, for this young man was a man of the land, a farmer. He had committed a crime and is now in prison and will be for another few years. But he will survive and go back to farming.

He prayed and asked to know why he had "fallen," as he put it, "to this level," how he could have ended up like this. He asked for inspiration to know and understand so that he could have something to hold onto during these years of this life. Because of his great need, the energy was immediately transferred to him and placed in the bone marrow of his legs, thighs and knees, partly because in these particular bones there is a lot of room for energy to park itself. Also, the marrow of these particular bones are greatly responsible for inspirations that lead to actions. The marrow of other bones might be information or energy that leads to theories, for example, but these bones lead to action.

While he slept fitfully during the night the energy was packed into his leg bones. Now, because his cell is so small and because he is a man of action, every day he exercises in this small closetlike cell. He runs in place and jumps up and down and does many physical exercises. Because of this physical action, you see, he will release from the marrow of his legs (hips, knees) a great deal of this inspiration over the next two or three years. When he gets out, and even before that, he will be a man of philosophy. He will have read a great deal of the old books they have in the prison (unfortunately, they do not have many new philosophy books) and will become a very spiritual being. He will be of a religion, yes, but he will be very spiritual and philosophical and have a greater understanding of how many ways the Earth feeds beings. This can make life very inspiring for him as a farmer. This was the best possible way for this man.

You see, it matters not who the beings are or what they have done. It matters what they need—and for us, how we can provide it in the best possible way, in a way that does not harm them and is completely secret to others, yet is readily available for the person's sustenance.

You have such a knowledge of the individual's feelings! So you aim it at the Earth, yet you can direct it from within Earth to individuals.

Yes. Imagine that you are walking around in what you call airspace. There are many components within this airspace. We are here in the space you are in right now; this is how we can communicate through this being. Because we are here, we do not have to send our energy great distances to an individual. We are omnipresent, so if any individual needs something and there is a way to reach that person, we are already right there.

You are omnipresent in all of creation, all worlds everywhere?

We would say yes, but we are more so here (perhaps that is not the correct term). We are omnipresent on Earth because the need is so great here, but in other creations we are present and available.

How many years before we see that the need will not be as great?

It has begun to taper a bit already because you are receiving your natural selves—your natural brain, as you say (your natural thought system, we would say), your natural heart energy. Even your instincts are coming back to you. It has begun to taper a bit, but not measurably yet. I would say that we will have to be omnipresent for perhaps another 25 to 30 experienced years, which is slightly different from calendar years.

More or less?

It depends upon your experience and which direction you go. That is why, when experiential years are referred to, it means a year in time based upon the experience of that particular moment, measured moment to moment on the basis of how one grows, changes—zigs and zags.

What percentage of our heart energy do we have now?

We are not sure, but it seems that everyone has no less than 11% and some people are up to 28%. It appears that there is up to 28% available for all individuals, but not everyone has been able or comfortable to integrate it. But it is there.

The people who read this book can ask to receive more?

Yes, and remember to ask no matter what your circumstances in life are. No matter who you are, what you think you are, what you've done or not done—let that not be a barrier.

Because it belongs to them, in other words.

It is yours for the asking, but you must ask and welcome it when it comes and, perhaps not unlike a new puppy, nurture it for a time so it will *want* to stay.

Asking for Your Heart Energy

How do we ask for it? How can we receive it?

You would simply ask. You would say, perhaps in a quiet moment with as little stress as possible, "I welcome my true total heart energy and embrace and celebrate its arrival." In this way wait, relax, notice if you feel the warmth in your chest or near there. You can hug yourself or stroke your auric field gently, with your hands moving down to bring that heart energy down farther into your body, vertically speaking. Stroke downward because it is easier for energies to access your head, neck and heart area, but sometimes more difficult for them to access below the solar plexus. Although the intestines are an area where you release, you also store there. So you need to nurture the energy downward and welcome it.

Another way is to move your feet around while you are welcoming it. The physical body is an instrument to which energy will naturally gravitate when some part of it is moving. If you have no feet, then the lowest extremity you have.

Once we receive the energy, what changes in ourself should we expect and what should we be doing with that energy?

There is no should, but if you wish to allow it to work for you, then do for others in some simple way, not complex. Pick something simple—perhaps brush your wife's or daughter's hair or even brush the dog (if they wish, of course). Do something simple of service that is gentle and loving for another, but let it be an unconditional love, not an intimate love. In this way that new energy will be educated about the levels of love here, which are many and varied. It is like training wheels on a bicycle; one must learn, and to do something simple is perhaps the easiest way.

Our Presence on Your Planet

You said that after the world war you were needed here most. Have you been here during all the eighteen civilizations on this planet? Have you been coming all that time?

We were available, not unlike being available for other civilizations elsewhere. But it was not the type of availability that is omnipresent now, because the previous civilizations did not have the level of drama or trauma that you have had. Oh, they had birth and death, and sometimes even catastrophes, but they were for the most part quick and fleeting. No, it is only in this current civilization that drama/trauma is so extensive.

From your perspective how long has this civilization existed?

Oh, I would measure this current civilization back perhaps not much more than 100,000 years. I do not include Atlantis or Lemuria in your civilization because they had their own agendas, their own purposes, and they were not really directly integrated into the Explorer Race experiment. This does not mean the lives that some of you had there are not impacting you in some motivating way now. I am going back perhaps no more than 79,000 years, and I include the rudimentary beginnings of your civilization. I am also not including some beings who are still tribal today, because in many ways these beings, at least initially, were also not involved in the experiment, but were sent here to assist the planet in gauging what a human being would need. Thus there are some tribal people who have been here much longer, but are not directly involved in the Explorer Race experiment.

What specifically happened 79,000 years ago when we started to become?

Oh, I would say it was when the human being as you know it was physiologically present. I am not including pre-prototypes.

Was this when they came from Sirius?

It is right around that time that the Sirian prototypes you now live with arrived.

Not when Jehovah brought the beings?

Oh, I'm not going back that far.

Sometimes it's nice to have reference points.

It's well you understand that these points of reference are liquid, but . . .

Yes, we've talked about the fluctuating nature of time lines before. You said that on other planets you worked with children two years old and under. Can you explain why? They've just gotten into a body and they're not sure about it?

Oh, no. It is typical in other creations, even the most benevolent creations, that beings are not required to survive. They have the flexibility and the opportunity to say, "Well, this is not quite right" and choose to pass out of that being and perhaps try it slightly differently. In order to maximize their feeling welcome in the body, we broadcast more energy to them at this young age than they would receive afterward so that they can accommodate the culture in which they live and the expressions they must utilize to communicate and feel the connection to their total being. In the first two experiential years of any being's life (granted, I am speaking of beings who will live a minimum of 150 years or—to include you—a minimum of 75 years) it is really essential that they feel welcome. If they do not, they will generally not live to the end of their natural cycle.

Ribbons of Light for Suicides

On this planet we now have so many children who are unloved, unwanted, you know; there are too many suicides and drugs. Do you spend extra attention on them?

Yes, especially those who cut their natural cycles short. They require something like a ribbon of light so that they can find their way. If a being were intended to live, say, 65 years and suddenly stops living because of his own actions at, say, 13, the door for his physical exit is not there yet. We provide a ribbon these beings can follow (it is not just a vague ribbon; it is comprised of gold and white light), and by touching the ribbon they will feel energized, invigorated and, most important, loved. Then they can move along the ribbon of light to their natural exit.

If we did not provide this, they would be walking the Earth in spirit form until they were 65 (in terms of experiential years), meaning that the difference between 65 and 13 would have to be lived by others on the planet—that many years would have to go by—before they could find their way to their next place. We provide a ribbon of light so they can find it more quickly.

Unbelievable! They can then go and be counseled and loved, then reincarnate.

Yes. Ofttimes in circumstances such as this they will choose to exist somewhere for a time before they incarnate again. It is usually like this because they need to understand and perhaps replay every moment of their life (without the pain, of course) to understand how they came to do what they did, even if they swear (between lives, you know) that they would never do that again. Sometimes one needs to understand these things by living them more than once. We neither condone nor judge suicide, but we provide support. Sometimes the light ribbon is unseen or unrecognized by individuals. And there are other beings who will go to rescue them in spirit form. Sometimes this does not happen immediately, however, and they are confused and uncomfortable for a time. But they will be rescued eventually.

So all we have is another 20 or 25 years, then the level of negativity and despair that drives them won't exist on this planet?

Oh, no, you do not understand. It is not a switch—it is a gradual thing. Over the next 20, 25 or 30 years or so it gradually changes, so by the time 25 or 30 years have gone by (assuming all goes well, yes?) it will be gone. But you should notice a significant difference even in 15 to 20 years. As a matter of fact, it will be so significant that you might not consciously remember how it used to be (for those who live through those times, and there are several here who will). The fascinating thing about this phenomenon is that wisdom changes as your place in space and the function of time-space changes. Even when you have accumulated this wisdom, if it is no longer needed within the time-space you occupy, it will simply return to the greater you as unnecessary and no longer be available for you here because you will not need it.

I guess I don't want to feel the pain, but I want to keep the memories.

But you know, sometimes the details of the memories themselves churn the pain. Once it is no longer needed, then why be attached to it? It is understandable now that you would feel that way, but later you will not be interested.

I understand. There'll be so much more to think about then.

You will have plenty to keep you occupied.

I will say that perhaps some other time we can speak, but we will end now. Yes?

Thank you very much.

Good night.

❖ Robert's Comments on His Experience

How did you see the Heart Council, Robert?

I didn't actually see them except at some point when they were trying to describe how many they were in number. I saw something like a fountain of individuals at one point and then just three big, tall beings at another point. But they were very distinctly this gold and white light. When they were describing the beings who were making the gold and white light, I could see the stuff that they make it out of. It's like looking through Saran wrap. You can see right through it, yet you feel the substance of it.

Creators of Gold Light and White Light

September 19, 1996

e are the creators of the invited matrix that provides gold and white light to all creations. (We're not referring to a combination of the two; there is both gold light and white light.) We are very busy these days. Once upon a time, before the creation of your universe, we used to have moments here and there where we could check and see what others were doing—travel about, you might say. But since the creation of your universe, your Creator's needs and the needs of that which your Creator has created have been keeping us working overtime.

A great deal of gold and white light is needed by your universe right now. Approximately 58% of what we create is going to your universe; all the other universes get what's left. To put a finer point on it, of that 58% almost 40% of the gold and white light comes to your planet. This is perhaps because of the wondrous action taking place there. The tension that allows the universe to grow will come about as a result of many inside-out cycles of your planet. If you were able to slow down the mechanical means by which your planet and its peoples are moving between dimensions while you are alive, you would see your planet turn inside out and back again every half millisecond! This requires a tremendous amount of gold and white light so that all life can sustain itself. However, it does have consequences in your life.

Reincorporating One's Discarnate Parts to Move to 4D

As far as we perceive from our point in the universe, since this pace has picked up, almost everyone is involved in the reincarnation of their discarnate selves. This means that all portions of you, whether it be portions of your now self or portions of other selves you have had anywhere (in this universe only), must now be reincorporated in some light mass and within the individual cellular structures from whence they came. This is not as easy as it might sound, because sometimes portions of one's light become attached to other beings. Also, sometimes even portions of one's physical self might be lost somewhere, perhaps in battle or "by accident," as you say. All of these bits become parts of the discarnate you.

Now, for you to be able to move from third to fourth dimension, it is necessary that all these bits find their way back to their points of origin within your incarnated selves. This requires the assistance of ourselves and other beings of light as well as the shamanic abilities of many others, some of whom do not even realize they are involved in such activities. The sleep states you have now are sometimes so deep and complex that some of you, especially those who have repetitive lives, feel that your sleep state is more adventurous than your waking state. Ofttimes this is because you are fetching pieces of other individuals in your light-body while your physical self sleeps. Not everyone is capable of fetching these pieces for themselves, and because we are talking about any incarnations that your souls have had in this universe, we are talking about lots of bits and pieces.

This turning out and in, inside and out, is the only way in which physical, living life forms can move between dimensions. If you were to move between dimensions *without* turning inside out as a planet and as beings, the natural order would assume that your deaths had taken place, and all beings would either die simultaneously and move on to their natural next lives, or (and this is much more complex and troublesome) they would move on as if one were moving past one's physical life. They would move *while alive* into what is beyond the veils, which would create chaos both for the individuals moving on and for what is beyond the veils.

Solution: Creating an Alternating Life Current

Therefore, in order to keep you from going into a natural loop of evolved energy, which happens when anyone passes over, it is necessary to create what amounts to an alternating current of life. Those of you who understand the way electricity is used in your modern age know that alternating current is basically that which pulses. Using direct current for a moment as an analogy, moving from one life to another uses a direct current of energy. To break that natural cycle of the direct flow of energy, we must have an alternating flow. So by turning your planet and all beings on it inside out and back again every half millisecond, the energy of the natural motion through the veils is thereby thwarted. You are then able to move as an anomalous body through the veils without either affecting or, more important, being affected by what is beyond the veils.

This information is most important for you to understand now, because it is one of the functions of creators to know how to do what is impossible within a system that works in a well-ordered way. Though you might look at the universe and say, "This is something that seems chaotic," I can assure you it is very well ordered. It is even systematic. Certainly from our perceptions this is so. Yet what if it is necessary (as it is with your Creator) to move an object with many beings, such as your planet, through a well-ordered system in such a way that it goes some-place it would not normally go? In other words, how do you create an anomalous motion in a safe, practical, loving way? This was the way that was devised.

We are familiar with it because when your planet turns inside out it uses white light, and when it turns back it uses gold light. Remember that I said fully 40% of the white and gold light, for which we create the matrix, is now coming to your planet. Fully 37% of that light energy is being used for the inside out and back—over one-third of the total.

I mention this to you so you will understand the complexity of moving between dimensions while still alive. It is not what I would call a burden, for it was a challenge that your Creator rose to. But as you can tell, it was necessary to call upon other beings who might conceivably be able to assist.

What do you use to create gold and white light?

The reason I call this an *invited matrix* is that gold and white light is not like other light. This is light that has direct physical effects as well as spiritual and emotional effects on any individual body or mass it encounters. This means that this light must, of its own nature and qual-ity, *want* to do what it is doing. It can't do something temporarily until it can go on and do what it really wants to do; it must be dedicated and excited and joyful, but also focused on what it is doing.

So we invite a matrix of energy to come to us. It comes to where we are from all universes, all creations—even beyond creations—and con-denses itself. Our area of creation is measurable, an oval (not a circle) approximately a thousand miles in diameter. This matrix compresses itself and literally shows up, volunteering for duty. This invited energy is mostly transparent. Sometimes there is a slight waviness to it; if you were to look through it, there would be a slight sensation of motion, for what is behind it has a ripple effect.

We then ask it whether it wishes to inspire spiritually, or spiritually, physically and emotionally (the first being the white light, the second being the gold light). The gold light has more responsibility and flexibility and at times has to deal more with consequences and results rather than supporting, nurturing and sustaining.

Of its own free will, as you might say, it will then form into two separate parts. We have found that most of it comfortably forms into what will become white light, and only energy that is experienced (ofttimes from the bodies or the masses of creators) forms into the matrix that becomes gold light.

The Filtering That Produces the Two Kinds of Light

Using a focusing technique, we then move the matrix that is prepared to come as white light through a filter of total unconditional love. It passes into it as it is, but when it comes out it is white light, if one were to look at it. Within this filter it is enjoined as focused, loving light and it tends to attract what needs it and be attracted to what calls for it—two slightly different variations of the same inspiration or truth. The moment after it emerges from the love filter, it will immediately go to where it is needed—some to your creation, some to the creations of others. We do not send it, because it knows where to go. Our job is done once the matrix has passed through the filter of love.

The portion that wishes to become gold light will first pass through a filter that familiarizes it with responsibilities; then another filter familiarizes it with consequences that require further action. It will pass through a final filter of pure, unconditional love. It knows where to go and moves there under its own power with the desire to help and the authority to do so. Because it has been authorized through this process, it brings about the change normally associated with creators. As I say, most of this matrix comes from creators, and what does not, comes from beings who are very, very advanced. So there is a tremendous amount of expertise present. This is what we do.

How does the planet use the other 63% of the white and gold light sent here?

A good question. Most of this is now going directly to beings who are coming in to be born. Because the new generation (all babies being born now) has the greatest capacity to carry this energy, this white and gold light goes to them when they are conceived, even if they do not stay to term and be physically born. Most babies who arrive are loved by someone, and the love that is given them, generally unconditionally, has the immediate effect of amplifying that white and gold light ten times. Thus the baby is able within its first two years of life to broadcast ten times the amount of white and gold light given to it. In this way the energy of creation, unconditional love and responsibility, and of actions based upon consequences of other actions is spread all around your globe to all peoples—to whoever is having children, no matter who or where they are. It is very evenhanded.

There is another small portion that is sent to various individuals who request it or who, in moments of sudden crisis, need to have white and/or gold light present to support them through that crisis. But mostly it goes to the young.

You might ask about those babies who for one reason or another are not born. Perhaps the pregnancy does not go to term for some reason. If they do not survive their birth, then for no less than three days of Earth time a portion of them will stay in spirit form and broadcast that white and gold light on the Earth, though it will not be amplified by ten times since they did not arrive as a loved being. Still, they will take that time to broadcast the white and gold light they have, so high is their feeling of responsibility to what you all are doing here.

When there is a workshop and the workshop leader brings in gold light, do you cooperate with that?

Yes. That will come through what is basically left over.

You said that some of these energies, besides coming from creators and advanced beings, came from beyond creation. Can you amplify that?

The Matrix

Yes. Beyond what you recognize to be the actions of creators, even the action of the point of creation itself, there is a matrix of energy. If you were able to hold it in your hands and look at it, it would appear watery, yet also plasmic. Hold it in your hands and it is clear. If you look at it, you immediately go into it. You feel all things and all things feel you. It is on one hand hypnotic and on the other, totally universalizing.

Imagine that all creation, including the point of the emergence of creation, is surrounded by a liquid, and that liquid, while it has a consistency similar to water, is also such a potent living being that it is *of* all and *contributes to* all creations. Everything was originally created from this material. This is the material of which portions come to us to be transformed into gold and white light. It is plasmic, in the sense that it can be readily activated toward any benevolent goal or purpose. One might conceivably hold it in one's hands, look at it, imagine a beautiful place to be with beautiful beings, even God Herself, then go immediately into that pool of liquid love and be with God. It would be a timeless experience. One might spend a conceptual feeling of many lifetimes there, yet emerge from the pool within your hands and have been gone for only a measurable moment.

So who created it? Is that the God you're talking about?

In my understanding that is what exists in perpetuity for the purpose of all creation. However, it does not have to do with discreation; that is something else.

But who created this Matrix?

I am not able to see that anybody as an individual created it. If you were to go to where it is created, you would see only yourself in reflection. So who created it? All beings. Everyone, if they were to go and look at this, would see only their own reflection, though they could still go anywhere within it because it is physically all around and about you. Yet you are it as well. *It is the liquefied consciousness of all loving creations and creators* who have existed, who do exist and who will ever exist. Naturally you will see yourself, because it is unconditionally loving, which is personal and impersonal in the same moment. You will see yourself in it because your immediate reaction as an encapsulated being would be based upon that which is truly God. And since you are made of God, can you not *be* that?

Do you know what your point of creation was?

We did not come through the point of creation; we came from that Matrix before there was much here. [Chuckles.] So we have been here for some time. We were naturally one of the first arrivals, because love is one of the first things that the place of action of creation would need. This is why we were initially the Heart Council. Then someone replaced us and we moved a step back closer to where we had come from.

As you look back, can you see any other consciousness between you and where you came from?

No.

In your understanding, there is no unit of consciousness we could talk to beyond where you came from?

I could not say that. I can only say what I know to be so from my personal experience and wisdom, speaking for both of us here. I am not aware of anything beyond that.

All right. We're on a hunt for the creator of everything.

Seek no further than yourself.

When Bentov talked about God realization, did he get that far when he saw himself? Was everything in him?

Certainly. This was why he was able to speak with assuredness. Think for a moment. Rain comes from the sky, percolates through the soil and becomes a stream that falls into a river, then into an ocean, either evaporating to become rain again or becoming underground water. This is the perfect analogy for who and what is Creator. Creator is always that which is in motion with loving intent, absolute responsibility and a desire to continue. Can you not say that, devoid of the structures of difficulty and challenge here on this planet, this is certainly a good description of your true souls?

Can you explain a little more about the planet turning inside out?

It is happening physically. You know, half a millisecond is very quick. Even now as we've spoken these few words, the planet has turned inside out and back again several thousand times. It breaks the current. If you as a planetary body and people were moving along without that, you would all be dead. The system requires some brake; basically you might call it short-circuiting. Without that brake one cannot move through dimensions.

I might add for you engineers out there that this is obviously part of the systematic engineering of space vehicles that travel through dimensions. That is also why space vehicles with unlimited capacity to travel through dimensions are piloted by loving beings of creator consciousness. (Those who do not travel unlimitedly through dimensions are not piloted by beings like that.) This functions as a safety mechanism to keep beings who are not sufficiently evolved or heart-centered from blundering into territories where they might unintentionally harm themselves or others.

Other than the Earth now, what are some of the more interesting uses for your energy in the rest of creation that come to mind?

The Mopping-Up Procedure in Sirius

Well, in this creation of your Creator we are still involved in what you might call a mopping-up procedure in that area of the galaxy [system] Sirius where the planet became overwhelmed by negative energy associated with the culture [negative Sirians] that once predominated there. I believe this is referred to in another volume [*The Explorer Race*, chapter 22], so I will not elaborate. There is a significant amount of mopping up there now. When an entire body of people moves from one spatial reference to another—this time to your galaxy [solar system] to reincarnate as a whole without going through the normal cycle and incarnating wherever they choose—it requires a tremendous amount of gold and white light to move into your 3.0 dimension without infiltrating accidentally to where you are [3.47].

It is also necessary to re-form the matrix for the planet that will temporarily replace that destroyed planet in Sirius. That replacement planet will be a gold and white light-energized body visible to those living in Sirius. They will notice its emanations of gold and white light; it will look about three times the circumference of your moon. That area where the gold light is will emanate a comfortable warmth; the area where the white light is will simply be loving, but not emanating a felt physical warmth. This will make it possible to heal the space around that former planet and radiate its energy for healing, love and physical creation and to welcome into its space the planet that will eventually replace it. I mention this because of the correlation between those beings and yourselves.

The Spot That Regulates Discomfort

Another example perhaps? Let us see what else is of interest and is perhaps appropriate to you. . . . Oh yes, there is a place in your creation that regulates discomfort. This means that your Creator intends to use discomfort in small doses to function as a teaching tool for your own culture in its higher-dimensional self and, more to the point, other cultures that have not yet experienced discomfort as a wide-ranging cultural phenomenon (ruling out the occasional individual).

This spot in your universe, which is several million light-years from where you are, is a very small spatial reference. It fluctuates from about 500 feet in an irregular, rounded mass to no more than a mile. This mass requires a significant input of gold light, with a certain amount of white light for its feeding and maintenance, in order to be constantly reminded that it is here to perform a function, not to become a force unto itself. It has had billions of years of reminders, so it is now dogmatically aware of its purpose and is quite clear that when your Creator begins to spread minor degrees of discomfort to stimulate growth in other planets, galaxies and individuals, it will not integrate more than 0.5 to probably 1% of itself into any given system.

This is not the 2% that your Creator discusses, because this discomforting energy has a tendency to expand slightly. Therefore a margin of safety is built in. It will not integrate more than 1% at most of the total mass energy of the planet to which it's going, because the energy tends to expand to slightly less than 2% (perhaps 1.9 or 1.985%, but no more than that).

We provide energy to this discomforted mass so that it is fed, cared for and can, through the light vision, see what is going on elsewhere—why it is needed and the loving reception it will receive because of what it can do in small quantities. As your homeopathic physicians know, sometimes the subtle is much more long-lasting in its educational impact than more massive doses.

The Explorer Race came from a point of curiosity within the Creator. Would you say that this mass came from a point of irritation or something in the Creator?

No. That discomforted mass was imported by your Creator for the specific purpose of Its intentions in Its universe. Your Creator does not have irritation, so this mass had to come from someplace else. I believe it came from a point of discreation. Discreation is not uncreation; it is basically *creation turned inside out*. It does not create something evil, by the way; it simply creates something that is under extreme tension because it is the opposite of what it naturally is, thereby unintentionally creating a small amount of discomforting or negative energy. This mass of discomfort was borrowed from this point of discreation.

That was part of the plan to bring some of that unresolved negativity here and resolve it?

Yes, but also to give it its own gold and white light through its own creation, meaning that it is basically allowed to redeem itself. This sense of redemption means that it discovered a loving, benevolent and valuable purpose while still being itself, without having to transform. If a being must transform in order to become loving, it feels that it is up against conditions. Even as human beings, you know how annoying and often outrageous conditions can be because they limit you. Thus this dark energy (as it is called) is transformed by *being itself!* It is unconditionally accepted; it is allowed and encouraged to be itself, and at smaller doses it functions as annoyance or minor irritation—just enough to stimulate growth but not so much as to cause pain.

That's incredibly important, because that's one of the purposes of this creation.

Yes.

How the Negative Sirians Doomed Themselves

Did the negative Sirians somehow pull too much of that in before this mass realized that it shouldn't have sent out so much?

The Sirians started, like other places, with a small amount. But because the ruling parties at the time on the old negative Sirian planet felt that they might be able to capitalize on the negative energy, they would sit around and go into it (they managed to isolate some, you see), feel what it was and do a negative meditation to amplify it. Afterward they felt very powerful. It was power without love, which, as you know, is not responsible and does not follow up and act on consequences. It was doomed to failure from the start.

I might add that the discomforting energy that was being used this way was outraged, because it had come there to be redeemed, yet here it was being forced to be what it is and was given nothing; rather, something was *taken* from it. So it continued to expand, because when an energy or life or being is looking for something, if it does not have legs, it expands until it finds what it's looking for. It expanded, but the powers there did not recognize that. That expansion eventually caused the destruction of their planet.

In our Earth years, roughly how long will it be before the negative Sirian beings move up?

Oh, I think it will take a very long time. They measure time differently; I would say (in terms of how long it has taken you) that it will take them perhaps 3500 times longer, because they have to learn by slow trial and error. Coming here en masse, they didn't really have a chance to learn much on the way. Normally one learns things on the way to where one is going to incarnate, but the Sirians did not have much chance to do that. They had the chance to be somewhat healed and become prepared for about 50% negative energy, which for them is a reward (less than they had been exposed to), but that was about it. So it will take them a long time to discover the value of cooperation and love and so on. But there is no rush; they have the time.

A Cosmic History and Chronology

All right, you were the Heart Council. That is what you did when you first became aware?

No. When we first came to the place where all creation as you know it is now in existence (before the point of the emergence of creation) . . .

What we're calling the Center of Creation was not there?

It was not there. We came to pave the way.

And you knew that?

Oh, yes. We were conscious before that, when we were in the Matrix of the plasmic energy. Besides having our own personality, we were blended with the personalities of the total capacity for personality of that Matrix, which is beyond anything that you as an individual or an individualized personality have experienced, but not beyond what you as a mass being have experienced.

If there was no one to inspire you, then how . . .

No, no. We were inspired . . .

To become the Heart Council?

Yes, by that which surrounds all that you know as creation. It wasn't a message that came to us; it was, in your space-time reference, over several thousand years that we became slowly more aware (myself and my other part here) of being individuals rather than a portion of the mass. As we became slowly more aware, we didn't so much move as become aware of what to do. I believe that we didn't actually move spatially. I believe that as the creation and all these different creators began, that liquid creation of all things [the Matrix] simply expanded outward. I remember that when we started, we were close enough to . . . well, if you were looking at it and you had hands, you could reach out and touch it. (Of course, we have to reach out in our own ways to touch it.) It is now expanded and farther away spatially.

What was it, another inspiration to move? Who created gold and white light before you did? You must have replaced someone.

No. As far as I know, gold and white light was perhaps in the Matrix. It was not our job to know that. I think whatever preceded gold and white light was in the Matrix, but as far as I know, gold and white light did not exist before then.

So when you were the Heart Council there was no gold and white light as you know it?

No. It was our job just to broadcast love unconditionally, both personally and impersonally.

But at some time you became aware that that's what you should do?

No, the moment we realized that we were individuals, we realized that it was our job to do what we normally did. The Matrix does that too, but it does other things. We were perhaps nominated to do that in this space-time reference. Therefore we did it until we were notified to do something else, and we did that until we were replaced and are doing what we are doing now.

So there are two personalities here: you and your partner?

Yes.

The Heart Council said their numbers could vary from 3 to 473, so they must be expanding and merging.

Well, we have no need to do that. [Chuckles.]

How did you find a replacement? They somehow knew they should do that?

They showed up. We had thought we would do that indefinitely. We were surprised; and suddenly we were doing the thing we are doing now.

So it's possible you might suddenly become aware that you should do something else?

I should imagine that since we have moved back toward the Matrix, we might rejoin it. But until notified otherwise [chuckles], that is what we will believe.

I know you say it's the total of all of us, but I'm still looking for somebody that does the notifying.

The notifying, as far as I know, has to do with intention and purpose. One must remember that to fundamentally change existence, it is necessary to have at least illusionary separation so that the pursuit of what is owned but not felt creates tension. From what I've observed and felt, the tension is that which precedes creation. One might ask what stimulates the tension.

Why do you speak and not your partner? Are you the spokesman?

Oh, we are really one. My partner does not function in the world of thought.

Have you ever spoken through a channel like this?

Not a human channel.

What kind?

Once through a gold-light being and once through a silver-light being who was exploring the fundamentals of light.

Who were they talking to?

I believe they most often talk to extraterrestrial races.

Is it possible to ask the Matrix if it has a spokesperson?

The Matrix has nominated myself, but you could . . . a moment. It will speak, but it will be halting at best.

Well, maybe you can do it next time?

Maybe this time, because it will not have much to say. The Matrix is feeling, but it is not symbolic thought. It is primarily feeling. Feeling, in my understanding, is the foundation of all personality.

The Center of Creation: A Gate

Let's back up to the creation. When you came here there was no Center of Creation, so how did that evolve? I didn't know enough to ask that when we talked to that being. How did it start?

It did not seem to start on the basis of anything we did. We noticed after a while, broadcasting this love, that at a distance there was the Center of Creation. We saw it; it was very active. One could not miss it (with optical creator eyes, as it were). We saw it, but we did not initiate it ourselves. We were here functioning for quite some time before we saw it. So we think perhaps it was our job to create the condition of welcome so that what would emerge through the Center of Creation would want to be here. After all, why would you, as part of the Matrix, have any desire to leave it in any form for something for which you would not feel at least the love of the Matrix? I think perhaps you would have no interest at all. This is why we were sent here—to establish that love, both personal and impersonal, by which those who might choose the adventure of passing through the point of the emergence of creation would even wish to come here.

It presupposes that those beings came from someplace else.

They come from the Matrix.

Ah. So when I asked the Center of Creation where he came from, he said he didn't know; he had always been there. He had no idea.

The Center of Creation is a gate.

A gate. So there's a being who is embodied and who functions as that gate, yes?

Yes, a creator who is very specifically focused.

But he said he didn't create it; he had simply always been there.

Well, he emerged from the Matrix. We saw him form in bits and pieces. Your friend likes to say *"pouf! and he was there,"* but we saw him form more slowly; we saw the bits and pieces form.

I don't know how big our creation is, but when you look at the Milky Way galaxy, is it a thousand times bigger, a million times bigger? How big is the point of emergence at the Center of Creation? Does it have a diameter or a radius? Is it a sphere or a round emergence point?

Well, it is not so very big. I suppose about half the size of your moon.

Half its size? And he said there are 500 trillion beings in it?

Well, certainly. You know the old theological argument about how many angels can stand on the head of a pin. It is not so much the mass. What creates a being is essentially personality. And what creates *that* is feeling.

So in the Matrix, focuses of feeling will form and differentiate, then emerge through the Center of Creation.

If they desire to do so. If they do not, they still have the option to stay in the Matrix. There is no requirement; they are not shoved. [Laughs]

Nobody says, "Okay, it's time"?

Nobody says, "This is your draft notice; you are classified."

What else interests you? What else would you like to talk about that we would like to know?

Most likely you will have a better idea what to ask me when you see the transcript, I think.

Oh, you mean you've put out some leads I've missed?

Yes. But it is all right. I would say this would be enough.

Can we talk to you again if I see what I missed?

It's possible. I must tell you that to hear from the Matrix would be brief indeed, but it might be able to shove out a few words.

Is it okay for the channel?

Perhaps briefly. Good night.

Thank you very much.

Zoosh: Those are some of my favorite beings. I am so fond of them that I go to visit them often. So you are interested to hear from the Matrix, which reflects back yourself? Yes?

Oh, this is Zoosh?

Yes. I must screen, you know, because the energy is too powerful. So when I come back to speak through Robert I speak a little bit like those you have heard because I am screening. My personality takes on elements of their personality for a short time.

It looks like you're channeling the Matrix rather than Robert.

I am screening it, because if its total energy were to come through Robert . . .

We'd all fry.

It would be a barbecue. I think our friend here knows this. I must tell you that the Matrix will probably have to be the last part of the evening. I might not be able to come back after the Matrix because of the dynamic effect.

Matrix of feeling: I am this to provide you with the sense of self. This gift of the sense of self prepares you to want to *do*, but it never eliminates the desire to be of the total being that I am. You would see yourself in me because I am that which has sanctified your individuality in order to provide you with the ability to create bountifully.

All right, Zoosh here. It is not possible to continue with this because the Matrix truly cannot separate itself from being what it is. Even screening through me, I can't take it for longer than that because I have to focus it into something that it is not. All right?

Thank you.

Good night.

❖ Robert's Comments on His Experience

What did you see when we were talking to Matrix, Robert?

It was sort of like a plasma. It was watery and thick at the same time. I felt that if I were to examine the thicker areas I'd see microclusters of individual beings. I felt that the watery areas fed those beings. At one point its energy started to build so strong, I knew I couldn't take it. The term doesn't apply, but I felt sort of abstractly or artificially that beads of sweat were breaking out on the back of Zoosh's neck and steam was coming out of his eyeballs.

Did you get a color?

There weren't any stars there. The Matrix was not exactly the color of water, but the color of clear light. It was a curved mass, curving around all creations. But it was pulsing, like breathing, which reminds me of what light-energy bodies do around mountains—or people, for that matter. I felt that it could be any color but that it was basically this clear light phenomenon, for lack of a better term. Yet there were these moments when there were denser spaces where personalities were, which had a fuzzy whiteness to them. I had the impression that the color had more to do with their being densely packed than their actual color.

When I saw you pop out at the end when he left, your body was flooded with blue light.

That's interesting. Maybe that was something to help me. Blue is a color that I'm particularly fond of.

All of you were in blue. I told Zoosh once, "No guts, no glory." I'll have to tell him he's exhibiting guts. The sweat on the back of his neck . . .

Yeah, I felt like he was close to overload.

I wanted to push back the borders of reality, but I didn't realize we were going to go this far. It's like the rest of us are saying, "Okay, Mikey—here." Zoosh tried to make that joke once, referring to the little boy in the cereal commercial. That's what you are—you're Mikey. You dare to go—Zoosh, too.

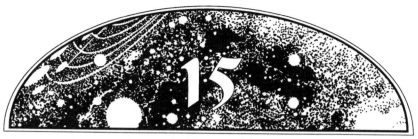

Creator Talks About Itself and the Explorer Race

September 24, 1996

hen did you first become aware of who you were and your plan for this creation?

You know, that's a good question. I became aware of the plans, the idea, the glimmer of a plan before I became aware of myself as a separate being within the scope of all beings. This is because it was perhaps inspiration. When I was a portion of other beings I remember a scenario drifting by (they always do, you know). Inspirations are readily available, and if one is more entertaining or interesting than the others, then in the matrix of precreators or even combined creators (they're all mixed up) individuals are born on the basis of their reaction to these streams of inspiration like threads coming through a cloud, the threads being inspirational scenarios. A sudden flash of light happens when an individual creator identifies with the scenario.

That's what happened to me. I was observing this particular scenario for a long time—actually past the sequence you're in now. I think it was, in terms of experiential time, perhaps a few thousand years past this now time when I saw the value of it. Also, no one else had shown any interest. The scenario was just about completely gone; it was just threading on by, and if no one became interested in it, that would be it. It would be gone for a time and then perhaps be floated by at some other future experiential moment.

I thought, " I can't let this go by. It's too good." So I individualized and hooked onto the caboose of that inspiration. Then I absorbed the inspiration for quite some experiential time, but remained within the matrix of previous and concurrent creators. Then I began to notice—it wasn't a willful act—that I was on the move. I thought perhaps I could stimulate this universe in a small way. After I noticed that I was moving, I realized this universe had to be created in such a massive way that it would be necessary to travel to some portion of available space with enough room for such a creation. It would also need to be far enough away from other creations that it would not disturb them.

This would make it necessary for other creators to make an effort to see what I was doing. I did not want to show off with this, because it was potentially very fascinating. I wanted to create this universe far enough away that I would have plenty of moments to consider how to proceed, but close enough that other creators could, by their interest, seek it out. And if they chose to, they could potentially become in some way amalgamated with this creation.

Zoosh's Initial Role

Many of them chose to become amalgamated by saying that if this creation suddenly provided enough expansion, they would be happy for their universes to expand as well. By that commitment they would make available to me any energies or wisdom they might have attained or could connect with that were not readily available. I believe it was this prediscussion with creators who were already involved in creations, as well as those who were getting ready to do them, that sent out the signal to my (now) old friend Zoosh, who then made arrangements to meet me on the way. Zoosh would act as a communications link between myself and other creators to create a network of the inspirational expansion of a universe.

Your networks largely disseminate information or feeling. That is intended; you might call it instinct. Your technical networks disseminate knowledge, but your initial network is *how you feel*. Because I needed to focus my complete and total attention on this creation, it was always my intention to allow Zoosh to remain as a link for this communication. But there came a point when Zoosh said he would need to become more involved personally and directly with beings within my creation as well as with other beings, and he asked if I could please find somebody else to function in that networking capacity.

Your Unconscious As News Broadcaster to Other Creators

That's when I hit upon (as you might say) the inspiration to let *you* do that. That is why you have always been born with the potential for feelings that were stronger than thoughts. Your feelings are so strong that they are stronger than your minds, your bodies (if one could separate them, but they are fully integrated) and even your spirit. Your feelings form an individual link for each and every portion of you. Universally (not only on this planet but throughout the whole universe of my creation) you form a sum greater than that of your individual parts. A small group of ten, with their feeling selves, might be expected to be ten times stronger than an individual, but that isn't so. If you get ten individuals together, you have a sum equal to *fifteen* feeling selves. This continues to multiply as one expands into higher numbers of created beings.

Through this system I was able to incorporate the primary function of your unconscious. Your collective unconscious and to some extent your individual unconscious, should it be important to do so, continually broadcast everything going on here on Earth (as well as other parts of the universe I've created) to other creators so that they know what is going on here. You literally took over Zoosh's task, and you have been doing that ever since. That is why so many entities will tell you what wise, wonderful and godlike beings you are, because no one here is born without that ability.

I'll tell you something else. No matter what else you get up to [chuckles] in your life, you always perform that function. This is how creators in other far-flung areas of creation know about both the benevolent and fascinating things as well as the more discomforting and tough things that are happening here. You don't all have simple lives of beauty, as you well know.

I also felt that if you had this responsibility at the unconscious level it would then be impossible, in spite of any corruption that might conceivably happen to any of you in this universe, for that thread to creatorship ever to be entirely broken. It could be twisted and bent, yes, but since this was truly an automatic function built into you, you would be unable to prevent it. This is what I would call a safety mechanism to keep you from getting too far off track. For most of the people in my creation that is not a concern. Such is not the case for those who are exposed to polarized conditions to stimulate growth as they exist here on the Earth and over the time of this creation a few other places that have had some levels of polarity—including one or two cases of even more extreme discomfort than you have had (negativity, as you are prone to call it). Even so, the automatic function that was broadcasting (not receiving, but broadcasting only) to other creators for the networking effect has always been in place here.

It was my belief, and still is, that this would give you a level of responsibility and intent to establish yourself as creators, for even though you were not receiving wisdom in return from these other creators, simply by constantly broadcasting to them you would create a momentum toward creatorship for yourself.

Even though you have slid back sometimes, that is to be expected in the learning process. (One does, after all, fall off the bicycle now and then as one learns.) Still, you have inexorably been moving forward. And in the not-too-distant future you, as a body of souls, will replace me and I will join with my equal parts and move beyond, perhaps to the place that stimulated the flow of inspirational threads through the cloud of creators and precreators.

I know you have an interest in what is beyond the level of creation. Because I have had to look at and tap sources beyond my own personal experience, I'd have to say there is definitely something beyond. It might make another book after this one [Explorer Race and Beyond] at some point in the future, because there are larger systems. As one expands through the levels of creation, one continually reaches more and more feminized levels. The polar (not even bipolar) feminization layers become more densely feminine as one moves beyond the levels of creation discussed so far in this book. I don't want to go into that myself because I think it is better for you to hear from these beings directly. I'm mentioning it because I know you're interested.

When you first became aware, were you in the Matrix around the Center of Creation, in the Center of Creation, or in what we call the Void?

Bringing in the Spirit of Adventure
and the Energy of Discomfort

I think that when I first became aware in this translucent cloud, I will call it, I was beyond the Center of Creation. I believe I might have routed my path near, if not through, the Center of Creation. This might have been helpful in rounding up souls to volunteer—because even though you are all portions of me, I needed to collect more volunteer souls when I came here to do this creation. Most of my soul makeup from which have sprung individual souls was very benign, nothing even bordering on adventurous. To be involved in such a creation it would be essential (especially to give birth to such a race as the Explorer Race) to permeate this universe with the spirit of adventure, even on a totally benign planet where everything is almost like heaven. It is essential that the spirit of adventure be there, or there would be no growth at all.

The whole purpose of this creation is to stimulate growth for all who desire it. Therefore on my way I think I passed through the auric body of the Center of Creation and collected a few rowdy souls (from my perspective in those days)—maybe I should just say hardy souls—who were more likely to be willing to stir the pot. In order to permeate the energy of those souls, I asked them if they would be willing to create a multidimensional diversity of their being within all potential soul beings within me that would be absolutely transformed with this spirit of adventure. Although these hardy souls had started out as what you would call individual souls, they were sufficiently well experienced and well advanced to be able to readily see and feel the value of this particular creation. So they did this.

It was also necessary, though not immediately, for me to pick up some energy along the way that was basically an outcast energy, an energy for which other creators had not found a useful purpose. I must admit that in order to get the level of cooperation I've received from other creators, I might very well have . . . I don't want to say *bribed*, but I was willing to find a good use for the energy of discomfort and turn it into something wherein it could be itself and be loved and cherished for being itself without having to transform itself in any way—which is essential for all creation.

All creation must know that it is thoroughly loved for being itself even though it might be many things at different times. Of course, everyone wanted to transform the energy of discomfort. A child always wants to be loved *for itself*, so after a while this being did not want to be loved conditionally anymore. I told the energy of discomfort, "Come along with me and I'll show you how you can be of benefit."

Early Experimental Use of the Energy of Discomfort

This energy was not a tremendous amount of discomfort—it was not pain or negativity as you understand it today. It was in its infancy then. It was basically what you might call the merest, the slightest, the most infinitesimal level of minor annoyance, just enough to stimulate growth. And it stayed at that level with me throughout all my travels until I got to this creation. At various times I completely let it go to seek its own level. Initially I tried to create with it an individual planet whereby beings could, at a higher level of their meditative states (I think most of you understand that), go in energy through or around or near the planet, depending upon how much growth they wanted. They could absorb just enough of that energy of minor annoyance so that they could then have the system within them that could stimulate or promote growth, because when something would annoy them, they would want to change it and would take action.

Now, that worked for quite a while. But as the Explorer Race concept began to jell and become less theoretical, I began to realize that in order for you to prove what you had learned and be sufficiently challenged, it would be necessary to let you have this energy of discomfort in a little more wholesale quantity. So various planets (this is even before Earth) were given the potential of, say, half to three-quarters of a percent of their full experience as this discomforting energy.

Before I did this I realized that there was always the potential for individuals to misuse it and build a force of what you might call negativity. Yet I realized that the cumulative effect would be that you, as a universal brain, a universal feeling heart, a universal spiritual consciousness, a universal inspired being, would absorb a significant amount of this wisdom that would result from what initially would have to be called mistakes.

At first, when this discomforting energy was having effects that were never intended by me, I felt that it might be better to eliminate the memories of that discomfort. But I was guided by a wise being who indicated that in order to build up a certain anathema, revulsion or even polarization, you would have to be able to retain, at least on the energetic level, a knowledge of the wretched excesses of extreme discomfort or negativity.

It was a tough decision, very tough, because everything in my heart said, "I can't let them go through this." But I had to make a personal sacrifice—that is, I had to sacrifice a certain amount of my moment-to-moment peace of mind so that you could learn the hard way, realizing completely that with the cumulative wisdom you would build, you would in time realize the value of minor discomfort, yet recognize quite clearly where the line ought to be drawn.

I must say that I allowed discomfort to become an extreme situation in very few settings, because it became almost immediately apparent that because you as souls in my creation, my universe, had not had any experience with such discomfort, you treated it as you would anything else new—you experimented with it. So I needed to limit discomfort somewhat, which I did. It was perhaps not until this current time in Earth that you had accumulated sufficient experience in the extremes of discomfort that you could accumulate no more without basically repeating everything. You had gone as far as you could in the dynamic of understanding discomfort.

I must admit a personal sense of relief there, because it was hard seeing you through it. And it was definitely hard for the welcomers (you call them angels) to assist you beyond the veils at the end of your physical lives, because ofttimes so many of you would have so much discomfort or misery. The welcomers were trained well, and even they were able to grow simply from your needs. So I do see the value of discomfort, though I am quite certain that no other creator in the future (or even yourselves as you take my position at some point) will ever allow discomfort to go beyond 1.75%, perhaps 2%, because of its potential for exponentially expanding through the curiosity of beings.

Discomfort: The Fast Track to Creatorship

This is not by way of an apology; it is more an explanation so that you will understand that discomfort was used so that you would learn much more quickly the level of responsibility required to become a creator. The usual method of becoming a creator takes ten billion[180] years in your concept of experiential time. To get you through the sequence faster, it was necessary to give you opportunities to make serious mistakes that you would have to make some effort to correct, even if it would not be possible to do so completely. The ramifications of this type of mistake can go beyond a single lifetime, which tends to support and even drive the soul on its journey toward balance.

Was the original inspiration the plan for expansion that the Center of Creation had with a couple of other creators? Did you then put that together with finding a proper use for discomfort?

I don't think that was the original plan. I think it was something that we realized could happen. I must admit that I felt it could happen early on, but then I did not have anything else to do but consider the creation I was planning. I don't think other creators had to consider it because of their responsibilities. I believe I was well into the creation of this universe before other creators realized its potential for expanding the sphere or, I must admit, the entirety of creation beyond what has been discussed so far, expanding the Orb of all creations. I think this was like a bonus, because when as a creator you're exposed to the vastness of creation that exists now, it is so magnificent that the concept of expanding it would not normally enter your consciousness. It always seemed unlimited to me and to other creators I've discussed it with. We did not then realize that doing something new would exponentially expand even the unlimited, because the moment something new is added, *all the ramifications* of that new thing immediately go out to all creation and necessarily expand the Orb.

Creator's Beginnings

Was the first inspiration for this creation that trailed by you just the idea of expansion?

No, the thing that trailed by me contained the foundational elements of the Explorer Race idea—not in its complexity, I must admit, but the foundational elements were all there. If I look back even now I'd have to say that if you were to look at it as blocks on the ground, it might look like a crossword puzzle without the blocks filled in, but with a definite pattern, recognizable as something that was attempting to become something. Like stepping stones, they were all there and I mainly just built on them.

So you were aware, then, in the Void. Through what they call your grandfather, you were aware of yourself then?

I was aware of the mass beings. I was in what I'd call the cloud of creation and I was aware of us as being. So I was a portion of an "us," but I did not feel a sense of individual identity.

But you were aware, when you went through the tube with the Creator of the Void?

Yes. And I believe it was the thread that caused me to become individualized. You must understand that my experience of something might not be the same as another creator's, just as your experience of your life might not be the same understanding that your mother's experience of your life might be.

I was just trying to see if you were aware during the Void and then the next generation was the past and the future.

I don't think I was aware of what you are calling the Void. I think that I was aware of being a portion of something. It is as if a portion of your brain would suddenly become individualized, jump out and start a creation of its own, yet your brain remained intact, still functioning normally.

So in the next generation—the creator of the universe of the past and future—you were individualized from that?

I was individualized in the way I have described—by following the thread. You'll probably be able to understand this much better when you get into the material on particle consciousness *[Explorer Race: Particle Personalities]*, because particles are continuously coming into you and going out. The particles that come out of you, even airborne particles, have the *entire consciousness of your being.* Granted, it might not last, but the consciousness is there, and it goes into their deep memory. Every particle that has passed through one being into another retains the full consciousness at a deep level of the being it was once a portion of. This is a theme I am aware of throughout *all* creation.

You have to understand that I'm putting it into a singular concept. When you become aware of any new bit of knowledge, the part of your brain that is involved in knowledge simultaneously becomes aware of it. If we say that a cell or a small group of cells in your brain are the localization of inspiration, that inspiration immediately spreads to the rest of your brain to portions that might stimulate action or thoughts about past and future memory and so on. It goes out to all portions within the level of their function; they all become aware of it. I became individualized when I latched onto that passing scenario.

So you came out and created this creation. Zoosh said that it was about 98.6% of the total time of creation before the Explorer Race was born. Why did it take so long?

Well, you have to understand that in order for you to want to leave me [chuckles], you had to be sufficiently bored, for starters. And the portion of me that launched into the Explorer Race was the portion that was the most adventurous. I might add that it was the portion I originally scooped up on the way and asked to permeate the rest of me, which would be individualized as souls with adventurousness. It took that long for you to say, "Oh, not another creation—same old thing!" It's pretty dynamic for the first few hundred thousand creations, you know. But you had to be self-motivated, because you weren't going to be shown.

It was different for me. I was shown the foundational elements of that which I would create, but you would not be shown that. I was attracted to something (the feminine principle), but you would need to utilize the masculine principle of pushing yourself out there without a clear purpose in mind, yet knowing you were ready to do something new on your own. Children leave home when they are ready to begin their own life; so it was necessary to wait until you were ready.

Explorer Race Beginnings

What was the beginning? How did the Explorer Race experience itself? Were there just a few at the beginning who split and fragmented?

Yes, just a few, and of course, since you were absolutely, almost densely adventurous (dense in terms of full-bodied experience), the first thing you did was go all over this universe I had created as a group, but not my total being (for the purpose of the analogy I'm separating my total being from the creation of this universe), flying around to see if it would feel better, look different, seem more interesting when you were basically on your own. In any family it's one thing to look at something as a youngster when Mom and Dad and brothers and sisters are there. In your secret thoughts you might think, Boy, what I'd love to do with that if I were alone! That's what happened. That analogy is apt. Children are patterned directly on the prototype of the Explorer Race concept. That is why they want to leave home. That is why they want to go out and do it themselves.

That's what you did. Initially there were not many of you, just three, and from those three sprang all that you have become. It's easier to travel in smaller numbers [chuckles] and keep track of your luggage, as it were. And you discovered, not unexpectedly, that when you were on your own things looked very different. You could experiment (which I encouraged you to do) a little bit in the creation of your own worlds, dabbling in worlds that were already partially created or in what I would call basic worlds—worlds that were waiting to have their specific direction encouraged. You played with that for a while.

After you had had enough personal freedom, you set about to expand yourselves into multileveled souls and so on, becoming greater numbers of those three initial beings to allow yourself the pleasure of the discovery you had when you noticed things anew.

Remember this: When you were with me completely (understand that this is an example; you are *always* with me), in the totality of me—my love and light, if I could put it that way—you saw all these things. But you discovered that when you went out on your own in this trinary group, the same things you had seen through me were new from that perspective—not completely new, but there was a great deal of newness to them. You discovered in time that that was because when you departed from me you did not bring all of me. You didn't bring the vast memory, the entire vision and so on, the entirety of my being. You had what amounted to blank spots because of the initial experience of ignorance, so you had the opportunity to discover. Discovery is the reward for adventurousness. I believe it was this moment of philosophical discovery that prompted you to believe that ignorance could be a very valuable tool, not only for re-creating, but to stimulate creation itself.

That leads to the fact that you chose to be partially ignorant; you separated yourself from your higher levels when you created this creation.

Yes, and it was by way of preparing *you* to have that motivation. Any being's ultimate motivation, regardless of what they have done or what they have created, is to go home, to return to one's total self. How could I expect you to have that experience without giving myself some level of that experience also? This precursor stimulated you toward seeing the value of that while you were still fully ensconced and functioning within my personality.

The Decision of the Nine for Seduction

So the three had become the Nine when that decision was made?

There were already many, many beings by that time—beings all over the universe—many, many beings beyond normal numbers. It was my intention that you not have such extreme negativity for your present creational episode. But the nine beings felt that in order to maximize the potential growth for the total Orb (which intention was the foundation of their decision) it was essential to have not only ignorance, which was already there, but to also create seduction. Seduction, as you know, is that which attracts you in some enticing way but which inevitably becomes something you wish you hadn't done. The Nine felt that including sufficient discomfort would establish a further tension of seduction.

Now, that is true mentally, but it didn't take into account the impact it would have on your loving selves, your heart being. I think when the Nine have to decide over again, they will choose to let that one go. You are in this loop of time, as you know, and you'll arrive back before that decision is made [see chapter 21 in *The Explorer Race* and the diagram on the next page]. I think they will choose to let that go, thus allowing the level of discomfort to be maintained at a minimum sufficient to stimulate growth but not so excessive as to cause harm.

But these Nine, were they some sort of chosen representatives, or how did they get in a position to make a decision that affected millions, billions, trillions, whatever? It wasn't what we call the Council of Nine?

No. The Council of Nine has more to do with the spiritual development. This particular network or council or group had to do with the *physical* becoming more. From their knowledge and wisdom of physicality they felt . . . I use the term "physicality" to apply to that portion of one's being that can grasp and hold something. (Although *you* can't grasp and hold something in the fourth or fifth dimension, people who are in those dimensions can do so.) The Nine felt that their decision would essentially compound the expansion. They decided to allow seduction because they felt that if the physical bodies had the opportunity to experience this level of potential mistakes, it would be possible to grow faster. It was a decision perhaps based in the *mild* influence of impatience.

Now, I can't say that these beings are impatient, but I can say that they were quite well aware of an experiential timetable. They felt (and I understand their feeling) that there would not be enough experiential time to learn everything you needed to learn before you had to replace me as a creator without speeding up the acquisition of your experiential wisdom. I believe they now understand that that was unnecessary, but I can completely understand their decision.

Strands in the Loop of Time

Can you explain some of the different versions of our history that we've heard? You created or suggested the loop of time, yes?

I created it. I felt that it was a decision worthy of having another opportunity to make, with the full awareness that they might very well make the same decision again (which they're not going to). But it *could* have gone that way. If they were to make the same decision again, then you would just go for- ward from that point. But here in this loop of time you have the oppor- tunity to discover the 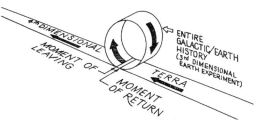 total ramifications (and so do the Nine) of what this decision would mean.

Help us understand. We came along and then there was the loop, but it wasn't really a totally focused single loop; was it various strands where different things were tried out? Otherwise we wouldn't have all these various histories.

I'd have to say that there are always those strands everywhere; that's another ongoing factor that some beings refer to as possibilities and prob- abilities and so on. These strands exist to ultimately give you the freedom of choice and the potential for variety, which I find particularly attractive.

To visualize it, instead of this wide loop, can we see it as a dozen skinnier loops?

If you were to look at it under a magnifying glass, you could see it as a braid.

Oh, really? So you go in, you go out, experience something, come back in and loop around like that?

No. We've drawn the loop of time here. Let's examine the cord of that loop. If we were to say it was a physical cord (which it isn't), you could see the loop of time. Then one might in the next sketch hold a magnifying glass over that loop of time and see that the line that creates the loop is a braid not unlike a braid of hair, in which many hairs are braided together to form . . .

Oh, hairs! I was just seeing the three strands of the braid. So we would try something, it wouldn't work out, we'd move over onto another strand, try something else?

Yes, that was always available. It wasn't something that was ongoing hundreds and thousands of times thrice. But it was available to you to have many opportunities to try many different ways so that you could thoroughly experience the full ramifications for yourself as the Explorer Race and gain wisdom as a potential creator. When one is a creator and experiences consequences, one can't just say, "Oops! Doggone it!" You have to take action, understanding that by the time you get around to taking action, there might be increasing consequences affecting many beings and you might have to take many actions.

Let's say you have a creation of a thousand beings (for the sake of simplicity) and something happens and you realize it's an *oops!* It would have been better to do it differently, but during the moment of oops! you realize that these thousand individual beings have individualized that experience. Therefore you need to create at least a thousand potentials, or maybe even 10,000, to give them ten choices each by which they might at some point resolve it and then utilize it in some beneficial way. Resolution is not sufficient; you have to turn it into something benevolent or beneficial *because that is ultimately a creator's authority or responsibility.* It's got to be worthwhile; it can't just be a slow, tortuous lesson. You have to get something out of it so that you'll learn, grow, become more and be able to apply that in some wise way in the future.

Thoughts Chosen over Feelings

There are many who have a different understanding of that decision. There's the idea that the Zetas . . . it's been explained in many different ways that that decision had to do with choosing thought instead of feelings.

If you are asking whether the Zetas chose thought instead of feelings, yes, they did.

No. My understanding of the point at which the decision was made by the Nine came from being told that the Nine chose thought instead of feelings.

Yes, that's another way to put it. Understand that if you focus in thought, it's very easy for thought to deny the feelings. But feelings can never deny the thoughts, because feelings are universally aware. Thoughts can be very focused in a very small space. One can discipline oneself to think only of a small number of things while vast realities are happening within and without.

So choosing thought would allow more negativity just because the feeling tool wasn't there.

That's right, because you wouldn't be using your greatest feeling instrument or your greatest sensing instrument, which is your feelings based in your heart selves.

You gained the ability to create, even to conceive of this loop of time, from the universe you were born in—the past and future, the inverse universe?

Yes.

This hasn't been done before, right?

It has certainly been done many times for individuals, but I do not think it has been done in such a massive way.

I am very interested in learning about your friends. Would you like to talk about them, or would they like to speak for themselves? Which would be best?

I will probably talk about them.

Wanting to Go Home, to Be Whole

Let's ask right now: What is pulling you out and inspiring you to this movement into something beyond?

Well, not only do *you* want to go home, but so do I. When you have experienced your creation as thoroughly as I have, there is the pull to go home. Because of my confidence in your ability to take over soon, what is really keeping me going is the next place. I feel I'm going to be moving into someplace in the Orb that I have not visited yet, something I have allowed myself to be ignorant of so that I will have fun. [Chuckles.]

That's like us, where we're cut off from the other levels of ourselves. So we're looking toward that, too.

Yes, and it is entirely synchronistic that we are feeling this. You are feeling this; I am, too. It is not an accident.

From your perspective, how will this work? First there were three; now there are trillions? Do we coalesce back into some kind of a small group?

Most likely the essence, the combined experience of the trinary being, will, as you say, coalesce. But the individual beings who exist on the planets and who will be portions of yourselves then, will remain in place. Nothing will be lost. But your combined experience—from what you were in the beginning of your experience as an individual and all that you have done—will probably re-form initially as that trinary unit. It is possible that you will remain in that form. It is also possible that you will become a binary unit or a single unit. But I feel you will probably like the trinary unit and stay in that form when your responsibility as a creator begins.

Will every being everywhere stay the being they are, but somehow holographically pass their experience up to this triumvirate?

You must understand that the constant automatic broadcast through your collective unconscious to other creators is going to reflect back at some point. You will have access to all of that, basically. You might say that it accumulates and is waiting for you, so at some point you will have all that wisdom mixed with equal parts of love and humor. I might add that wisdom, love and humor make up the foundation of any creator. You can't be a creator without humor, because when things happen that you hadn't planned [chuckles], you don't have the time to suffer about it; you've got to be able to laugh it off and turn it into something better.

No one has to die; nothing has to end. It is just distilled, but that does not take away any memories or wisdom from any beings who exist. It's kind of like a big photocopy.

The Unexpected, Proof There Is Someone Beyond

You're saying that creators need to be prepared for unexpected effects.

Yes, because even on the creator level, the unexpected is granted to us. This is a way creators know that there is something beyond, because something happens that is not of our own creation. I suppose a creator might be neglectful in a moment and something could happen that is of that creator's creation. But mostly it happens because something else takes place—something unexpected. Something will be added or subtracted. It's almost as if we are expanded for a moment and our responsibility is expanded as well; then there is an opening for greater wisdom and greater love and humor. When this occurs (this is common knowledge amongst creators), we know that someone in the outer bands of the Orb (if it can be quantified) has given us something. [Chuckles.] So we act.

Can I ask you to clarify the word "orb"?

I'm using the term "orb" because an orb is basically a sphere, and I like the term because you can readily see it as spherical layers around other spherical layers, yet illuminated both from within and without. If you were to go to the outer boundaries of creation, you might think there would be just some dark mass beyond. But that's not true; I have visited the outer boundaries. Although I was unable to fully . . . "experience" would be a portion of it, which is what I'm striving toward doing now. I was well able to see that not only was light coming from where I was, but there was light coming *to* it. This suggests either the potential for other orbs or something else. Something else always drives us on even at this level of responsibility.

Can you humor my ignorance for a minute? Here's my picture: There's a Center of Creation with all the creations built up around it, and then there's this matrix from which all the beings come. How does that relate to your Orb?

The Center of Creation has to be a dot in the center of the sphere, and all levels of creation beyond that become spheres around that sphere in increasing sizes, yes?

And around that is what we're calling the Matrix—beyond that.

You are calling it the Matrix.

The beings who create love and light used that term. They said that the Matrix is around the Center of Creation.

I have heard that, but I do not call it that. I'd prefer to call it "that which is to be found out." It doesn't relate directly to your language, but is more like "what is beyond." I do understand the use of that term, but for me, "matrix" feels too limited.

The way they explained it was that beings were individualized there, came into the Center of Creation and then went out.

It's as good as any other.

Well, it's going to be a hell of an adventure, right?

Hopefully, it will be a heavenly adventure. Think of some good questions for next time and we'll say good night.

❖ **Robert's Comments on His Experience**

The last image I have is of someone sort of hurtling through these spherical mists that are layered upon each other, getting to the outer boundaries of this sphere that is like a cloud, and looking beyond.

And seeing a light?

I didn't get that part; I was sort of interested in passing through the levels. The funny thing is that each level of the sphere, although it's made up of individuals, also has its own mass personality. I found that interesting.

It would be the personality of the Creator, right?

No, I think it's more than that. I think it's the mass personality of all the creators in that sphere, because it's like . . .

Is it like tiny cells making up a bigger cluster, all within the main clusters in the sphere?

No, not clusters. My understanding of clusters would be like many circles all put together, but individualized circles. It's not like that. It's like you draw a dot, then you draw a circle around that, then another circle around that and so on—outward like a bull's-eye.

That kind of layering.

Yeah, that is the system.

From a point in the center, which he said was the Center of Creation.

It's that, not clusters. Yet each layer is made up of multilevels of creations and it's just amazing to be simultaneously flying through millions or billions of creations. It feels so totally natural that it's like, "Oh, isn't that normal?"

Ah, that's wonderful!

Creator Talks About Its Friends

September 26, 1996

Well, we continue, yes. Comments on my friends who chose to accompany me on this journey?

Yes, but I have a question first. Did you see the light beyond the Orb before you created the creation? You must have, because you haven't left since you created it, right?

Yes, before. This was necessary so I could understand the role of this creation in all creations and be able to conceptually feel the effect of this particular creation on that light. Now, I have chosen to leave a little of the change unknown to me because I have the feeling that when I move up to that higher level I won't go up just one notch. It is more like taking an express elevator all the way, watching what happens and then going where I will find my next adventure. That's not unlike what people are doing this night, enjoying the celestial show [tonight's lunar eclipse], yes?

Yes. Has the unknown, beyond anything that's known, pulled you ever since you've created this creation?

How could I expect you to go through something that I myself would not be willing to go through? No, I had to have experiences similar to yours. Otherwise I would tend to become perhaps less interested in the outcome. Motivation is very important.

Can you talk about these friends in the same order that your creator [Creator of the Inverse Universe] gave them to us, so that we can keep them in the same order until we learn to know one from the other?

If you like.

1. Synchronizer of Physical Reality and Dimensions (Sephram)

He said the first one brought a total and complete understanding of all levels of physical reality.

All right. Yes, I'm not going to go into names or anything because I think that's been covered.

No, we do not know who these beings are.

Total and complete understanding of all physical reality? Ah, yes. This particular energy was most important to me. It's as if I had book knowledge and sense knowledge of physical reality (meaning that I could sense it and understand it), but not the personal knowledge. You see, I asked these individuals to come with me because it's one thing to know and understand something, even at the creator level, but it's entirely different to have personally discovered or rediscovered it yourself, experiencing the exultant joy of something new. I could not say I had that. My knowledge was experiential but not sudden and inspirational. This particular being had that knowledge. Almost everyone I asked to come with me had to have a certain qualification—enthusiasm about the project and a personal level of enthusiasm so they could exude that enthusiastic knowledge to develop this creation.

Advisor to the Angelic World Project

This particular being has that. This being has been known by many names but is not particularly well known on your Earth. I'm trying to get a name for you that would fit into your context. You know, this particular being had a lot to do with the stimulation of the angelic world, but I'd rather say that the being embodied this great wisdom. I'll give you the being's actual name rather than the name you knew it by—Sephram. The sound of this name is directly correlated to the angelic world. This being did not create the angelic world, but had a lot of motivation toward the creation of a level of beings who wanted to contribute to this creation beyond any physical life they might live or even an encapsulated etheric life. The angelic world was able to accommodate a great many beings who were interested in the project and wanted to contribute in some way. Sephram was very helpful in advising and guiding that project.

All of these beings had been creators before you met them and had created their own creation, right?

Yes.

So what creation had this being created? A creation with physical beings in it?

Yes, I think he did something a little different from what I've done here. Sephram began a universe that was created from the outside in almost as one would create a sphere and then start building spheres going inward. It was similar to the Orb, but Sephram was part way through the creation when it started creating mass that was more easily felt in the outer portions of the creation. If you were to go there you would fly through something like air, but the inner portions are much more substantive. We're talking about a single living creation that is not made up of individual beings so much as a trial run toward an unlimited physical being. This creation was an intensely personal experience for Sephram, and it was this particular level of personal experience whose cooperation I felt was desirable to ask for.

Is that creation still continuing, and does he run out and check on it every once in a while?

That creation is in continuance, and I must say that I used this model for the unlimited nature of your energy body . . . auric field, yes, but even more the energy body that is within you, that radiates about you and has the unlimited ability to bring some version of your senses to beyond. You can reach from here to the outer edges of the Orb and beyond. It is really an influence of Sephram. I decided to do that because Sephram felt that in the creation of physical beings such as yourselves, even with the intended built-in motivation, there had to be some means by which you could unconsciously in the dream state (but also consciously) reach into all creation and be able to have a sense experience. That was also influenced by Sephram. Even now you can learn to reach beyond what is reachable to your physical body and touch what is normally not touchable. You can touch the moon (which is basking in the shadow of Earth tonight) and you can equally touch the face on Mars if you choose. You can touch the stars. You can touch all beings. You can touch the emergence of creation. You can touch into the light field around the Orb, which is the combined energy of all creation, and by touching into this you can remind yourself of the eternal expansion of all loving light such as yourself.

If all of the friends of the Creator except Zoosh came into the creation at the beginning, did they fragment into souls and interact in various worlds?

Not really. Not unlike a tea bag affects water, they saturated creation with their energy to the desired extent. But they did not fragment, because I really needed their singular undivided attention most of the time. Occasionally one of them would choose to have a personal experience: be a planet, a sun, or now and then even focus into individuality as you know it. But by and large they remained complete unto themselves.

2. The Master of Maybe (Miriam)

The next one brought in a thorough understanding of maybe—the Master of Maybe.

Yes. Maybe was essential because, you understand, we were trying to create something here for which there was little precedent (none I know of, actually). It was necessary to create a potential to do something entirely different. Here maybe is the foundation of hope. I believe hope was firmly established, tested and found to be of value here on Earth by you, my Explorer Race. Maybe was a foundation for that. Understanding the limits of the language, "maybe" is perhaps the best term (you can even say that I like maybe better), because you could apply it to just about anything. Thus no matter what appears to be unmitigatingly limited, the minute you apply maybe to it, the edges become flexible and rigidity disappears quickly.

The Master of Maybe really has been tremendously influential as we come down the home stretch here, because you absolutely, positively had to have the capacity to hope, to get through difficult things and be able to look beyond what was known in any society, even what was provable in any society or reproducible as true. You had to be able to look beyond that, so you utilized hope. I think it has been very helpful.

Other beings on other planets must have this, too. For the most part they have maybe, and because you have perfected hope and radiated it out, a great many beings now have hope. Hope existed in a rudimentary form on another planet for a time, but it did not prove to be practical because it was applied to the pragmatic world. You cannot really apply it and limit it to the pragmatic world. You have to make it something that is a feeling, which is then built upon by the imagination. If it is something for which linear logic is applied, it does not work out. Hope is intended to be an inspiration, you understand, not necessarily to be played out in exactitude. That's how it was begun someplace else but not perfected. You have perfected hope largely as a result of the Master of Maybe, as we're calling that being.

Would we know him? Can we have his name so that we can interact with him?

Miriam in Atlantis

A moment. Perhaps best known as Miriam. "Miriam" relates quite nicely to the Old Testament, but before that the Master of Maybe influenced another being named Miriam who lived in a society many of you are interested in—Atlantis. Toward the end of Atlantean culture when well-meaning individuals tampered in places better left alone, it was necessary to have a voice (which turned into many voices, many individuals) with which to protest. Even though the society did not physically last, the lesson was learned by the individuals who were experimenting in genetic areas. Although they did not have the chance to present their findings—their recommendation that genetic experiments in Atlantis be suspended—they realized the fallacy of that pursuit. It was necessary, as you can understand, for your society to partially reproduce those Atlantean mistakes so your people can also recognize that it is not appropriate, and then complete it by speaking perhaps in an august body such as the United Nations or some such central educational facility, presenting not only the evidence, but their heartfelt feelings that this is an unworthy pursuit when done without love.

Now, genetic experimentation with love, kindness and compassion is acceptable, because then even the tiniest molecule or atomic structure being experimented with (not upon—that's the difference) is asked if it would care to volunteer. And only those particles who wish to be involved would then find themselves a portion of that experiment. However, particles, beings, creatures, are now drafted without their permission and sometimes treated in ways unworthy of you.

So the being formed someone named Miriam in Atlantis?

To be an advocate, yes.

Against the use of the experimentation.

Yes, and later on that being was known in biblical times. But I feel that the most important contribution of Miriam was that Atlantean experience, because she was a profound advocate for the return to heart-centered ways. This is the way Atlantis began—heart-centered. It was important to raise those points for discussion, which she did.

I'm not clear whether the Master of Maybe influenced Miriam, or lived the life of Miriam.

Influenced, not lived the life. Influenced in the sense of being so close to her that she could access that being as one might access a guide, for example.

Creating the Net of Light between All Physical Beings

What did Maybe create?

Maybe produced what I would call a "net" effect: a connection of light between all encapsulated beings in all creations everywhere. If you were to look at it from a distance you would say it looks like a net. It seems hard to imagine in terms of numbers, but it is just as easy on the creator level to create something for one being as to create something for trillions of beings and beyond; it's the same energy. That is what the Master of Maybe did.

How did the net work? Did it connect the lightbodies, the hearts and minds?

No, it connected the unexpected, meaning it connected that element of experience any person might have that related to the unexpected—the surprise, the unknown, inspiration, yes, all of that—but the best word is the "unexpected." One might describe an unpleasant experience as unexpected, but if you can understand that the intention was to initiate something new, it would have to come in through an experience of something already established. Because the unexpected was already established, the net utilized the experience of the unexpected to stimulate maybe.

When you have an aha! moment, when you have that rush and feel that connection, does that put you into that net?

You're in the net already. But when you do have an aha! moment, a sudden flash of insight, you actually feel different. It's an exultant feeling. If I may perhaps utilize a more down-to-earth comparison, it is not dissimilar to the experience of the sexual climax—not in its physical orientation, but like an echo of its exultant feeling on a physical and emotional level. This was intended so that the individual experiencing it would realize it was an important moment.

In the larger scheme of things this exultancy is something you receive in the same moment you project, so it not only stimulates the net but gives and receives at the same moment, which energizes the net under its own inspiration. The net is constantly being drawn from and stimulated at the same time. It has no source of external power, but is powered by all the beings it is connected to. When you think about that, it's quite extraordinary. That's another reason why the Master of Maybe was a very special person to bring along.

3. Master of Frequencies and Octaves (Ah-Nam-u-Ahn)
Your creator said that another being brought in a very thorough understanding of frequencies and octaves.

Yes, this was essential. Think about it: How can one even consider the creation of dimensions within the same space without having someone who can in a moment be all of those dimensions and all of the other dimensions that exist (as far as we know—I'm willing to allow that there might be more somewhere)? I could feel which dimensions were appropriate for any given planet, society, galaxy. In the larger sense any dimension that exists for any system exists for all systems, but in practical expression those dimensions might not actually be used and occupied by beings, sentient or otherwise, in every planet or system. When I was creating these systems—elucidating details, the imaging of these systems—this particular being would be present and be all dimensions during the creation, even the initial creation of any given planet. I could then feel which dimensions would be appropriately resonant for that individual planet or perhaps even entire galaxy. This was its manner of consulting.

Understand that when you're involved in a mass creation such as this, sometimes it is pleasant to have help and advice from such beings. I could have done this myself, but it would have taken so much of my attention that the creation of this universe would have taken much longer than necessary. So this was the means I chose to use.

Creating the Atonal Moment First to Make a Communications Web
What had she created before? What was she in the process of doing?

She was involved in something unusual. She created an atonal moment, meaning that there would be no sound, and even if you

attempted to make sound within that space, sound could not be produced. Then around that atonal moment—in an elliptical orbit, basically going around, ever expanding—she created all frequencies of all
tones and all potential future and past frequencies that these tones
might become, since she had that knowledge also. For instance, a
music might sound perfectly rhythmic, but as you move away only certain tones and sounds carry well, and if you get far enough away it
doesn't sound particularly like that music.

This was all done, in terms of experiential time, phenomenally
quickly, and it was wrapped around an atonal moment so that the
moment could act as a communications "web" to bring the experiential
knowledge of this creation to anyone who chose it. An atonal moment
necessarily attracts sound, and if it is overwhelmed by sound, it will
eventually accommodate it. When the atonal moment began to accommodate this sound, it also accommodated all sounds in all of their frequencies and dimensions. When it became saturated, it was sent as a
messenger to other creators (and at times even to other planets or
beings) for them to consult as a library of frequency or tone that might
be useful. Then this creator would replace it with another atonal
moment in the center.

You might ask, why use an atonal moment? Why not simply create
something with all tones and all frequencies? If that had been done, you
would now lack both the joy of discovery and the elation of moving
from one thing to another thing within the same range of experience.
An atonal moment could be seen as the opposite of tones and frequencies, so that one is enthusiastic about it when one suddenly moves into
one's opposite and has the knowledge and wisdom of being atonal as
well as being filled with tones and frequencies. When one goes out,
then one tends to exude the wonderfulness of this. However, if one
were simply programmed with tones and frequencies, one might perhaps be a bit more dry about it.

*Fascinating. How would we know this Master of Frequencies and Octaves in our
world?*

A Being Who Was a River

Perhaps the most well-known being we can mention is not human.
Is that acceptable?

Yes.

This being was perhaps best known as the Tigris River.

That stretches my mind a little.

Well, you have to understand that although a river is constantly
exchanging itself, one could say very much the same thing scientifically of
yourselves. You are constantly changing elements of yourself, and science
has come to the conclusion that most of your cellular structure changes

from time to time in your lifetime. A river simply does this more quickly.

Its spirit feels everyone who comes, looks at it and enters it?

She was the Tigris River back in more ancient times during the flowering stage of societies that promoted sacred pathways. She chose to do that to create a means by which physical beings could actually immerse themselves in the river, which they did. (Many sacred societies understood the total sacredness of that river then, and some do even now.) By so doing she was able to heighten their personal, individual experience of their multidimensional selves through the exposure to frequencies.

From time to time I will have to describe the known aspects of these beings in your culture as what you would think of as things, because many of the best known beings on your planet, although influenced by various beings, correlate to beings other than those who came with me (to portions of myself, if you don't mind).

Does this being have a name you can give?

I understand what you're saying. It's a tough one; I'm going to get it in your language as best I can. Why don't you bring me the tablet? I'll see if I can write it out: Ah-Nam-u-Ahn.

Do you want to go onto the next one?

Yes, go ahead.

4. The Spirit of Youthful Enthusiasm (Pan/Tri-Ahsk), Master of Variety

This is the one who is the spirit of youthful enthusiasm.

A moment. Right off the top I will say that you have come to know this being best as Pan. This being's youthful enthusiasm was also critical, because it was necessary that children or even offspring of cloned societies be born with the desire to fully experience life in the way that is most natural to them. This level of enthusiasm is essential, because even if you were on a planet where things were relatively benign, the project would make great demands of all beings.

If the beings are not in growth on planets where the society is stable and perhaps even very spiritual, you might ask, "What are they doing besides their daily affairs?" They very often do a deep, planetwide meditation to unite with each other (because all beings want to unite with all other beings), then with all of their people and generations everywhere. Ultimately they will unite energetically with all beings. It requires a certain amount of enthusiasm to do this, and it tends to stimulate a certain level of joy. I bring this up so that you do not come to think that beings on other planets are selfishly focused only on their own existence.

This particular being, whom you know best as Pan, I invited to come for its enthusiasm, and also because it brought something essential that sustains enthusiasm. Ofttimes you come up against a wall where you can't go any farther. Sometimes you continue to repeat experiences and bump up against that wall. What can sustain you to find another way around or through the wall is the sustained enthusiasm that is most obvious (or at least epitomized) in youth. How many times have you had an experience where you saw that something could be done in a better way and said so, but the people were satisfied with the way they were doing it? And as you worked your way up in this organization and reached a level of authority or influence, you began to initiate some of your ideas. It takes sustained youthful enthusiasm to do this, regardless of your age.

For the creation and sustenance of the Explorer Race it was necessary that people be able to have sustained youthful enthusiasm regardless of age or condition in life, because although hope is useful and even essential in prayerful situations as well as imagination, actions based upon hope will, on the physicalized feeling level, come from sustained youthful enthusiasm.

What was his creation?

The Creation of Variety

One moment. Oh, yes—another reason I found this being compatible was that it created what you know as variety. As this being traveled around the universes, becoming aware of the creations of others, if a particular creation seemed stimulating or exceptional, this being would create a variety of that experience or being that could apply in every frequency, pulse and dimension to that creation. Then it let other creators know that although a certain being or experience from someone else's creation might not be appropriate in their creation, it might become so with a varietal application. This being was and is a master of variety, and as such had a great influence on me. You've experienced that no two snowflakes (or even atoms and molecules) are precisely the same—certainly their personalities are different. It was this level of variety that I found more than appealing, literally stimulating, so I asked this being to accompany me on my journey to bring about this creation.

This being has a name I am more familiar with. I have written out its actual name here in symbol form [see illustration] because that is the way I refer to this being, an affectionate name—Tri-Ahsk. Transferring that to your current language it would sound very much like *tree-osk*.

You will notice that I separate syllables with dashes. That is because syllables are really separate sounds that make up the physicalness, the personality, the immortality of any being. For example, if you were to take your spiritual names, the individual syllable sounds would have a great deal to do with how you see yourself and how you feel yourself to be. If one were to consider for a moment one's own given name, it might be amusing for you to write it out, separating the symbols, and notice which symbol most appeals to you. Notice it mentally, then on the feeling level. You might discover that the mental is attracted to one and the feeling to another. The symbol that has the best feeling will most closely resemble the foundational sound of your actual spirit name. In fact, almost always some sound within your given name will correlate directly with your spirit name. (There is some fun homework.)

How did this being bring varietal energy into the creation? Did he do something; did he saturate the energy?

I really met this being along the way. I think it was shortly after my awareness of being an individual that I met this being. Although this being did not join me at the time we met, the infinite thrill of variety stimulated, encouraged and sustained me regarding the value of the creation I would do and its potential on other levels. You have your creation that you understand and know, yet there are many other levels of this creation, some of which are evolving and moving, not unlike yourselves. Some are actually moving toward completion—moving backward in time to the point of their inspiration. That specific level of this creation you will probably not have much to do with, although it is a level that includes Earth as you know it.

These people are not talking backward [laughs], but their evolution, the ultimate zenith, the intention of their world, is to get back to the core of their being. Society is not collapsing; it is simply moving back along the branches of a tree to the trunk, then to the taproot. And the taproot itself might be constantly searching for its seed self. This version of your universe will at some point reach its seed self, where it will be exultant for a time, then decide what it will do next, because once it has achieved that, it's on its own!

How do we know this being? Why did he choose to be known as Pan?

I'm giving you the name by which you would most likely know this being. Pan is a mythological being and the name was applied. I don't want to say he chose to become Pan; I'd rather say he chose to become what he is and that the characteristics of her personality would resemble Pan in terms of Pan's joy and in terms of Pan's desire for all beings to express themselves in all potential ways. This could, of course, lead to mischief, but this being is inclined toward a benevolent expression. You know this being by that name, but it would not be that being only.

Has that being individualized in any way that we would recognize?

That is why I gave you the name Pan.

That's the only instance, then.

Yes, because that concept of Pan (Pan is actually more of a concept) is immortal. It is ongoing, so there's no need to be individualized as anything else.

5. Master of Imagination: The Universal Mother

The next one is a total master in the field of the imaginary.

You obviously can understand how this builds on itself. How good would an inspiration be if you could not imagine how you might apply it? As this particular being illustrates, imagination is profound in the sense that . . . well, I already had the ability to think infinitely and I could picture, but I didn't have that sense of personal joy associated with these pictures. The thing I wanted more than anything else in the creation of this universe was for it to be a personal experience for all beings. Thus the imagination—especially evident here on Earth now because of the unnatural veils applied here so you would learn—is essential so that you can remember. Imagination is truly more a recollection of the things you cherish most. I felt that this being had a certain level of fun to offer.

Your creator said it helped you appreciate the level of potential involved in imagination.

That's right. Potential was more fully realized by me in terms of imaging, seeing and . . . you understand, with your imagination you cannot only see, but you can bring your senses into it and be in the imagination. You can have a sensual experience in the imagination. You can touch, smell and taste; in some cases a person's imagination is so powerful that you can even taste it. It becomes a multidimensional or perhaps multileveled experience, taking imagination beyond the conceptual into a full-bodied experience (again, the levels).

We gained that very quickly?

Well, sometimes you gain more from an experience by having less. You see, on other planets where life is benign and there are so many beauties, you do not need to use your imagination much because life itself is so pleasant and beautiful. But here, where life is not always as pleasant and beautiful as you would like, the imagination is used quite a lot, far more than on many other planets.

The Light Crystal of Spires

What had this being created before he came?

A moment. This creator created something you could somewhat identify with at a distance. If you were to see it, it would look like a large light crystal, though it would not be broken off at one end. It would seem to have spires moving out radially. It would be like seeing something that looks round, but whose roundness is based upon the spires. You could draw it by putting a dot on a page and drawing lines out from that dot, creating a circle. Imagine that in a spherical pattern, and you would have an idea. You could look (as one might look into the eye of a microscope) into any point of this light crystal and see anything that any of the other crystal lobes (comparing it to the lobes of your brain) knows of, produces or experiences. It was like a living brain wherein each crystal spire, or lobe, contained a separate personal experience and were connected with each other in the center. Each lobe could experience anything that any of the other lobes had done. The intention was to create a magnitude of imagination.

To put this in your context, a small group of people could do an exercise in imagination, such as pick something you find desirable—perhaps Earth as it might be in its beauty in the future. Each individual would imagine it, then everyone would compare notes. You would discover that many different imaginations will be presented and that each individual's imagination can be literally felt by the others, especially if the group is familiar with each other and in tune. That was built in, you see. So imagination can reach beyond thought into immortal spirit.

Do we know this being on our planet?

A moment. [Chuckles.] Perhaps it is best known as the spirit of giving. Look toward any culture that has created stories of Santa Claus and the like. I'd say the spirit of equal sharing, but that is perhaps too vague for you. Perhaps it is best known conceptually as the Universal Mother.

6. Zoosh, the Storyteller, the End-Time Historian

Now we come to our friend Zoosh.

Zoosh, as you know, is the storyteller, perhaps even the mythmaker. Because with Zoosh myths have a tendency to play out in fact, I like to think of Zoosh as the artist who conceives of something, communicates it, and during the communication it begins to form as a creation of its own. Zoosh is that which influences you toward your best or greatest potential in any given area. Zoosh encourages. Yes, you know Zoosh as the communicator, but that is not why I asked Zoosh to come. It is more that Zoosh loves what he's doing so much and is willing to take responsibility for being an influence. I have to tell you that taking responsibility for being of influence was the most important quality to me. Yes, I am used to this myself, but there are times when I would like a comrade that I can schmooze with. I asked Zoosh to come along so I'd have somebody to schmooze with. (I have to utilize a different language, because the full meaning cannot come across in English).

What had Zoosh created before he came with you?

Over the moments of experiential time, Zoosh has provided for creators all levels of the loving parent, one who encourages, supports, sustains and sometimes prods. I believe it is that level of creation that I would prefer to apply to Zoosh rather than discuss Zoosh's creation, which has already been discussed in previous material. Zoosh, you know, does this for creators as well as individuals, as I'm sure you have noticed. Sometimes we all need to be prodded a little bit.

That's not the name you know him by, is it?

Zoosh? No, I think not. But it's similar. Ah, give me the tablet. [He prints the name Zoosh with about 25 o's and exhibits it, eliciting laughter from those present.] Zoosh shortened his name a bit because he felt most people would not care to be bothered with the pronunciation.

Has he ever individualized?

Was not Zoosh a planet once? I believe Zoosh was a planet and wanted to see and feel within this creation how it was going. One cannot really tap into the totality of the concept of how it's going without being a varietal, physical and energetic being. You have to have that focus in the physical to truly understand, because the physical has everything to do with results. You see, in other dimensions one does not necessarily exist for results, but in the physical one is dealing with results all the time. As far as I can tell, Zoosh existed as a persona before I was individualized.

7. Master of Feeling: The Goddess

The next one is the Master of Feeling.

You can understand that this totally feminine energy (I don't want to say polarized; it sounds too limited) was also beneficial. Now, I understood this feeling, but I wanted to have someone to consult with, especially when my creation began to produce more beings of a polarized nature (man and woman, for instance). I wanted this being with me because she is so capable of ascribing the levels of feeling, the nuances, the subtleties. She was able by her very nature to stimulate feelings in entire universes or in a given individual in the moment. This being is sort of my first lieutenant; she sits on my right hand, as it were. If I am entirely focused on something else, she can run the store. She can take care of my creation if I am momentarily needed elsewhere.

Your creator said that you called for her during the latter portion of this creation, when you launched humanity for the sequences from our birth until we replace you. So she had a lot to do with the Explorer Race?

I'd say that she has quite a bit to do with the motivation of the Explorer Race, "motivation" meaning its movement or expansion.

What was her creation before she came with you?

Her creation was the energy you know as heart. As Zoosh likes to say, "to put not too fine a point on it," she created love as a felt experience. Love has always existed, but she created it as something that could be felt. If one existed in something that was a preponderance of a single feeling, one might not know any other feeling. Perhaps that feeling would be calm (such as the Zeta Reticulans possess). Yet the moment one instigates the feeling of love, there is an immediate physical reaction within any being, even in a nonphysical being. So she created love as a felt experience.

So love as a felt experience is not a part of other creations?

No, no, you don't understand. She created it in the beginning. There are some creations in which the society experiences what I would call a calm rhythm. Before she created love, that feeling of calm rhythm was more the practical application of love. She created the feeling of love, which is unmistakable. For example, when you're feeling love, you know it. It is quite discernible from, say, desire.

So this feeling has been created for a very long time now?

Certainly.

How do we know of this being?

I think you would perhaps know her most likely as the Goddess.

8. Master of Plasmic Energy: The Rainbow

The last one is the Plasmic Master.

The Master of Plasmic Energy, yes. Here we have a being who experiences light in all forms, including its liquid and solid forms. This is the full range of light in every color, tone and frequency in a way that can be felt as a plasma. Even the blood that runs through your bodies is a plasma, a physiological term for a combined total of many beings. Every cell is a being and has its own personality—even every neutron and particle. Air is a plasma of its own; it allows singularity within similarity, so one would say that it feels like air. You can't actually feel it, although you feel the friction as you move through it. Yet every point of energy that creates the air (not just the gases, but the foundation that supports the gases) is a plasma, because plasma represents the continuity of similars.

This was important, because I knew that in my creation there would be not only an individual experience of many things, but there would be beings on your planet and everywhere in this creation who would be so unusual, so far from what other beings are, that something would have to unite them, not just through love and creation itself, but something tangible. It is plasmic energy that unites all beings. So I asked this being to come along to disseminate itself within my creation so that if there should ever be even a single being who has moments of feeling alienated, there would be, at least on the physical level, absolute connection to other beings. You might say this being is a fail-safe organism.

What had he created?

I think before he came along with me he is best known for the creation of the light around the Orb. It is always nice, you know, to bring along someone who has preceded everyone else.

Aha! So you got sort of a guide when you brought him.

Yes. And having preceded everyone else, he not only knows what has been, what will be, what might be and so on, but I believe he might very well know what preceded him.

Has he ever individualized so that we would know him by name?

No, I do not think you will know him by any name, but you would most likely recognize her most famous aspect on Earth as a rainbow.

A rainbow?

A rainbow is, in fact, plasmic. A rainbow is liquid light, yet it celebrates its existence, however fleeting. Now I will tell you something: Rainbows are always with you, although you have the opportunity to see them only when it rains and the sun shines through. But know that they are always there.

So you and Zoosh were traveling around looking at creations, and you simply met these particular individuals and invited them along.

Yes, sometimes they came along. Zoosh and I were palling around and they joined up at different times, creating a little group—not a gang, you know [laughs], but a group. The foundation of the group experience, a group of friends, even a gang, is associated with this. One could have a gang of friends but . . . oh well, it is a polarization of a potentially good thing.

Was part of what you offered them like, "Come and help me do this awesome thing never done before, then we'll all go off and see what's out there?" They're all going with you, aren't they?

No, they will probably go their separate ways.

Really?

Certainly. They are creators in their own right, are they not? They'll go on and do what they wish.

They'll go back to their creations and you will then go alone looking to see what's out there?

I will go on. They are welcome to come with me. One or two might, but most of them will likely go on to whatever they would care to do.

They will be incredibly enriched by everything they've experienced in this creation.

Possibly. Or perhaps I am the one that is enriched.

I'm sure it goes both ways.

Possibly. I'm not certain of that with all of the beings. Certainly not with the Master of Plasmic Energy. I think perhaps I am the one that is enriched in many of these cases.

But they have enriched every living being in your creation.

Oh, yes!

We're all so much more because of them, right?

Yes.

How do they influence us? I don't understand this tea-bag kind of energy. We seem to have their qualities in our DNA and in our very life force.

Your DNA has less to do with your life force than your persona, your personality, who you are, which tends to be rather the same from one incarnation to another. They tend to influence your personalities more than your DNA. Your DNA is merely the formulaic expression of your physical self.

I see. So they've given us hope, imagination, potential—all of these things.

Not given them to you; you actually perfected hope. They have laid the foundation solidly upon which you could build.

You said that one of the beings, the Master of Imagination, was known as the Universal Mother; and the Master of Feeling, who created the feeling of love, was known as the Goddess. Is there a distinction? Some people might confuse them.

Yes, the Universal Mother would be greatly influenced by the other, yet the Universal Mother is beyond the mothers of yourselves and the animals and even the tree that seeds or the pod. The Universal Mother has to do with that which loves without condition or attachment, that one who loves throughout all time. It is that which is absolute nurturance.

Whereas the Goddess represents what?

We have already said this [creating love as a felt experience].

I mean in opposition to the nurturance.

No opposition; complementary. The purpose is that all of these elements complement each other. There is no opposition. If there were, things would not work.

Does the Goddess carry on the feelings of the Mother?

She carries through.

Does she impart them?

She laid the foundation upon which the immortal Mother might take action, so I'd rather say they're more of a team.

Let's end now.

❖ Robert's Comments on His Experience

Did you see anything you want to share?

It was a challenge, because every time the Creator spoke of each of these individual beings, my resonance to these beings shifted. It was as if the Creator shifted Its focus, so Zoosh had to shift his focus. Even so, I felt different. It was a xylophone effect, sort of different tonalities for each being. It was a bit of a strain.

You would stop and move your consciousness for each one?

Yeah.

What did you see when he was talking about Pan?

I thought he was going to talk about animals because I kept getting this flood of pictures of varieties of beings, including lots of animals we don't

have here, though maybe they've been here before—horned animals something like cows that fly or swim, insects with antennae that are big or little and fairies and solid beings, more the higher-dimensional beings.
The rainbow must have had a beautiful appearance.

Oh yeah, right. I saw the liquid-light effect that I've seen on the Pleiadian ship, where you see and feel it—it's a full-bodied experience with all your different senses. Within the color there are these little sparkling points of light. The rainbow's like that, too. If you've ever been really close to a rainbow, you'll notice that there's some sparkling stuff in there, so it's like fixed liquid light.

Creator Speaks of the Stuff of Creation

October 1, 1996

reetings. I would like to share something with you tonight before we take questions. Then I'd like to give you a brief but intimate tour throughout some of my functions.

I want you to understand why the familiarity between you on Earth here is so common, why the idea of meeting a total stranger is rare, but the idea of meeting someone for whom there is a feeling of distant familiarity is common. For the sake of simplicity, imagine for a moment that you are no longer dispatched from me but are within me as a being. Here you are, all your individual personalities encompassed within some massive light (if you wish to think of me that way) and millions of conversations going on at the same time. It would be like a low murmur within a room that you could notice if you wanted to, but that you don't usually notice unless you need to.

Imagine for a moment that you are having a conversation with other parts of myself that have personality like yourself, a stimulating discussion. Suddenly one of them says, "Time to go!" and out it goes to do some task. Although the absence might be grand in terms of experiential time (several thousand years or so), it comes back at some point and you resume the discussion exactly where you left off because the connection within me is timeless.

During all of this is sort of a light show, so that you are being bathed in different colors of light and are moving around within me while the communication from one portion of me doing this or that is affected by another portion doing something else. I mention it to you this way because it is most easily understood if you can picture me in a spatial way or if you can see me as some "thing" rather than a vague sense of personality or perhaps (even worse) an idolized sense of personality. Oh, I want you to feel good about me, naturally; I feel good about you. But to place me on a pedestal is not something I would choose you to do. I would prefer that you perhaps appreciate me and think of me as a friend rather than place me so high up on a pedestal that you necessarily cannot be equal.

You Are a Plural Being, a Whole System

I mention this because it has always been my intention that you follow in my footsteps—not only my footsteps, but your own. And it has also been my intention that you do so mostly by what you yourself have discovered. Oh, you've got your primer here within me; but on your own, with the gift of ignorance, as your friend Zoosh likes to say, you have managed to achieve a great deal—much more than you can imagine at your current manifestation. When you pass through the veils you will remember all of these things you have accomplished in previous lives and current lives as well as that which all other parts of me have accomplished. You have your individuality, but in essence you are a plural being. I am a plural being, and because you are a portion of me, that is what you are. As a plural being you can accommodate in linear, circular or spherical ways any type of thought or feeling that any portion of me has known, felt, understood or experienced. In this way you are not invaded by the thoughts, feelings and so on of other portions of yourself (identifying yourself as me), but you are accessible to others and others are accessible to you.

I tell you in this way because I want you to understand that your questions, even at the end of this life, will instantly be answered as you move through the veils. It is intended that all of you here on Earth, functioning within the veil of ignorance, have more questions than answers so that you would be driven to achieve and understand, and also so you would leave those questions as a legacy for others when you move on in your immortal path. Perhaps some of the best things ever left to anyone are questions that encourage others to live their lives to the fullest in whatever their chosen field might be, and to discover answers to these questions or define those answers in the manner of their own personality.

It is true and necessary to understand that when you are beyond the veil, you realize that the reason you have more questions than answers is because other portions of yourself (I and that which is totally you) have all those answers and more. Yet when you are in the veil of ignorance here, often it is the simple questions like *why*? that keep you going. Sometimes you cry out *why*? in agony and other times in humor, or even when feeling miffed. Yet it is the very act of questioning that reaffirms life. If you can ask the question, you give yourself permission to find the answer. You thus reaffirm your immortality to seek the answer personally and you also stimulate others—other parts of you, other parts of me—who have the answer to get it to you in some way so that you can appreciate it.

I want you to understand that you are a part of a whole system, not some disjointed, leftover thing that is permanently cut off because you failed to please me at this time or that—never that. You are on a journey, an adventure, to create, to invent and to sustain creation. It is truly the sustenance of creation that all creators live for.

Let's start with your creation. First you have the inspiration. How do you then go about it? We've had a lot of these outside consultants. Do you say, "Bring me tools to create dimensions"? What do you do?

It is an interesting question, that, because it obviously asks, "What is the stuff you use to mold this creation? Where do you find the stuff?"

For starters, very often creations are built backward. First one sees what one wants to create. Remember that I looked at that thread of inspiration and I had the feeling, like a formula, of what to do. On my eventual travels with my companion and then multiple companions, as I was moving toward the general area where I felt my particular creation would be most welcome, I reviewed, as you would say, potential scenarios of what my creation might look like. I wanted it to be something that would have the maximum amount of flexibility for variation, meaning that I didn't want it to be rigidly fixed. I didn't want it to be too simplistic, either. I wanted it to have simple basic building blocks that were exchangeable through many of the planets, galaxies and so on, but I also wanted it to have sufficient capacity for variety so that I or anyone who succeeded me would never be bored and would feel a complete sense of freedom to adapt this creation to its own vision (meaning you, of course).

Looking at My Potential Creation from Its Midpoint

Now, in the course of those scenarios I happened upon one that I would call a median scenario, one in which I could create any of many different versions from that midpoint, as one might start out building a wheel from the point in the center. When I reached that midpoint (and it was quite vast), I did something that many creators do: I focused entirely upon that creation, almost like one might create an imaginative thing. You would see something, perhaps something you knew, perhaps something you didn't know, and while you were holding that picture in imagination you would examine all the details.

Now, you have been told by my friend Zoosh that imagination is the divine part of the mind. Now I will tell you why. While I held that picture I invited any and all bits of material from any creation or existence anywhere that wished to come and be involved in this creation, to come and take a place in this imagined picture that is like a template. I held this picture, in terms of experiential time, for perhaps several million years while I examined its details minutely. It is a picture I have created, yet the closer I examine it in the smallest detail, the more complex it seems to become, for I've invited not only light, form and shape, but also personality. Some come directly from me, some from other creators, some from the mass light of creation beyond all spherical expressions of such creation.

At some point it filled in sufficiently and I begin to utilize various levels of time and expressions of dimension through the use of my imagination of how this creation, as it looked in that moment, came to be that way. So I worked my way backward, utilizing that mass and that material. The mass and material basically became the players, as in an actors studio. They played different parts, and we re-created it back to the point of its beginning. (Not to put any great damper on the idea of the big bang theory, but that never happened. It's a nice idea, but it needs to go back to the drawing board.) It started as a thing of beauty; we traced it back to the point where all that came was merged in one mass of energy, then to that point where I imagined it and allowed it to go forward.

Very often creations are created from a midpoint—in this case, a midpoint with the most flexible variability—and then go back to a starting point to unite and go forward to the midpoint and beyond. That's how I did it.

Matter Responds to Loving Invitation

As you can see, imagination is the divine part of the mind, and when you go beyond the veils you understand that your imagination truly does create reality. The sooner you know this the better, because it is not just a picture one holds; it is also the complete understanding that everything is alive and wants to be what it chooses. A molecule might want to be a stone. Perhaps it would like to participate in the manufacture of something man has made, to be a full-time chair, for instance. Or perhaps it would like to be a person. But never is it drafted and told, "I don't care if you're a typewriter; now I want you to be a book"— never. It is always done only on loving invitation. As you learn to understand that, you will be able to do the thing you have always wanted to do ever since you have been manifested in physical form—think something and thereby create it.

The reason you have not mastered that is because when you're struggling with that which is destructive or creative, you cannot be allowed to create something destructive, because no molecule wants to be a part of that. No piece of material, no matter, wants to destroy something against that something's will or be used against its own will. So it won't do it. You have to have total cooperation from the matter itself; it must want to do it. When you are able to do that with love and harmony, then you will be able to do as our friend says—*pouf!*

When you called in matter that was intelligent, it presupposes that some of it came from beyond the creation.

What makes you think that the matter was intelligent?

Sentient? Conscious? What's a good word?

Matter Has Love and Personality

The reason I want to pick at this point is that I do not want to limit matter to being only of thought. Rather, matter is recognizable when it has *love and personality.* Thought is not a factor of immortality. If one could condense love outside the realm of any being, you would find within it masses of threads of personality. Love is by its very nature all-encompassing, and as such, personality is attracted to it. That is obvious, is it not? You have personalities; you are attracted to love, especially unconditional love. I know of no Earth person who is not. No matter who you might offer as an example, they're all attracted to it. Certainly after life they rush toward love.

I understand that the common idea is "sentient" or "conscious," but I want to help you move past that limit because it would limit the reach of this material in printed form to only those who think. I would like this material to go beyond those who think to those who primarily feel, because those who feel even more powerfully than they think are likely to be the first who can lead you (or at least show you how) to truly be yourselves. After all is said and done, you are, at your root, love and personality.

What I was trying to get at was that you called this forth from other creations, but also from beyond anything that had ever been created. That's the "beyond" we're looking for, right?

As one goes beyond, there is something like a cloud of a sort of pre-ordained material. It is a cloud of personality and love waiting to be inspired to go somewhere to manifest and be manifested. It's like a line outside a movie theater with no movie listed, and suddenly one is listed and a bunch of people say, "That's for me!"

Have they never appeared in a movie, or have they already been in a movie but got bored and went back and are waiting?

At that level they have not. They are simply love and personality, totally pure, with no impact of anything that you would call experience beyond that love and personality. They are not a blank slate, but the makings of all things.

Participants from Outside

But in the Center of Creation you have personalities that have had experience and are coming to look for something else.

Yes, sort of a recycling area. [Chuckles.]

When you called forth, did that bring to you what I call the outside consultants, the beings who make dimensions and who come from outside your creation?

The beings we referred to last week?

Not the friends, no. Before that we talked to beings who said they had created dimensions. They were called in, you know, as outside consultants.

Yes, that's when they came in. Even though the message goes out instantaneously to all creations, one must understand that these beings are occupied. They might not be able to show up immediately, so I waited until I felt that everyone and everything was there that I needed for the building blocks of my creation. I had to wait a little while for some beings. [Chuckles.] You know, good consultants are hard to find! [Chuckles.] If you have to wait, you wait.

Are the personalities in your creation generated by you, or are they generated by the eight friends? Or are those eight friends simply adding personality to the soup?

They're not generated by my eight friends. They're not even adding personality to the soup anymore; they've done that. It is more that they came because they are welcome in that initial template and they were interested in the movie, as in my analogy.

Are there beings in the Explorer Race whose original essences were not generated by you but come from other creations?

No one comes to this creation who has not passed through me. This does not mean that other beings from other creations cannot come. But they must pass through me. It is not exactly a safety mechanism, but it is by way of saying, "If you are interested in this project (to put it in linear terms), then please come and participate. If you are interested in some other project, know that this isn't the one. Thank you and I'll see you around." But they must have a desire to participate. They can come with their own agenda; that is all right. But they must be able to express that agenda within the plot line (if I might use that analogy) of this creation.

If it is an agenda that is perhaps more easily fulfilled in someone else's creation, then I will steer them in that direction. If, on the other hand, it is an agenda that will work against my creation's intention, I will ask them to wait. I do not necessarily send them away. If they wish to observe, I will say, "Be my guest." But I do not let them pass if they have an agenda that works against this agenda. That is why you are often told that you are protected. You are protected from those who would turn this creation into something that I did not desire for you or me. So you are protected from taking meandering offroads that might lead to the fulfillment of some other being but not necessarily yourselves.

Let me pursue that a little further. When you move up, the Explorer Race will become the Creator. What percentage of the beings in physicality would go back to other creations?

That's not decided. That's entirely up to them, but you want a rough estimate, yes?

I just wondered how that worked—whether you could go back and forth in different creations, like visiting different galaxies.

It is possible that some of the beings will say, "Well, that's enough, thank you very much" and go on to whatever else they choose to do. I think most of them will come with you because it's an exciting thing, a great adventure. As far as I know, it hasn't been done before. I can't imagine anybody participating in this creation for this long and saying, "I'm not interested in the culmination of this experience." I would be very surprised if more than one or two go somewhere else, but there's always the person who wants to beat the traffic.

In the scenario you painted where you had a midpoint and filled in that matrix, then went back to create within that matrix and continued forward, where does our Explorer Race fit in?

You must understand that you came with me. You were me; there was no separation—there's no separation now, either. For the sake of the explanation, you and I were one. If you wanted to say you were cells in my brain, that's it. You are a portion of me that I have birthed, do you understand? You're asking where you fit in—you arrived *with me.*

The Explorer Race's Position in the Time Sequence
Where does it look like we are at this moment? Are we near the end?

You're near the beginning. You're near your beginning of self-motivated intention. Right now you're a mass of individual personalities, but as you remerge and . . . you know, after you go to the fourth dimension, you are not going to become the Creator immediately. For me it's like the blink of an eye, but for you it will be quite awhile. During that time you will go out, explore the planets and so on. But at some point you will become very much more aware of all of the portions of you, whether they be billions and billions of trillions or whether they be smaller numbers. And you will realize that with the slightest motion, almost without any effort on your part, you can be complete.

Sometimes the feelings come up for you now—not just for people on the spiritual path—that you are not complete, that there is something missing. But by that time in the future you will be beyond that feeling. It will be something that everyone knows and understands, and when you are beyond that feeling you will be at the point where you will easily be able to change your mind and be complete and total. When you do that you will remerge into the complete being of a creator, with all of your individual personalities sharing all the combined knowledge, including that which *I* know, and you will go on and replace me. This will take a little experiential time, but when you look back on it, it will seem very fast indeed. Do you know, even now when you look back on something, especially looking fondly back, it seems like it was over too soon. Yet when you were in the midst of it, it seemed like it would never end.

You said that we're almost at the end of the loop?

Yes.

But that means we're near the culmination of the Explorer Race.

That's right. You're near the end of what it took you to get here, and you're near the beginning of what you will do when you get to the next stage.

Elongating the Sphere of Creation

One of the beings who was called in said that you had stretched your creation out from the spherical so it would not be balanced. When we become the Creator, are we going to put it back in balance?

It's in balance. The advantage of elongating a sphere is this: All balanced creations, from the biggest to the smallest, tend to be based on the spherical shape. But the minute you pull and expand it, you allow for fundamental shapes and more variations. It is natural for all life to want to be spherical; that is the natural shape. When you take something spherical and pull it out, it wants to become spherical again, so there is a stress. To utilize the stress you will create whatever shapes you need to in order to reunite. You could cut something that looks like the shape of a pie slice. On its own it would look almost triangular, but if you shove enough of them together you'll have a circle. That need to reunite will stimulate further creation and allow for other shapes. That is why I felt it was perhaps a good thing to do, for if the creation were entirely spherical, you would have had no need to create as much as you have created.

Understand that I am not creating a great deal of boundary between myself and you; you and I are a little interchangeable now. But we had to do more. We couldn't just sit back and let the natural process take place. If we had done that, you would not have had the opportunity to accumulate so much experience because there wouldn't have been anything to strive for on a physical level.

You know, when a snowball rolls downhill it does not become square. It tends to become rounder [laughs] as it goes down the hill; it has a natural propensity for that spherical shape. Yet if we take something that is born for that spherical shape and stretch it out, just like an elastic it will tend to return to its natural shape even if it has to take a long path to do it. This forces those who are stretched out to be creative, be they few or many. So from the beginning you were urged out of necessity to be creative in the most fundamental ways.

If I understand right, your creator, who created the past and future where there's no now moment, made motions partly over here and partly over there, but nothing in the middle. That's not a circle, is it?

From Past and Future Came the Present, Where One Learns

If we look at it as a line, it doesn't seem to be a circle. But let's change that line to a tube. The minute we do that and set it on its end, it certainly is circular even though the tube is hollow. The outer part of the tube is what will be and the inner part of the tube is what was. But what goes inside the tube? Anything that's flowing by is and goes through the tube. You see, shapes really do apply in terms of your creativity. The moment I said "change that line to a tube," explaining for the sake of the book, you got it immediately. Do you understand? That is how shapes can be self-explanatory.

So is your creation in the isness of that creation there? I got a feeling that it was within . . .

Within the context of your description and your question, yes, because my creation has more to do with what is. I am able to use past and present because of my birthright, yet it takes place more in the present because it is in the present moment that one learns. One might accumulate in the past and anticipate in the future, but one learns in the present.

You had this idea long before the creator created the Void and before its offspring, your creator, created the past and the future. You had to wait until they did that—so there was a timing involved, right?

In terms of experiential time, yes. That waiting is really the main reason I had the leisure to travel about to look at other creations. You see, I could feel that it wasn't quite the right time; the moment wasn't there for my creation. I must admit I didn't consciously think about why it wasn't. At that level and at your own natural level, you don't think about it. You don't analyze it; you don't justify it; you just know. It is either that this is the right moment, or that the moment isn't here yet. That's it. You accept it and go on.

Because that moment didn't arrive for a long time, I had the luxury of traveling about to absorb other people's creations, to look, to feel, to sense, to be in them for a moment if I wished. As it turned out, that was very helpful. Not only did I meet beings I was destined to meet, but I also had a chance to reconsider my own creation based upon the variety of creations I was seeing. All in all, my particular travel was broadening.

Most of the creations you went to were not individuality-oriented, I understand, but had more of a group concept.

Yes. I wanted to create something whereby every portion of the creation would have its individual personality, yet could assimilate within the personalities of every other portion. From the smallest cell, particle, neutron or even energy that makes up a neutron to the most massive galaxy, everything has its own personality. Your Earth has her own personality. Everything has it, yet when united through love and personality, there is a union, a bond.

I wanted to create that. That was always my vision. I didn't quite realize how much variety was at my disposal until I took my tour. So you might say that while I was waiting for these other things to happen (though I didn't consciously think what I was waiting for), I made good use of my moments.

There's so much more we need to know.

Responsibility

In this creation that you are currently involved in, you will perhaps have the responsibility of creation thrust upon you sooner than I did. When you think about it, I had a chance to be a portion of some other mass of creation. Since you were a portion of me then, you had that chance, too. But when you became singularly your own, when you were birthed into this testament that I intend to leave you, then you started this voyage. It has been long and at times arduous, but I believe the rewards will more than make up for it.

After I have gone on to my next level and you are involved in running this show, you will find that it is necessary to pay attention and be responsible quite quickly. It is important for you to know that many creators are interested in this creation; you will have a great deal of help. And very often parts of you, different bits of your total personality, will not have to be present all of the time. Bits of you will be able to wander about for even thousands of experiential years, taking little side trips on your journeys to go here and there, not just on errands but often for the sheer pleasure of it. You have decided, and I believe you will carry it out, to continue to accumulate and grow beyond this creation so that you can keep up, as you like to say.

You created the Explorer Race to broadcast from their unconscious level to all of the other creators. At what point does that unconscious become conscious? At what point do we become that whole being, not whole with the highest self, but the whole consciousness?

Prolonging the Pleasure of Becoming Your Unconscious

Remember that I said there's a time in the future when . . . it's almost like changing your mind; it's going to be a feeling. Not only are there other parts of you that are right there, but with the slightest effort you can be united in those parts. For me it's like a twinkling, but for you it might be a thousand years or so while you establish that unity where you as individuals are your complete self. Then there will be no death, because when you are your complete self you will be able to manifest any physical form for yourselves and it will not deteriorate in any way. You will live like that for a time, and when you realize that you have accomplished all you can do singularly, you will naturally choose to come together and take over. You will experience just the slightest change of perception in which you basically become your unconscious, which allows you to feel very comfortable with the level of responsibility.

Right now you are not consciously responsible for your autonomic system in your body; it runs on its own. Your unconscious causes it to run. When you become your unconscious, it will be easy to run your autonomic system—your heart beating, blood moving through all the vessels. Your lightbody is a little different, but similar. It will be so easy that it will require less of your attention than moving your little finger slightly now or humming a tune you can't forget ("Rock of Ages" or some such thing). You will become your unconscious in stages. It will seem like stages to you, but this is mostly to prolong the pleasure. You see, we want to prolong the pleasure so that the gift is enjoyable and does not pass so quickly that you can't savor the joy of it.

Have some beings accomplished that now, like Babaji and Sai Baba? Are these beings at that level?

Not quite, but they are very close, because these beings are able to, at a moment's notice . . .

. . . to manifest a body.

Yes, be other places physically and so on. They are very close to that level and at times can maintain it. But they know better than to maintain that level all the time. If they did, they would be unavailable to you, you see. They know that they are here to help, and in order to help they must be a part of you; they must look like you. If they don't, then they take the terrible risk of being perceived as a god. Your society right now is still hanging onto the idea that any god is to be looked up to and revered, untouchable by man. It is that very acculturated thought that is stifling the feelings, and it is truly the feelings that make up who you are. But you will get past that. That is why this book and others, to say nothing of teachers and your own observances from living your life, are necessary and perhaps worthy.

Are there others you could name besides Babaji and Sai Baba?

I'm sure there are several others that the readers could think of. I don't want to single individuals out for unnecessary media attention. Why complicate their good works?

Individual Emergence

Bentov, on his way to God realization, saw a cosmos with three chakras and 49 universes on a chromosome, and he said that was Alpha. Is that something he just saw? Is that a cell in you, or is that your creation? Where can I place that?

You can place that within the point of emergence of his personality. If you can understand that the grandeur of each and every person or personality is so magnificent that it is beyond the capacity of any living language to describe and can only be felt, then we can understand where such an image might be found. Words can give only a pale description. It is always found in the heart. How do you describe the most magnificent sunset? Words cannot do justice to it, but you must try.

If other beings took the trip through the levels to God realization, they might not see that?

They might not see it from *that* angle, but probably from their own. That is appropriate, for it is intended that the route be familiar. You see, that route was familiar to your friend because that is his unique route. For you it would be Iyour unique route, and you couldn't get lost because you would know your way instinctively. Never worry about getting lost. No one is ever lost; sometimes you take a side trip, but you are never lost.

Origins of Seven Teachers

We work with a teacher . . . it's turned into a set of teachers. I'm going to name some beings who are the chakra forces we've been told about. Are they part of you, or from outside your creation? Are Agni, Shiva, Jehovah, YHWH, the Logos, Lucifer and Id created by you, or are they from someplace else?

One at a time for the sake of the functional mechanics here.

Agni?

Part of myself.

Shiva?

We are such old friends, but I suppose I must say from elsewhere.

One of the eight?

No.

Jehovah?

Part of myself.

YHWH?

A first cousin of myself. Part of myself, yet with connections elsewhere.

But not one of the eight friends of the Creator.

No, I don't want to identify the eight with any of these beings you mentioned. Let's just go on and finish the list.

Logos?

Part of myself.

Lucifer?

Not part of myself, but a very important invited guest. Obviously, how could you grow without Lucifer? You couldn't grow without there being tension.

Id?

Not part of myself, but a worthy creator offspring.

The Teacher for the Eighth Chakra

Who is the eighth chakra, the soul star?

[Chuckles.] What is the most worthy of all the beings? It is always that which is felt.

But this is beyond those seven I named; this one I don't know yet.

You know it; it is not a thought, not a word, but a feeling.

Someone who exemplifies love, obviously.

Yes. Essentially, it is affection. Affection is that which can be universalized. You can have great affection for a cat, a dog, a horse, a pony, certainly a person, even a thing; you might even have affection for your car. And while your car cannot return your affection, the love you have when you sit in it almost makes it feel as if it does.

Is there a name for the soul star, the eighth chakra?

It is a feeling: the warmth of eternal love, which is a physical feeling as well as a feeling that knows no bounds in any universe. So it is always that which unites all and is a constant. You might say it is *the constant*, for without that constant, why bother?

Will we need a teacher with a name, as we have with these other chakras, when we're ready for that level?

The teacher is within all of you. Bring in the warmth that you can feel physically in your chest or anywhere in your body. The warmth that is within causes you to relax, to feel for just a moment that there is more and that the more loves you. It is a feeling; it is a constant that is there. But you must seek it; you must look for that warmth, and when you find it, go into it. Embrace it and let it embrace you. In that way it is simple. It does not require a great code to understand. It does not need to have a cosine or sine. It is something that is there for you at any moment, yet it is something you must choose to look for. You can feel it if you are physical or nonphysical, and you can feel it now.

I can feel it right here. Ah, even when we are nonphysical, we still have a heart chakra or something in that area.

Yes. That is the center of all creation.

Oh, even in our lightbody.

Beyond and before. It is the center of all creation, for without it no portion of matter would desire to be with any other matter. If there is not love and affection, why bother? If there were no love, why would you as a molecule wish to join any other molecules, even if it were to create the most magnificent instrument to save all life? Why bother?

Did the beautiful poems that Van Tassell channeled come from you?

Well, I would like to think that it was his creation on his higher level, his overall total being, but perhaps I provided the bits and he put them into forms. He was a great visionary, some would say a person before his time, but I think he was right on time. He waved a flag and said, "It's here, now." And others said, "Oh yes, you're right." They couldn't destroy him, though.

No, though they tried.

Yes.

Can we talk to you again next time?

Yes. You wish to continue?

Sure.

Then we shall. Good night.

❖ Robert's Comments on His Experience

Is your heart chakra nice and warm?

Yeah. I really could feel that. The Creator is getting more personable. I feel like He's letting out bits and pieces of His personality. I have the impression that He's going to show up in the particle book, because when He was talking about particles, I could see an atomic structure. Then it zoomed in and I could see a particle within the particle and it zoomed in even farther. There were uncountable billions of bits within that particle. It was as if you could go in and discover just as much as you can going out. It was infinite.

Creator Discusses Successes and the Outworking of Negativity

October 3, 1996

reetings. We continue.

I would like to know what you are most pleased about in your creation or in the springing forth of the Explorer Race.

I'm so glad you asked that. I'd have to say that I am particularly pleased with the way things have turned out. In the beginning (understand that the beginning was sort of the middle) I must admit that I was considering that perhaps I had taken on too much. Maybe it wasn't going to be quite as direct a route as I had thought to accomplish my purposes. But something wonderful happened: the matter that came here to become the planets, the people, everything, became so joyous to be involved in this project that gradually after time went on (experiential time, you understand) I needed to give less and less energy to the project. The mass of the material that came from elsewhere to join me in this creation had brought with it the capacity to greatly energize the project. I had not thought they would do it because they had their own agendas, as you say.

Your Ability to Forgive

What pleased me more than anything else was the level of cooperation from the tiniest atom to the largest galaxy. The cooperation in this project was wonderful, but I suppose I am most pleased about the capacity to forgive, which was really expanded well in this creation.

Many people and beings have come and gone in this creation, and most were benevolent, benign. But there were times when things happened that were a little more dramatic (to say nothing of what has happened on Earth). Yet I would have to say that what I am most pleased with (even though on a daily basis you might not agree) is the marvelous capacity of your souls to forgive the transgressions of others.

There have been other struggles between planets where a misdeed was done and the planets or cultures never forgave each other. They remained enemies for so long that it was necessary to intercede—something I do not take lightly. I won't do it unless it's absolutely necessary.

That's where the "prime directive" would have come from?

Yes, that's right. But here on Earth the capacity to forgive has been most impressive. For example, in recent history your country was able to see the German people at the end of World War II as human beings apart from what their representatives did, even though the people of Germany got caught up into pretty heinous things during World War II. But right after that war your government sent food and assistance to the people of Germany, even though there was a price to pay in your political alliances with others. Now, that might seem like something other than forgiveness, but it is forgiveness, because the decision was made from compassion. That forgiveness was rapid.

I'm not saying that everyone has forgiven the German people of those times for doing what they did—or, for that matter, those on other sides and in other wars. But I'd have to say that your society has worked out a means by which people can pay for what they've done and be forgiven. This really sprang forth from religion. I believe it is in human nature (or the nature of the soul) to let go of the past and be more optimistic about the future. What has been done here—the acceleration, application and expansion of forgiveness—is something I'm particularly pleased with.

See Things As They Are and Celebrate Your Differences

As the Explorer Race continues in its training to become your successor, what do they most need to focus on in terms of developing character traits or preparing themselves?

Absolutely without a doubt what is needed is to be able to look at things truthfully as they are, and by all means have your optimism, your dreams, your ideals, your goals—that's fine. But you must be able to *see things as they are!* You can't turn a blind eye toward something simply because you do not want it to be there. As a creator you must be able to be absolutely honest. I'd also say that you have to be able to see past the disguises others wear and respond to their real needs. By real needs I do not mean the needs you project on them because you have an agenda, like changing their minds or something, but you need to be able to sense the needs of others. If it is something that you can assist with comfortably, then do so or find others to do so. A creator must understand that if one amongst you is suffering, you are all hurt. This is a reality. You have discovered that you can put on your suit of armor, but in reality there's no suit of armor; you are all hurt.

Other traits you might develop? Perhaps it is something you have worked on, especially in this country (though there are other countries as well)—the ability to enjoy the differences amongst people and even celebrate them. I think you've made significant progress there. You don't have to like everyone or everything, but giving respect and appreciation is essential. Just because you don't like it (I'm not saying to like it if it isn't likeable) doesn't mean that there isn't something or someone or someplace that it is appropriate for. If something is not right for you, let it go, recognizing that it needs to exist for some reason, and that when it no longer needs to exist it will no longer be there. This does not mean that you accept it and say that injustices and cruelty are all right. I'm talking about people and their personalities. If you don't like someone's personality, you don't have to hang around with that person, but recognize that it's there for a reason.

The last thing is that every chance you have, get together with groups of people these days, especially divergent groups who might not ordinarily gravitate together, people who are trying to do something for the greater good or who battle forest fires or what-have-you. Try to find the good in things and groups and try to enjoy cooperating as much as possible, because when you all come together again you won't have better-than and less-than; you will all be equal. You will all have opportunities to cooperate, interact, learn and develop new wisdom from others. Learn how to cooperate and enjoy it even if it's for a moment. If you can't stand the person you're cooperating with but you know it needs to be done, just say, "Well, it's a good thing. When this is done we can look at it and admire it and then tip our hats to each other and go our separate ways.8 On the creator level you really have to be able to do that. Let me give you an example.

Bringing in Discomfort

When I was coming here to do this creation, it was crystal clear to me that this creation was intended to stimulate growth, not only for you but everyone—even for other creations, if they wished to participate (which they do, as it turns out). I was not capable of providing discomfort (negativity, as you call it), so I knew that I was going to have to attract someone who could. This has been mentioned before, but I'm going to mention it again because when I asked this being to come, it was originally intended to provide just a minor degree of discomfort, enough to stimulate change and growth. But because of what people got caught up in doing and because of the extremes and the exploration of what *not* to do by example, this being was forced somewhat into becoming something really quite awful.

As a result, I had to be able to look at this being with love and compassion, even friendliness. This being has often come to me and said, "How can I get out of this job?" [Chuckles.] "This isn't what we talked about when we were talking about your creation as you wanted to do it." It wasn't what we talked about, of course, so I feel a little personally responsible. You have to be able to see past what beings have become, not necessarily through their own choosing. That's not only forgiveness, but redemption. Since I've had to do this, I've actually seen you do that as well. That's why I mention that I'm happy about what you have done with forgiveness. Very often you've had to forgive people you would never imagine forgiving. I [chuckles] have had to do the same thing.

And we've had to forgive ourselves, too.

Most important.

The Negative Sirians

That brings up the negative Sirians who somehow got caught up in that ghastly negativity. They'll be lovingly nurtured now through the system that will follow behind us, right?

Yes. When people go through some kind of a trauma here you have people come in (it's a little more enlightened nowadays) and counsel them and so on. This is a good system; in many governmental circles this has been activated (in education, law enforcement and so on). This is a really good thing. This is also the case with these individuals [negative Sirians] who are spreading out somewhat on third-dimensional Earth, of which you are no longer really a portion. They will have many teachers and guides, most of whom they will see in their own level of physicality, who will not be like them but who will come and speak to them in great gatherings to inspire them, to radiate loving energy and, most important, to stimulate and bring up the loving energy within them.

These people are being initiated, and this is the manner and means by which they will be nurtured. They will also be given the foundational elements of principles by which they can live. I would say that it is not that far away from the commandments referred to in the Bible (though they weren't commandments as much as guidelines, urgings or suggestions). Those "commandments," as it were, will be provided to them in the most basic things of life.

Here is a typical commandment: "It is safe to tell the truth." It is so much different to have a statement like that. That's not a commandment; it's really a nurturing statement. This, by the way, is how the original commandments read, but they were changed to something more authoritative because the people who received those commandments felt that the people would not accept suggestions, that they had to be told what to do. I understand that. It wasn't my intention to have it done that way, but I do understand why it was done.

So these beings who have come to 3.0 Earth are being nurtured and supported, and basic suggestions are being given to them, such as the most useful and valuable character traits to support and the ones to be tolerant of and so on—sort of a foundational ethic given with a great deal of love and support. So yes, they are being supported.

I've felt their energy. I know how far love and support are from the way they were living.

Yes, it's going to be a climb for them. But it will be a pleasant climb.

Will they take the same path out of here that we do, then go out as partners for a race to other planets?

No, I think not. I don't think they'll become the Explorer Race. I think that they are more likely to pursue an avenue along the lines of what you call avatar or philosopher. I'd say the philosopher-avatar spread would be more appropriate. They will go into teaching, explaining. They're going to be inspired by those who come to see them in these early days, and they will want to be like that. To them that will be God, and they will want to be like God. That is more likely the path they will choose.

They deserve it.

They certainly do.

Thoughts from Hindsight

If there is anything that you could change in your creation in hindsight, what would that be? Negativity?

Yes. In hindsight, if I could do it, I would not have allowed so many extremes of discomfort and suffering. I think this perhaps could have been done more quickly, or at least the levels of suffering might have been done earlier on, but it's hard to say. Within the scope of the entire project, all of the experiences, changing even the slightest thing would inevitably change the outcome. Regardless, I'd have to say that I regret the level of suffering that individuals felt they needed to go through, and I hope that this will not occur again. I must admit that other creators certainly looked askance at this. They said to me (perhaps rightly so), "Is the reward worth the price?" I must admit that I replied, "I don't know."

It might be hard to imagine a creator saying "I don't know," but because what you will do in the future will largely be affected by what you have experienced, I believe (I am 99% sure) it will be worth the price. I can't say that unequivocally, so if I could change it and still have the same results of what you are now, I would do so.

It might be part of the process that one can't go one way without going the other.

It might very well be; I believe it is. I wish that beings did not have to suffer so much. The knowledge and wisdom gained from suffering will last, whereas the actual pain that might affect an individual's soul will not. Even so, I think that as a creator you will be highly motivated to support and sustain even minor annoyance. But I think you will put a check on the system that I did not, to keep it from getting worse than that. Minor annoyance does stimulate growth, but it can get out of hand, sometimes so quickly that you cannot imagine.

Free Will

With your policy of not interceding and giving free will, there's nothing you can do about it?

That's right. The reason for not interceding is that once the soul has started out on a path of exploration to learn something completely, you cannot intercede until absolutely every level and possible variable of that experience has been learned. That's why I didn't intercede. Please, I want people to understand that when they asked for relief from their suffering, that's often why they did not get relief. Interfer-ing would be tantamount to interfering with another creator's creation. I had to grit my teeth (if I had them) and hang onto the edge of the seat and take the wild ride with you.

This issue of free will: I think there's only one or two planets in creation that have beings on it with free will. This was given because creators need free will?

Yes.

But are the rest of the individual beings in your creation automatons?

No, no.

How does free will work in the rest of creation?

The rest of creation is simply not exposed to things that could put them on a tangential path. Their philosophy very often is one that is impossible to challenge. The philosophy of a planet is akin to religion. It is not dogmatic, but the way a society lives is wonderful and spiritized and filled with love and support and nurturance and everything you hold dear. Individuals are encouraged to have the best possible time, as it were. It is crystal clear to them that their philosophy is obviously the cause of this joy, and the idea of adding anything that might corrupt the system would appear ridiculous at the very least and, more likely, outra-geous to an individual of any of these societies. Even the littlest child or the greatest rebel of one of those societies would never do that. They might want to have greater freedoms or perhaps look at other societies. Some of the more rebellious members of a benign and benevolent soci-ety might become anthropologists or social scientists, flying around to other planets, perhaps even to Earth, to see what the benefits and the costs of free will are. Invariably they would decide that the benefits do not outweigh the costs.

You would consider these planets to be heaven, as it were. These beings are not automatons; they just pursue a lovelier lifestyle, and they are not really in school. There might be a minor lesson to learn in a lifetime, but this minor lesson is learned in the most benevolent ways, and it doesn't feel like school at all. As a soul you might gain some minor wisdom from a given life on a planet such as this, but it does not interfere with your lifestyle.

Your goal for the Explorer Race is to spice up those societies a little—not to change their societies to something corrupted, but to give them that spice of discomfort, just the slightest annoyance, so they can grow and continue to expand their philosophies, perhaps have a life in which they will resolve some greater challenge for the soul in a benign and wonderful way, yet learning. Never is the Explorer Race intended to add more than the slightest degree of annoyance, perhaps 0.5% to 0.75%, which might on its own expand to no more than 1.75%. There is a check on it so that it can't go past 2%. Some might be allowed to go to 4%, but that's likely to be isolated to the Pleiades, because they have indicated a desire to grow at a more accelerated rate. Ruling out that exception, you will be encouraging this growth cycle for all these beings, but it will not interfere in their lifestyle.

The Redemption of Negativity

What about the whole issue of negativity? Surely, for the first time in all of the creations since the beginning, you took negativity and made it a worthwhile thing without transforming it. Is there more out there to be worked with?

Now, that's an important point. I told the being we're calling negativity [the Master of Discomfort] that *you* would redeem it, but I would not. I wanted it to have a stake in the outcome so that it could experience true redemption for itself and have the complete knowledge that you as the Explorer Race would be the one (combining you as one being) that would bring that about.

So negativity bided its time until you, as the Explorer Race, began to emerge. And when that happened, it was for this negativity being like a fiftieth anniversary and birthday party and Christmas and New Year's thrown in. It was a wonderful thing. It said, "Now I'm finally going to be redeemed!" Redemption for negativity is not being changed to positivity, but being loved and appreciated for what it has to offer without having to become the extreme of itself. Negativity in its own right cannot stand to be its extreme. Of all the beings who have the most discomfort with negativity, it is negativity itself. When negativity is at that minor level of annoyance and so on, it feels all right with itself, because it is crystal clear that it stimulates something worthwhile. On the other hand, when it becomes extreme and is simply involved in suffering for other people, it suffers, too.

So you yourselves have an obligation to yourself and all beings—but also to negativity—to rescue it from having to suffer with you. You want to know if there are other great issues to be resolved. I think you will find that there are. I really don't want to interfere in your discovery, because you're going to have an opportunity to travel (though not as long as I did) when you come together as Creator. Yes, you're going to have to take over from me when I leave. But as I said before, parts of you are going to be able to go off and travel around. You'll come back and then other parts will go off and travel around. This traveling will allow you to discover certain other elements of existence that are largely unappreciated or unavailable for the full expression of their potential, because they too have been shunned due to the nature of how they're felt and so on.

The Redemption of Ignorance

You will redeem many others, but one of the more grandiloquent ones that has the potential of becoming really appreciated is ignorance. You all know that the moment that precedes great inspiration (inspiration for something you're already working on, like a puzzle or something that can't seem to change, and you're stuck) is really a form of ignorance. And when that inspiration comes through and you then expand on it, you resolve that ignorance. In those moments ignorance is redeemed.

I think you will pick ignorance and a few others to redeem, to help them become appreciated for what they truly are and to pass them on to elements you will create in your creation. Let's say that you produce a planet with beings on it who have minor annoyance available to them, but their culture is basically beautiful. When they get an inspiration, because their lives are so inspiring already, they don't necessarily act on it. But when they're given a little more ignorance, they will perhaps appreciate that inspiration more.

Now, you've done some work on that here. The veil of ignorance that has been placed here has given you this opportunity so you could re-create or reinvent reality. I think you will take on ignorance and other beings to redeem them through experience.

I think Zoosh said that you're going to take 97% of you with you, so you leave us like your real estate. What are we moving into if most of you is leaving?

Yes, I'm leaving the real estate. I'll be leaving the physical planets, the galaxies and all of this business. That is not the mass of me; it is the others, it is matter, only a portion of me. I'm also leaving you with the essence of myself. When man and woman get together and have a baby, they stimulate the growth of another adult; their baby grows up to be an adult, having all of an adult's capabilities. You have my essence within you. You are growing up now to be the adult. If I were to take *all* of me, you wouldn't have anything left over. Some of the matter might wish to return to its previous business, but I think they are really interested in what you're going to do and that most of it will stick around to see. You will certainly create new planets, new galaxies—possibly even life forms in dimensions that exist but which I haven't put anything into. It's almost like an empty storage box—the dimensions are there, but nothing is in them. I'm leaving those for you to see what you'd like to put in them.

Some of the outside consultants have stressed how carefully you created these dimensions as potential. And you're leaving them as potentials.

Yes. I think that not only will you play around with this dimension, but you'll probably put your main focus into those dimensions that contain nothing other than the matrix that supports them.

If spirit creates the soul and the soul creates the physical body, can you explain how it works? You seem to use the concept of soul as if that is the top level.

It is the top level to me. I would say to change the word "spirit" to me [Creator], and we're in good shape.

So the souls are our first-level creation?

They are to me. When you were birthed out of me, you were birthed out as souls, not as spirit. I do understand that some beings are isolating the individual portion of soul within an individual life and saying that all of those lives combined with all of the knowledge of all of those lives might be conceived of as spirit. But I would rather say that spirit is *me*. That would be the point of agreement.

Lucifer, the Loose Cannon

Lucifer was a great light. How did he become connected to negativity?

Well, let's just say that Lucifer was a *portion* of a great light. Lucifer always was interested in growth and change, not necessarily for the better, but for what you would call basic research—to see what could happen. "Change this and see what happens." With that kind of personal agenda, if you're acquiring elements of growth and change, you would inevitably acquire discomfort or negativity. That's what happened to him. He acquired it, and because it added such a tremendous realm of experience, he got fascinated with it. He began to explore more and more within it.

That is how he became involved in such extreme discomfort. The responsibility at the creator level (which happens also for other beings) is that once you start something, you can't go back. You don't uncreate it; you go forward until you close the loop. If you choose, you can deal with it at a higher level or a parallel level, but you have to deal with it. That's what he did. He created so much of it, then suddenly realized at some point that he had become obsessed with it and had let go of a lot of his love and light.

At that point he said, "Wait a minute! This is not for me," because it was out of control, from his perspective. It was now reproducing on its own without any stimulation from him. At that point he said, "Wait, I've got to set this to rights." He realized that he was part way down the loop already and couldn't go back. He had to go forward and see it through. That's when the signal flags and flares came up saying, "Help!"

Do you consider him one of the friends, or was he an outside consultant?

He was an outside consultant, but I could not have done this without him—that's very important to remember. Even though it got out of hand, it got out of hand for him, too. It would not have been possible to have had this level of growth without him. He was essential. He had to remain a consultant, because here was a being who was basically a loose cannon. He couldn't say, "I'm going to do something" and deliver on it, because he was so out of control that he himself didn't know from one moment to the next what he would be dragged into. So he couldn't possibly be involved in the inner circle of this creation, though he would have liked that. Once negativity has been checked to the point of minor annoyance, he might be able to be involved in an inner circle of creation, but not when he's a loose cannon.

When Jehovah says that he and Lucifer came from the Father, who or what is he talking about?

You must remember that Jehovah is a portion of myself and that he has somewhat of an agenda and is a little polarized. Jehovah is the masculine polarized version of myself, whereas the Goddess is the feminine polarized version of myself. So from his perspective the ultimate in the Creator is masculine.

So when he talks about the Father, he's talking about you.

Yes. Just as when the Goddess talks about the Mother or the Grandmother, she's talking about me. And the Goddess might conceivably be talking about even beyond that. I have my portion, which is the Goddess, but I have also seen other creations and other creators, and I do not know any other creator who did not have its version of the Goddess. I know other creators who do not have a polarized masculine version, but I felt the masculine would be useful for what I wanted to do. I don't think it's possible to be a creator and not have the feminine, but for what I wanted to do I needed to have the polarized masculine as well.

He has said many times that Lucifer declared to everyone that he was greater than the Father and that's what created doubt in those who were there. Was that here in this system?

It is not my perspective that the being I know as Lucifer declared that. But it is certainly possible that some aspect of Lucifer said it. After all, we know that extreme negativity is always confrontational, even in yourself. I would have to say that it happened in Jehovah's polarized reality, but in other portions of me at that same precise moment, Lucifer was not speaking and saying this. That would have been more of a vignette happening in a portion of me.

Jehovah has the capacity at any time to be totally united with all of me, but he is still completing some of his personal odyssey, so I think he will not be completely conjoined with me and go on with me. When I go on, Jehovah and the Goddess will come with me, but you will also have the Goddess. I don't think you're going to create Jehovah; I needed to do that. But Jehovah is very linked to what you are doing here on Earth and to the Explorer Race, so I think that he will be with you for a long time yet.

We can stop now. There will be more, so for this moment, good night.

Synchronizer of Physical Reality and Dimensions

October 8, 1996

am the individual in charge of balancing, leveling and synchronizing physical dimensions so that your Creator does not have to be responsible for this. Your Creator's job is creation, but your Creator is also an individual who enjoys variety. And when creators enjoy variety I've often found they like company. I have signed on for this creation to give your Creator a little relief and provide such energies, primarily focusing in the physical dimensions.

I have most of my focus in the second, third, fourth, fifth—and I'm going to include between the fifth and the sixth, because a certain amount of physicality is there. By the time you get to the sixth dimension you really feel yourself if you're there with substance, although you don't have to. I'm not including the first dimension; because there is no motion there, I don't really need to put forth any effort. I put forth the effort once, then that's it; I don't have to do anything further. My primary energy goes toward the second, third, fourth and fifth dimensions.

What did you do to create the second, third, fourth and fifth dimensions?

I did not actually create them; your Creator set it up. It's as if your Creator set up a filing system and I came along like a good clerk to make sure that everything was in order, then I maintained the creation. I don't want to take credit for the creation, because that would not be appropriate. What I do more than anything else is maintain certain pulse vibrations that allow beings to exist in these dimensions and, perhaps more important, keep the dimensions sufficiently separated so that beings from these dimensions do not casually fall into other dimensions.

Now, these barriers must be sufficiently amenable to certain functional transit shapes and certain light and sound frequencies so that beings with the proper authority can travel interdimensionally. From my point of view it takes authority to do this. On the rare occasions when someone accidentally or capriciously travels through these dimensions, because they do not have authority to do so, they are either pulled back into their own dimension or brought back to their dimensional point of origin.

It requires a very specific pulse range to accommodate, create and assist the dimensional overlays to merge and at the same time resist each other. Under most circumstances they resist each other. However, if beings travel under authorization, they must be able to merge sufficiently during that light, sound or pulse transfer so that this resistance will not block their passage.

Earlier Creation Experiences

How many creators have you signed on with before?

This is my third time. In the one previous to this I was involved with another creator in the creation of many different varieties of physical beings who could adapt to physical dimensions. As a consultant in that creation it was necessary for me to create within a small space the vibrations of physically expressive dimensions so that this creator could very quickly, as one might sort through a deck of cards, go through its inventions of beings and see if they could not only survive, but thrive in these dimensions.

For example, you as physical beings in your dimension can survive, but interestingly enough, your Creator has set it up in such a way that you do not *thrive* in this dimension. I believe this is because your Creator did not want you to live too long in your physical bodies here. He had a purpose in mind and did not want to create a physical body that could do so well in this dimension that you might live comfortably here for 1000 or 1500 years (which is not unusual for beings in other dimensions). I mention that as an aside not because your Creator does not love you, but because your Creator seems to have set it up so that you would be exposed to this experience for a limited time only.

The creation before the one I mentioned was very interesting, because it was a creator who was creating dimensions. I acted as a consultant for this creator and offered advice and suggested possible expressions of physical dimension. That particular creator established *over a thousand* separate and livable physical dimensions! This gives you an idea of how many possibilities there are to exist physically. I'm talking about physicality as you know it as well as dimensions that are close to yours—perhaps slightly higher or lower in physicality, but close enough for you to recognize as a physical existence. These thousand physical dimensions were but a small sampling of what this particular creator was involved in, for he also established well over 1300 nonphysical dimensions. When this creator got to a few more than 1300, it was way past the time I was needed, because he had created the physical dimensions first. I was interested, but I moved on because I was no longer needed.

You must have created your own universe with physical dimensions to get the experience, right?

My Origin

No, not really. I did not do that. I *will* do that, but I have not created what I would call a universe. I did come from a place of varying . . . if you were to see it in space it would be very interesting, and you might see this in time. It looks very much like a thick wheel spinning, with more spinning happening within the . . . a pen, perhaps? Thank you. A poor artist am I, but I will attempt. [Draws.]

Recognize that there are no [straight] lines. (This is for the sake of future artists so they don't have to be baffled by what this means.) This is a rough idea, you see. If you were to approach this, you would see the spinning. The interesting thing about it is that no matter from what direction you approach it—even if you had a thousand people on your ship and all compared notes at the same 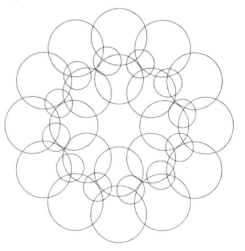 time—nobody would ever see exactly the same thing. Everyone would see it based upon their particular expression of themselves. It would be something you would see (assuming you had eyes) physically or else sense, and no one would sense it, feel it, see it or even hear it (which is possible) in the same way. I was able thus to experience what I felt was the ultimate (in terms of your existence) in sensual reality—feeling the senses, the "sensual" that means feedback: something you would feel or be aware of in infinite varieties.

This is really where I came from, what I am a portion of. Every time someone would see this creation, those of us who were involved in it would be able to feel what they were feeling and see what they were seeing, which would add to the variety. I think that this is most likely where I mastered the physical dimensions, because of the tremendous varietal experiences and reactions to the sight. It is quite stunningly beautiful, if I do say so myself [chuckles]. In all the time that I was aware of myself being there (well over a trillion of your experiential years), I do not recall one single time when any individual who saw it did not feel wonderful about it. It is inspiring, and as a result they were filled with sense experiences of it; it was a sensual experience. I was able to fully experience all of the physicality of the whole wheel, of the wheels within the wheel and even the wheels within the wheels within the wheel.

You might think that if you wander around to the side you would see it on edge, but you don't. If one could approach it from the side it would not be as beautiful. This we knew and we know still. We wanted people to have a good experience, so no matter which side you approach it from, it looks exactly the way I drew it. It is quite interesting that way. It is not really an illusion; that is how it appears. This is a creation that wishes to present a certain face of itself to all beings, because we of that creation know that this is the most beautiful face, the best way to see it and understand it.

How beautiful! Is it filled with physical beings?

No, that is the interesting thing. Each vortex within the overall wheel is a being unto itself. And then within those vortexes (wheels within wheels) there are other wheels spinning—your artist would have to indicate that—and each of those is a being. We are a combined being, but when considered in terms of numbers, our number is quite small—I should say fewer than 10,000. Yet observing this from space, it would be at least the size of your galaxy—quite stunningly large so it can be seen.

An interesting thing, however, is that if you wish to explore it, fly into it, you can't. [Laughs.] It's not because it's a reflection or an optical illusion; it's just that we need to protect beings from the overwhelming impact of the *totality* of physical experience when they are focused in an individual physical experience. So it's like a huge thing you can see, but as you direct yourself toward it, it becomes farther away or isn't there anymore. This is a built-in safety factor.

Has the Void gotten that far? Is it bright-colored lights with the Void around it?

I do not think that the Void is around it, no—nearby, though.

But it's so bright you see it even though there is no darkness around it?

Well, there is some dark space, but it is so brilliant and the colors are so eye-catching, if I can use that term, it is seen from very far away.

So were you birthed from that creator?

Yes.

When did you become aware of yourself?

Just about the time that my services were needed. I think this often happens in creation: when what you have to offer that is uniquely your own is needed, then the chances of your becoming aware of your individuality and your persona are very good (if you aren't already aware). I believe that's why I was called.

My Contribution to the First Two Creators I Consulted For

To that first creator who had a thousand physical dimensions?

Yes.

So what was your contribution?

The one who created all those dimensions? My contribution was primarily broadcasting a pulse of a physical "frequency" that would not be a dimension this creator had established, or would have been a variation sufficiently far from others this creator had used that it stimulated a flow. It was like one might give an inspiration to someone, and they then create a great deal of variety from that inspiration. Then I waited until this creator needed another inspiration, and I would pass on another. That is how I was the consultant.

Did he have beings in those thousand physical dimensions? Did he experience them or evolve them?

Not right away. First came the creation of the dimensions. I inquired before I left whether beings would be established, and my understanding was that when this particular creator had finished doing all it could do in dimensions (he also had a consultant for nonphysical dimensions, but not me), it would then begin to establish a few beings per dimension to see how they worked out. I believe this creator wanted to see how many dimensions it could create and whether individuals who were perfectly attuned to that dimension could live or incarnate forever. I think this creator intended to create just a few beings in a livable world to see if that kind of physically immortal existence is possible or desirable.

Then you were called to the next creation.

Yes.

You felt a call, you knew the creator, or . . .

Well, I was really done there. I knew I was done. I actually had been hanging around past my time of need and I began to feel somebody needing me.

So you went there and provided the same kind of inspiration?

No, I kind of bowed away from the inspirations from the other creator and basically reproduced all of those thousand physical dimensions for this next creator, not because it was going to create the same thing the first creator had created, but because this creator wanted to try out different physical beings in different physical dimensions to see which ones it would be most fond of or most interested in. So out of that roughly thousand physical dimensions it picked no more than eight in which it felt it could keep a good feeling or understanding. This particular creator wanted to create many planets and galaxies and beings within those dimensions and obviously did not want to focus *only* in physical reality.

Joining Your Creator

How did you happen by here?

I got to the point where I was done. What happens with individuals like me is that if you're not called anywhere, you just hang around unless you want to go back home or go on and do your own creation. I wasn't ready yet, so when your Creator was traveling about (I wasn't hitchhiking) your Creator told me as It was going by what It intended to do and asked me if I would like to come along. At that point She was not too far from reaching Her destination to begin Her creation. So I went along.

First He created the midpoint, right?

Before He did that, He took a look into the levels of dimension, you know. We went over that first, then we created the midpoint. After that there was another review of the levels of dimension. It was my job to pay attention only to the physical dimensions, and I think He took good care of the nonphysical ones. Then He started out in the middle and went back to the beginning. Back at the beginning we paid a lot of attention and started creating the subtleties of the dimensions—who goes where, what goes here, what goes in between the dimensions, how we could make it accessible for beings. At that time when we were talking about it, I didn't even know about His idea for the Explorer Race. He had reviewed the possibility, but He didn't call it the Explorer Race then.

He would say what would happen if and when He became ready to birth a creator—a creation of His own that was meant to be a creator—and how they could travel interdimensionally and make it available for interdimensional travel for other beings who were properly able to do so. We had to get into the details and spent quite awhile doing that.

Starting at the Midpoint and Laying Out Dimensions

Then we began to lay things out. I thought it was interesting that He would go to the midpoint first. I hadn't experienced that before. The other two creators I was with started at the beginning and went forward. I don't think I've even heard of a creator who started at the midpoint, went back to the beginning and then went forward. That was *very* interesting.

What was your understanding of the purpose of that?

My understanding was that your Creator would get a strong feeling for what . . . it was as if your Creator didn't want to lose His way. In the variety of such a huge and varietal creation it would be very easy to get fascinated with something out here and something out there. But my understanding (which came much later) was that your Creator wanted to feel the midpoint as an anchor so that He wouldn't lose track of where He wanted to go. I think that ultimately *you* are where He wanted to go. So basically He took a chalk and put a mark in space [laughs]—x marks the spot—then went back to the beginning.

Once it was created, then you stayed there to maintain it.

Yes. I've stayed here to maintain it. Your Creator has several consultants; I believe this is so your Creator can be more intimately involved with His creation than I have seen with other creators. For instance, the other creators I have been with do not usually create such a variety of beings. How high can you count? The variety is *unbelievable!* I do not know of another creation like this. The interesting thing about your Creator is that He is personally involved with every tiny bit of your creation, from the tiniest particle to the biggest galaxy and everyone and everything in between. Because your Creator is so intimately involved, I think it is helpful to Him to have consultants to take care of some of the mechanics. We're kind of like a middle management that helps run the creation because of your Creator's intimate involvement with so many beings.

I can almost feel that. You said that the first creator you worked with was more interested in the mechanics and the building of its creation than the beings and the consciousness that would live in it.

That's right.

And this creation is totally the opposite.

Very much so.

If from the beginning to now is 100%, how long was it before there actually were physical dimensions?

I see where you're going. We went to the midpoint of creation and then we went back to the beginning, and from the very beginning we were laying out physical dimensions. But if you want a percentage and say that creation started at zero and finishes at 100%, it was about 1½% into creation when the dimensions had been well laid out and beings could be created. "Beings" includes planets and galaxies and particles.

Physical Beings

So there were physical beings all during the creation, long before the Explorer Race, which is a very recent thing.

Oh, yes.

They were physical beings—nice, benign physical beings.

Oh, certainly. Even beings who basically looked like you, with maybe a few variations [chuckles].

So they lived their life, evolved up through the dimensions and went back into spirit? How does that work?

Well, understanding that your Creator loves variety, I think most of them lived their existence. Some of them moved from one existence to another. For instance, some of them ensouled planets or even what you now call animals. Some of them moved from one type of being to an entirely different type of being. Some of them existed simultaneously in multiple dimensions, in one dimension as a humanoid and in other dimensions a lightbeing or an animal or a cloud (which has perhaps a brief existence, but clouds of light live longer) or even a building block for a genetic expression (roughly, a gene). The variety is far beyond what we can spend the evening talking about. Your Creator (this is a joke) doesn't know the meaning of dull! That's the consultants' standard joke with your Creator. Your Creator doesn't know about dull; It can define it, but that's all. Your Creator would get very bored, for instance, in the creation of the Void.

But He needed the Void and the past and the future and the particles for His creation, right?

Certainly. Whenever your Creator is exposed to anything that could be used in a varietal creation such as this one, well, if it looks good, if it feels good, why not?

All of the things that you eight had been exposed to were also brought in.

Yes. There is very little excluded from this creation. When you cast about and compare the expressions of other creations to this creation—in terms of both physical and nonphysical variety—there's a lot of stuff that's used and not much that isn't.

The Explorer Race Begins

Zoosh said that about 98.6% of the creation took place before the Explorer Race was birthed.

Yes, and it was just a little before then that I realized what your Creator was up to. It's not that it was a secret; it's just that your Creator did not want to distract me. Your Creator is this way, I think, with most beings. You know, if you're thinking about something else, no matter how involved you are in your own project, you cannot help but be affected by it. I believe this was your Creator's idea of keeping us purely involved in what we were doing as consultants.

So how did things change when the Explorer Race was birthed and negativity was birthing?

Oh, this was very interesting. It helped us understand a lot of what your Creator was up to. Perhaps in its most interesting connotation it helped us all to realize what was next. When we realized that you were intended to replace your Creator when He went on and that our services might not be required anymore, we started paying a lot more attention. We realized that this creation was coming to an end and that even though you would take it over, you would change it, probably quite a bit, because you are sufficiently different from your Creator.

Any expression of who you are as a total being, the Explorer Race, is bound to be at least 1½% different at the beginning. With your capacity for going on to being maybe 50 to 55% different, I think you might not simply add things on, but change things. You have discovered the value of change and are not afraid of it as a race, so I think that will permeate this creation. And when you've been exposed to a creator like this one for so long where variety is infinite and you *add change* to that variety [laughs]—well, it's a quantifier, just that much more. That's one of the reasons I got personally interested.

Did your duties, responsibilities or actions change?

No, not at all.

You're in charge of the dimensions, not the people in it.

That's exactly right. I will say as an aside that I have noticed that since you as a race of beings have been birthed, there has been a lot more travel between the dimensions to come here and observe what you are doing. Before then only an occasional creator would come by, and that was about it.

This is the hot spot.

Yes. Now every day thousands of visitors come—time travelers, creators, individuals from various galaxies, even some beyond this creation. [Chuckles.] It's just busy, busy, busy.

Does that make more work for you?

No, no more work for me. I simply have to pay attention, so that these authorized individuals can pass through the dimensions without harming the dimensions and without being harmed.

Shapes That Can Travel the Dimensions

You mentioned certain shapes when we started talking. What is the process?

Certain shapes function as long-distance portals—for example, the diamond shape.

Ah yes. The maker of that talked to us.

Yes. The diamond shape is particularly associated with traveling through dimensions; when we feel that shape coming, it very easily passes through. But some beings come from a significant distance, where they do not use the diamond shape. I have seen everything from the diamond to the spiral to even a cone. These are all authorized. Occasionally a shape will come along that isn't authorized—for example, a two-dimensional square. Now, that's not authorized. I've seen beings attempt to come here in a two-dimensional square, but they were prevented from doing so. This usually means that they are not sufficiently evolved to see and feel here without leaving something behind. Should they evolve sufficiently and still be attached to that shape, they will probably arrive in a cube, which is an authorized shape.

Is your energy in these dimensions? You feel what goes through.

Yes. That is how I can maintain it. If, for example, a two-dimensional square or a two-dimensional line comes (that's also been tried), I can immediately feel it. I can feel it approaching from quite a distance, and I can immediately put up a pulse that notifies your Creator if necessary, but most often I just deflect it. They are not simply shunted away without explanation; they are given an explanation in the politest terms and are told to try the authorized shapes—but they are not told what those shapes are in case they are not sufficiently evolved. They are also told that if at a later time they wish to come in an authorized shape, they will be welcome.

I've mentioned that certain shapes are authorized, but of course I haven't given you certain keys that are necessary to use these shapes. I have mentioned these shapes so that you will be able to visualize the experience.

We talked to a wonderful being who created shapes as portals. He called himself the Shapemaker. He works with you?

Yes. We are cohorts. [Chuckles.]

He is an outside consultant, too.

Yes.

So there are dimensional overlords who are created within the system who work for you and with you, and there are some outside consultants who are here from outside the creation who work with you?

Yes. They don't call themselves overlords, but I understand the meaning of your term. It is not an inappropriate term even though it is a little too grand.

They patch up and fix things when we get some holes in the dimensions.

Yes, there is quite a variety.

Do you have a staff?

Yes, but we think of ourselves as your Creator's staff. It's not hierarchical; we don't salute each other. [Chuckles.]

You have beings who work with you and help you.

Oh, certainly. And we help each other. When I saw my first spiral approaching, I needed to talk to the Shapemaker about that to make certain it was an authorized shape for interdimensional travel. I had not seen the spiral used for that purpose before. That is an example.

So who was in it? What did they want?

They were coming from another creation entirely. They weren't the creator from that creation, but they were coming because they were involved in the exploration of fringe beings. From their perspective that means beings who exist physically for a short time only to accomplish a very specific purpose. In terms of the infinite levels of time and existence, you as the Explorer Race are embodied physically for only a very short time. So according to their definition of fringe groups, an unusual group, you definitely qualify. You're an unusual group. You're physical for only as long as it takes you to learn what you have to learn, then you will recombine, become a creator yourself and go on as that. They came to study you, and they were here for quite a while.

Did they take some ideas back with them?

Oh, I think they did, yes. They were here for several thousand years.

The Zeus Connection in Atlantis

I know that you don't necessarily use names, but is there a name or a vibration by which we can refer to you?

Well, I'd say this: for a time I was known as Zeus.

Oh, I hadn't even got that far yet—your overall name, such as the name you use on your level.

Oh, Creator gave me . . . but that was a spiritual name. I'd say the spiritual name the Creator provided for all of us is absolutely accurate, but I gave you something by which you could have a recognizable landmark. I was Zeus, but not for the entire time of Zeus. I got Zeus going [laughs]. Zeus was someone who truly existed, truly represented itself to the people, was seen in visions by the people of that time. He was also involved in times before that, and even today is still of assistance. But I am no longer focused as Zeus; someone else has taken over the job.

Was that the first time you appeared in this creation as an individual entity?

Yes. It's the only time. Creator felt it would be good for me to have some kind of a personal involvement so that I could feel His intentions, but also I think Creator wanted me to become personally involved with you the way He is so personally involved with each of you. Zeus is and was a very personal god, if I may say so.

Those who interacted with Zeus felt personally touched by him and very often inspired. It was a physical experience. When you were in touch with Zeus even in a prayer, you would feel that vibration, I believe. That was possibly because of my overall work here, but I was willing to use that. So I was focused into the Zeus entity for about 10,000 experiential years—not that long.

Where did it start? What civilization? What area? What dimension?

Well, Zeus was not a continuing being. Zeus started out in Atlantis, because a lot was going on physically there. Zeus was an inspirer on the masculine level.

Did you have a physical body?

I was able as Zeus to physically manifest myself, usually as a very tall being.

How tall?

Oh, anywhere from 50 to 200 feet tall. The people wanted a guide who would be recognizable as a god to them, so I had to do that. If I had been five feet tall, they would have said, "You are a wise being, but you look like us." So I couldn't look exactly like them; I had to play dress-up a little bit, you know [laughs]. It was a good experience. When Atlantis ceased to exist, I think I was able to help a lot of the souls who had lived there to understand and come to a greater feeling of what they had accomplished.

Because the civilization ended so suddenly, a lot of people felt that they had done something terribly wrong and that they were being punished. I had to tell them that it was never intended that their civilization come to a natural ending during its own time. It was always intended that the civilization of Atlantis end during *your* time because you were intended to be even more involved in technology than they were, perhaps at a slower level. I was able to transport many of those beings from that time to these times to observe what was going to happen and give them the option, as the result of their observation, to incarnate in these times in order to feel they they were picking up the thread of their former existence.

I wasn't really involved much as Zeus in the times written about in the ancient world. I was involved more personally during Atlantis because that's where the action was. Much of what you are doing, in terms of resolution, application, even redemption and wisdom, started in Atlantis, and now you're going to finish it in some good way. Atlantis stopped because the creations coming after that required the planet to be more whole and complete. You see, toward the end Atlantis was doing a lot of mining, and the planet needed its physical self intact because some of it would be needed later.

Now.

Yes.

It stopped in what way?

It stopped to start up again later. Because the people were involved in experimental things, some of which were not so good, they felt that their civilization had been destroyed by the gods. Thus many souls during that time spent quite a bit of time with me and others (just as one might spend time with a counselor before they incarnate again) so that they could understand and feel why their civilization needed to have an abrupt end. As a result of that abrupt end, it created what you call karma, because it was unfinished business. It created so much unfinished business that it became almost a stress for your civilization to go in such directions as technical mining and a separation of life (not realizing that other beings like yourself are really a portion of you) both consciously and on the heart level. More of you are now realizing that mountains are actually a portion of you in the heart, that machines are living organisms, in terms of their particle makeup.

All this separation of energy, you see, created a stress of energy for its resolution. That is why your society from its beginning as the Explorer Race has always been very philosophical, even in times you would consider primitive by your current standards. There was always the philosopher and storyteller, sometimes in the same being.

So what did you do next? Was that the only time you actually acted again?

That's the only time I was (if I may use the term) incarnated. But I let that being go after about 10,000 experiential years and someone else took it over. [Laughs.]

Who took it over?

I basically birthed the being that took it over; I totally focused into the Zeus consciousness in that moment and birthed that being. In that way the portion of me that was Zeus could carry on, but I don't consider it me anymore; I let it go. It was like what you consider a child; your child is your child, but not you specifically.

When this shop closes up, is Zeus a separate entity who goes with you? What happens to that being?

That is entirely up to him. He's still available and sometimes is still called upon by members of that civilization. He's still alive today, you understand, and the heirs of that civilization and those who read the classics who are interested in such things occasionally call upon him. But he is also available for much greater duties. For instance, Zeus is particularly able to help interpret the feelings, expressions, thoughts, ideals, dreams and so on of stone to human beings. So those of you who are very interested in stone might wish to call upon Zeus to act as an intermediary for explanations of this form of life.

The Gods of Olympus

What about all of the incredible stories about the gods of Olympus? Did he play some of those games, or was it all fiction?

Let's just say that most of these stories represent ideal qualities. It was hoped that the physical beings would imitate or wish to imitate ideals. When the stories occasionally indicated failings or frailties, that was to identify the gods with the people so the people could feel the direct connection and that it would be possible to live up to such a god's ideals because some of them had feelings like people. These are hints, you know. These stories were intended to inspire and create a sense of personal identification for the people who received them.

So the Greeks just sort of took over something that was already old.

They took it over, but it was aimed at them. This is largely because at that time they were very philosophical people, and this was meant for philosophical people whose stories would live on after the golden era of their civilization—which they have. Many civilizations have come and gone that you are not aware of because their stories have not lived on. But you cannot say that about the Greeks.

Did you give them the stories?

I was involved in some, but only peripherally in most of them, because by that time that portion of me I had birthed to perpetuate the Zeus god was really in charge. I think we consulted a bit, but mostly it was that being's creation. Those stories were passed on to individuals to write down, so it was connected to the human beings who were inspired.

So that's the only time you got to go down and play with the people?

Well, not all the time, only when it was necessary for me to show myself in some physical form so that the people could say, "Oh, a god!"

But you inspired a lot of beings?

That was my intention, yes.

How long ago would you place that? How many Earth years ago, even though it was in another dimension?

It is hard to give that, but certainly well over 100,000 experiential Earth years. It's hard to place it past that point.

Since then do you feel more of a connection to humanity?

Yes, I have more of a sense of awareness of the intimate subtleties that you represent. When you look at your race from a distance, it does not appear to be all that subtle, but as you get closer you discover the tremendous subtlety involved. Even though human beings do not always consciously act on that subtlety, it is very much omnipresent.

The Next Step

What's the next step for you? What is the plan, the dream, the vision?

Well, with beings like me it is always where we are needed. It remains to be seen whether you will want to utilize my abilities. It is certainly possible that you might pick a portion of yourself to do what I am doing to maintain the creation. Perhaps I might consult a little bit. If you want me to carry on as I have done with your Creator, I am available, but I think maybe you will not want that. It is too soon to say.

Is there some way you can communicate with the soul of humanity or the oneness?

I see no need to inflict this decision upon you before it is necessary. It would only be a distraction for you, so I will just wait. When you take over your Creator's position and your Creator moves on, then you are likely to review the consultants. I think your Creator will not need most of the consultants to go with Him.

What is your feeling for what He's looking for? You were not created exponentially; you are a whole being, right?

Yes.

So what is your sense of what He's looking for and what He will find?

Well, I can't say without His knowing, but much as I understand, He is looking for something entirely new. [Chuckles.] And when you realize that this Creator is involved in variety and is very attracted to it, the only way He can find something new is to go to a dimension He's not aware of.

Well, that's where the rest of Him is waiting.

Yes.

You came from your creator, so you didn't go through the Creator of Creators, too?

No, I didn't go through that route. I just signed on with your Creator. Off we went on our merry way.

But in your travels have you seen what the Creator describes as beyond the edge of the Orb?

I have seen this, but only through your Creator's memory. I might like to go there. If my services are not needed, I think I will go there and see what that is about. It sounds thrilling.

Beyond it there must be something. You see, we're looking for who created the Matrix. Do you know anything about that?

Nope. [Chuckles.]

Why are you laughing?

Because my job is so specific. You know, I've accumulated all the knowledge along the way, but I don't know certain things, probably because I don't need to know at this time.

All of these friends of the Creator have specific duties?

Yes.

And most of them except Zoosh have been down here in the creation, right?

I couldn't say. It's better for you to ask them.

So you're focused very specifically; you're not always even aware of what they're doing.

I really can't take too much time off to see what they're doing. As a matter of fact, I can't take enough energy to channel directly through. I'm just talking to Zoosh and Zoosh is basically passing it on. I cannot spare the energy to do this directly.

Oh, I see. That's an incredible focus.

[Chuckles.] It is what I do.

The Explorer Race is so varietally focused, they might not have the ability to focus the way you do.

That's another way to look at it, but that's not your job. If it were your job, perhaps you would be able to do it just as well.

I've run out of questions. What else would you like to tell us?

Not that much, you know. I'll just say this: Your work here is drawing to a close, in terms of the experiential time of this creation. You will have considerable time to explore the galaxies and perhaps even to the edge of this universe while you are still physical or reasonably physical—perhaps an expression of yourselves somewhere between the fifth and sixth dimensions and from there perhaps a little more, as you are lightbeings.

But your task is really quite wonderful. I don't know of anyone who's had this responsibility before. It is in some ways very responsible, but in other ways it allows you to do it as you wish because there's no basis of comparison. No one can come back to you later and say, "You should have done it like this, the way *they* did." [Laughs.] You would say that that is the way *you* did it. Maybe if people follow you they'll be told, "You should have done it like the Explorer Race," but they can't say that to you. You have a lot of latitude and a lot of flexibility in what you can do. This is not surprising, because your Creator is interested in variety and will naturally allow you to have latitude. So I'd say that if you keep that in mind, you will be able to feel free about your expression of yourself. On that note I'll say good night.

Thank you very much.

All right. Zoosh speaking. How did you like my friend?
He's wonderful! What would you like to tell us about him that I wasn't wise enough to ask?

I mostly signed on to say hi and good-bye. As for me, I would say that he is modest, not unlike beings of his type. There's really no more to tell. You saw a little bit of it, but he has a very good sense of humor. Yes, it helps to have a good sense of humor if you're going to be a consultant—as any consultant knows.

You have to be ready for anything.

Yes. So next time we will strike off in the direction of another consultant, yes?

Can we say which one it is?

Oh, let's take them in order.

Okay. Next is a thorough understanding of maybe.

Sounds like fun. Then I'll say good night.

❖ Robert's Comments on His Experience

Did you see our friend

I did. I didn't realize until just now but it was like looking at a blank space and seeing something like three-dimensional lines of light between the space. The lines themselves were varied. It's hard to describe it, but . . .

His energy evidently is what creates the dimensions.

I couldn't see the individual dimensions per se, but I could see the separations between the dimensions. I didn't realize until just now that that's what I was seeing.

When he was telling about the stint of Zeus, did you see that?

Yeah, I did see a picture of a being. I guess that was Zeus. I didn't really get a sense of proportion. When you see one being unrelated to anything else, you can't really tell.

He had a sense of humor.

I think a sense of humor might be an across-the-board way of knowing and recognizing evolved beings.

Master of Maybe

October 10, 1996

ll right, Zoosh speaking. Well, shall we shove on?
We're not shoving—we are flying the breadth of the cosmos!

A Trip to the Circle of Light outside the Orb

You know, before we go on tonight I want to share with you a little adventure I took somewhat because of our conversations about these books and especially as a result of a comment you made last time. I went out to the edge of the Orb and I noticed the light coming in. When you have light here in your dimension or even in most dimensions within this creation (actually, all the dimensions I've been to within this creation), it radiates outward. It might radiate in different patterns and shapes, but you can all agree that light begins at a certain point and radiates outward, yes?

The interesting thing about the Orb and the end of it is that the light is radiating inward! That caught my attention, so I went out beyond the light (you *can* get beyond it). What I saw first were sort of large renditions of human beings who looked very much like people you'd see on Earth. It was a curious phenomenon, because it reminded me of the factor of everything being one.

There is a circle of light, which I believe encompasses the entirety of everything (otherwise known as the Orb). That circle of light is not very thick when measured in terms of universes—and there are a lot of universes to go through to get to the edge of the Orb. In terms of your universe, it's perhaps one-tenth of your universe thick, which, in terms of all the other universes, is a fairly thin shield. The light looks very much like a cloud, and it's radiating inward. There is apparently nothing pushing it in.

I realized that the light is radiating inward because it *wants* to come here. When I went beyond the light I saw all these beings, and when I went beyond those beings I saw points of light. When I studied those points of light (I can't call them stars; they were more like points of light within something that I'll call space), I could see that there was a feeling of great interest coming from these points of light. I believe they have something to do with the cloud of light that is coming into the Orb. I thought I'd pass this on to you.

Can you go farther?

I'll go farther another time, but that's what I did so far.

Wonderful! And you were never interested in looking at it before?

Let's just say I was sufficiently busy not to have looked at it before. Now we're going to move on. What's our next stop tonight?

The Master of Maybe.

Oh, yes [chuckles]. All right. A moment.

I represent the link between the impossible and the possible. Welcome.

The Development of Hope and Bridging to the Possible

Thank you. It has been my duty for some time now to provide the impetus and the energy toward your development of hope. You have been told that you have largely invented hope here. I would say that you took hope to a new level, meaning that no matter how impossible something looked, if you had hope, not only would that hope be manifested in prayers or devotions, but it might also be easily associated with the possibility of creating that which would resolve the impossible. Hope existed before, at least in theory, but you developed it, and that is most important.

Now, it is my job to provide this bridge, but my job also functions on the intimate level. As your recent friend discussed the other night, we consultants are very much like middle management. It is our job to keep things running if a creator is busy elsewhere. For my particular job I need to help bridge the impossible to the possible (otherwise known as maybe) both generally and for the individual. I often find myself functioning as the energy of inspiration, sometimes with individuals at individual moments.

For instance, a being such as a tiny ant might look at a puddle. You would just splash through it, but for the ant it is an ocean. The ant naturally knows how to swim, but it has never swum through such a large puddle. Yet it must get to the other side, for that is where the ant lives. My job is not to force the ant into the puddle, but to encourage and support that individual (ants *are* individuals even though they might look like a well-synchronized team) while it is hoping that it has the strength to swim across this mighty ocean (which is how it feels).

It is not my job to save the ant, you understand. But when it is hoping that it has the strength and endurance to get to the other side, it is my job to provide the energy of possibility. Maybe this being has not tested the limits of its strength before. Maybe it can go beyond what it thinks it can do. That is my job: to encourage and to provide the energy to sustain what could be or what might be. This is something I find most inspiring. I have had the privilege of observing many individuals and whole groups accomplish something that they never thought they could. This was largely because they could go beyond hope, beyond beseeching and really try something.

I have found that working around and near your world has been fully 60% of my effort, because you are attempting to accomplish so much in such a short amount of time, and therefore my inspiration is needed by many. Your Creator, guides and angels will provide the coding of that inspiration. This means that if there are words, thoughts or pictures that would guide an individual or perhaps many individuals to something, I do not provide them. But when the Creator is busy elsewhere, which is often these days, then I provide the energy matrix upon which this coding is laid.

I have had other jobs to do, especially in the beginning. There was a time when your Creator began to doubt the possibility of success (as He would define it) in this Explorer Race of which you are a portion. Your Creator was not sure whether you could do as much as He needed you to do in so short a time even though you had been prepared well. So much responsibility was thrust upon you, but without much of the normal preparation that any creative being would have for making choices. From time to time your Creator would feel there was something He hadn't done and needed to do, but wasn't quite sure what. Because He felt stumped or simply discouraged from time to time, it would be my job to cheer your Creator up. From that tiny ant to the mightiest, wisest beings, *maybe*, in my experience, has been applied with equal success regardless of a person's individual responsibility.

Your Evolution in Orion and Maldek

Once upon a time your Creator was watching your evolution as souls. This was after you left the great and powerful wisdom keepers of

Orion. I call them wisdom keepers because even though it was some-what of a colonial empire, one of the main forces that drove them to cre-ate an empire was their desire to have in one central location all the available wisdom for themselves and for anyone with whom they inter-acted—in other words, the ultimate library. What drove them onward in their colonizationwas their desire to contact civilizations and provide services to them, bringing them under the wing of the empire for the protection and sustaining of their cultures—but not to destroy civiliza-tions as might have happened here on Earth. This has been largely reported, but I must tell you, because even with its excesses toward the end of that empire, the Orions started out with a good idea.

Your Creator became discouraged when you as the Explorer Race left the Orion empire and went to another planet upon which errors (lack of forgiveness) were applied with such rigorous predictability that the planet exploded and your Creator had to reconstitute you. All of you weren't there, but a significant number of the Explorer Race went through that.

You mean Maldek?

Yes. You went from Orion to Maldek. Now, it happened over many years, but most of you had a life there—some a long life, some a short one. Most of you were a portion of that. And after Maldek blew up, your Creator had to literally pick up the pieces for a long time, because both the planet and your souls were shattered by the experience. You were very depressed because on the soul level, beyond the physical manifestation, you knew that you had gone to Maldek to put things right. What is happening here now on Earth was intended to happen on Maldek, but it didn't. So when everyone was killed on Maldek (only a few got away) your souls, as you went through the veils, remembered immediately what you were supposed to have done, and you were utterly devastated by the sudden and full realization. There were so many realizing it at the same time that it was as if you needed years of psychoanalysis to be put back together so you could have the desire to do it all over again on Earth and do it right.

Your Creator couldn't stop to feel discouraged while He was busy re-forming you, encouraging you and sustaining you through the angelic light and the totally polarized Goddess, giving you the feminine nurturing you needed, which was a massive amount.

After it was over and things were up and running on Earth, Creator paused for a creative moment and wiped Its brow, if you would, and said, "I'm glad we got that going again. How can I have any true hope that they will not make the same mistakes on this new planet?"

Well, it's never good for a creator to become discouraged, especially when a creator has such a specific agenda as your Creator does. Some creators (and I've worked with others) have a creation that they totally allow to go its own way to see what happens. Your Creator is not like that. Your Creator has intentions, purposes, goals and even values that She wishes to perpetuate (Zoosh wants us to mix the genders there sometimes), so She cannot afford to fall into a pattern of discouragement or be sorrowful for too long about what Her children are doing.

Encouraging Your Creator

That's when I stepped in and spent time with your Creator's memory. Your Creator, you see, was discouraged in Its memory, not in Its heart or Its love. So I went into the memory of the Creator and pulled up every good thing you ever did even before Creator birthed you to go on your own. I reminded Creator of how you have always learned only by making mistakes. Even before mistakes were widely used as a way to grow, you were always the portion of Creator that would eagerly jump into something even if you didn't understand it. You might blunder around for a time, but with your youthful enthusiasm you would see it through.

Now, some people might consider that being stubborn, but from my perspective it simply means that you don't like to leave things undone. You like to complete them before you go on. And if you don't, even in individuals there is always stressful energy to complete it. I reminded Creator's memory of this. It was a particularly enjoyable experience to see Creator's memory recall all of these good things. When a creator recalls things, we don't recall them in sequence, but in layer upon layer, you see. Therefore everything I reminded Creator of exponentially expanded, because Creator would remember an individual instance and then apply it to many individuals. After a while Creator got over that sorrow and felt a sense of reinvigoration for His experiment.

I mention this to you not in any vainglorious way but to let you know that there is support for you here, whether you are the tiniest ant or at the level of a creator. "Maybe something could be better" is a useful feeling. Of course, in a polarized world some of you have decided to polarize me while you're at it: "Maybe things could be worse." But to your credit you will often say, "Maybe things might get worse, so we'd better enjoy it while we can," putting a brighter tone on it, which is what's intended.

I recognize that as a polarized experience right now things are difficult. But know that you are never too far from hope or potential or even maybe.

My Origin: The Emotion of Potential

How did you become the Master of Maybe? What did you do before this creation?

For a long time I existed beyond the Orb. Actually, I existed beyond even the light. Zoosh spoke to you briefly of his recent short journey beyond the Orb. He spoke to you of the points of light. If you go back a little farther you will discover that the points of light all represent supportive, nurturing or positive emotions or feelings, If you go into one, it is like passing through a doorway into a well of that feeling. They all stem from love, but as you know, there are many nuances to feeling. For instance, you could go into one that would be joyful and you would be overcome by the feeling of joy. You could go into another that might be gaiety, and you would be overwhelmed with laughter. You could go into another one marked compassion, and you would feel and know all there was to know through your feelings.

I mention this to you because beyond those points of source feeling (I believe this is where feeling comes from) there is an intermediate space. Picture all of your creation as a circle [he draws, 1]. Then here is the cloud of light [3] around the Orb [2], then a gap [4], then the individual points of light, which I'm drawing as little intermediate lines [5]. Beyond that is a significant space [6]. Within that space exists primarily the emotion of that which could be, or potential. I came from this space of potential—an unlimited basis of what could be. I was there for a *very* long time. It sounds like maybe is very close to *what could be*, but maybe is actually based upon *what already is*.

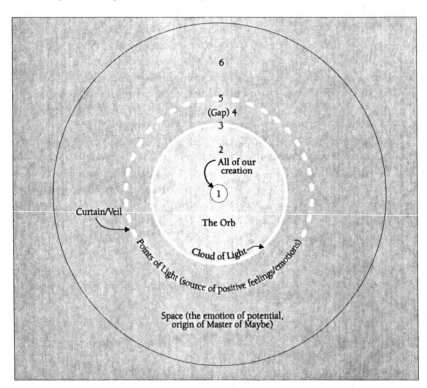

And a little more.

That's right. What could potentially be really precedes what is. I became aware of myself right around the time when I was needed for creations that were going beyond what they were and needed support within a matrix of energy. I fit into creations that already existed, but I came from the space of potential.

When I began to get involved in supporting what is to become more through the energy of maybe, I began to move out of the space of potential. I went through what is almost like a curtain or a veil, where these points of light are associated with the emotions. I went through the space, I went through the light, I went into the Orb. I was in major transit for quite some time and was moving very quickly. Even though the voyage was in time, it still took awhile. Even though I would go through a universe in a second and a half, I could acquire all of the potentials for why maybe was needed and how it could be used.

The Universe Where Individual Souls and Free Will Began

I traveled through several universes before I got to the one where I was needed, which preceded this creation. In that particular universe there was the beginning of what you now know as individual souls. In experiential time this is so far back that years don't even count—not even centuries or eras or eons, it is so long ago. It was before creators began to fragment themselves into bits called souls. In this universe they were beginning the experiment with souls, but the souls had not yet manifested physically.

The souls had only limited capability, not as much as their creator. These souls needed to grow on their own within the fairly narrow structure of this particular creator. They actually needed to go beyond the narrow structure that this creator was applying to them, but that creator could not or did not at that time perceive this. So I was really called by the souls themselves. When I arrived, that creator acknowledged my presence and welcomed me, but really did not know why I was there.

Working with that creator and those souls, I was able to support the souls to move beyond the very narrow expression of personality that was applied to them. When that creator realized that the problem came from the need of the souls, it was able to allow very wide parameters for souls to express themselves, from an individual being to something as massive as a planet. The function of individual souls was in its infancy then and very much experimental. That's how I got my start.

So you stayed there a very long time?

Quite awhile. Compared to the length of this creation, I stayed there approximately 75% of that measurable length—which, as you know, can't really be measured in years, but it was a long time. In the process I was able to learn my job better, because although the creation was nowhere near as large as the one you are in, that creator was working with something that every creator everywhere was fascinated with. It was something entirely new. No creator had ever fragmented itself before. It was as if all creators everywhere stopped and watched— that's how thrilling it was. I feel very privileged to have been involved in that.

What were some of the ways they were able to go beyond?

They needed to be able to express themselves beyond being points of light and become motivated to reconceive themselves as a smaller or a lesser creator, which was that creator's original intention. "Let me break off a piece of myself here, fragment it and see if it could come back into a miniature version of myself." That is how souls got started. You can see what a narrow range that is. But once these souls got broken up into pieces, even though they were being dragged back together to re-form and become one thing, they didn't want to do that. One wanted to go here and one wanted to go there; they wanted to explore and experience. They wanted to go and do other things.

Any parent understands that with children. I could feel their need to do this, and I provided the matrix of maybe, which is sourced from potential, as you know, but has to do with things already created. The souls were able to visualize and emote their feelings as to what they wanted to do. They didn't know they could communicate separately to their creator. They "thought" that their creator knew everything they knew, because the communication was totally telepathic. They thought that their creator understood everything they were feeling, not realizing that they were different from their creator. They were a group of individual creations who were developing separate identities, but their creator had only one identity, which included them. They had already become different from their creator, and their experience in life had gone beyond what their creator had known. Thus their creator could not hear, feel or know what they needed.

I provided the matrix of energy by which they could feed back to their creator on another level so that their creator could understand that these beings were not simply a portion of itself, but separate entities entirely. This creator needed to allow them to do what they would—within given benevolent parameters. That was the very beginning of the concept of free will.

What happened to them then? They evolved and became separate?

They all evolved and became creators themselves. Remember that this creator wanted them to come back together and re-form a sort of mini version of itself. However, by allowing them to go here, there and everywhere, acquire experience and then become creative, when they rebirthed themselves they were inclined to produce many, many more individuals, because they appreciated the experience of individuality. They gradually evolved into creators, each and every one of them, rather than merging to become a smaller version of their creator. In this way their creator was able to go to a much higher level of creation through being networked through all the other creators it birthed.

And they have their own creations out there now?

Yes.

What do you mean by higher level?

This creator went to the higher level. It was very interested in reproducing something that would become a multiple of itself, then re-form into another version of itself and return to being itself, as it were. It was experimenting with the idea of individuality, but was not particularly aware of what it was doing at that time. When it went to a higher level of itself, it was able to achieve a vision that allowed it to . . . well, I'll make it personal: it was able to go to where *your* Creator is going to go. It was able to move beyond the need to create individually, yet still be in observance and respect and love of individual creation.

Creators will often say to you, "You are me; we are all one." The creator's bias is to look at all portions of itself as being an extension of itself. There is still the need by creators (creator psychology here) to express itself in various forms. At the higher level a creator does not express itself in various forms, but it observes, advises (if necessary) and sustains all creations everywhere. It acts more as a *source energy*, supplying the nutrient of self-awareness that creators need in order to create and before they are aware of themselves as something or someone that they do *not* create. This level provides that self-awareness. Remember, I said that I became aware of myself. Many of the creators who have spoken already have also said, "I became aware of myself." That's where they get the energy to become aware of themselves.

When you say they go to a higher level, is that within the Orb or beyond it?

I believe it is beyond the Orb, because the Orb itself is made up of all these universes, these creations.

So we've got lots of exploring to do yet.

There is no reason to limit yourself (you would naturally hear this from me, of course).

This Creation

You tell me that! So you basically brought here the idea for Creator to create the freewill, individual souls in this creation?

By that time your Creator had already heard of this. Your Creator was going to be so involved with such a tremendous variety of individual souls that He wanted to have someone who had an intimate knowledge of the motivation of individuals to become individualized. For instance, you have billions of ants on this planet right now and they all have individual souls and personalities, even though they've mastered the ability to work within a team; add to that people and plants—everything is ensouled. Your Creator didn't need anybody to say, "This is what to create." But It did need to be reminded of that motivation, that constant desire to do and be something that might not necessarily be the most benevolent potential.

For example, here you are now in a polarized world where you have positivity and negativity, or comfort and discomfort. Because the world is so strongly polarized, within you sometimes you have individual portions of yourself that have such a strong desire to create that they are willing to create within you even though it goes against the primary function of you as a physical organism.

Like cancer?

Yes. Cancer and the growth of any tumor or any organism that wishes to express itself, even to the detriment of the total organism of which it is a portion, is a direct result of your present level of polarization. At a minor degree of polarization—1 to 2% discomfort—that doesn't happen. That happens only past the 30% mark.

The Future 61% Negativity

How deeply did we get into negativity? What's the most we had on Earth?

In terms of what you've had and the potential for what you still might have—and looking back from the future at this point—61% is as far as you will go. I know of a time in this creation here on Earth where you have had 60.5% discomfort. Since I know that you will at some point go as extreme as 61%, this leads me to believe that in the future you will go to 61%. Knowing you as well as I do, however, I believe that the only possible reason you might do this would be to create a springboard, something that builds a tension you will use to blast off. I think that is the only possibility. This leads me to believe that you will not maintain that 61% negativity or discomfort for very long.

But it's probably likely to be in the next couple years, then.

I should think it would be sooner rather than later, because you are really moving beyond that potential. I suspect it will be within the next three years.

So did our Creator put forth a call, or did He go through your creation, the one where you were?

He was already under way when I was called to be with him. I'd have to say that He had a place reserved for me. He could say, "Well, Maybe came in with me," but it's like hanging a sign on a chair that says "Maybe"; the sign was hanging on the chair before I had fully arrived. Your Creator arrived sufficiently motivated that He did not need me right away. It was after several brief skirmishes, from your Creator's point of view, with the complexities of what I'd call compound individualism (meaning many different types of individuals who did not have the same agenda in mind, but who were a team in the same world) that He needed to be reminded of the motivations of individuality and their need to be sufficiently nurtured so they wouldn't be thrown into chaos once they became aware of themselves.

Expanding the Creation to Separate Individuals into Groups

When you are not aware of yourself at this level and you are basically part of the whole, you can be in chaos and love it. You'd just feel, "Well, that's the way it is. It's wonderful! Isn't it exciting?" But once you become aware of yourself and you have a necessary separation from the whole in order to develop as an individual, chaos will be frightening indeed. Therefore I needed to remind Creator of the neces sities of the psychology of individuality, the nurturing of individuality and the need for compound individualism (which means many different kinds of individuals in the same place)—that this needed to be separated out somewhat. This actually played very nicely into your Creator's idea, because She wanted to have the most variety in the most space.

Initially Creator started out with the most variety in a fairly small space. It was my suggestion that if the individuals were separated at least spatially, they would have the opportunity to develop and be nurtured by individuals similar to themselves and wouldn't diverge indefinitely by being exposed to individuals unlike themselves.

At what point in the creation was this? What percentage of the total length to now?

This was pretty close to the beginning, perhaps around 10%, maybe 13% into it. So in the beginning it all looked like . . . well, if you ever looked at a slide teeming with life under a microscope, it was very much like that conceptually. I encouraged Creator to separate the microbes a bit.

Do you mean physically expand the creation then?

Yes. The creation moved way out then. That's why this particular universe has far-flung star fields. You can go from one end of this creation to the other, and it has more in common than it has dissimilar—stars, planets, shapes. Basic foundational principles are the same from one end of the universe to the other, but there's lots of variety within the individual context.

In the sense of personalities—if we can apply that word to beings as vast as you and the Creator—had you conversed and discussed the possibility of joining Him, or was it that He put out a call?

I think He put out a call. He put it out before I was available; that's why He had a chair with the name "Maybe" on it. I wasn't available right away.

My Contributions

You had to finish what you were doing?

That's right. But He put out a call, feeling that He would need me to cheerlead Him onward. I couldn't come right away, but I did send what amounted to a library of knowledge. I was sort of there, because I had sent everything I could that I thought would be useful to Him. That's why there was a chair there. As it turned out, because I wasn't quite aware of what He wanted to do, I could have sent other things, too. But we got it worked out.

You encouraged him to expand the creation; you pumped him up and gave him hope after Maldek.

Yes.

But what were some other contributions that you made to the creation that would not exist without your energy?

The interesting thing is that what I've been doing is so ongoing. As I say, as your Creator has become more involved with the massive level of creating and individualism here, also paying attention to what you are doing here. But He is being somewhat pulled away from here right now. I have been very much responsible, as other consultants have, for what's going on here with you. The reason I mention what is going on here is because I've been close to you.

But other events with the Creator? One particular one that is interesting but perhaps not totally relevant is this. Every once in a while creators get together. They won't leave their creation, but they do transfer some of their personality to talk things over. They usually do this in a totally merged state, as you might pour liquids together to become something of their own, then afterward separate and go back from whence they came. Communion can be total and unique because they become one thing unto themselves.

When your Creator sent that portion of Himself to this conference, because He was so involved in individuality He couldn't merge into becoming one thing. At that point I had to wrap myself around that portion of the Creator and provide an encapsulization of connection or a bridge and be the network between what Creator was and what everybody else needed your Creator to be. I was able to create a synthesis that allowed the others to feel your Creator as a portion of the one while at the same time protecting your Creator to remain focused in individuality.

What percentage of your energy is directed toward the Explorer Race and the planet right now?

Oh, I'd say anywhere between 70 and 75%.

Your energy is used to give us this sense of hope, that we can do more, that we can make it?

Yes. It operates on all levels, including the feeling self, but it is perhaps most compatible with the mind, because the mind can easily fall into patterns where it perceives limits as real. This is more the case than with other parts of you—the physical self, the feeling, the emotional self, the spiritual self. Those parts do not feel any sense of permanent limits, certainly not the physical self, absolutely. Because the mind very easily becomes involved in an artificial concept of limits, it needs maybe more than any other part of you. Therefore fully 40% (not of the 75%, but fully 40%) of me is involved with your minds, which need a lot of support to move beyond limited applications.

How do you do that? Do you work with the mind of humanity? Do you work with individuals? Do you work in the dream state? Do you work as energy?

All of the above. Perhaps most of it happens during your conscious state, but a little bit in the dream state. When I work in the dream state it's when you're going into it and when you're coming out. Others are responsible when you're at the deep dream level. So mostly it is when you are conscious.

Working through Levels of Consciousness
to Resolve Problems and Inspire Faith

So 40% is with the mind. Then how does the other 35% work with us?

The other portion of me is largely involved in mass changes. There are many things that all of you are upset about—violence and so on. You want things to be better. You want Creator to make it better for you, but unconsciously you all know that it's up to you. So I'd say that most of the rest of my energy is laying down a matrix of maybe that allows you to have a vaguely conscious feeling—beyond the unconscious, permeating the subconscious and coming up into the conscious as a feeling.

Feelings can come through the subconscious to the conscious mind. This is the only way right now that feelings can come up other than through direct physical evidence. So I will work through the unconscious and the subconscious to the conscious mind in order to provide you with the feeling/thought that maybe you can go beyond and resolve some major problem such as violence. You "know" in the mind (though it may not be true) that you've tried everything. This often comes up with individuals, but it comes up just as often with governments. You've "tried everything and nothing works" because they (whoever "they" are) just won't listen to you, are too stubborn—whatever the excuses are.

What you need now more than ever in mass groups is what I would call faith—that things can change, that somehow you can do it even though you don't have the tools and ideas and don't know how, yet you feel like you can and it's almost there and you're ready—that kind of energy. It is necessary to permeate you with that kind of energy so that when the tools do arrive and are recognized by a select few, they begin saying, "Hey, look! This works!" More and more people will adapt to those tools and say, "Yes, you're right. This *does* work."

Working for the Rest of Creation

What about your other 25% energy for the rest of creation?

Those are much more benign. That's the stress-free part of my life, where I am able to work with beings who have much more benevolent lifestyles—you know, peaceful, fun. I'm very often functioning on the playful level, because the beings in those other worlds are at their most creative, adaptable and changeable when they are in their youthful state. Once they get indoctrinated into their civilization, no matter how benign they are, they will come to believe in the value of their civilization by the preponderance of evidence that supports the idea that maintaining their civilization as it is produces happiness for everyone. You can't ignore that.

But when they are young in their cycle (I don't want to call them children, because it does not quite apply) they need to be supported in their individual potentials so that the energy they have as a person will not be lost when they merge with the society. It requires a lot of maybe energy to do that. You know, in your world children go through adolescence to have an actual energy that allows them to define their personality (however rebellious or benevolent it might be) apart from their immediate society so they can feel like they are someone separate. In more benevolent societies the "child" feels a loss of self-identity as it merges with the rest of society. So I need to support the maintenance of their sense of self-identity after they merge with society even though their society might be very similar to themselves.

Working with the Explorer Race

I would bet money that you have either been in the Explorer Race as a psychologist or that you have strongly influenced some of them.

Well, let's just say that I've had some interesting conversations with some of your more renowned thinkers, philosophers and—all right, a psychologist or two after their life cycles. Just because you're no longer a psychologist or philosopher in your physical life doesn't mean that you lose that point of view after you go beyond. That usually has to do with your personality.

Have you been here as someone we would recognize? In history have you been a human?

No, I haven't been a human. How could I stop and be a human when I had lots of stuff to do?

You could birth a part of yourself. You have never individualized?

No. Why? Did you think you recognized me?

I don't know. It just seems that your knowledge is so vast and wonderful that some of it must have filtered down here into individual teachers.

Well, you know, I talk to souls not only after life but sometimes before a life. And I certainly communicate with individuals energetically, very often all the time.

So some of your knowledge has been used here on Earth.

Well, it is certainly possible that I might have inspired or provided the energy or encouragement that someone needed in order to create some accomplishment of their own.

But when you say you put out a matrix, that's your beingness, right?

Yes.

So your beingness is focused. You talk about these percentage points. That's you?

Yes. It is personal, yes. I might be scattered all over in bits of myself, but I do not lose any portion of myself, nor do I actually live through the individuals. I am only with them to the extent they need me. When they no longer need me, for whatever reason, that portion returns to the totality of me or goes elsewhere where it is needed. So I never lose any portions of myself, but I might be all over the place at any given moment.

It sounds like the Explorer Race is going to continue to need your services, and that you won't get laid off when the Creator leaves.

I think you'll probably want to keep me on because there will be other beings within this creation who will need lots of that kind of encouragement—though I am certainly open to training an apprentice or two. [Laughter.]

The Future

Okay. Let's talk about when you finally leave. You've worked with creators in their creations, but you come from a place of potentials. With everything that you've learned, do you see yourself becoming a creator and creating your own creation?

Let's just put it like this: As of this moment I feel no personal motivation to do that, so I don't see myself doing that. I enjoy what I am doing now and I believe I will continue to do it. Barring any tremendous change in the future, I think I will stay with what I'm doing. I like this. I've found a home.

Well, you're wonderful with what you're doing. Would the trigger point to expansion affect you in a way that might cause you to change your mind?

Well, I couldn't say that. I fully expect to have more mass of myself available when the expansion occurs. It is certainly possible that I might change my point of view, but at this point I have no inkling that that is so.

But you've looked from the future.

The interesting thing is that this goes all the way up to and beyond the creator level, in my personal experience. One can stand in the future and look back in any past. Yet your *personal* future, your *personal* evolution, is necessarily veiled to you because if you could see what you will do, it immediately limits you. No matter how far in the future you go, it is much easier to see your immediate future, a short period ahead, rather than your long-range future. That is because limits immediately come up, and you will simply tend to have a bias toward a given future rather than an openness toward your potential future. Even creators have somewhat of a limit.

I see. It's a matter of making that fantasy true, making what you saw a reality.

Yes, or else you have a bias against it, not seeing that it might take you someplace benevolent. The main thing is that you might develop a bias pro or con, or even be disinterested in that particular potential for the future, because you don't see everything that it means. Because it can create a bias, the veil is present for all beings (every creator) that I know of. I don't think it's present beyond the Orb.

This means that a creator has a purpose, a plan and a goal, and he sets out to do it. But he doesn't really know how it's going to come out.

Well, that's the fun of creation. That is why beings who are creators want to be creators. If you knew exactly how it was going to turn out, can you imagine what a short line would form for becoming creators? It would be totally boring. The fun of it all is being able to do something magnificent and wonderful, with surprises available, and having to rise to the surprise or simply enjoy its pleasantness.

My Growth

You've helped the Creator, but in what ways have you used this principle in yourself, where you did something you didn't think or know that you could do? Give me an example.

I think the biggest growth I've had is along the line of individuality, because when I look back at what I've been doing, I realize I've been very much involved in that concept. It was very much conceptual before I got here. Your Creator is enamored of individuality; there's no other way to put it. I grew in its application because I had to provide maybe to everything from soup to nuts; I had to provide it to such a wide variety of beings. I had to form, re-form and multiform myself in ways that I had never had to do. As a double-jointed person does, I had to basically bend around backward and tie myself in knots. I had to do things I didn't think I *could* do.

Because you couldn't lead them to the impossible unless you could feel in yourself that it was possible.

That's right. I had to do this kind of thing. I might be doing something very simple in one place and something highly complex someplace else, and everything in between. I had to do it all at the same time, whereas in previous creations there was very much a rhythm, a synchronicity.

One thing after the other. But here you had to do it all at once.

Yes, the simplicity was very much there in other creations. The complexity in this creation is just beyond enumeration, so I had to really stretch.

Which is wonderful.

Yes. When we stretch, we discover we can do more. That is really what I'm involved in.

But you had to do it with yourself before you could invoke it in others and inspire them.

Well, it made me so much a believer in what I was doing that I could do it much more enthusiastically.

I'm running out of questions. Tell us whatever you want.

All right. In order to fully appreciate maybe, the most important thing is to know that it does not always have to be applied to this life, that it's just possible that the unsolvable might be solved at other dimensions of yourself. Yes, try to solve it. Yes, make the effort. Yes, involve others in this to the extent that they desire resolution or growth. But know that if maybe is present, no matter how unsolvable it seems to be, *a solution is available.* It will happen, and you will know about it. Good night.

❖ Robert's Comments on His Experience

I really had a distinct impression of beyond the orb when he was talking about it. I could see the points of light and the well of feelings within those points. Then I felt his frustration in trying to describe what the space felt like beyond that. I also felt the word "potential." It was as if the word included a physical, dynamic energy. So I felt the potential as a thing rather than a concept. I felt the tension of all this stuff that was waiting and excited about becoming whatever. It was a physical feeling.

Zoosh started it out by saying he went out there to look beyond the orb. He got only as far as the points of light.

He told me this afternoon, I remember. I was driving somewhere and I had a flash (maybe he was doing it at that moment). I could see light from here radiating outward and the light around here radiating inward. I think that might have been the moment when he was on the road again.

Master of Frequencies and Octaves

October 15, 1996

provide the frequencies and to some extent the pulse harmonics and the necessary octaves for each dimension as required by your Creator. It is important to note that creators, regardless of where their creations exist, must have some assistance because this job is so vast. It certainly is in this case, where the number of embodied individuals within this creation is higher than you can count within an understandable mental sequence. Without getting into Fibonacci numbers [chuckles], I will simply say that my job is to coordinate frequencies, octaves—generally speaking, harmonics—so that your Creator can apply them. I do not apply them; I create them somewhat in the same way your music teachers might have given you a perfect pitch in school. I provided this, not unlike a transmitter, then your Creator used these harmonics to establish the matrix of each dimension.

For example, in the sound-pulse harmonic of the third dimension, you have something akin to vibrations. You might remember that thirty years ago in experiential time things were calmer. Human social systems were different, but you could be in the middle of a busy town then and still experience calm moments. But now that you are moving between dimensions while you are alive (an unusual circumstance for physically encapsulated beings, ruling out traveling in ships or in light, which you do not do extensively yet), you are experiencing something similar to what a pilot's body goes through when his plane moves through the sound barrier. One of those feelings is a stimulation to the nervous system.

It is my job here to carefully—*very* carefully—apply certain overlays. I have to provide the basic tones for the third and fourth dimensions, but you are moving through the dimensions and are now right around 3.49. When you got to about 3.36 [for information on the dimensional shift in 1995 see *Shining the Light III*, chapters 30–32] I started applying tonal overlays within the dimension that would allow your physical selves to move through the barrier between dimensions and physically survive the experience. If this had not been done (at the request of your Creator) you would not have survived. You as physical beings (including the planet) would have arrived right around 3.47—and that would have been the end!

That is why in so many documents, some of which survive even today, visionaries and psychics have predicted the end in these times. You are *living through* the times predicted to be the end. If Creator had not requested these overlay harmonics, then it *would* have been the end. These "borders" between dimensions are very firm so that individuals from different dimensions do not accidentally fall through.

Here we have an exception to the rule (rules are made to be broken, yes?) whereby an entire planet and its people (and to a lesser extent the rest of Creator's universe) are moving through the barriers between dimensions while you are alive, and doing so with a minimum of damage (considering what would have happened otherwise) to the planet, the physical selves, the animals and so on.

Harmonic Overlays That Protect Angels and Lightbeings

I will make a sketch of harmonic overlays. Imagine dimensions as concave funnels. These harmonic overlays provide a tonal bridge that functions in a very specific corridor, which keeps your planet and all the beings on it isolated from the comings and goings of all beings in your creation and to some extent other creations. We cannot much afford to have holes in time, although there are beings who can repair them. We also cannot much afford to have holes in veils (there are several between dimensions).

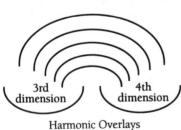

Harmonic Overlays

It is not possible to allow a hole the size of a planet and all its people, because there must be someone in charge of every individual, whether it be a human being, a tree, a mountain, a dog, a cat—anyone. That's a massive project. We cannot allow this kind of tear to take place without that kind of vigilance. Multiple harmonic overlays are required because beings will have to come here to be with you as you carefully move through this opening between dimensions.

There is a fourth-dimensional Earth. To some extent we have you traveling on Earth as a bus, and at some point that Earth will come part way, then fall back and lock into third dimension and you will find yourself on fourth-dimensional Earth. Or else (Creator has not decided this yet) you will ride on a pseudo-Earth, which changes gradually from its third-dimensional to its fourth-dimensional self while third-dimensional and fourth-dimensional Earth are here. I think this is most likely the decision Creator will make. (Creator is actually doing this now, but the decision is still optional.) In this way other life forms on both third-dimensional and fourth-dimensional Earth can exist in safety.

There is a great deal going on. These harmonic overlays also provide safety zones for the multidimensional beings and the billions of angels and lightbeings who must come to help out. Therefore every individual has, in addition to their usual guides and teachers, a guide through this process because it is so unique. It has never been done this way before. Your normal guides and teachers cannot take you individually through this process from the third to the fourth dimension, so there need to be very clearly established angels and lightbeing guides who can lead you and your individual entourage through this process. The harmonic overlays provide a narrow opening, or gate.

Because there is an element of what I would call harmonic vacuum involved here, we are dealing in tolerances like those you would find in a product very carefully machined for a specific task. Here is a measurement so you get the idea: You're slipping through a gate for which the tolerance (in terms of machining) would be .0 plus another 24 zeros and 1 [0.0000000000000000000000001]. We've got something here that's tremendously precise, and between that tiny little space and the rest of the universe I have to squeeze vast amounts of what I would call erratic sound substance. Both I and Creator and everyone are pulling this in. Now I'm going to tell you what that's about.

Erratic Sound Substance Protecting Your Dimensional Shift

Erratic sound substance is made up of energy particles similar to quarks, but they are extremely small. What has been categorized and somewhat documented as a quark emanates a light that is, at any given moment, anywhere from 1000 to 5000 times its actual size. So it leaves a light signature that can occasionally be imprinted as an image that has been somewhere; that's how they know these exist. These erratic sound particles make up that very thin barrier I spoke of, because they are the only kind of particle that can exist in such an extreme of sound. If you were exposed to the actual harmonic pulse it would cause instant deafness and death. That is how extreme it is.

Erratic sound particles can handle that. They exist in it; it is their nature to be in it. Not only can they handle it, they actually thrive in it.

With the Creator's assistance they are creating an actual systematic life form that links together, quark by quark, what I'd call a light film. They are constantly moving around, but it is their light trail that is actually protecting you so you can slip through this gate unharmed. These particles are actually consuming and living on the harmonic that Creator and I have placed there (we provide it and blow it in). They exist on that sound, and what they leave behind is a form of light that is particularly protective to you.

This envelope moves very slowly from one dimension to another, allowing you to make this move safely. I give you this example so that you will understand it within the context of your journey. In other dimensions there is a tremendous amount of focused material of sound or harmonics that keeps the dimensions well established. Anytime you make a move through a dimension, there is tremendous effort. But in other dimensions of this creation there is less vigilance required because the basic system of the dimensions is sustained by the original program placed there by your Creator. Beings who are reasonably evolved can pass through these dimensions because of the evolutionary light cycle that they establish. They can pass through as light without causing any harm. If someone passes through unintentionally, as occasionally happens, then individuals assigned to these tasks will go to these dimensions to repair the holes.

Your Tolerance and Intolerance for Certain Frequencies

In order to establish the various frequencies that you can hear and feel, I also must provide a certain basic pulse upon which you build a certain tolerance for frequencies. As you all know, some frequencies are comfortable, even sounds you can make. There is also sound that you can only feel or sense, if you are reasonably sensitive, and still other frequencies you are unaware of. As you know, some high-pitched sounds are uncomfortable. Most of these very high-pitched tones are your natural state of being, and it is intended that you deflect somewhat from your natural state of being.

Creator wishes you to get the most out of your experience here on Earth as you pass from the third to the fourth dimension. Since it is your nature to be lightbeings, to exist at the higher dimensions and the higher frequencies, Creator has established an artificial barrier such that when you are exposed to those higher frequencies, there is just enough discomfort to move you away from them. I'm not talking about ultrasonic here, but about higher sounds that you can actually hear.

These tones and frequencies are important to understand, because you, in your natural state of being, are of the higher frequencies. What is new to you, what you are stretching to learn, what you are attempting to accomplish here as the Explorer Race, is how to create and be responsible for what happens in what you call the denser dimensions (for example, the second and third dimensions). You are having this education here as a portion of creator school because experiences at the higher dimensions always have echoes in lower dimensions. Conversely, there are practically never echoes from what is created at the lower dimensions. Anyone in creator school must be able to deal with the repercussions, the results and the consequences of creations at higher dimensions that will greatly impact the lower (the slower or more material) dimensions.

To fully grasp what this means, I must remind you that at the higher frequencies you are unwelcome because you are a physical being. At the end of your natural cycle and even in some deep dream states, these higher frequencies are home for you, but when you are awake and conscious, you plow along in the lower frequencies so that you can directly understand what happens when A goes to B or when C goes to D—results, consequences. You are here in these material planes to experience direct results and consequences having to do with your or others' actions applied within this realm.

No one is allowed to become a creator without going through this level of the school, because what goes on at the first dimension is basically an imprint of what goes on everyplace else—a permanent record. In the second and third dimensions is material existence, where you're actually functioning. To some extent you as souls have not really existed in the second dimension as you know it, but some of you have had a little bit of latter second dimension (2.7 through 3.0) and all of you have existed from 3.0 on.

Progressing Slowly to Discern Dimensional Impacts

On the basis of what I've said here, you could extrapolate that there have been many creations at higher levels that have existed in the beginning for some time without its creator (creators do this) or without beings who are working on being a creator. For example, one of the final stages in becoming a creator is coming together with other beings to manifest things (pouf! as your Zoosh likes to say). But many of the pouf! situations that created something out of "thin air" have had an unintentional but mischievous impact on the more material dimensions.

You are going very slowly through the dimensions so you can feel impacts caused by people in your dimension and occasionally even impacts caused in your dimension by beings in the higher frequencies. This is also why your Creator has invited many higher-frequency beings to come and visit, because they represent a group or even a world of beings who have established a benevolent creation at a higher dimension that has detrimentally impacted the more material planes.

That's another reason you have so many lightbeings visiting here all the time—this is not only a school for yourselves but for others. It is also why you don't have as many physical ET contacts as you once had, although you are getting a significant amount of ET contact right now in the form of symbolic interaction at the deep dream level, on the teaching level, on the sensitive level and, more physically, crop circles, which are the establishment of signs and cosigns by which certain tribes and families are identified.

As we move on in our understanding here, we need to recognize that within this artificial environment of accepted frequencies in which you currently exist, you must notice not only the impact of what you do but also the impact of what other beings do. This is why you are conscious of politics, not just as you know it (elections and so on), but personal politics—what individuals believe, what they do on the basis of those beliefs, how they act, how they gather with others, how they achieve what they achieve, how it affects you. This is what I'd call the body politic, because it has to do with how you conduct your life and how it affects other beings.

This is also why you have such a very good communication system. On higher dimensions the communication system is much different. Yes, there is telepathy, but it is on the feeling level. Language is nowhere near as complex and precise. It is more associated with what you can see in thought pictures, what you feel. Communications are much simpler compared to the wide variety of language you have here. You do not have ready access to telepathic mental understanding, though all of you have telepathic emotional understanding, albeit not largely applied in a way you can understand. Mental telepathy is not readily available to you, so you must have very specific languages, signs, symbols and so on.

Within these frequencies you are constantly reminded of how you affect each other. This information is important because it is something that is *intended* to happen. You are not intended to come here to have only a pleasant life. This is guaranteed at almost all other places, but you are intended to come here to learn, to have your nature restricted by Creator so you can learn the impact of what you do. At higher dimensions you could have very evolved, loving lightbeings creating something that seems to be wonderful and magnificent—yet entirely unbeknownst to them, it is in some way negatively impacting the more material planes where cause and effect are more readily recognized.

You As Educators

You will educate many of these lightbeings who are here to learn. You too are here to experience it, but when those lightbeings come, they observe, but they do not feel. They are protected from feeling because they could not handle the energies here and because their frequencies do not fit into your frequency range. Thus they can visit without affecting you or being affected by you, and you are similarly screened from them. You are learning by direct education, whereas they are learning by watching—one step removed. You will go out and teach them someday as the Explorer Race, which your Zoosh has spoken to you about.

As you gradually merge to become Creator's replacement, you will then have experienced the consequences of what you do. I cannot tell you how complex, complicated and almost unconscionable has been the impact upon other creations that have not had material planes such as this to make these discoveries. There have been earlier creations for which I have been a consultant, in which the creators were evolved in their time and experience, but these creators did not understand the impact at lower material dimensions where they were uninvolved. Lower dimensions existed for any beings to explore within their creation, but after beings went there they said, "You can't exist there. The energy is awful there. There are constant rips in the fabric of time and space. It's impossible! If you go there, it's like a pit: you get lost."

That is why for many, many experiential "years" creators regarded the material planes as being inferior. Anyone who went there, including their creator, glancing at it himself/herself/itself, would feel that this was somehow a backwash of the creation, a sort of garbage dump, not understanding that anything that happened in the fifth dimension or higher would directly impact *all dimensions beneath it.* The impact was felt not so much in the fourth dimension, but in the third and second dimensions it was like a truck driving through a china shop, very devastating.

Joining Your Creator, Recommending 2nd, 3rd and 4th Dimensions As a School

When your Creator established this creation, He rounded up a large team of individuals—not only myself, but others—and had lots of consultations before arriving at this space to create this universe. I joined up because I had consulted with and helped other creators clean up the mess in their fourth, third and second dimensions. They had not understood the impact of light and its well-intentioned effects on the slower dimensions, which are basically what I'd call substance, or form.

So when I arrived with your Creator I had an agenda, which was to see that such things would not happen. I advised your Creator to use the second, third and fourth dimensions as a place of schooling, because the immediate impact of what one does (though not always recognizable, it is there, I assure you) might be highly beneficial as a teaching tool. I will not take credit for the creation of these dimensions, but I believe that your Creator ultimately decided to use these dimensions in birthing you as the Explorer Race, to give you a place where you could learn the consequences of your actions.

This type of applied creationism is new, and it's another reason other creators are paying a lot of attention to what is going on here. They are all taking another look now. Since the beginning of this creation they have taken another look at their own second, third and fourth dimensions to see whether they might wish to establish these areas of their creations as a school or a place where other beings, even from other creations, can come and learn about consequences and the impact of their creation and so on.

You must understand that what's going on here within your creation is not only unique throughout all creation as I know it, but is quite revolutionary in its integrity. Now, we all know that in order to maintain functional integrity, barriers are needed. You have a barrier, your cells have barriers, your bones have barriers. Your skin is a membrane, a barrier that keeps you within your physical self. True material integrity requires at least the appearance or the assumption of separation in order to learn.

If you as an individual do something and it affects another person, you could say, "Well, *you* did *this*" (pointing at the other person) or "I am reacting to what the other person did" and explore all those avenues. But at the very least you recognize that something apparently outside of yourself has had an impact on the material self, on you as you know yourself to be. In this way you learn a great deal as an individual about integrity on the material plane, on the light plane and on the creator plane, because what you do affects others as well as yourself.

Universal Ramifications: Applied Spiritual Integrity

All of this is very important when you consider that the ramifications of this affect everyone in not only this creation (and this is absolutely the vastest creation I've ever participated in) but in all other creations that I am aware of within the Orb. It might even affect creations beyond the Orb. In this context you can see how what you are doing is so very important. I'm not saying this to make you self-conscious, but so you will realize that even if you feel you are living some kind of innocuous or boring life, you would not be allowed to be here if your Creator did not have absolute faith in what you are doing and learning and, perhaps most important, in what you will do in the future.

So no matter how exciting or mundane your life might seem, every one of you without exception will be involved as Creator in the future, bringing not only the vast depth and array of your experience, but also the ability to know and understand applied consequences. At the end of the natural life cycle you shed all of the pain and suffering, but you retain the wisdom you gained. You will sometimes even review your life to see how things came to be the way they were, and within that review you will add even more wisdom to the total you and thereby to the ultimate creator you will become.

It is intended that the issue at stake is truly *applied spiritual integrity*. If a creator is totally conscious of all dimensions of its applied creation, it necessarily follows that that creator will be the ultimate in responsibility. From my experience of existence (which is a long time), I'd have to say that your Creator is the most responsible creator I have ever been aware of because It was willing to do something I have not seen in many other creations: Before your Creator created anything, She rounded up beings such as myself who had lots of previous experience and skills, invited us to come along and contribute to the extent we wished so that we could accumulate experience like your Creator and learn along with Him. Your Creator was willing to say, "I Am . . . yes, I Am," but also to say something beyond "I Am" (which is the standard rejoinder of any creator). Your Creator was willing to say something most unique and wonderful: "We Are." I am not aware of any other creator before yours who was open to saying that. This is one of the most magnificent, wonderful things to say, to provide and to associate oneself with.

The Miniature Galaxy that Physically Changed Earth

As often happens in the fifth dimension, there were once some beings who were moving beyond what you would call physical substance into the realm of functioning in light more than substance. This was a group of 100 white lightbeings who gathered to create an artificial (temporary) creation of a miniature galaxy within this creation. This was allowed because they were learning and it was important for their growth.

So within a space unoccupied by other galaxies they created over time a small spiral galaxy, about half the size of your own. It took about 150 experiential years to establish the whole thing. But what they didn't understand was that anytime you displace space [chuckles], it is felt on *all* the dimensions. As one goes up, it is celebrated: "Oh! A new creation!" It is wonderful, it is felt very well. But as it goes down in dimension, on the fourth dimension it was felt as a very slight discomfort, such as in the following example: If you've ever been on a bus or in a theater occupied doing something and someone comes along and sits next to you, even if there is no attempt to strike up a conversation or become involved in your life, it's still a slight discomfort. But you get used to what you're doing and you forget about it. That's how the beings on the fourth dimension felt this new galaxy.

On the third dimension it was felt as if someone you didn't know came up to you, put a hand on your chest and shoved you about five feet. It was felt as a very strong intimidation. This occurred several hundred thousand years ago, right around the time when tremendous volcanic activity was going on. Earth was impacted so strongly that volcanic activity began to die down and several mountain ranges that would have become continents within the sea didn't do so. A few continents that existed were undercut by erratically moving volcanoes. (A volcano has a given path; it is going to move in a certain direction. This is somewhat set within its creation, as a volcano is a part of Creator.) The path of these volcanos, these beings, was deflected and several continents were severely undercut, changing the way they look.

For example, there used to be a land bridge between the islands of Japan and the continent now known as China. This land bridge was damaged, undercut so much by deep volcanoes that it fell into the sea. Even today, and certainly in the past thousands of years of your history, both Japan and China have felt strongly that one ought to occupy the other. This has greatly affected the politics of the region, to say nothing of the history. That is why there has been great political and historical unrest between these peoples—China sometimes invading the islands, at other times Japan invading China. None of this would have happened if the land bridge had remained. The peoples would have been homogeneous. There have been other impacts, but I mention that one because even a casual understanding of history would demonstrate that it has indeed been a powerful consequence.

There was also tremendous impact in the second dimension. Something wonderful was created in the fifth dimension that all other dimensions in it and above celebrated, but because of the displaced space and the lack of knowledge and understanding of consequences of those 100 white-light beings, the more material dimensions were impacted. In the second dimension the connection between consciousness (awareness) and spirit (permanent existence) was severed for over 3500 years! This is part of the reason that certain second-dimensional beings were able to make mistakes and perpetuate them for so long that they strongly impacted the second dimension.

Tremendous assistance arrived. Lightbeings from all over—angels—rushed to the second dimension, and with all of their efforts it still took about 3500 experiential years to repair the damage that had fractured their dimension. You can see how those white-light beings—no matter how wonderful they might be and no matter how sensational that miniature galaxy might have been—with their simple lack of knowledge of displaced space, impacted the rest of existence.

Loss of the First Dimension's Historical Records and Slow Repair of the Four Dimensions

This impact was so great that it was even registered in the first dimension—which is a record of all things in any creation. It registered in the first dimension as a loss of records. If you were able to hover over it as one might look at a map from above, it would be as if a huge asteroid slammed into a topographical map, leaving a big hole where once there was history. Those 100 lightbeings were not only responsible for dealing with the consequences in the fourth and the third dimensions, they had to repair piece by piece within the first dimension, which is not easy for a white-light being to do, but possible when there are 100 or more. The loss of that historical record was not only about what went on in the second, third and fourth dimensions during that time, but in *all this creation!* They're still working on it, although they're just about done. (They can hear me saying this and can laugh about it now.) It has taken them all this time to repair what they did to the fourth, the third and the second dimensions, and they are now just finishing up the first dimension, probably completing it within the next three or four experiential years.

You might ask, "What happened to the galaxy they created?" It was a beautiful miniature galaxy and was intended to be a model of what they might create someday when they achieved creator status (not realizing that they would be delayed for some time). They had not created living beings on any of these planets or stars or systems, so when they realized what had happened, they simply uncreated it. But they did not disappear it, as you might say. They recompacted it into its original point of light just like one might fold up a piece of paper and store it in a small slot (the Creator had said, "It's safe to put it here"). They will re-create it once they have finished repairing the damage on the first dimension. They will then heave a collective sigh of relief and probably take a little vacation. Then they'll go to the space where they wish to go and, much wiser for the experience, begin their own creation, starting with that point of light of their miniature galaxy.

Asking Permission of the Space

What will they do that will have different results? What did they not do the first time?

Well, there's nothing like having to repair the damage you've caused. What did they do the first time? They created the galaxy without asking permission of the space that they were creating in, so the space was displaced without its permission. When somebody displaces your space without your permission it is offensive at the very least, to say nothing of potentially destructive, as you might have noticed in any car crash. After repairing the damage, they are perhaps more understanding of what goes on in the first through the fourth dimensions than most beings at this time. Although their particular experience was more dramatic than they would have wished, these were a sort of prototype Explorer Race (this is largely why your Creator allowed this). When Creator was considering speeding up your evolution, She said, "Okay, they want to do this. I'll let them do it and if they're successful and do it right, we can speed up your evolution greatly." Well, you know what happened. Afterward Creator said, "No, I think one step at a time is just fine."

After a significant rest they will leave this creation (the creation of which you are a portion), go out and begin again, with a rightful claim to be masters of the first, second, third and fourth dimensions (though perhaps not the fifth).

Is it just a matter of asking permission? Is that the one thing you need to do?

Well, you must *receive* the permission, too. You can't stand in space and say, "I'd like to do this" and then just go ahead and do it. You must receive the permission, and that might take a little time. Maybe that space is occupied with something. Maybe you need to go to some other space nearby and ask that space, "Is this all right?" The main thing is, you need to go to all of the space where you're going to do this, asking its permission, asking whether it's all right to begin, then work slowly enough so the space can get out of the way in its own time. This was not done.

That would prevent repercussions.

Yes. Of course, you must know how to hear the response as well. (By the way, you hear the response with your feelings.)

My Education in Sound as the Structural Integrity of All

So how did you gain all of this wisdom, knowledge and skill?

Once upon a time I existed in the cloud of light that surrounds the Orb. That cloud of light is motion coming toward the Orb, and I believe there is a degree of individual perception in that cloud of light. I began to move away from the Orb, not toward it. I moved through the points of light that are established as the tide pools of emotion. I moved through a fairly thick barrier, taking a little experiential time. I did not realize at the time why the barrier was so thick, but once I got to the other side I was fully cognizant of why it was necessary to patch up the space behind me as I moved through it. It was basically a one-way thing: you go one way, but you return by another route.

Once I got through it, I moved into an area that was what I can only describe as a constant impact of felt sound. I believe this is where I got my initial programming, my understanding of the incredible variety of sound. Sound is not just within *your* perceived ability to hear, for I did not have that limit. Within this sound they were constantly creating and uncreating beings, creations. There was an unbelievable cacophony of sound creations that would come and go so fast as to be unmeasurable by even your best electronic clocks.

I have come to think of this coming and going of creations as the reservoir of thought inspiration. Anything that has ever been thought, pictured, felt and transmitted through inspiration seems to come from this place. I took that to be a wonderful thing. I stayed there for quite a while, experiencing uncountable, soon-to-be inspirations—never the same, always varied, always associated with the combination of sounds within the space of that creation at that moment.

It was then that I gradually understood that without sound—from your perception, to the felt, to the imagined level and beyond—it is not possible to maintain the structural integrity of anything that can be thought, considered, seen, felt or perceived. I felt that this would be a good way to conduct my life, so I moved back toward the Orb (it took me a while to get back through the barrier) to bring this to whichever creator wished to incorporate my knowledge and see what might come of it within the Orb. (I remind you that the Orb is *all creations* within where we are.)

That's what I've been doing, where I came from and why.

Which creation called you first?

It didn't work like that. I realize it has worked that way with some other beings, but this is something I did on my own. I wanted to go beyond; I wanted to see what else there was. That's why I functioned that way. You might say I was self-motivated, because I wasn't called by anything external. You might also say I was pulled. That would suggest that I probably passed that way at some time before I had a sentient consciousness. This is likely anyway, because anything associated with creationism within the Orb passes through that.

Once you got back to the light around the Orb, then how did you choose where to go?

I didn't actually choose. That light radiates inward, as you know. I just let myself radiate inward. I decided that the light knows where it's going, so I allowed myself to be radiated inward wherever I went. When I discovered where I was, I started moving around until I came across a creator who could recognize my sound picture. I didn't broadcast myself as if to say, "Here I am. I have come to save your existence." I basically moved slowly enough (though pretty fast by your standard) that any creator could see and feel who and what I was and would have the option of saying, "Stop! Come over for a visit. Who and what are you? Let's 'talk.'" In this way I did not impose myself on anyone, but waited to be asked (which, I might add, applies in many other circumstances as well).

So who asked you first?

The Split Creator of a Spiral Creation

I was asked for help by a creator who was involved in a spiral creation that was moving inward (not outward). This creator is a very interesting being. It had split itself into two parts—imagine a tornadic action that moves very slowly. Let's see if I can make a very rough sketch. It moves inward like a pinwheel, but very slowly, then goes someplace

Spiral Creation
through a Gate
at Its Center

else. One creator had separated itself from its other part, and neither part knew what the other was doing. This creator was creating its version of ultimate beauty and spinning it slowly inward, passing through a gate to the other creator, who would create its version of ultimate beauty from what passed through.

I thought this was rather unique, so I took the voyage myself to get an idea of what was going on. In the gate from one creation to another it was riotously uncomfortable! I came back to the creator who had originally requested my assistance and informed it that the gate needed to be changed. Pulse harmonics was needed there so that when a creation came out of the gate on the other side, it would not be so traumatized that it would be uninterested in participating in some new creation.

Although I communicated with that creator and the one on the other side, I could not tell one what I told the other, because that was their arrangement. As a result, they literally replayed their whole creation. They ran it back to the beginning and did it all over again so that none of that material would be uncreated. The trauma was thus uncreated. Then the whole creation started again, and within that gate I provided and maintained certain pulse harmonics that the creators were able to understand on both sides. The material that passed from one creation to the other (as a part of what would ultimately be the same creation) could then pass through pleasantly, comfortably and benevolently. Most important, the material started out as something more expansive, then became more compact, but experienced it as nurturing birth as it moved from one portion of itself to the other. By the time it got to the other side it was excited and interested in what it was going to be.

I might add that it is ultimately intended that birth for you here will be experienced the same way. You know, if something is learned in one creation, it tends to pass on to others if it works. At higher dimensions birth is very much like that. It is something that is celebrated and there is no pain. The child is excited and happy, looking forward to seeing what it will be when it passes through its mother. It comes out the other side welcomed. It is a joyous adventure, not always the way it is here in your current dimension for any of you who have had children. But that will change.

Where did you go after that?

Joining Your Creator

I moved on when I was done there, went through about three or four other creations, during which I provided very much the same kind of consulting I provided in that first creation, adding to that creator's understanding of the value of frequencies and harmonics. By this time your Creator was moving near me—because, you know, your Creator had been on a long voyage before I came to this space. I had already done these things and had developed a pretty strong agenda about what I felt was important for creations. Because of my personal experience I could be a source by which your Creator could tap into what was beyond the Orb, in the space where I had been empowered. Your Creator appreciated the value of my agenda. We had many worthy communications before your Creator established this creation.

Ah, this is the first time we knew He talked to somebody from beyond the Orb before he created this creation.

Yes, it gave your Creator the wisdom to proceed with care and allowed It to understand a little more of the personal choice involved in the creation process. Creators, when they become aware of themselves as an individual, often do not recognize that their birth into personality is a personal choice and not something that simply happened.

Because of my visual, felt experience of what was beyond the Orb, your Creator began to examine a little more His role in personal choice. As a result, your Creator might have become more personally empowered, feeling She had a significantly broader avenue of what She could do, based upon what She personally chose rather than what was simply right and proper (using terms you can understand). This is very important, because your Creator wanted to do something very revolutionary.

Before we had these discussions I think your Creator had qualms about whether what It would create would be right and proper. Beyond our initial meeting, your Creator was able to understand and feel good about not only the value (which He was quite charged up about) but the principles by which She would establish the ordination of the Explorer Race through channeling and impactful dimensional experiences.

Your Creator knew there was a very good chance that you would suffer as a result of becoming embodied as the Explorer Race. Your Creator felt uncomfortable about this, even though that suffering would be lifted from you at the end of your natural life. How could It impose suffering that ranged from mild to great upon any beings? So by way of the permission that comes with personal choice (and there's a certain degree of impetuousness involved in personal choice), your Creator was able to say, "I'll take the chance." And chance really was involved. If things had not turned out as well as they have (you might not think it looks like that, but it really has), your Creator would have to, bit by bit (remember my explanation of those 100 lightbeings having to repair the inadvertent damage they created), repair the damage to each and every one of you. The amount of experiential time it would have taken (in terms of the length of your creation as it has existed to now) is about

400,000%.

Unbelievable!

Yes. Your Creator would have been a busy little being for a long time simply putting you all to rights. Let's just say that your Creator is mightily relieved that you are turning out as well as you are, because He has other plans for what to do in the future. [Chuckles.]

Did you ever choose to birth part of yourself you could embody into the Explorer Race?

No, I haven't done this. It wasn't intended. I didn't need to do it.

Did you work through inspiring some of our composers or musicians?

No. that's not my job. My job is to provide the mortar; I don't have to be the bricks.

Oh, I thought you had inspired some of the great composers.

No, not true. Other beings did that. I provide the mortar and other beings provide the bricks. I'll say it twice—I like it. [Chuckles.]

You're an incredible addition to this creation.

Thank you very much. I will close by saying that the incredible complexity of your being is what makes up the universal choir. When you pass from this dimension to the next at the end of your natural cycle you will hear, feel and rejoice in the universal choir. It is the voice of all beings who have ever existed as well as those who are currently participating in your existence (perhaps ringing a little louder). It makes such a sound as has been described by the term "heavenly choir." This is something you participate in. Just because I have provided the means does not mean that you have not provided the manner. And the manner in which you hear it (and you will all pass through that veil) will be the song that welcomes you home. Good night.

❖ Robert's Comments on His Experience

That was pretty awesome. He had a lot of knowledge and he seemed to have a pretty good command of the language.

And a great sense of humor.

Fortunately. It seems to be a mark by which we can recognize . . .

. . . the more evolved, the more humorous.

Yes.

You needed to adjust yourself because he was impacting you physically.

Yeah, that's right. I felt it; it was really uncomfortable, then something happened and I was okay.

He said he was lessening the electricity he was putting in you.

Yes.

Spirit of Youthful Exuberance

October 19, 1996

et me tell you a little story about how I came to be with your Creator. Once upon a time I was involved in the creation of a prototype planet that is now the model for the Pleiadian cultural star system. I did not create this planet alone, but my essence was transferred to the body of the planet itself. In this way all who would manifest there, utilizing the fabric of the planet for their body, would naturally be filled with enthusiasm and fun. If you're going to have a culture where there's not even annoyance, you've got to have some reason to go on. If you're not going to have problems to conquer, then you need to have some kind of reason to live, yes? That was the design.

My contribution to the fabric of the planet had to do largely with the outer skin, about the outer eight to ten miles of the planet, which was permeated with a light blue crystalline substance not unlike fluorite—which is, even in its current state on your Earth, capable of being programmed with fun, excitement, happiness and youthful energy. (For those who are growing older and deteriorating more than you would like, use fluorite crystals, especially if you can get pale blue ones. If you ask youngsters to carry them around in their pockets and then put them in your own pockets at the end of the day, it will tend to uplift you, making you want to do things and enjoy life more.) That was my contribution to that planet, and it was a challenge as well as fun.

Joining Your Creator to Create Human Preadolescence and Advanced Senility

It was about the time when I was getting ready to depart from my work on that planet that your Creator meandered by with a fairly somber group of consultants in tow. I naturally felt that this party needed some cheering up, so when Creator "interviewed" me to see whether I would be interested in coming along to . . . well, I assume to cheer up their little quartet, I said yes. I thought I was going along for the ride, not realizing until much later that your Creator had some vast universe It was about to generate. When I heard about the project I thought, This is something I want to be involved in, especially because I'll be able to work on the Pleiadian star system.

That, you know, is really my favorite accomplishment, although the fifth dimension of the planet that occupies *this* space—the fifth dimension of not exactly Earth, but Terra—is something I'm also very proud of. It has a very lighthearted, fun-filled manner of being and is something I am particularly fond of. The beings, I might add, are very similar in culture to the Pleiadians as well as the Orions in their youthful stage (which is right around the first 150 years, because the average Orion nowadays lives 750 to 780 experiential years). They are also very fun-loving, very Pleiadian in nature.

I found that this attracted me. I was involved in that a lot and also in the creation of two stages in the life of the human being as you know yourself to be—preadolescence (perhaps early twelve years old) and advanced senility. Although senility has its downside, it also has a great upside because people are getting in and out of their bodies a lot. When they get out of their bodies, they often need to go through a veil of youthful invigoration, because at that time of their life their bodies are pretty worn out and most of them are upset and confused about many things. After they step through this golden sheath of youthful enthusiasm, adventure and happiness, they are very capable and easily transformed to their most vigorous selves.

Now, an interesting thing is that people who have been wounded or injured (or even born injured) will also be vigorous, as if never injured. They will be whole and complete. Those of you out there who might be reading this and who are missing limbs or have handicaps, know that you are quite complete sometimes in your deep dream state or in the good part of senility, should you experience it.

The Prototype Planet: Invitation to Fun-Lovers and Adventurers

Was the prototype planet that you were creating when Creator came by your first effort at creating, or did you have other experiences?

That wasn't my first. It was a cooperative effort. I was involved with another being I'd have to call the crystal formatter. I was involved primarily with the outer eight to ten miles of the planet, but the rest of the inner planet was a mass of crystalline substance. The outer band took the form of crystal, not because of my creation, but because of my programming. Because the rest of the inner planet was also crystalline, it enabled the planet to act not only as a beacon but an antenna to radiate into all creation to invite beings who would like to have lives of fun, adventure, happiness and discovery to come and manifest on this planet. The whole planet was really a giant radiating antenna.

What was the purpose of the creation it was in?

One might think of a creation as an envelope, as it is in this universe. Many creations I have seen do not have envelopes around them at all. But that universe is purposely separated from other creations. Because what is going on here is so unusual, there needs to be a boundary.

I and my friend, the crystal formatter, had gone to a place that was roughly between universes and created our creation in a way that made it clear to anyone in any of the surrounding open universes (no boundaries) that they would be welcome on this planet. This planet is known, now that it's well established, as a planet where you can come to play. Even beings from far-off places will come to this planet to play and have fun. It's known for its good times, perhaps mainly because of the planet's capacity to hold and store as well as transmit, like all crystals everywhere.

If you come from a culture that loves music and there aren't any people there to play music with or who have memories of previous enjoyable musical events, that will be created as a living experience, and you will simply step into it and enjoy it. Because different cultures have different experiences, the planet can serve all their needs as long as they fall within the parameters of the planet's values (meaning no harm, no pain, pleasure, fun and so on).

What did you do before that?

Studying Enthusiasm in Particles

Before that I was involved in a long-term study of the elements of youthful exuberance within the tiniest particles. During this study I discovered that the place to go to find the most joy was the tinier particles, because they were less likely to be interfered with by some mass creation. One tends to find more pure emotions in these infinitesimal particles. This study was sort of a particle-counting research adventure with my trinary self.

There are two other parts of me; one part is still in residence within the core of the planet I mentioned, absorbing and sustaining certain energies I can draw on that I might need here. Another part of me (I decided to play the game with Creator) is waiting somewhere with your Creator so that when we go on (I'll go on with your Creator because it sounds like fun) I'll meet up with that other part of me. That will be fun.

You separated only at the time of this creation?

No. When your Creator happened by that planet, I left a part of me there. I was a binary then. When Creator said He was going to leave part of Himself someplace else to come here and do this, I thought that sounded like fun, so I became a trinary. Creators can do this.

What did you do before that?

My Beginning as Liquid Color beyond the Orb

Before that I existed as liquid exultant color. As far as I can tell, this color came from the place where color enters. If you go out past the end of the Orb, past the light and the points of the emotions and the thought flashes, there is a place where perpetual moods exist. This is where I'm from, and if you go there without a mood, when your personality arrives you experience all colors and all moods. Moods are sustained emotions, and sustained emotion is colored by other emotions or states of being (a better description of moods). If you go there with a given mood or a predominant feeling, you will discover that you become certain colors.

I had never seen colors before this place. When I left, I didn't come toward the Orb, but went the other way. Consistently I noticed that there wasn't any color. Oh, there was feeling, there was sensation, there was intonation (sound), there was love—but I did not discern any color. Now, this could mean that there isn't any color, or that beyond that point I simply did not have the ability to see it.

In any event, I explored that for quite some experiential time, going a long way in that direction (for lack of a better terminology). I was trying to find something familiar, because I could see that color was easing toward the Orb, but I wanted to know what preceded it. By moving outward I gradually came to the conclusion that *anticipated feelings* preceded color. This suggests that there is something beyond that, but I didn't go any farther because it took me so long to get to the cognizance of anticipated feelings that I didn't want to spend any more years going in that direction. I returned as fast as I could, and it took me only about half the time. Then I went into the Orb.

What did you travel through? Was it a dark cloud, was it white, or were there beings?

It was dark, but it wasn't substantive. It would be as if you could go very fast but there would be no wind. There was no friction; there was no substance that I could notice. Nothing was moving. It was like a vacuum, but a vacuum associated with a precondition. I call it anticipated feelings because it was something that existed before feelings. There was no white light because there was no color. Perhaps one could say that the dark would have been a color, but I'm referring to it as dark because it was more like the absence of light. If I had to describe it as black or blue, it wasn't that.

There was no light.

That's right. There was the absence, but there was the absolute permeation of love, which suggests that love comes before light. [Chuckles.]

Is that when you first became aware? You became aware, then you went that way?

Well, I was aware all along; I don't ever remember *not* being aware. But I became aware that I could go somewhere on my own at some point when I was in the color. That's why I went the other way. I was curious to see what was beyond. I had heard about what was in the Orb, but I hadn't heard anything from anyone about what was the other way. I've always been aware of my personality, but I had never felt any particular urge to go anywhere. Yet at one point I realized I could go. I think this was probably the preamble to being invited somewhere.

While you were there in the color and you were aware, there were other sentient awarenesses that you could communicate with?

Yes. Everyone there was equal. One would not be, say, red for years and years; you were constantly changing color. As you changed color you would change mood, so it was a place of constantly fluctuating moods. If you found a particular mood/color that you liked, you could maintain that as long as you wished. I know some beings who have been gold for as long as I can remember, a few blue, a couple of pinks and a green; that's what they've always been and that's what they are now. (I check up on them. One tends to want to see what people are doing sometimes, you know.) But almost everybody has changed.

When you came back from anticipated feeling and you went into the Orb . . .

I went through the usual process, passing from mood into the wells of feeling. I chose feeling that was associated with what I like—joy and happiness—and then went through the opening, which is like a point of light. I went into the cloud of light and thence into the Orb by the happiest route I could find. [Chuckles.]

So then you met the Creator.

Well, not immediately. Then I went to work on the planet.

Traveling with Your Creator, Taking a Different Route

After you met this Creator, then what?

Then we traveled about. I met the Creator pretty early on and we traveled about for quite a long time.

Who was with Creator? You said a quartet.

Discomfort . . . let's see . . .

Zoosh had to be there.

Yes, that's right. Zoosh was there. Somebody else was there, somebody very feminine. You see, I don't think of them in the way you have them defined. I think it was octaves [Master of Frequencies and Octaves].

So you traveled around—then what?

A thousand, million lifetimes worth of what-what.

Then you decided to do this creation. Did you come here with our Creator?

When Creator said, "We're getting near the area where I want to do this creation," He asked everyone if they wanted to accompany Him in by that route. The route Creator took in the final few years to get here was a strain, because Creator had to take sort of a tortuous route. It felt like it would be too serious for me, so I asked Creator if I could meet Her just before She got to that point and if I could take a different route. She said, "Okay, yes."

And I did take a different route. I quickly returned to the planet, then I came back. I suppose you think it's silly, but it's kind of like hide-and-seek. I turned my back so that I couldn't see where Creator was going—that makes it more fun. Then I went back to the planet and stayed for a while. You see, then I would have to find Creator and Creator's consultants on the basis of color and feeling. Creator left a trail, but I didn't want to follow the exact trail because that would be too boring and too serious. I managed to go around a creator who tends to be a bubblelike aperture, sometimes visible and other times an empty space. I went through several star cascades that are near this creation. A star cascade is the most beautiful, wonderful thing to go near because it's a point of exit from a creator's . . . usually star cascades are where galaxies are formed. When you go near them there's an incredible joy and happiness and light. I can't describe it. It's ecstatic. So I tried to take the route that took me by various star cascades.

Sounds like fun.

I think so.

What happened when you got here? How did your skill work into this creation?

What I had to offer was designed to build a happiness to be physical into all beings. Thus I've been involved very much in the physical planes. I'm defining the physical planes as anything from the second dimension through the seventh, because toward the upper end of the seventh dimension and beyond one starts getting into beings who *could* be physical briefly if they chose, but usually tend to be in lighter substance. Beings who are physical usually have a more fixed lifetime. Even at the seventh dimension you might have a lifetime of 1500 or 2500 years, but it's fixed, because to be physical at all is a little bit of a strain because of its limits. The boundary of yourself is a limit to some extent, and most personalities can live with limits for only a short time.

My Veil, Which Creates Enthusiasm for Physicality

It was my job to build into the fabric of the existence of any given race an amplification of their natural happiness so that they would want to be physical. Otherwise nobody ever would be physical, especially in the second, third and fourth dimensions. I can assure you that no one would want to be physical if that fabric weren't built in, because it would be like, "Oh, heck, going to work now."

Up to this time beings had been creating environments for the generated beings from the Creator. You're the first one who has talked about having an influence on those beings. How did you do that?

Mostly you've got to get there early, before the movie starts. Being there at the beginning, I placed myself in the point of emergence of all life. A portion of myself is always at the emergence of all life within this universe so that anything that will be manifested must pass through a veil of my existence, affecting it like a tea bag affects water passing through it.

Beings at the higher dimensions would have that feeling anyway, but all of the ones at the denser, more learning dimensions must go through my veil, so the very fabric of their souls is affected. No matter how they're influenced by the planet or the culture to which they're born, the essence of their soul is affected by the veil. Even if a soul does not manifest itself physically, once it has gone through it, if it goes anywhere in the second through the seventh dimensions, it will have a degree of enthusiasm for being physical.

So even when you leave the Explorer Race, they'll still have what you gave them.

Yes, because the veil is there. I'll leave the veil.

After you had done that, did you interact in the creation?

That is my primary interaction. I wasn't willing to come along with Creator unless He could promise me plenty of time off to pursue my own interests, because otherwise it would be *boring*! That's it. My main job is to maintain the veil, and I do it mostly remotely. Every once in a while I have to show up and punch in for work, but most of the time I can just go about. This universe of your Creator is so vast, and it is constantly expanding. Your Creator does not believe in sitting still. It's not like, "There, that's done!" Your Creator doesn't know the meaning of "there, that's done!" [Laughs.] It's more like, "Oh, it's to *that* point! What's next?" That's another reason we're compatible, you know. I spend a lot of my time exploring the universe of this Creator just to see who and what is out there and whether they need a fairy godfather (or is it godmother?). Whatever they need, you know, I'm available.

Pan

But the Creator said you had manifested as Pan.

Oh, I've been known to do that, but I am not exclusively Pan. Pan is a three-part being. Pan must be made up of a portion of me, because

Pan is, at its essence, a happy self.' It must also be able to pass on that happiness to living beings associated with the natural world, which is anything on your planet, including yourselves, and anything on any planet that is individualized. Even if it's a part of some larger thing, if it's individualized, Pan is available.

However, doing something indefinitely, constantly radiating energy —that's not me! That would be the octaves [Master of Frequencies and Octaves], because she's more involved in radiation and long-term application. I think there's some element of what I would call star energy within Pan. Pan is like a mini sun. The reason Pan gets along so well with the fairy world is probably because the fairy world is fed by a youthful sun. That's what they live on.

Where's that?

In their world wherever they are. It's not a "down the corner, turn right, up two blocks."

Fairies are all over the universe, the creation?

Yes, not just here—everywhere.

Things I Like to Do

What do you see in your travels? There are people, planets, galaxies, solar systems. What do you see out there that's unusual?

Well, I'll tell you one of the things I like the best. When you can see whole systems (which you can do at this level), some interesting things take place. Looking at the universe, sometimes you'll see for a time entire galaxies that look from a distance like stars forming at least temporarily into a fantastic shape—you know, a recognizable being. It's like when you look at a cloud and say, "Oh, there's an elephant" or "there's a giraffe." It's very similar.

That's a constant I've noticed. This suggests to me that in all life forms, be they massive galaxies or universes or planets or a single cloud, the element of fun is there. Sometimes there will be light rays that extend. If you can look in the sky sometime and see clouds, it won't be long before you see faces and interesting things. The clouds are *really doing that* in cooperation with spirits in or near them! That is something you see in the universe a lot. Sometimes you'll see light stretching between them.

The other thing I like to do is go into the particle world (I understand you're going to take that up next). The vastness of this universe is equaled only by the vastness within a single particle. Now, I realize that that doesn't follow your laws of physics, but at the level of research physics it really does follow. If you can go out at the same velocity as you can go in, the outgoing velocity of a mass is equalled only by the incoming velocity of that same mass—which, by the way is the formula for star drives. I don't feel worried about your understanding that and getting out there too soon, because it will probably take you another sixty years to resolve. But that is the formula.

Questions and Answers

We'll pass that along. What have you learned in this creation? What are you going to take with you that you wouldn't have had if you had not come here?

Undoubtedly, it is variety. Your Creator does not know the meaning of doing the same thing twice. I have never seen anything in this creation (as long as I've been here and that's forever and before) that is absolutely identical. Oh, I know you could say identical twins, but even they are not identical. No, your Creator just loves variety! I understand that very well. Probably nearly every creator being who comes here is impressed by that because when you go to other creations you don't see anywhere near this kind of variety. This is phenomenally more so than *any* other creation I'm aware of.

Do you have any regrets?

That's an interesting question. No, I can't say I have regrets. I don't know any creator who does, because creators are not allowed to have regrets. If you have regrets you have to do something about it. So you can't say, "Oh gosh, I wish I had . . ." The minute a creator says, "I wish I had" (and this goes for you too, by the way), *you will!* Be careful about saying, "I wish I had." *It is guaranteed that you will!*

Have parts of yourself gone up to become little pieces of the creations of the Creator?

Do you mean, have I ever become someone individually?

Something, someone.

No. I'm pretty happy being what I am.

So what's the goal, then? You and the Creator will go out beyond as far as you want?

I'll tell you something interesting. Goals are an objective of finite beings. I have no goals.

What's the plan? When you and the Creator leave, you're going to go exploring?

We are going to see if there is more, what form it takes and how we can put our mark on it. [Laughs.]

You became aware of yourself. You didn't really have a creator like this Creator?

No, I didn't have that. I've always been aware of myself, but I became aware that I could go somewhere without being in the mass of everything that I was. Everybody in that mass of color—*everyone* there—is aware of themselves and always has been, as far as I know.

They haven't gone anyplace yet?

They haven't gone anyplace. Apparently they have not felt any urge to go anyplace.

That's beyond what is called the Matrix around the Center of Creation? The Matrix is only within this Orb, right?

Yes, as far as I know. One might consider that the light shining in from beyond the Orb is part of the Matrix too, but it depends on how you define it.

So there are numbers beyond numbers of incipient and potential sentient beings everywhere?

As far as I know. *You can't get away for a quiet moment anywhere* unless you can create a universe like that.

But can't you sneak into the Void? That's quiet, isn't it?

You can sneak in there, yes. But the reason the Creator of the Void made the Void is because that creator wanted quiet. But if *you* went there, it would not be quiet. They would ask, "When are you leaving?"

Can't you go there and be quiet?

Well, possibly. You have to be quiet in your thoughts and quiet in your feelings. You have to match yourself totally to that Creator of the Void in order to be respectful—*and that is just not in my nature!* [Laughs.]

Most of the other creators we've talked to, the friends of the Creator, maintain things like frequencies and dimensions. Are you the only one of the eight who is relatively free?

I can't speak for the others, but your Creator knew that I wouldn't come along unless I would have plenty of free time, because I like to have fun. I really do not feel responsible for the others, but I've seen the others gadding about a bit now and then.

Ah, so they sneak out. Do you communicate with each other?

A lot of them are so serious, you know, that I don't really communicate with them too much. But sometimes we have lighthearted visitors from afar, and then occasionally, if your Creator is busy, I might be assigned to take them around and show them a good time. [Chuckles.]

How would you do that?

Well, I generally ask them what they would like to do, and as long as it falls into what *I* like to do [chuckles] (because that is who I am), we'll go there. You see, I know where everything is in this creation. That's another reason I explore it. It's hard to imagine, but your Creator has created something so vast here that it's hard even for Him to . . . well, that's why She has middle management. (Although I don't call myself middle management, the others do. That's their joke, I know.)

Well, can He move around within the creation?

The Creator *is* the creation.

When you say you want to show visitors around, you have to do that because He can't, right?

No. He's everywhere; He has to be everywhere. She can't suddenly focus Herself in only one spot. What would happen to the rest of the creation?

So that's why you take them around and show them?

Yes. I take them around if they fall within my purview.

What are other creators most interested in? The variety?

Mostly they're interested in the variety, yes. Sometimes they come to get ideas if they're working on something. You know, it's not at all unusual to find creators coming here just for the tour like this Creator did. That is typical. One wants to have as much input as one can.

It's like, why re-create the wheel? Let's go out and see what's out there.

That's exactly right.

Other than this wonderful job of putting joy into souls, have you had any other little projects or ongoing things that interest you?

It's hard to imagine this, but this creation is so vast that . . . now, think of this; it will be amusing: I've been in this creation since the beginning, yet I spend no more than 3% of my experience maintaining the veil. Therefore I have 97% of my experience (you would say *time*) to explore this universe. Do you know how much of it I've managed to explore since the beginning, allowing for its constant expansion?

No.

No more than 3%.

Really?

When I go somewhere, I like to really get into it and explore. In the beginning I could say, "Well, I've explored 50% of it. Aren't you going to make any more?" But [chuckles] I can't say that anymore! No, your Creator doesn't mess around. Now, even moving at the quick pace I do, if I see something I like, I want to be with it for a while. Now it's only 3% that I've explored.

Is the creation expanding, or is there just more of it?

Everything is getting bigger *and* there's more of it.

So that's why our scientists say that the red shift proves the universe is expanding.

Yes, they're right about that. It *is* expanding.

So it's going to expand until the Creator leaves?

Yes. Then you will decide whether you wish to continue it or whether you wish to maintain it and see what you want to do with what you've got. It won't continue expanding, nor will new things be added at the moment you take it over. It will just stay, you know, like you say to your dog, "Stay." It will stay until you decide what you want to do. You'll basically be in maintenance while you decide what you want to do with it.

Exploring and understanding, because all of the beings are leaving, right? Creator said He was going to leave the real estate.

That's about it, although they have the option to stay. *You* have the option to ask portions of them to stay and they might or might not. You could ask, you know.

I don't mean the friends of the Creator, because they might stay. I mean the beings that the Creator generated, that are a part of Him. He will take them with Him, but not the Explorer Race, right?

Oh, you're talking about the beings who are living on the planets?

No. Every being that the Creator has generated except the Explorer Race—all the beings that are unmanifest are all part of Him, right?

You're going to have to rephrase that one. Let's put it like this: All the people who are living on all the planets will stay there. Creator is not going to take them with Him. You're going to take over. Creator's not going to lug everybody off the planets and say, "Time to go now."

So if they've individualized, they stay?

Absolutely. What are you going to do? Say, "Whup! Time for your grandpa to go!"

Well, I didn't know.

No, no. Everybody stays. Otherwise what are you going to do? Be in charge of planets, just sitting there? What point is there in that? Where's the challenge in that? Anybody can take over and watch a warehouse. That's why there's only one guard at a huge warehouse. How many people does it take to look at a bunch of boxes?

That's what I'm asking, how it works. What part of the Creator is going? What percentage is He taking with Him?

The Creator will take the essence of Its personality that It arrived with and any of the consultants who wish to go with Her as well as beings who have come with Her to help out—that's it.

Zoosh once said that most of him would go with Creator.

Not that I know of. He can't do that. What would be the test for you?

I see. You're going to go look around and then see what happens after you leave here?

If I could tell you, then it wouldn't be a surprise.

What do you want to tell the Explorer Race?

It is your nature to be happy. Here you have to learn how to be sad. When you go past the veil at the end of your natural cycles you are naturally happy. You leave the sadness behind because you don't need it past the veil. Know that any sadness from whatever cause will not follow you. It won't go into your next life. Besides, lives that have sadness for you, the Explorer Race, are really pretty much in the past. You have only a few more years in which you can experience that. I just want you to know that that is coming to an end. It will be all right.

Do you have a name by which we can refer to you?

Well, my cohorts, my consultants, have a nickname for me. They've called me this for as long as I can remember, and it's really

kind of comical. They call me Junior. [Laughter.] They've always called me that. So good night.
Good night.

A ll right. Zoosh here. Well, Junior does not always agree with me, but that's what makes the book interesting. If we all agreed, well, we'd be pretty bored. We are not Creator's soldiers; we are Creator's friends.
Is he called Junior because he is so much like Creator himself?
Yes. He's a chip off the old Creator.
Even though they are not related, in the sense that he came from way, way beyond.
No. It is an affectionate name. I don't think he really has a name, anyway. If you were to see it, His name would be Color, and constantly changing color—because that's his native land. You know, sometimes we like to have symbolic names for each other. Junior has always been our favorite name for him.
I feel a little frustrated because I didn't ask enough questions.
Junior is not known for his patience, and talking to you as long as he did is surprising. So don't feel bad about that. I was very surprised when you were able to turn the tape over. I was surprised when it went past a half-hour. Junior is not one to hang around in the same place. He is like a child; when the sun is out and it's time to go out and play, well, Junior has a reputation for going out to play every chance he gets.
What does Junior look like? Does he look like a burst, is he spreading, emanating, like arms of light, color, sound?
That is one of his apparitions, yes.
Because I saw him changing a lot.
Well, let's call it a night, eh?

❖ Robert's Comments on His Experience

When he was going through the nothingness away from the color, I could see the color real well. It was a liquid-light type of color, meaning that if you look at it in its infinite particles it twinkled, but as you pulled back from its small particles, it was like rolling colors expressing themselves by some unknown method. When he was going away from the color toward something else, the feeling of it was like looking at something that was just empty space—the space between the stars. It seemed to have what looked like a bubble around it, though it's hard to describe. There was like a thin sheet of something over it so it looked like something that was both there and not there. That's a strange way to describe it, but I don't have words for it. It was something that was more of a void rather than a specific thing. I could feel him moving through it very fast, but there wasn't any sense of motion. I could feel the motion he was creating, but not any sense of . . .

He said there was no friction.

Exactly. It continued to look the same, so it looked like he wasn't making any progress. There weren't any landmarks.

But we're only speaking to one-third of him. When he came in, he played the same game the Creator did—he left one-third of himself in the planet he created and one-third of him someplace else. That's the third that knows what's going on. This is just an aspect of the being

I can't get the third with the planet.

Leave the planet. The other part is the one that really knows what's going on.

All I can tell you is that I can't channel him, but I can tell you what he sees. It's like the Cheshire cat, in the sense that I can see this big smile in the midst of all this light, if that makes any sense. There's a tremendously happy, sort of a I-know-something-you-don't-know feeling about it, but he's emanating a lot of light to cover it. I can't speak of it for him into this reality without our Creator knowing what's there. But he knows what's there. Our Creator doesn't want to know so that He can experience the discovery for the first time.

And Junior is just a part of the being.

Yeah, Junior's the part that came with Creator to this place.

I thought maybe we could get that other being. I can see that he can't be channeled without ruining the surprise.

The one on the planet is very involved with what it's doing.

So Junior is not the whole being. I just want to make clear that there's much more to that being than we're seeing here.

That's what's available for the manifestation here.

Master of Imagination

October 22, 1996

I am Master of Imagination. Your Creator requested my assistance when He was voyaging to this space before this creation. He had a pretty fair idea that He would create you at some point, intending to replace Himself. He could provide you with a significant amount of imagination, but not beyond His own ability. He brought beings with Him who were not a portion of Him so He could get other needed energy inputs, thus endowing you with more imagination than He could pass on on His own.

The Silver Thread of Imagination

It is not my job to inspire you, to pass on ideas. It is largely my job to expedite the thread of imagination that connects you with your Creator. The thread itself is not Creator's, but the connection between you is. The normal connection between you is gold thread, but this thread of imagination is a silver thread within that gold thread. It allows you to go beyond what you know, beyond what you have ever heard of in this life, and in some cases beyond what anyone has ever heard of.

Since your Creator is around and about you, the thread functions primarily as an antenna to the source of this creation—the center of it, as it were—allowing you to thread beyond this creation. The gold strand connects to your Creator; and the silver strand runs through the center, through your Creator, through your Creator's center and beyond into the Orb itself. In this way you are able to imagine and envision things beyond this creation and Orb that your Creator has no previous experience of.

I was called early on by your Creator and asked to observe Its creation. Since I would not directly participate before the emergence of the Explorer Race, I did not have to be here all the time. I observed with a distant eye and have been elsewhere until your ensoulment, your birthing out from your current Creator.

The Tube of Vertical Thoughts and Colors

Before I needed to be here full time, I traveled through other creations to see what principles or energies of imagination might be useful for you beyond what your Creator can offer. I found two places that were especially important. One was another creation within the Orb. It is a very small one in terms of mass, but it is involved in the ultimate (from my perspective) in vertical thought. This encompasses all dimensions ever experienced in this or any other creation within the Orb and apparently even some beyond the Orb. I've tracked vertical thought from one end of the Orb to the other, and there were thoughts and colors in this small creation that I'd never seen before. Unusual thoughts are contained within this self-generated vertical tube.

Vertical
thoughts
and colors
⟶

There is a center point in the tube, and thoughts travel from that point of emergence in all directions, meaning that since it is a tube, they travel in both directions. I examined very carefully the point of emergence. The thoughts seemed to go out into the Orb and become available to anyone who has a creation or is a portion of a creation within the Orb.

The Thin Triangle of Electrical White Light, through Which Buddha Breathes Light

When I tracked back from the point of emergence I noticed that what came into this creation looked initially like another tube but was actually a long, thin triangle without discernible colors. If I were to call it a color, I'd have to say it is a version of electrical white light, one that can move and act on its own and can choose where to go and where not to go, unlike most white light. This triangle went well beyond the Orb into another space entirely, and what I can only call a massive creator was, for lack of a better term, blowing into this triangle.

This being has a rough shape and looks like the Buddha looked toward the end of his life. This being, however, is visible only from the waist up. It's massive, fully one-quarter the size of this creation. Although I don't feel air moving about, it is making all the gestures of breath, breathing out this electrical white light. When he breathes in, he doesn't take the light back in; he breathes the light outward only, keeping it moving toward this creation.

I inquired of this being and found out that it is in fact the immortalization of the Buddha. This is where Buddha went, for those of you who are interested in these things. He's out there right now, breathing all foundational elements of thought into this thin triangle, which go into this very thin tube that is indescribably long. (If you were to stand in front of it, it would be about 80 feet wide.) Coming out of the ends of the tube are colors that I believe contain foundational thoughts.

You can see why I felt it was important for you to have a thread running near this. Foundational thoughts are thoughts that begin something upon which other things are built. When this is provided to any being, that being has a chance to create upon one of those foundations. The foundation gives you a sense of direction and purpose, possibly even goals or outcomes, depending on the direction of your civilization—whether it operates in time and space or whether it is permanent, or circular.

The Vibration That Precedes Sound

There was another creation well beyond the Orb. To discuss it you must fully understand the integrity of music as a language or at least have the foundational basics. You know what sounds you can hear; even trained musicians cannot hear much more than other individuals. Some animals have a much higher range, of course, and some plants have both a much lower and higher range. But the sounds you need to hear are fairly narrow so that you will not be bothered or distracted by life forms you need not integrate or interact with on a full-time basis in this incarnation. That is built in by your Creator. That's why you do not always have an awareness of the subtle energies around you.

I had to run well beyond the Orb, beyond all previous mentions here, to an experimental creation that is involved specifically in the vibration that *precedes* sound. It is not actually sound as you understand it, because in the absence of something that can vibrate, no sound can be heard at any octave or frequency. But you would feel it. I felt that you needed to have a connection to the feeling that precedes sound so you could better integrate your ability to imagine higher (and in some cases lower) dimensions.

The Master of Frequency and Octaves has spoken already, and although this being is doing a great deal of good for you, you are somewhat limited in perceiving or even feeling what it is doing. In the not-too-distant future it will be very important for as many people as possible on this planet to be able to sense vibration. Most of you will do so at least initially through the imagination, sensing something that feels or seems like "just my imagination." The word "just," however, is a demeaning disqualification of the value of imagination, which has always been intended to provide you with the means to leap beyond what you know mentally.

The intention here is to give you something that will help you to be in touch with spirits, with Creator, with gods/guides and the angelics so that you would have every opportunity to be in touch with those beings who can help you.

By the time you read this there will be a much greater opportunity to feel these vibrations. You will be surrounded by them and in some cases encompassed by them. You will think initially that it's your imagination, but as you attune to it—listen and feel for it more—you will find that you can quickly integrate this onto the feeling level. It will move from what appears to be imagination into something more attuned to a *felt instinct*. This is very important. Those who have not yet mastered or understood how to use your instinctual selves will be able to grasp this, and from then on you will have the opportunity to know how to find whatever you need, who is safe and desirable to be with, who is intended to be with others, what to eat, when and how—basically all survival decisions: food, shelter, family, friends, situations that now have clearly defined *mental* patterns.

Your Coming Ability to Instantly Grasp the Future

As many of you have noticed, the mind that you have been using almost since the beginning of your voyage as the Explorer Race is changing radically. You no longer have the access to the past that you once had because the aspects of memory are dwindling. By our giving you this preharmonic vibration, you have a way to tap into the future. Whenever you *know* something, you get an instinctual feeling based on this vibration. To know who and what is right for you, you tap into the ultimate outcome of interacting with the who or what, which energetically puts you into the future. If it is a person, you feel everything that you might do with this person, and you can tell by the energy whether this would be a good person to be with for a short time or a long time or at all. You are becoming much more sensitive on the feeling level, and it will begin seemingly with your imagination, but the imagination will be used as a *felt* resource rather than something unquantifiable.

I bring these two things [foundational thoughts and the soundless vibration] to your attention because I feel that they have been most helpful in your current dilemma where you are losing what you call your memory. Understand that your natural thought process is vertical—you know what you need to know when you need to know it, as Zoosh likes to say. This is instinct, but it is what I call creative, constructive instinct, which means that it's not solely body instinct, but body instinct combined with spiritual instinct. This gives you the ability to grasp the future in a split second without being burdened or interfered with in terms of future memories (which can really clutter your mind). You will have a feeling in your physical body that tells you "this is good, at least for now." And if at some point in the future it is no longer good, then you will get the feeling that it is not good and turn from that to something that is good.

The ramifications here are powerful. You will know what to eat and what not to eat. If you are going somewhere traveling, you will know which is the route for you and which is for others. It will make all the difference in the world to your personal safety, to say nothing of meeting all the people you ever wanted to meet or felt you were supposed to meet. How many of you now might ask, "Where is my true family? Where are my true friends?" With this new skill you will be able to find them almost at once. They will also be able to find *you* almost at once, and there will be a bias to do so. This means that everybody will be looking for everybody else at the same time, and when two objects are moving toward each other, the distance between them is (as the mathematicians say) greatly decreased.

To fully appreciate that, I want you to realize the long-distance thinking your Creator had to do to allow Herself (as Zoosh likes to say sometimes) to know Her own limits. Is that not a fascinating concept? Your Creator, with all of Its abilities to make planets, people, loving beings, angels, everything, has, at least for the purposes of this creation, built limits into Itself. Thus It requires assistance from others so that *you* will not be limited. It was always your Creator's intention that you be totally unlimited in your capacities, but that you have plenty of time to discover the fallacies of pursuing unlimited, self-destructive action. Thus when you achieved creator status you would not in any way be enamored of self-destructive tendencies—meaning hurting yourself or others, because others *are* you, of course.

When your Creator recognized His own limits, He said, "I want my children to be unlimited." Think about that. That's really quite exceptional. The reason your Creator came in with so many assistants was to make doubly and even triply sure that no stone was unturned. Sometimes these assistants and helpers were able to do things that other assistants were doing, but your Creator wanted to make sure that *all* potentials were covered. That's why so many beings came in with your Creator or joined It at a time convenient for both parties.

How do you connect that silver thread? What are the dynamics of it?

Spreading the Veil around the Explorer Race's Physical Lives

Connecting this thread involves very careful preparation. When every soul is coming and going between the veils of what you call life, the thread needs to be connected to you all the time you are physically incarnated, even the deep sleep states. But when you are not physically incarnated and rejoin the totality of your being, it is not necessary. I need to spread a very thin veil all around wherever the Explorer Race might be. Because you incarnate on other planets and solar systems and galaxies, I will send some of that veil there as long as you maintain your status within the Explorer Race.

Right now you don't incarnate all over this universe, but only in places whose people have at one time or another visited Earth. With few exceptions, the veil I'm spreading is no larger than 40% of this universe. This allows me to maintain fully 60% of myself either for other projects or to pay attention to what I'm doing with that 40%. It is basically an automatic function: You pass through the veil into physical life and pick up the thread; you pass through the veil away from physical life and you leave the thread. It's really very mechanical.

What about the other end? How do you connect way out to where the Buddha is and to the other creations?

Remember that the limitations of space (and time, for that matter) are only limitations within the context of your current incarnations. You will immediately see and feel the results of what you do (if not immediately, others will). In other words, you need to have physical evidence because you need a lot of feedback. When you go beyond the point where you don't need physical evidence, the physical effort that it would take, for instance, to close and open the fingers of your hand would be the same amount required to move instantaneously from this planet to the outer edges of the Orb. Even if you don't know where you want to go, if you have an idea about what you want to experience (within certain boundaries, if you wish to be specific), you will go there just as quickly. It is really very simple. In this case I do not connect every single individual. I connect a bigger cable (so to speak) to these areas, which is connected to the veil so that I don't have to run all of your threads to these places.

My First Awareness in a Creation beyond the Orb

When did you first become aware? Where were you?

I think when I first became aware, I was aware of my personality. Unlike the others, I was physically born. I was in what I would call a perfect state of balance, where thought was not a factor but where the absence of thought was noted. We all felt that something was missing, but since thought wasn't present, we didn't know what it was. This might be part of the reason why I'm particularly enamored of thought, because when you don't have it, you miss it, and when you have it, it's pretty wonderful.

I was physically born on a planet that was part of a distant creation where an experiment was taking place beyond this Orb. The intention was to birth into being individual personalities—in my case, that which would become an individual personality, which I am now—who would choose to participate in all manner of applied becoming. *Applied becoming* is that which supports, sustains and otherwise assists anyone or anything toward becoming. I and other members of the being I was before being birthed are very much inclined toward that. Because I lived in something that is more associated with a constant feeling rather than any sense of knowing, I was perhaps a good candidate for this experiment. The beings who were involved in this particular experiment could see me and identify me from the rest of the beings I was with. They culled me out (as well as several others), so apparently we are creators or spiritual masters in training—it is hard to say.

My Physical Birth and Death in a Universe Made for Testing

In any event, I was then allowed (that's the way I look at it) to go through a birth process very much like the one you have on Earth, except that no one, neither the birthgiver (the mother) or myself (the baby) was allowed to have any discomfort felt by one party alone. If there was any discomfort, we both had to feel it or neither of us. This was designed to create an absolute bond between both the birther and the birthee, if you would. It was the intention of the experiment to prove the ultimate validity of loyalty.

Later I came to find that this is a small universe where emotions and thoughts and so on are tested to prove their validity—or in occasional cases, their destructiveness. This is where negativity was proved at one point to be destructive, although you are now proving that it has benevolent abilities when given the chance to be appreciated for itself and when it isn't blown all out of proportion, meaning present in only a very small percentage of your existence.

That is when I first became aware of my existence. The life I lived there was not like a life you would have here. It was a form of what I'd call multidimensional physical life. If you were to look at me in that life, you might have a hard time following what I was doing, because I was functioning physically *and* with conscious awareness in 33 dimensions at the same time! This was designed into me as well as my birth mother so that we would be absolutely united in intention. Even today when I discover something new, which happens now and then, my physical mother knows about it. That is the ultimate proof that these beings in this universe wanted—to see whether such a bond would be immortal (or everlasting, as you might say). That they proved, and it is still in existence.

So you were birthed as an immortal and you've been conscious ever since? How did you leave that life?

I went through what you call a death process in all 33 dimensions at once, thus experiencing what it would be like. They didn't really think about what I'd be doing later in life, but it has proved invaluable for my understanding and appreciation of you as physical beings. So yes, I went through the death process. This was most useful, because in the first, second, third and fourth dimensions the difference between the day-to-day life and the transference through the veils to what is beyond is quite profound. But once you get up to the fifth, sixth and seventh dimensions of where I was, it becomes more subtle because of the higher-dimensional expression. It's a very subtle transference, yet worth appreciating.

In terms of our life, how long was that one?

Oh, in terms of experiential years, perhaps 80—not very long.

Then what did you do?

After having that experience, I was basically given a free ride. I was told I could do whatever I wished and that if I chose to do something with thought, these beings would be most interested to be kept informed. I began to wander about in my spiritual-life self, and I was definitely interested in thought without their prompting. I was not interested in what you call "end" thoughts (which you are constantly aware of and functioning with), but in what *precedes* thought. That's part of the reason I came across these other creations I've connected you to.

Imagination Becoming Another Sense

I also was interested in what could be done to bring about a greater capacity for thought even when there are seeming physical limitations. That's when I came across the inspiration of imagination: the ability to go beyond all the senses available at a given moment—allowing the imagination itself to become another sense. Thus imagination could produce physical evidence. It was important to me that imagination not be regarded as strictly entertainment, though it is that, too.

For physical beings I evolved my perception of imagination, so that it could stimulate either memory of feelings or physical feelings for which there is no conscious physical memory. In this way imagination would be ultimately recognized by any evolving race of beings as another sense, which is its intention. It is another sense. It is not what I'd call the sixth sense, but it is in there with the other senses.

What was the adventure? The physical birth, then you found that first creation, then the second. Did you do something else before you met our Creator?

Moving through Creations inside and beyond the Orb Gathering Thoughts

I had spent a lot of time in that place beyond the Orb (mentioned by one of your previous guests) where thoughts and inspirations are manifest in pictures, so I had acquired a lot of thoughts. Wanting to have depth to my character, I spent (in terms of your experiential time) approximately 4.5 million trillion centuries moving about all of the creations of the Orb and those beyond it who had some connection to this Orb—such as the Buddha. I assimilated thought and senses (including visualizations, smell, taste and so on) from cultures fully 10% of which have a relationship to you. Basically, I did my homework, although I wasn't thinking of it as homework at the time. I was thinking, This is just great—something to do, pleasurable, interesting and, yes, exciting! Only now do I realize, having worked with your Creator, how valuable and necessary that was.

How are we able to gain by that 10% of those other creations? Can you project thought to us? How do we learn from that?

You learn because it exists. The thoughts in that 10%, wherever they are, can be felt by your sense of imagination. The imagination has an electrical/magnetic component that goes well beyond the electrical capacity of your brain. Your thought organism, as you know, consists of your entire auric field, not just the brain and nervous system. I mention it because the brain and nervous system are better known for their electrical conductivity. The imagination is primarily magnetic, but it has to be somewhat electrical or you would never *feel* anything that the imagination stimulated in you.

The range of magnetics, and to some extent electrics, of these 10% of civilizations falls nicely within your electrical and magnetic capacity of imagination. I refer to the imagination as a sense because it is one.

Because you've experienced these things, do we tap into your experience?

All Solutions Readily Available

No, you don't understand. If it exists somewhere, no matter how far . . . remember that once you get past the need to have space and time, thought travel can be just as fast or even faster than travel of a being. For instance, right now there are a lot of people, not only scientists but average people, who are very aware of crises in your civilization that need to be resolved. As you all know, when many people become consciously aware of a crisis that needs resolution, that crisis is soon resolved. If just a few people (10 to 15%) on Earth are aware of it, it will eventually get resolved. But if, say, 80% of the people on Earth are suddenly aware that you need to have more oxygen available or that the atmosphere needs to be repaired or that you need to find a quick, benevolent way to neutralize radioactivity, this can be done very quickly.

All of those solutions exist somewhere. It doesn't make any difference if it is so far away that your numbers cannot count it, because it is readily available. However, it requires a great many people to have that sudden need. You must be aware of a need either on the unconscious, the subconscious, the conscious or the imaginative level—one of those four. If it's just a vague thing that other people are aware of but you yourself aren't, you don't count in that 80%. There has to be some cognizance. I'm including the unconscious here in terms of its psychological description, not in terms of the collective spiritual unconscious, because you are always connected to that.

Meeting Your Creator

How did you meet the Creator?

When your Creator was on the way here, I was what you would call meditating. When I meditate there is a vast display of colors and what amounts to song. If you were to hear it, it would sound very much like harmony. I was doing this not to draw any attention to myself, but when I am in touch with all that I am it requires a slight sound, which produces colors as it interacts with the cosmic energy around me (cosmic energy being the building blocks of love). The rest of me was simply emanating my essence.

On His voyage your Creator stopped and watched. Then I became aware in my meditation that someone was present because they were watching (Creator had already collected a few people). I gradually came out of my meditation and your Creator politely waited. Then your Creator asked me (knowing and understanding who I was, since I was basically connecting to my total self) if I would be interested in showing up for Its creation. It gave me a basic overview of when and where and how much and so on. I said yes. Although in the very beginning of your creation I didn't have to be here much, now I'm here full-time.

We have an understanding of this Orb, of the light around the Orb, the points of light and potential beyond that. Then the one called Junior [Spirit of Youthful Exuberance] talked about going beyond that layer, but he didn't go all the way; he went so far, then came back. Did you go beyond where he went for an extremely long time, then turn around and come back?

Yes, because that layer is not that difficult to go through—well, it depends on what your agenda is. Since my agenda is to acquire anything that falls into the field of imagination but not to apply it, I can pass through something that might feel dense to someone who is more into the application. (Junior is more into application.) What I was doing was more of an acquisition for a later application. Something would feel dense to Junior because it was intended to slow him down, saying, "This probably isn't for you," but I could pass right through it without any sense of resistance.

A Description of Orbs and Creations

Then what? Are there other orbs? My suspicion is that there are a hundred orbs or a thousand orbs. Is that true?

I have no reason to believe that that is not true. The first thing I did was examine where I was—all beings do that, you know. You become aware of life and then you examine it. You examine your body, your crib or wherever. That's what I did. Then I had a choice. After all that traveling I could have continued to travel, but I had a feeling that I had accumulated something and would be able to contribute somehow. Since I had acquired so much knowledge within and to some extent beyond this Orb, I felt I ought to stay in the Orb because I've got that knowledge. I could have said, "I want to see what's beyond" and kept on going.

Since I am imagination, here is my vision of what's beyond as I've been able to imagine it, using the sense of imagination: There is a long time of travel where there is basically a peaceful zone, not much happening. Then one starts getting near an outer boundary of another sphere (or orb). Most of the creations within this Orb happen near its outer edges because it's there that love and light feed in—creation happens from the outside in. So as you move outward and get closer to the outer boundaries, you start running into more creations. If you go through the Orb, the process repeats itself—as far as I can tell, ad infinitum. It is interesting to note that if you were to go inward instead of outward, traveling to the center of this Orb, it would be very peaceful. Not much happens there. That's the way it seems to be. Growth and creation happen from the outside of the sphere, gradually moving inward.

I have examined only this Orb thoroughly and was able to see/feel other orbs beyond, and this one seems to be fully 30 to 35% filled up as one goes into it. But as I go in I can see other orbs inside it. You'll hear more about this in the particle book. I believe some of those orbs within this Orb are already totally filled. It's not a bad thing when they are totally filled. Life that wants to continue to expand or creators who want to continue to create have to go to the next outer orb. So one keeps going out, out, out.

I suspect that the orbs that totally fill up are the ones in which particle consciousness has achieved the ultimate level of conscious reality. When the particles achieve that, they cannot continue to create more there, so they go either inward or outward. Since inward would more likely be the completed creations, particles from filled-up orbs will go outward, bringing all they know, all they are and all their wisdom to this outer orb because it isn't filled up yet. They will contribute whatever they can of the knowledge they've gained in the ultimate creation within their original orbs. Your Zoosh will tell you that every single particle is an amazing being. You have all of that here. How many particles are inside of you? You have all their ability.

You've given so much here and added so much to the Explorer Race, what can you see yourself gaining from it?

Oh, you mean besides being knighted or some such thing?

[Laughs.] Yes.

Well, I'd say that it's like when I was traveling around getting experience. At the time I was doing it, it felt like I was just having fun. This is very much the same. I feel like I'm having fun; I'm doing something worthwhile and it's great. I'm applying what I've done, what I've known, what I've gathered. My feeling is that the next thing I do (since I don't see it clearly) is going to be based upon what I'm doing here. Not unlike your Creator, I don't plan my next move so much. I'm more inclined to wait and see what happens. If you no longer need me, at some point I will probably go off to some part of the Orb, meditate and wait and see what happens!

See who comes along.

That's right.

Do you have any beings within the Explorer Race that you have created or extruded or connected or . . .

One moment. Let's see who wants to be revealed and who doesn't. I have a few.

Oh, I'd love some names you know that I've heard of.

I understand. Okay. He doesn't want to be revealed yet. (I'm going through them here briefly, slowly, to give them the full opportunity.) No, she's not quite ready yet, either. Let's see . . .

Sometimes they don't want to be revealed when they have something *they're* going to reveal. And they don't want to be revealed as an incorporation; they want to be seen as an individual. One moment. Well, this doesn't probably mean much to you directly, but I am connected to the goddess of the Pleiades. That is a being who looks after all beings in the galaxy [system] Pleiades.

The Uncreated President/Avatar

Let's see who else will reveal themselves. I have to go through several here. Well, this one is sort of a nonbeing, but it's a being that almost was and will be. You remember that Zoosh discussed with you the president/avatar?

Yes. He's coming back, right?

Yes, he's coming back.

Oh, that will be exciting!

He'll be a world leader when he comes back, so actually the timing will be better.

The head of the United Nations or something. How did you feel when his time line got moved? Was it just another experience?

I was distracted, which at this level is less than one-tenth of 1% of annoyance. I couldn't get it out of my consciousness for a while. But we talked about it. Creator said, "This is probably what's going to happen," and then I felt better. Your Creator is very loving that way. If any of us or any individual is greatly disturbed about something, Creator spends time with us. You don't always know it then, but you always know it after life. I think that's really all I can tell you right now.

No historical figures?

Well, they don't really want to be revealed, but I'll see.

My Relationship with My Creations

But you have sent beings into physicality and felt through them what it felt like?

I have not sent them into physicality. What I like to say is that I am connected more personably with them. We have a sense of shared consciousness.

Do they come back into your beingness when they have completed their experience?

They just go on. I do not barge into their soul tree, but I connect with them on the personality level and they share it with me. To some extent I share with them, too. I don't try and give them an edge, but I will often help them with their visions. I have assisted some of the greater visionaries. There are a few native people, but they do not wish to be revealed. You know, very rarely do beings want to be revealed because ultimately they become revered. It's a very fine line, and we have to be careful. It's one thing for a goddess to be revered, but entirely another for an individual.

How does that work? They will be part of the Explorer Race, then? When the Creator goes off and you choose to either stay here or leave, will they be part of you, or will they be part of the Explorer Race?

They are always part of the Explorer Race, and in some cases part of whatever race they were involved in. I just sort of connect with them. It would be as if somebody reached out and touched you for a while, then let go at some point. I'm not connected with them for their whole life. I connect with their personalities, but it's a temporary connection.

I see. I thought you extruded souls.

No, I don't do that. That's not my job.

About Imagination

Beings who read this book can ask to touch into you for their visions and their own extra imagination, right?

Well, all you have to do is touch into your own imagination to touch into me. Just recognize that your imagination is a sacred instrument designed to be a sense that goes beyond your physical senses to what you do not know, but *could* know. It is also entertainment, what you would like to play with and so on. That's particularly important for beings who have a limited capacity to express themselves physically. Without an imagination life would be pretty boring.

As we go into the fourth and fifth dimension and are not limited physically so much, how will imagination work?

Well, in the fourth dimension you still have some fairly pronounced limits. On the fifth dimension and beyond you do not really experience imagination per se. It is more like vertical thought combined with instinct. Limits then are in more of a social or even religious context rather than a sensed physical barrier. It will be less important then for the imagination to help you to leap beyond and more important for the imagination to be a tool applied to day-to-day, practical problem-solving, if you should happen to have a problem. At higher dimensions you don't have them all the time, unlike here. [Chuckles.]

So imagination is most important here while we're in between third and fourth dimensions?

In this particular creation it is, yes.

Is there anything you'd like to say that I'm not smart enough to ask about?

Understand that imagination has always been intended to be a means by which you can move beyond—not just plan or hope or wish, although those are all valid, but to *go* beyond. When you are imagining something, don't doubt it just because someone else has told you it can't ever happen. If you need to resolve something, even if the resolution on the imaginative level cannot be attained at this time for one reason or another, write it down or remember it or use it as a basis to ask for an inspiration.

Remember that imagination is truly a memory of the future. It is true especially now, since your memory is fading so that you can come into more instantaneous thought (your natural thought). You have much more ability now to access the future than you ever had before, and when you combine your imagination with your instinct and inspiration, there's a good chance that you will not only know how to solve problems, but who to solve them with. Good night.

❖ Robert's Comments on His Experience

Oh, boy. I had some good visuals that time. I saw a tube with colors running through it. It was odd because if you went out to the end of the tube, it wasn't just color; it was like a feeling. It wasn't a feeling in the sense of an emotion, but more like a physical feeling. You could linger in it for a moment before it went somewhere.

Then I had a definite picture of the Buddha blowing into this thing. He had a big, round belly and it looked like he was in a state of perfect bliss. He appeared to be breathing in, then he'd exhale and you'd see this variation on white light. It was really beautiful. I had a really good picture of that.

Then I had another picture. I guess it was this being meditating. There were swirls of color, and if you focused toward the center of the swirl, you could feel something like a physical feeling. It was like the memory of a sound, not a sound that you could hear, but one that you could remember.

It was definitely an experience channeling that being. Sometimes it makes life here seem kind of abstract and other times it helps me to appreciate life here more.

Zoosh, the End-Time Historian

October 24, 1996

ll right. Now, way back there was a time and a place where what you know as material substance didn't exist. I can't call it the Void, because that word has been used. But it was where there was no awareness of feeling, no awareness of light or sound, no particular input. The best way I can describe it is that it had no recognizable form, no congenital existence and no apparent purpose. Yet within all of this existence, this seemingly nonexisting existence, there was a feeling (though it wasn't recognized as such at the time), a sensation of what I can only call tension. This tension existed for a very long time. Looking back on it, I realize that this tension was a call for help, because the basic nonexistence of it, the unexpressed potential of it all, needed to *do* something.

Remembering My Beginnings

Gradually a feeling began to develop that I can only describe physically for you—it was a tingling feeling. It was not unpleasant, but it was definitely attention-getting. It existed for quite a while, and so significantly that if one described it visually (though it was not particularly visual) it would seem as if there were points of flashing light and spaces in between.

Looking back at that again sentimentally, as it were, I'd have to say that those points of sensation (what I'm calling tingles) were really almost like dots that one might connect to create a form. At the same time they might have been considered synapses or even pores in one's body. While they were becoming something, they were not yet what I would call conscious.

Then gradually, very slowly, there came a sense of warmth. As the warmth began to spread, all of the tingling sensations turned to light. The warmth spread everywhere and all of the points of light gradually began to acquire a sense of awareness. My definition of awareness is a sense of unified personality and the ability to learn, grow, change, acquire and, yes, to think.

So within this great mass there was gradually this warmth. The warmth is, of course, love that sustains, unites and also anoints. One does not have life as you know it or even that you aspire to without love. It is essential. This place I'm talking about was quite massive. I know you like digital comparisons, so I will say that it was about one-fourth the size of the universe stimulated by your Creator, which is pretty big, because your universe is beyond big.

This large mass suddenly had points of light, it had love, it had awareness. And it began to move, because motion follows not long after the stimulation of those basics. One might say that motion existed before that, but one would not have been aware of it. One would simply have been moving and have felt nothing.

Let us have a timetable for this. The length of time that has made up your universe (U), combined with the length of time that your Creator (C) became aware of Itself and took Its journey and arrived here (C + U), is the base number. For all you numerologists out there, the base number is not zero or one, but a circle, a sphere—a complete number. Numbers are complete only when they are seen three-dimensionally, not flat. Flat numbers disempower you, but that's been intended so you wouldn't become too creative too soon.

So C + U is the three-dimensional circle, the sphere. Now, if we put that base number to the one-trillionth power, then that number shown three-dimensionally would equal the experiential time that this motion, this love, this awareness, began. That was my birth.

You as a point of light, or you as that entire creation that's one-quarter the size of this universe?

The me that was one-quarter the size of this universe. I've grown since then, but . . . you know, you've got to start somewhere.

Keep going. It's wonderful.

Well, the awareness of being is a wonderful thing. I have to tell you this—it has been a very long time since any of you have had this experience. We can trace some of you back to this time and some of you perhaps even before. In my personal experience (which is not forever, but it's been a while) one has this experience only once. At some point you are a portion of something, but you don't feel a sense of yourself. There is something there, but it is undefinable in conceptual terms or even feelings. Then you become aware of being something and then someone.

Coming to awareness is quite astonishing. You don't have this experience when you're born or when you die because there is absolute continuity there. Therefore coming to awareness is your true birth as a being. It's something you don't forget. I can assure you that when you're at the end of your natural cycle you will all remember that too, but you forget it when you're here.

When I became the beginnings of what I am now, I began to move, as I say. But I realized, looking back on it, that I had been in motion before but without purpose and without a sense of self or even choice, desire. The motion was not noticed; it was not of any great significance in terms of what you might talk about or even what you might feel and hold dear. It was merely a recalled sense of no-sense, or nothing. It is a strange feeling.

Did all the points of light wake up, and only you became aware of every point of light at one time?

My Search for the Origin of the Love Feeling

No, it was a gradual thing. As the warmth (which I've now defined as love) eased across my total being, parts of it woke up at different times as the tingles, then the light, then the warmth. Looking back on it, I realized that that was terrific. Waking up suddenly would be exciting but extremely disorienting. Here I had a great deal of experiential time to assimilate the acquisition of self.

Then, feeling myself, I began to move. The first thing anybody wants to do after they've been activated is to go out there and see if there's anybody else. Believe me, that's the first thing you do. That's what I did. For one thing, I knew that this love came from someplace, so I started moving in the direction it was coming from. It's only natural to seek out that which has loved you into life.

After a while I realized that it was not something associated with direction, but a feeling. I had to move toward the feeling. So I stopped and focused myself totally on that feeling. I tried to see if I could acquire a point of origin for that feeling, but I could not acquire a single point, as in a direction. However, I did acquire what amounted to a spherical sense, like being inside a perfectly round fishbowl that has no opening. I felt it getting stronger as I went out spherically, so I expanded spherically for a long time, expecting to find a point of origin, which I didn't.

Finally, after I had expanded (moving well beyond the speed of light and even thought), I realized I wasn't feeling that love any stronger. I wasn't sure whether there was any point in pursuing this, so I returned to my original size. Then I had the thought that I would try to move inward, condensing, as it were. I did that, and as I moved inward and became more condensed, the feeling became stronger. I was quite amazed. I wasn't sure whether I was simply concentrating the feeling within myself or whether there was something in there. (As physicists have suspected, you can take a single particle, expand it to the size of a universe and bring it back down to its original size again, but the mass does not change.)

So I moved into a smaller and smaller space until I was a size roughly equal to a helium neutron, and then I felt this incredible sense of love. It was just overwhelming. I didn't want to go inward any farther because it was so terrific. I stayed like that for a very long time, just basking in that total, pervasive, overwhelming unconditional love.

I think I soaked that up for at least a trillion or a trillion and a half years. It's hard to describe, it's a wonderful feeling, and when I looked back on it, I realized it was the first total awareness that I'd had of total unity with all—even though at that time in my infancy I wasn't even aware of how much "all" there was. It's a feeling, not so much a mental awareness, that the answer is not the beginning and the end, but what *precedes* the beginning and the end, otherwise known as the intention.

Initially I was floating there as nothing, then suddenly this great love swooped down and I became something, I became someone. That intention is the greatest gift one can bestow, for I have discovered that giving it gives the feeling, receiving it gives the feeling and being in it also gives the feeling. The great gift there was simply to enjoy it.

I must admit that as a being of thought and experience and a little variety (little compared to your Creator), I wanted to see what would happen if I got smaller. So I made myself smaller and the love actually didn't increase. It decreased a little, not because I was denser but because a certain pitch, volume or mass, (size, you could say) was just right for me. When I got to that size to experience the total love I had available for me, that would be the right size. This would be like standing in front of a fairly large and complete xylophone or big church organ, playing each note slowly. You would find several notes that were wonderful, that you just loved, that you could constantly play, enjoying just those notes. It is similar to my experience because that octave, that tone, that feeling, the complete experience of it, is so much a portion of you. Another person might sit at the organ and find completely different notes.

The Point of Perfection: The Sense of Home

This is fairly important, because I've come to realize that this point of perfection, the point where love cannot get any better, is a sense of home. You've all wondered about home. Where is it? Is it some *place*

—a star, a galaxy, a universe? In my personal experience home is that creation of yourself where you feel the maximum amount of pure, unconditional love, which I felt when I made myself the size of a helium neutron. If you consider my creation, where the warmth or the love came and provided me with a sense of awareness, this total, concentrated unconditional love must be home, because it is the concentrated feeling of that which created me, or at least allowed me to be aware of myself.

When we talk about home—and you all think of it, I know—temporarily it might be someplace here on Earth that is wonderful. The feeling is the same, yet ultimately it is that place, that size, that shape, that color, that tone, that taste, even, where you feel the totality, the maximum amount of unconditional love available for you.

That's so beautiful. Then what?

Well, I stayed there for a while, as I've said. When you have that feeling and are totally attuned to the feeling of home, you know that wherever you go and whatever you do, you can achieve home without having to actually go anywhere. You can simply reacquire that status (for me, it was about the size of a condensed helium neutron). It's a wonderful freedom, because you know that you can go wherever you want to go, as far as you want, and *home is right there*. It was that sense of permission that caused me to want to celebrate that love and tell somebody about it. This is perhaps the idea of where the messianic thing came from, meaning "I've got this wonderful experience. You don't have to *be* it, but wouldn't you love to hear about it? And if you're it too, I'd love to hear your story." It's not "Have I got a way of life for you!" but "I've had this great experience, and I'd like to hear your version, too."

Looking for Friends

So that's when I started traveling to look for friends. Once you've found home and total love, the next thing you want is friends. After I traveled for a long time without seeing anybody else, I realized that space was not the method to travel. I needed some other means because I was in this vast volume. No matter how fast I went, it didn't make any difference. What was around me was simply what I had been before. I realized that in order to go somewhere I had to find a place that could be *defined* as somewhere. So I stopped and reacquired that condensed state of love, and while I was in that state I thought very purely, "I'd like to go someplace where there are wonderful beings to meet, where there's variety—things to sense, feel, see. And I'd like to do that just as soon as I'm done doing this." I stayed in that state again for about a hundred years' experiential time. (Time just passes; this is only a frame of reference. You don't think of it in terms of time passing.)

How did you know there were things and other people?

I didn't. I was basically expressing a need. How often have you noticed that a person can need something, even the richest person and happiest person, but not know what it is? I was expressing an undefined need. I wanted to meet beings if they were out there. I knew that *I* existed, so I had to believe that others did as well.

After about a hundred years' experiential time I began to feel that it was time to emerge from my cocoon, so I began to relax that condensation and move outward. Without having traveled at all, simply being in that condensed form of light (love, in this case), I suddenly noticed that I was surrounded by many points of light. I hadn't gone anywhere in terms of space, yet I was surrounded with points of light. There were clouds of light and stars; there were clouds of color. I was surrounded by feelings that would come and go and that I've since recognized as being many possibilities, many things—sometimes beings, sometimes a feeling on its way to where it's needed. I was surrounded by universes.

I felt so thankful, so joyous to have other beings I could communicate with that I spent quite a while just moving around from being to being—not what I would call individual people like you, but beings of light like myself—telling my story and hearing their stories, the sort of comradeship that comes as a result of need and the celebration of being alive.

I did that for a long time and talked to a lot of beings. I didn't get bored with it. Everyone I've talked to all had a similar experience. They became aware of themselves and went through similar things, but not all of them the same way.

Creating a Small Universe of Beings

Then I decided that it was time for me to create something, so I had my fling at being a creator. I created a small universe. Compared to this universe, it was much, much smaller, but within it beings could feel all of the nurturing emotions and pass them on to other beings who would be fragments seeded from the original beings like a dandelion going to seed. They could allow those seed selves within them to have a long time of no awareness, from one to three years' experiential time. I don't like to deny beings the awareness of themselves, but I wanted to give them those moments so they could have the great joy of experiencing the awareness when waking up from the seed stage to the full range of being. I must admit that becoming aware of myself has been the most wonderful experience of my life.

I put a lot of my attention into that. After a time the beings within this universe (a universe of beings rather than planets) had gone through as much of the experience as they wished. So you might say that my universe was a celebration and a re-creation of my own coming to awareness. When that was completed I reacquired all those parts and reassimilated them into my total being, condensed myself down to my small size and then experienced another several billion years' experiential time of that total condensed love and went on.

Since we don't have a hundred years to talk about it, hitting the highlights (from your point of view), I had an interesting experience. It's only interesting now within the context that we're in, but at the time it was just another experience. You've had creators talk about (your Creator mentioned it) seeing at some point the construct of a potential float by as a thread. There are a lot of things like that out there in the All that I've experienced.

The Thread That Floated By

One of the constructs I saw floating by was also seen by your Creator, though it didn't resonate with me the same way it resonated with your Creator. In the long run this might have been one of the things that connected your Creator and myself, because we saw the same thing. You constantly see many, many things. After a while there are things that you just don't pay so much attention to. But I did notice that; I thought it was a very interesting construct.

Does it float by like a movie or a script?

No, it isn't like that; it's much more akin to a thread. Nowadays you put music and pictures and all of this on the tiniest little pieces of filmy substance; we're coding these very words onto a piece of filmy substance, a tape. If you've ever seen a flying spider go by trailing one of those long, silvery wisps, it's not unlike that—a sort of long, silvery thread of white or even gold light, sometimes other colors. It's very pretty to look at. Usually there are many clouds of them, but if you notice an individual one, then you acquire its fundamentals—what it could be.

Does it flow into you, or something like that?

Yes. It doesn't download so much; you simply know it, and you can do something with it or not. I did notice this thread, but I didn't act on it. Your Creator did. That might have been one of our initial contact points, as I look back on it.

Here's another interesting fact for you: Before your Creator became fully aware of Itself and went on Its long journey to this space, even before your Creator acquired companions, on my own I covered part of the trail that your Creator took simply because I was curious. When you have unlimited time, if you see something you like and if it looks interesting and you're not in a rush to go anywhere, you go do it. Many of you have done this at other levels.

I went on a similar voyage. It wasn't totally the same as that of your Creator, but that's another connection we had.

My Travel through the Orbs

Did you come from this Orb?

No, it wasn't in this Orb. As a matter of fact, in order to be in this Orb you have to have certain motivations. One is that there has to be a need within you: You must either now have the need or have been a portion of someone or something else that had a need to be a part of or create something that will last for a while.

Were you drawn here when you had that need to see other beings?

No, I didn't come there then. That was before this Orb.

You saw all those lights and all those other beings and talked at great length somewhere besides this Orb?

Yes. As you said, there are many orbs. As the Master of Imagination recently described, the orbs are spherical in nature, and as they get filled up, creations begin to take place in a larger surrounding orb, continuing outward indefinitely.

So I was well out. Part of the reason there weren't other beings to meet when I became aware of myself is that I was in an orb very far out from this Orb. This can be roughly drawn [draws].

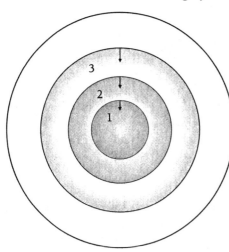

So one might fill up this orb [1], then in time fill up this orb [2]. You'd fill each one from the outside in, and in time you'd be filling up the next orb and so on.

I saw them like cells side by side.

No, it's spheres within spheres. I had created something that had a lasting effect, but I wanted to be exposed to beings who have what I would call an intention to create lasting reverberations (this is a musical thing, really) of value and beauty.

Now, that's a pretty good descriptive definition of your Creator. Your Creator wanted to create something like that. Because It got interested in that particular strand, It wanted to perpetuate that in the form of offspring, which the whole Explorer Race here is about. It was right around that time that I started to feel myself in motion. Now, this is a particular motion where one does not experience moving through space or even time or dimension; it is more a feeling that you are moving toward something or someone

But it acts like a prime attractor?

Yes, there's something attracting you. You're not moving through time or space, but whatever is attracting you becomes more noticeable. You are in some form of motion, but if you looked at things around you, they would be in relatively the same place. Looking back on it, I was moving from the outer orbs, which were not as packed with creation as some of the inner orbs, gradually toward that point in the inner orbs where I would meet your Creator.

Moving Toward and Meeting Your Creator

I realize that it was at that point that your Creator needed a friend, a companion. I could understand that completely, having gone through it myself. That's when I went to that point of intersection and met your Creator. The rest is history. [Laughs.]

Your Creator really needed someone to commiserate with who had had previous experience and who could occasionally provide your Creator with a feeling or vibration that stimulated Its answer. To understand this on the practical level, before you receive an inspiration from Creator or any of your teachers, there is a slight feeling (if you could slooooww the process down physically) that precedes the inspiration. That is what I would pass on to your Creator. I add the fuel and then your Creator, from Its own sources, would flash the fuel into the light of creation.

When you met the Creator He was not exponentially separated? Was He a whole being?

He was aware of Himself.

No, but He left a part of Himself when He started this creation so He could go find it again.

When I met Creator He was whole and had not separated. That's right.

So you know Him in His entirety?

Yes.

Whereas He doesn't.

He does, but He doesn't.

Well, He chose to forget, right?

He chose to forget so that He could have some identification with your process. That's right. If She needed to acquire it for any reason, She could, but She hasn't so that She could have some of the fun you're having. (Hah-hah-hah! *Some of the fun you're having!*)

But He forgot even His own creator, according to his creator [Creator of the Inverse Universe].

Well, it was actually helpful to forget that, because even here when one is fully aware of one's lineage, it can at times be distracting. Your lineage can take you off your track sometimes. Your Creator needed to have help and assistance to bring about this creation while at the same time not have anything to distract It. So being less aware of Its lineage was a benefit in this case.

The only other one we heard about who did that was the one you beings call Junior [Spirit of Youthful Exuberance]. Did he separate after he met the Creator, too?

Yeah. Junior did that, probably having something to do with what Creator was doing. Junior wanted to go along with Him. Well, youth and enthusiasm rush in very often where . . .

"Oh, you're doing that? I'll do that, too." Something like that.

Yes. It's like, "Oh, that looks like fun. I want to try it."

That's the one. The other six companions and you are all whole beings; you all know yourselves completely.

I think so, yes, from what I have assimilated from hanging out with these individuals for a while. I don't think any of them have any residual bits of themselves they've stored someplace else.

But this Creator has a creator and a grandfather . . .

Ad infinitum.

But you have no one to go back to.

My Home: Love, Which Is Not Somewhere but Is the Foundation of All Being

That's not true at all. Remember, what came originally was the warmth, the feeling, the sensation. When I went on that search for home, I wanted to find who had created me. In order to find it I had to make myself small, because the way to acquire home was to get to that resonant size, shape and (for me) vibration by which I could feel the overwhelming sensation of condensed, unconditional love. *That* is what created me or allowed me to be. Instead of going somewhere to find it I *became* it.

I understand that. It wasn't like going to another being who in full consciousness birthed you in the same sense that this Creator has someone like that to go to.

Simple logic would tell you that yes, this is how you can acquire that feeling. Yet doesn't logic suggest to you that somewhere *someone* sent that love to me?

Oh, absolutely.

It just suggests it. But you know what? In my experience I haven't been able to find that "somewhere." This leads me to believe that love is self-perpetuating and self-motivated and goes where it's needed.

And you called it?

Since love is my home, I can go home anytime I want. I can feel it around me all the time, and if I want to condense the feeling, I make myself the size of a helium neutron—and oooohhh, it's really there.

Someday you might start looking around for where it came from. It might be fun.

What do you think I did for the first part of my life? Do you understand what I'm saying about love?

I know—that it is self.

As much as I've been able to reason this out, I believe that it is not somewhere . . .

Or someone?

Or someone. It's not that. It is the *foundation of all being!* Yet if love was not made by anybody and if it is the grandmother and grandfather of all beings (which I believe), then one might ask, is it possible that there is a point where creation began? I'd say that this energy is the beginning of creation, because I have made every effort and asked everyone I've met if they've ever gone to the point that preceded love or might have been the source of it. Nobody I know has gone in as far as I have. But I'm not ruling out the possibility. I'm just saying that I believe that it is ultimately . . .

Self-sufficient.

Yes.

My Gain and My Contribution

What do you feel that you have gained from being involved with this creation, and what do you feel you have given the most?

It is hard to put in a brief statement, but if I condensed it, I'd say I have seen what can be done with very specific motivation or intentions. Your Creator had a very specific agenda when He came here—and that is unusual. Usually creations are a little looser than this one when they begin. So I've seen what can be done within the concept of a major agenda, and I had never seen that from the get-go. I've also acquired lots of new friends.

And I suppose I've given a sense of purpose, the value of companionship. Because your Creator needed a companion, your Creator realized that within Its entire creation this is a worthy thing to need and a wonderful thing to fulfill. I think I contributed to that, though I'm not going to take sole credit for it. I'd say your Creator and I contributed to that equally.

The Creator said at one point that you had been delegated to network, to be the communicator. Then at some point you were going to take a more active voice, and that's when He used our subconscious and unconscious to radiate out to all the other creators. What did you do at the point when you quit being the communicator and took a more active role in the creation?

The Agenda for Acquisitiveness

I suppose He's referring to that time when I acted as an advisor to a group that was creating the motivating consciousnesses for all encapsulated beings on the individual and the societal level. I was interested in helping mold the way people's acquisitiveness would utilize an agenda(I was learning from your Creator)—if not before, then after. Even at the most mundane level, you buy a dirt bike and then you want to get a bigger one. Or you discover the world of ideas and you want more ideas, so you read. It was the foundation of the way acquisition works.

Who did you advise? What group of beings?

Oh, I advised the Council of Nine. It was their job to set up the way individual people on all of the planets would think, feel, act, not how they would function societally, but at the very core of their being.

Is the Council of Nine generated, or are they outside consultants?

Oh, the Council of Nine is generated.

By the Creator?

Yes.

What you're calling acquisitiveness is really part of the lust for more that we have.

Oh, I can understand why in a material society you would perceive it that way—the lust for more, but . . .

But it's wonderful. It's like a lust for life, a lust to see what's beyond the next cor- ner—curiosity. It's like a lot of our best traits, isn't it?

All right. I can accept that definition, yes.

Did that take a long time?

Not in terms of experiential time. It was being done because it was a pleasure. The Council of Nine did not do it quickly; they took their time. Laying it down for the individual beings all over this universe took maybe 1000 or 1500 experiential years—just because it was fun.

Is that a quality in the soul? Is that how do you do that?

Yes, I'd have to say that. It's a quality within the immortal personal- ity. Allowing for the fact that some of you beings preceded this crea- tion, it would be added to you as you began your first chain of lives, as you were spawned by the Creator as an individual being, becoming aware of yourself. Or as you came in from another creation it would be added to you. Therefore it happened either when you were being spawned or created by your Creator; or if you came sailing in from someplace else and wanted to begin a chain of lives here, it would be thrown into the pot that made you up.

Later Jobs Here

Then after that you went back. You didn't have to be a communicator, so did you take on other challenges or other chores?

No, I think your Creator wanted me to do that so I would have a per- sonal stake in this creation. I think that was really Her motivation. I said, "Okay. That's enough of that. Let us resume. The Council can handle all this by itself if it needs to." After a while you don't need advice; you do what you're doing well. They didn't need it anymore, so I made myself available to them should they need help. But they haven't needed it since. After that I simply hung out with your Creator and went other places if needed.

As an ambassador, or as . . .

No, as more of an advisor. Understand that when there is an interesting creation going on, other creators are aware of it, especially within one's own orb, but sometimes even beyond one's orb. Occasionally other creators would like to have threads of this creation. Remember that I said your Creator saw a thread of *what could be*. Threads are like that, sort of the foundation of the foundation. Yet when other creators want information on a specific creation rather than the foundation of the foundation, when they want to have someone to elucidate about it rather than simply get a creator data printout, as it were, if we have a personal relationship I'll go and talk to them about it. (But I stay here at the same time.)

Ensouling a Planet

At some point you ensouled a planet, right?

Yes, but that was just to get a more physical, hands-on feeling. It was an interesting experience. I wouldn't do it again, because it was too confining. I admire beings such as yourselves who are willing to be confined in encapsulated time experience, even though it is not even a drop in the bucket in terms of your immortality. I know what it's like to be encapsulated, and I needed to experience that perhaps on the planetary level. I figured I wasn't ready to be encapsulated as an individual. I didn't want that much condensed restriction, so I tried it as a planet for a while.

And we blew it up?

Yes. But before you blew it up I was just about ready to pass it on to somebody else. I had already said, "Well, that's enough of that," and was getting ready to pass it on to a feminine energy who was going to take it over. But because the planet blew up, she went on to another planet within this creation and ensouled that planet at a higher level.

Dimensional level?

Isis, My Intended Replacement, Chose Venus Instead

Yes. A higher-dimensional level so the planet would not be uncomfortable. At the third-dimensional level that planet Venus is uncomfortable.

That's the one she went to and ensouled.

Yes, as an option. It was, after all, within the same solar system, so she went there and ensouled it but not at the third or even the fourth dimension. Once you get up to the fifth dimension, the sun (which is still there, by the way) becomes a radiating source of light, love and all of this, but one does not experience heat. You might feel the love as warmth, but you don't get sunburned.

Is it like musical chairs to take over the ensoulment of a planet? People, beings passing through?

No. With your analogy to the game, it's not sudden or even external in its stimulation. It's something that happens now and then. She knew that I didn't really care to do it anymore. The entirety of me wasn't doing it, obviously, because I had other things to do. But the part of me that was doing it had completed the experience. If you've completed an experience—finished working on a book and there's no more to do and you're done—you want to go on to the next thing. The part of me that was done wanted to go on to the next thing. And she was interested in ensouling a planet and working with the deities she might bring in to interact with.

Someone was ready to leave Venus to her?

Well, Venus at that time and place was not ensouled—meaning that the planet had its own sense of purpose but was prepared to have someone join it with an agenda. Isis had that agenda.

Isis is ensouling Venus?

She did at that higher level for a while. She found it interesting and fun. She had a chance to play with a lot of the beings of the devic or fairy world. I think she did a lot to develop the variety of life and physical expressions there. A lot of cultural influences from Venus, certainly in terms of the fairy and the devic worlds, were applied on what you now call Earth. She had done lots of things before then and she will do many things after. But she did it for a time; she felt that was interesting. She saw that I was doing it and she said, "Well, that's nice, Zoosh, but this is the way I'm going to do it." We have our little jokes. She did it her way and I watched for a time. It was very interesting.

That could be another book—the real story of the people in mythology.

You have to remember that people who wrote down the original mythologies were inspired, were they not? They didn't find these names scratched on a cave wall somewhere. (Well, a few of them did, but that's another story.)

Is there a reference to who you are in our current literature, history or religions of the world?

Meaning, is there some portion of me that is referred to? No, I don't think so. It's a good question, because I think it is so for some other beings, but I don't think for me. I haven't had recent enough direct contact with you as beings on this planet for this to exist. In the time records or in the library or akashic record you might see some reference, but I don't think there's anything physical.

Why do you make yourself known now?

Currently Giving You Hands-on Instruction

It's not so much that I'm making myself known out of my own need, but it is my job, though it wasn't assigned to me. I've made it my business to be the end-time historian so I could help you ease back into the fullness of your being by guiding you. I've decided to take it past the original vibration that precedes inspiration given to your Creator and actually give you some hands-on instructions. "This is my version of your background" (not making it mandatory that you believe it) "and here's what you can do to . . . " An owner's manual, if you like. I decided that I want that much of a stake in it. I want to help you.

I still remember what it was like before I had my beginning awareness of self, and it's not fun. I don't want others to have to go through that.

In a sense, we're going through that now.

In a sense, yes, because as you move through from one dimension to another the rules are constantly changing, even how one learns and applies. So I think you need a little guidance. Although you're getting a lot from many other sources, I'm perfectly willing to throw in my two cents' worth as well.

Well, it's worth more than two cents. What are some of the stories in the time records that would be interesting to us? Did you interact with ancestors of ours, with souls who were in the Explorer Race before they came to this planet?

Aristotle

Well, let's see. I interacted with the being you now know as Aristotle before he came to this planet. Before he came here and did all the things you know about, he was very involved in quantification. The study of quantification is less involved with theories and ideas than in numeric values and principles. Because he was involved in the quantification of values, principles and to some extent numeric values, he found himself ultimately attracted to various crystalline objects here and there in space.

At the time he and I met he was quantifying a floating liquid crystal. If you were to examine it under a microscope you would see the microcrystalline substance floating about and you would be overwhelmed with thoughts, data, words, ideas. Simply coming within a thousand miles of the liquid crystal you'd be overwhelmed with potential. You wouldn't want to come too close. But he was inside; he could do that and he was quantifying it.

We spent a little time together visiting. He was not at what I would call the creator level, but he was at a point where he could become a creator if he wished. But he did not wish it. He was still involved in the acquisition of foundational reference points.

By the time he got here he had become known for, and was really a master of, comparative reference points. So when his soul came in he intended to encourage the foundational elements and practices of a well-ordered society; he wanted to provide foundational principles by which a society could become well-ordered if it wished. I think he ultimately achieved this within that life. He didn't so much tell people what to do; he laid out what could be done and a lot of those ideas were integrated.

The Accessibility of Creatorship

Are you saying that an individual soul can go out in this creation and become a creator on its own, separate from the mass Creator of the Explorer Race if they reach a certain level?

Yes. And there's a point at which you can do that even beyond this individual physical life. If you decided (free will is a real thing) to go out within this universe and make some small creation that would be harmonious with this universe, it would most likely be granted if you had proven that you could do so within the harmony of this universe. Your Creator would know if you could do that. If you wanted to do that, you would have some idea of what you wanted to create and you would run that idea past the Creator. Creator would say, "Okay, give it a try. Fine." If you had been spawned by this Creator, you would basically need to prove yourself.

On the other hand, if you came from beyond this creation and had been a creator before, then Creator wouldn't even review your idea; it would be an understanding between the two of you that it had to be harmonious within this creation. Creator would say, "Have fun!"

That's within this creation.

That's within this creation. But if you wanted to leave this creation and go back where you came from (if you came from someplace else and had been a creator before), certainly there would be no restriction. There is only a restriction if this Creator had spawned you.

But if He had spawned you and you created something harmonious, then you would be allowed to go out and create a whole new place?

Yes, it's kind of like qualifying. "Well, you got your M.D. Now you can go out and practice."

What is your relationship to Progenitor, who, I understood, was your ancient lineage?

The Progenitor is really not so much before me. I know that Progenitor says, "I am that which preceded Zoosh," and in that context you might say, yes, Progenitor preceded me. But I think maybe we had better hear from Progenitor itself on this one. I don't want to speak for him.

All right. I am Progenitor of Zoosh. I can speak only briefly at the moment. I will say that I am the oasis of the energy that Zoosh was a portion of before he had awareness. I continue to exist at that level. Zoosh was simply a portion of the mass of my being who became itself through the use and exposure of immortal love. I can add no more to your understanding of where love might have come from because I became aware of the love, that energy within me, and it transformed me from being the pure precursor of thought to being intimate thought. When I became aware of that, I activated portions of myself to become beings. Zoosh was one of the first of these. But you can see that from my own experience, I can tell no more of where love has come from than Zoosh.

Are there other beings Zoosh could communicate with who came from you?

Yes, but they would be more like twins, so not much more could be acquired. He has not indicated an interest in doing this, though it is available for him to do so.

Well, he didn't know it was available.

He knows what I know. There are no secrets between us. I'd rather say that I am the matrix from which Zoosh was originally made up. So in that sense I preceded him, and if anything precedes anything, it also follows it. That is why I have defined myself that way.

Zoosh: Well, we had a little spoken word from Progenitor there only because I did not wish to speak for him directly. But I can assure you, he's still there and is available. He occasionally comes through to speak to individuals should it be necessary or if he has the proper words and feelings for that specific individual. Sometimes it is because he has known them before.

But did he go on in experience? He didn't just stay where you were when you became aware.

Progenitor does not have to go anywhere to experience anything. Being the energy that precedes pure thought, this means that any thought that happens *anywhere* is immediately available to him. So he does not have to go anywhere; anywhere comes to him.

What's the latest word now? You were going to go on with the Creator, but then a couple of months ago you said that He had asked a part of you to stay with the Explorer Race.

That's still up in the air, because until you [the Explorer Race] recondense as a total being of your own, you won't be able to tell me collectively whether you want me to stick around. I need to hear from everybody at a time when you are more conscious of your total self. So that decision will be deferred. But I can still stay here and help you out while I go with Creator.

It's not either/or.

That's right. The only question is, would you like me to stay here with you, or will I go with Creator? I could stay here with you *and* go with Creator, or just go with Creator for a time.

All the other friends of the Creator are in pretty much the same position, right? Their services might be needed. I would think they would be needed to continue.

They might be needed, that's right. If they are needed and there is a desire for them to stay, they will most likely stay. I can't speak for them. Most likely they will stay, but as with everyone else, they will need to be politely asked.

And the contract negotiated. This is absolutely awesome. Thank you.

You are most welcome. Good night.

❖ *Robert's Comments on His Experience*

Did you see anything that you hadn't seen before regarding Zoosh?

I had a pretty good visualization of things he was talking about, like his condensing himself. I didn't have the feeling so much, just the visuals. It's kind of like seeing something at a distance but not being it. That's what I saw, although I remember some of the feeling of vastness and I have a pretty good picture of the orbs now.

Master of Feeling

October 29, 1996

I am that which understands all manner of feeling—not only what you call emotion, but that which precedes emotion (inspirational feeling) as well as physical and even spiritual feelings. We might discuss this a bit.

In order to deliver the clearest possible messages to anybody, especially you here, the best way is to give you a message you can't ignore, even though in your current times you have learned to ignore feelings. This kind of learning must be integrated into the structure of your society because it is not natural to learn this. You have been regulated in such a way that you would seek physical evidence either to lead you to thoughts or conclusions or to support them. Your ongoing personalities have been placed carefully into physical instruments that also register feelings well. It has been designed this way.

Your Suppression of Feelings

When you consider it, it is ironic that your society, so pursuant of thoughts, ideals and even desires, would in recent years give so little credence to feelings, the one true manner by which you can know. I do understand that through years of invasive attitudes there has been a fairly all-encompassing suppression of knowing what feelings mean. The explanation for feelings has always been passed on through a feminine chain either through direct lineage (learning from one's mother or sisters) or through a religion based within a feminine sanctity.

Some years ago your cultures declined to perpetuate the easy way and decided to take the opposite way, which is the obscure (not hard, but obscure) way, as if to lay down a challenge in front of you, saying, "Life is too direct, too simple. Let us complicate it to make it more challenging." Well, that might have seemed like an interesting idea at the time, but now you are reaping the crop that is abundantly at your feet, which is bundled nicely into confusion.

I am here to remind you tonight that your feeling self is not reactive only to your external world. It was primarily designed to be a physical chain of communication stimulated through your instincts, which are related not only to your physical world, your emotional world, your spiritual world but also to that which *precedes* your direct linear spiritual world, which is perhaps most important.

Sometimes you want and need advice, asking it from your teachers, guides or whoever can give it to you. You have known different teachers throughout the years, but beyond this plane there are teachers, guides and others waiting to advise you appropriately, considering the challenge you might face in any moment. Therefore there is what I would call *pre*spiritual or *pre*inspirational feeling.

The Broad Range of Your Feeling Self

Preinspirational feeling comes from beyond a direct knowledge from your total self—defined as the total accumulation of wisdom from all your lives or any chain of lives as well as all the guides and teachers within those lives and their experiences on up the line. But there is more!

Before you were a fragment of Creator—a personality unto yourself—you were a portion of something else that also accumulated wisdom up a different line. [She draws a diagram.] The wisdom of one's individualized personality that I'm showing on the diagram has been accumulated as a result of what you as an individual personality have been exposed to [shown above "Self"]. You were a part of something else before that, perhaps not individualized into the personality you are now, but you were there [shown to the left].

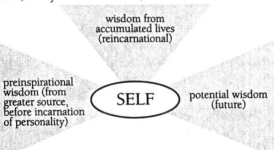

wisdom from
accumulated lives
(reincarnational)

preinspirational
wisdom (from
greater source,
before incarnation
of personality)

SELF

potential wisdom
(future)

There is also the potential wisdom you could have available in the future [shown on the right], preinspirational wisdom. Through this one can be touched with a physical message felt as an instinctual feeling from teachers and from experience beyond your immediate knowledge. Initially this always comes through as a feeling *before* the feeling.

You might get inspiration on the feeling level from your own accumulated reincarnational wisdom [top of the chart, vertical wisdom], but if there is nothing there to apply to a situation or if it is only partially applicable, something like a circuit is triggered to access another source of wisdom that comes from outside the boundaries of your personally accumulated wisdom. I call that preinspirational wisdom, because it fills in the gaps of the wisdom available to you. This comes in as a feeling, as raw data before it is interpreted into understandable language. This feeling supplements the inspiration from your reincarnational (or vertical) wisdom and enters your physical self via your emotional body.

Your feeling self is the part of you that gives you your physical evidence. Before and after anything else, you are here to learn about physical evidence, because if you do not pay attention to physical evidence, you will continue to make the same mistakes over and over again. Any student of history will back me up on that.

So the only way to truly sustain yourself in the most benevolent way possible is to "listen" to your feelings and learn to interpret them. This is why I recommend gatherings of people who have the ability to share and interpret feelings. Sharing does not mean worded communication. One tends to use many, many words to describe a feeling, whereas the feeling itself is sufficient.

Homework

I recommend that groups of people make an effort to share physical feelings with each other without touching—pairing off, perhaps, and choosing a feeling. Let's not do this telepathically. Let's choose a feeling and say, "I want to share with you how I feel this particular emotion," then attempt to *be* the feeling. Don't send it to the other person; let that person reach into your auric field to sample it. Afterward compare notes about what you physically felt in different parts of your body. Don't try to get into what thoughts or memories it engendered, but keep it strictly on a basis of physical feeling.

If you have access to the outdoors and if weather permits, go outside and see whether an old tree or a mountain or the sea is available—some prominent, fairly massive object in nature. Pick a feeling within you (always benevolent ones for these exercises with entities) and say out loud, "I will now feel this," noting the feeling within yourself. Don't broadcast it, just feel it. It will broadcast naturally, allowing whoever you are communicating with, be it a mountain or a tree, to choose to sample it or not.

If that feeling becomes heightened, look around. Is it the tree that is heightening that feeling, feeling it within itself and broadcasting it back to you, or is it possibly something else? Move your physical body around to see; don't just turn your eyes or your head. Turn to the left slowly to see in what direction the feeling becomes heightened.

When you find what direction it comes from, you know that the object you face is communicating that expanded feeling. There might be something in the way, perhaps a house or a car, but don't assume that it is *not* the house or the car. Walk around the house and see if it is something beyond that. If it is the house itself, then so be it. The main thing is, do not question it as long as it feels good.

The key to utilizing this homework is not getting caught up in worded explanations or even mentally enthusiastic responses, but keeping it simple: "I felt this in this part of my body" (if you're talking to a human being). If you are in exchange with an animal, a tree or an ocean, you don't have to speak out loud or describe it; just note where you felt what. Always remember to use a benevolent feeling. The idea here is to be reminded of an ancient method.

The Feminine and Masculine of Feeling

In ancient times the feminine, which gives its allegiance to feeling, generally passed on this knowledge. Several thousand years ago the negating of the feminine wisdom of feeling that had been taught to all beings began in some areas. Even today this wisdom is suppressed, though it is recorded in some secret libraries. Yet today it is taught instinctively by many beings. There is no reason you cannot re-create this wisdom today, utilizing the means I have discussed as well as others that you feel might be appropriate.

Since I do not wish to seem to eliminate half the population, what portion of feeling would be masculine? The preinspirational and the inspirational are entirely feminine, but the physical vehicle as well as your ability to experience physical feeling are masculine. One might say that certain parts of the physical self are feminine or masculine, but speaking generally, the physical self is a masculine element of creatorship training at the level of physical education. What caused the separation of the sexes was the need for something by which to feel on the third-dimensional level so you would know what you feel by being exposed to different thoughts and activities around you as well as what others are feeling.

When you are focused in your feelings, you will know (not by mental telepathy—that is the hard way) what is right for yourself and others on the basis of the felt message to you. If you feel good in interaction with the tree, for example, then the tree clearly feels good in its interaction with you. If either the tree or you feel threatened by anything, both of you will know it in the same moment.

Say, for instance, that a vehicle comes much too close to you. If you feel threatened, the tree will not heighten your sense of good feeling, but immediately drop its own feeling and broadcast *your* feeling. The converse is also true. You might be able to maintain your good feeling, but it won't be heightened by the feeling from the tree if it feels threatened by the car. This is important, because it suggests that if the tree feels threatened and you are still broadcasting that good feeling, you will also be broadcasting the tree's anxiety, which will warn other trees and people in the area. I'm not giving you this education because I expect you to understand or even assimilate it entirely at this time, but because I want you to practice.

Setting Up the Web for the Potentials of Discomfort and the Wisdom from Feeling

I wanted to start out immediately with a description of what I do, because the reason your Creator acquired my participation in Its project was that It did not have the prerequisite mastery of physical feeling at the dimensions in which you, the ultimate intention of this creation, would be occupying at the graduate level of your training. Your Creator could feel, yes, but It did not have the subtle capacity to feel the discomforting feelings associated with the learning process at the denser, more challenging octaves (the dimensions).

Because your Creator did not in Its own right have discomfort and had to acquire the Master of Discomfort, there was a need for someone who could attune to and provide the instantaneous wisdom of feelings and also act as an interpreter (as I do sometimes) between different beings—especially with the Master of Discomfort you call Lucifer. (I do not call this being Lucifer; he is better known as the Master of Discomfort.) Acting as an interpreter between them, I can provide your Creator with the subtle awareness of what it feels like on a personal level to have discomfort.

Your Creator would never have allowed you—portions of Itself—to experience discomfort without having experienced anything in Its overall being that you might feel. If your Creator had done that, It would be capricious at the least and at most, irresponsible.

Your Creator required consultants. By the time I joined with your Creator to come to this creation, It had already acquired the assistance of the Master of Discomfort, but was having difficulty communicating with that being because they had no common felt language. Communication was available at the mental level, but it was not sufficient. Your Creator needed to understand how to create the web by which you would be exposed to possibilities and potentials of discomfort (some meant to teach you and some to simply repel you) and where and when to place the strands of the web. This was largely my and the Master of Discomfort's job, as well as anyone within the Creator's aspects of Its personal self who had physical knowledge and the full range of physical wisdom.

Creator's Parallel Existence

It was necessary to create almost an artificial identity to do this. This allowed your Creator to have what amounts to a parallel existence in which communication occurs that does not need to affect all beings. This parallel existence is where most of the felt communication I've mentioned takes place. It has also allowed your Creator to play out certain scenarios and sequences which, if played out within this universe, might lead to mischief.

If your Creator communicates with the Master of Discomfort either through myself or some other means, the Master of Discomfort must project a degree of discomfort that would under normal circumstances affect your Creator's *entire creation*. But this cannot be at this time because other beings are unprepared for exposure to even the most minor degree of discomfort (1 to 1½%, the Master of Discomfort's normal state) and cannot tolerate it. So your Creator created this parallel existence in which It could communicate with such beings as the Master of Discomfort and screen out exposure to beings who are unprepared for such rays and feelings, with myself as an assistant.

Your Creator played out a dress rehearsal of your acquisition of wisdom through both traditional and more dramatic channels such as you are experiencing now. It played out many different potential scenarios in this parallel existence. Having had the opportunity to play them all out in this parallel existence, your Creator is interested to see which direction you will choose as the Explorer Race. It is fairly essential that your Creator not be too surprised. It had to react swiftly based upon an instinctual knowledge rooted in some discomfort . . . for instance, you might have a bad feeling as you're turning down a street and say, "I think I'll go the other way" and miss some major disaster. But your Creator cannot have a bad feeling. This tells you why your Creator must have consultants and why It had to play out potentials for the Explorer Race in a parallel form. Your Creator couldn't afford to be caught by surprise, or if It were, It needed to experience it safely, without affecting the rest of Its universe.

My Role As Interpreter of This Experiment

My job, then, has largely been interpretive. But sometimes it has been necessary for me to assume or even assimilate expressions of existence that allow a true understanding for all beings. For example, as individual beings—humanoid beings or other beings throughout the universe—acquire wisdom and knowledge and begin to have a greater ability to be their own creators, they will need less guidance and advice from your overall Creator. Many beings on other planets and galaxies felt wary and even suspicious of this experiment of your Creator. To be suspicious of a creator is not a pleasant experience. That's why it was necessary to have someone who could explain what it's all about to them without their feeling the slightest discomfort. That was quite challenging. I was able to do this by using their instinctual bodies as experienced through their past lives.

The ones who have had the most anxiety about the possible consequences of your meeting and interacting with them—even though they know it's for their own growth—are the same ones who originally sent expeditions to Earth to contribute to your eventual appearance. These are the ones you are genetically connected to—Sirius, Orion, Pleiades, Andromeda and a few others, even Zeta Reticuli. These and a few other races have the most anxiety.

I was able to communicate to them the value of their growth and reassure them that they would not be exposed to anything truly destructive or painful. I did this by bringing them back on a spiritual level into past lives in which they were exposed to some level of the Explorer Race by either passing through your total being unbeknownst to them or by being members of the Explorer Race. This has been particularly helpful for the Zeta Reticulans, who have in recent years discovered that you, at this time here on Earth, are their past lives directly and on the linear level. This was quite astounding to them and is more elaborated in previous books [see chapter 10 in *The Explorer Race*]. Other beings also came to realize that even before you arrived on Earth, you and they were entwined in some way as you weaved your way through the universe, eventually coming to the Earth for your graduate training.

It was very helpful to do this. Through the connection to their past lives and the discomfort associated with the Explorer Race, they were able to understand through the felt spiritual memory that discomfort is a stimulus to learning and growth. They were thus able to release their anxiety and understand how they had achieved their level of culture on their current planets, how their souls had led them there and how they had all grown in similar ways, having once been members of the Explorer Race. Their Explorer Race heritage, they understood, caused them to seek out where they are now and achieve their present level of culture and creatorship.

These ribbons of life allow all beings to feel the value of the Explorer Race. These cultures now realize that to some extent the actions and interactions they had with you in the early years of your development as human beings on this Earth—the genetic influence, the exchange of cultures and ancient contacts—were truly predestined. Having been a member of your tribe, the Explorer Race, and having gone out to other places, it was only natural that they be inexorably drawn to come and interact with you, who are truly the ancestors, in a sense the children of their past lives.

Now one can see the complete circle that once was obscure. This can be quickly accomplished only through *feeling knowledge*. Although one can study and accumulate mental knowledge for many years, there is always an opposing, well-justified point of view. But feeling does not lie. One knows that if one gets too close to the fire one will get burned, just as one knows that when one is in a loving, happy, joyful moment, the feelings associated with this are universal.

So my job with your Creator has always been to improve communications through the *felt physical reality*.

My Beginnings

Can we start back at the beginning and work forward? Where did you first become aware of yourself? When? How?

Once upon a time, when the creation of which I was a portion was but a flower of stars (if you approached it from a distance, it would look like a flower), I was a portion of the stem of that flower, feeding into that universe. As a portion of the stem I was aware of being not quite the universe I was coming toward and also not quite what preceded it (the root). I was so close to that universe, yet so far away from the root where I had come, that the only way I could experience either one, since I could not see them, was through the feeling senses—extended feeling.

When I extended myself back through the rest of the stem to the root where I was from, I felt a consistent feeling of nurturance, that which is feminine at its core. Then as I allowed my extended feeling or radiated sense of feeling to go forward, I felt the celebration of the emergence of any universe.

During my time in this stem out of necessity I became a master of benevolent feeling. That was the founding of my personality. As time went on I was moved from the stem into the universe and cycled around it, experiencing the celebration of all benevolent feelings. As I worked my way out to the edges of that universe, as is typical, I felt a need for me coming from somewhere. I also felt as if I did not have everything I needed to provide for this need. It was almost as if I were feeling a future need.

I bade farewell to the flower universe and began to move in that general direction on the felt physical level, still having no visual perception of what would eventually come to be my meeting with your Creator. As I moved toward it without being able to see, I had to fully use my radiated feeling, which has now come to be known as instinct. By using instinct I was able to feel the best way to go. Because my feeling was radiated so far and wide, I would sometimes feel which was *not* the best way to go. In this way I was beginning to be initiated into the awareness of discomfort—because when a way did not feel the best way, it was a slight discomfort that steered me toward that which was more comfortable.

Because it was a long voyage, I was able to master the feelings associated with all pleasant emotions, including some you don't have exposure to yet, and also many unpleasant emotions associated with places I was not intended to go but to simply know and understand. When one is on a trip, one often has time for reflection.

As I began to congeal the experience of pleasant feelings compared to some slightly unpleasant ones, I reflected on these as I moved toward the intersection with your Creator and your Creator's need. The need, of course, was to improve communications between Itself and the recently acquired Master of Discomfort. I did not realize why I had acquired this knowledge of discomfort, albeit somewhat slight, until I arrived to meet your Creator. Your Creator, quickly recognizing who and what I was, asked me to come along in the kindest possible way. Since I was up for the adventure, it felt like it would be worthy.

Perhaps the most important thing by which one knows at the mastery level whether something is appropriate to do or not is whether it *feels* worthy—whether the intent, the practice or the ultimate conclusion of any given situation or project will be beneficial. It does not have to be all three, but it must be at least one.

My Role As Mediator, Using Creator's Future Self

How do you communicate to the Creator these feelings of discomfort? How do you assist communications between Lucifer and Creator?

Since your Creator does not in Its past have any acquaintance with felt discomfort, the only way I can do this is to go in the other direction—well into the future when your Creator has total mastery of *all* feeling. I utilize a future life of your Creator that has assimilated the awareness of this present version of your Creator. Just as one acquires wisdom from past lives, one can as easily (certainly at the creator level) acquire wisdom from one's future, getting a glimmer of it in the process.

Because I do not wish to interfere with your Creator's joy at Its emergence into more, I have jumped far into your Creator's future, skipping over three or four incarnations (creators have them, too) where your Creator has achieved total mastery of all feelings.

Could we call them creations?

Yes. And when these communications take place between your now Creator, the Master of Discomfort and myself in this parallel universe, your Creator is able to understand the experience through the wisdom of its future self.

No one else has ever talked about that. How were you wise enough to know that

He had a future self?

When one reaches the level of mastery, the past, the present and the future are absolutely connected. The level of mastery has usually been pictured like this [drawing a triangle] in your current civilization, whereas the real level of mastery has to do with this [drawing a circle]. In the first diagram the triangle represents the godhead and a direct correlation to time, meaning that things are separated, whereas in the circle the past and the future are a portion of the present. That is why the circle is always used when referring to growth and evolution.

How did you mediate between them when it got so profoundly negative for Lucifer that he couldn't control it?

Whenever the Master of Discomfort experienced great pain and misery and was unable to communicate to your Creator the actual feeling of the increased discomfort that was being fed back to it, I asked your Creator to come with me to Its future. We would leave other beings in charge and go to Its future self, where It is the master of all feeling. We would find within that being the felt memory of pain and go into it, totally becoming the pain. Your Creator would always be moved to great love, compassion and empathy for the Master of Discomfort in those moments.

Creating an Echo of the Future in the Parallel Universe

It is interesting to note that one does not have a linear past memory of discomfort when that wisdom can be felt in the future, so this was not a retainable lesson for your Creator. Every time the Master of Discomfort would complain that the pain was unendurable, your Creator couldn't remember what this was, because it was as yet an unknown. So we would go to the future again. We went back and forth many times before your Creator was able to retain the echo of the future memory, although It still couldn't retain something from the future. The moment It got to the future and felt it, there would be total compassion and absolute resolution to do something about it the minute It got back to Its present self. Of course, the moment It got back to Its present self, It would no longer have that memory.

The only solution was to create a permanent echo of it in that parallel universe, which I was able to do, so that when those communications took place the permanent echo of the future pain and the knowledge of pain would be present for your Creator, allowing It to have an instantaneous means of knowing what the Master of Discomfort felt. This ultimately led to Its recent decision that you can feed back no more discomfort to the Master of Discomfort [see Appendix]. Your Creator is obliged—yes, obliged—to relieve the Master of Discomfort of all that pain because the Master of Discomfort's normal state of being is about 1 to 1½% discomfort, enough to know and understand, but certainly not enough to suffer.

What a chore you have had!

Without challenges, creators and even the purpose of being a creator is totally negated.

But you personally have had challenges.

Yes, but pleasant outcomes, because beings are learning and being understood. I don't have to tell you that even at the level you are currently experiencing, feeling that you are not understood is a terrible thing. Any child knows what it's like to feel misunderstood or not understood at all by its parents. Parents feel the same way when their children do not understand them. It is not a pain one can live with indefinitely. That is why you seek out peers who will understand you. This soothes the wound, although it does not heal it. The wound creates a tension between the parent and the child that needs an ultimate resolution, which usually happens after the child grows up and becomes a parent, when there is an aha!, a total understanding. Also, if the parent has had an experience like that of the child, the parent says, "Oh, yes, I forgot that," because the parent was also once a child. The tension brings them together.

In your opinion, would this channel be able to channel Lucifer?

This channel would be able to channel the Master of Discomfort before the time when he was overwhelmed with all of this. It would not be a good idea to channel the Master of Discomfort as it is now. My energy radiates through this channel and is felt in this room and elsewhere to some extent, and so would the Master of Discomfort's pain radiate through this channel. This must be done in either the past or the future when the Master of Discomfort is its normal self and feels fine.

Would that be productive, a positive thing to do?

I think it might be beneficial. Certainly Zoosh will stand between them if there is any discomfort.

In terms of the information that would come out, would it be worth asking the channel to get Lucifer's side of the story?

It's always worth asking, is it not?

How I Help You Master Feeling

I understand what you've done as an advisor to the Creator, but how do you interact with us? What is your goal in the creation itself?

Only to provide the avenue by which you can feel discomfort. My job is to create threads like a harmonic from my own being to your

Creator and connect them to the Master of Discomfort at its higher-level self (the 1½% discomfort) and to every one of you. If you do it for one, you can do it for all; it is no extra effort.

But that thread connects only to the souls of those in the Explorer Race.

Yes, or anybody else, should an occasional being within this creation be experimenting with discomfort. But for the most part those threads connect to the Explorer Race.

Can you see now? Were you forced to become the Master of Feeling because you could not substitute something like seeing?

It's an interesting question, you know, because I do not see now. I think—maybe I should say that I feel [chuckles]—that you might be right. If one is being launched with some responsibility, one must not only use the talents and abilities that one has, but one must also take them to their greatest magnitude to experience all they have to offer. This is one of those chicken-and-egg questions, is it not? Yes, I would have to agree with you. I might very well have come into feeling because I did not have other avenues to knowing.

Do you think it's a temporary thing and that after this you will go back to seek out the visionary aspects?

Why would I want to?

Well, once you've mastered the feeling, then . . .

No, no, you don't understand. You believe that once you've mastered something you can then go on and do other things. It is never that way in mastery. Once you have mastered something, then you help others who are attempting that as well. Here you are with all of your senses, one of them being feeling. One could certainly say that you are all attempting to master feeling, so I am here. When others are attempting to master feeling, I will be there because I can do the most good. One learns to master something, then one teaches. One does not say, "Oh well, I'm done with that." You do not graduate. Mastery *is* graduation, in my experience.

Do you interact personally with people? Do you interact with beings at our encapsulated level in the creation?

I do not. If beings, especially masses of beings, are in significant pain, I might blow in your Creator's ear, though it is not usually necessary. Creator will know because of Its connection to that parallel self. It has happened only once, I believe, when there was a dream of a future event. I will tell this story, yes?

The Armageddon Dream

Years ago there was a dream on this planet. It was a dream of what has come to be termed Armageddon. The dream happened to millions of people at the same time on the same evening. It was truly an attempt by your Creator to head off potential Armageddons that had occurred before. Your Creator did not want that to occur in this creation at this now time, even though this happened well in the past.

How far back?

Oh, perhaps 7000 to 8000 years ago. Your Creator put it into the network of feeling by allowing people to have the dream, which is an unpleasant one, of various aspects of Armageddon. It was like a mass nightmare, one of those nightmares that's so vivid and so real that when you wake up you're on one hand terrified and on the other, totally relieved to discover it was only a dream. Because so many people were feeling so much terror at the same time, I had to blow in Creator's ear and remind It that it was too much. "Let them all wake up now," I said.

This little story is by way of saying that your Creator was giving you a vision that would steer you *away* from Armageddon, which is an experience almost always caused by a lack of exchanged feelings between individuals, causing them not to feel the pain of others. When you don't feel the pain of others, you can easily make catastrophic errors.

This dream of a potential Armageddon (which I don't believe will happen) took the form of individuals being alienated from each other, not having shared feeling or what I call community feeling. I believe this is why certain things have been added to your civilizations and have flourished. One of them that you can all identify with is the theater. One goes to the theater to be entertained, yes, but ultimately one goes to the theater to identify with and feel the feelings, albeit a fiction, of the participants on the stage or screen. The audience experiences mass feelings generated by a fictional creation, even if it's an enactment of an actual event. Drama and the theater have flourished because of the dream that happened so long ago to let people know that alienation is not safe for *anyone.*

So the references in the Bible and some of the dire prophecies of Armageddon go all the way back to soul memories of that dream?

Yes.

Like Revelation and some of the others.

Yes. The text of Revelation was largely associated with a similar vision experienced by the being who wrote the text. Of all the texts in the modern version of your religious Bible, this is perhaps the most accurate.

Was it a retransmission of something that he tuned into from the past, or was it aimed at him again?

It was aimed at him again, because it was understood what he would do with it and that it would act as a reminder. Even for those not of that religion it is a fascinating read.

There have been eighteen civilizations on this planet [see chapter 1 in Explorer Race: Origins and the Next 50 Years], and many of them ended less than pleasurably. Do you remind Creator of the feelings of those endings, or . . .

It is only necessary to be involved in the present. All those souls have been redeemed, so it is unnecessary. But I congratulate your Creator on Its great wisdom to induce the dream to say, "Let's not do that again." The dream has truly driven you. Granted, there is still much alienation and you do not always feel the feelings of your neighbors and friends. But sometimes you do. In some circumstances you choose to feel those feelings in a theater or during events where many gather and where there is perhaps a speaker, and one is uplifted or even moved to tears.

At the fourth dimension will we be able to feel the feelings of everyone we come in contact with?

No.

At what point?

Now. It is acquired by doing the training. You can't wait until the fourth dimension. This is not something you're going to wait to experience. You're going to go out and do it now. I'm not assigning you to it, but saying that if you wish to achieve the fourth dimension in these bodies, *you must know what others are feeling!* This suggests that societies based in competition will not survive with that element in their society, even competition with yourself, because ultimately that leads to someone suffering. Although you have enjoyed much from competition, you will not have that in the fourth dimension.

Even the aspect of trying to do better tomorrow what you did today? You call that competition?

Yes, because it judges what you do today.

That's a totally new concept.

Well, that is our intent here, is it not?

Yes, that's true, it definitely is. Did you shorten the story of your journey? You covered the period when you left the flower creation until you met the Creator in just a few sentences. Did you interact with various other creators and learn much more in the process?

No. The entire knowledge came about as a result of having to feel my way and interact with my path, physically as well as expansively, to arrive at your Creator.

Does it seem to you like a destiny, in that you didn't describe any side trips along the way?

Yes, I think it is a destiny. Within the context of one moment I was a portion of the stem to the flower universe, then I was becoming more aware of myself. It was not a self-motivated awareness; it just happened. I didn't say, "Now it's time for me to leave the stem and go into the flower universe." I simply found it happening, just as I found myself moving inexorably toward my junction with your Creator. So I would have to say it's destiny. What I do know about destiny is that it is always predestined.

The same person who waved the thought by the Creator might have been guiding you to this point of intersection.

What little faith I would have if I did not agree with you.

You've given much to the Creator; what do you think you have gained from this adventure?

The Wisdom of Discomfort

I believe I have perhaps gained the wisdom to know when to intercede and when to do nothing. I have often stood by while the Master of Discomfort and people on your planet have been suffering, because it had to reach a certain level before I could persuade your Creator to go to Its future self and ask It to feel. Your Creator has chosen to separate Itself from other portions of Itself and be incomplete so that It can learn with you. I'm not degrading your Creator, but I am saying that your Creator had an objective in front of Its eyes, a mark It was striving toward on the horizon. Your Creator has until very recently been unwilling to deflect Itself even for a moment from that goal. But after several trips to Its future and with the anchored echo of that future memory now in the parallel universe, your Creator is more inclined to check in with that experience. I had to learn when to get Its attention and when not to do so. In other words, I had to learn a significant amount of tact.

And patience.

Yes.

Are you implying that you have felt the agony as much as Lucifer has?

Yes, because my job is to be the Master of Feeling. Remember my journey here? When I felt something uncomfortable, I was deflected from that toward what was more comfortable. But here I find myself in a universe where in this area discomfort is quite common, and I cannot be deflected from it because I'm required here.

Do you feel it at the same strength as Lucifer does?

I do not, but I feel it. And when the Master of Discomfort glances my way, figuratively speaking (he does that only when it has reached an unbearable point), then I act.

Since the level of discomfort is not supposed to get above 2% after the Creator leaves, will you be required to stay here then, or will you go with Him?

I will not be required to stay. It is up to you, who will replace your Creator. I think that like many of the other consultants, we will stay for a time. We will wait in the wings, as it were. If we are not called upon, we will feel free to mosey about.

Do you have a desire, or will you just wait to feel your way if you can go someplace else?

Remember that I came into being because of a need. If there is a need, I will likely stay. If there is no need, then perhaps I will be drawn by a need from elsewhere. A master is always drawn to where it is needed. It never goes on its own volition.

So those who seek adventure are not masters yet?

[She smiles and nods.]

Final Advice

You've given us incredible wisdom. What else would you like to discuss that I haven't been aware enough to ask about?

Please know that this Earth school, this place where there is so much feeling, some of it very difficult and challenging and some of it wonderful, is very temporary so that you would have the immediate ability to know yes or no—or sometimes maybe! [Chuckles.] Be aware that this experience is fleeting. Get the most out of it and learn! Practice the exercises I gave at the beginning, and if they are useful to you, share them with others. Achieve if you can the warmth of great love felt in your physical self. Share it with other beings and feel it amplify. Do not turn away from the discomfort that you feel from others. Know that here it means that something can be done. It doesn't mean that you *must* do, for they must ask. But if they ask, you might help or ask others to help. Because you all have this ability to feel well-ingrained within you now, ultimately you will teach more about feeling than you will ever learn about it in the future beyond the Explorer Race. Good night.

Thank you very, very much.

A ll right. Now Zoosh speaking.

The Master of Feeling said the Master of Discomfort would channel either the past or the future because right now he's so full of pain. Did you work that out?

I believe so.

He is mentioned so often by everybody that he will have to be included.

We might not be able to do it as long as the others.

Just so he can tell his story.

The only thing we can do is make a run at it and say maybe (not to be confused with the Master of Maybe).

But why is he not considered one of Creator's friends? Why isn't it "the Creator and nine friends"? He was the first one, and he's put so much into this creation. Why is it "the Creator and eight friends" plus the Master of Discomfort?

Because Creator can identify with all of the others with an equal experience. Creator can *feel* all of the others. Creator cannot directly feel the Master of Discomfort and is thus blocked from having a complete friendship with him. Although the Master of Discomfort can communicate to the Creator, the Creator cannot receive that communication. It is always a block in the way of friendship, is it not? If you can communicate with someone but they can't feel your communications, you do not feel they are a friend. More likely they are a relative! [Laughs] But that's another story. Good night.

Master of Plasmic Energy

November 1, 1996

am the Master of Plasmic Energy. It is my job to convert feelings, thoughts and even inspirations to a groundwork for physical mass, which is akin to liquid light, though not in the visible light spectrum. Plasmic energy is a building block. If you took enough of it and condensed it, you would be able to feel it as rubbery. When it is simply there, it functions as a form of amenable (liquid) magnetics. Amenable simply means pliable, flexible, in allowance. Plasma is a form of energy that functions secondary to the original stimulus. For instance, you might have an inspiration, whose energy is electric and magnetic. Yet before the inspiration takes form in thought or feeling, it comes in with an expedited mass of this magnetic energy, or plasma, which is the foundational element that interacts between the inspiration and your physical world. It attracts and stabilizes whatever is included within the inspiration—the subject of the inspiration and the materials at hand as well as the full coloring of the one who is being inspired.

If the person has limits, the plasma will conform to those limits. If he or she has more of an unlimited, wide-open approach, the plasma will be more magnanimous. The main thing is that inspiration is normally colored or influenced by the being through whom it passes into physical awareness to be thought or acted upon, thus becoming form.

Plasma is the foundational element for all that you see and know. Planets cannot exist without it, not only planets as you know them here physically, but even light planets. Suns and most bodies of creation require plasma and many creators are made up of it. It is the building block of life.

Now, it is possible to have thoughts without plasma being present, provided the thoughts occur in or are transferred through a vacuum of space (not the scientific definition of vacuum). If thoughts simply pass from one place to another, as might occur near and around creators, they do not require plasma because they are not intended to be acted on until acquired by someone who can do so. This might also be true for inspirations coming from a guide or even from a creator to an individual. They do not acquire anything as they pass through that space. They acquire it only when they are focused through something at the point where action might follow.

When guides and teachers tell you that you are all one, it is because you are all made from one original point of plasma. Plasma is also sometimes referred to as cosmic energy. I realize that cosmic energy has been called many things. The term is used to make it sound more inspiring and more nurturing [chuckles] than scientific, because "plasma" does sound scientific.

Practical Applications for Plasma (Magnetic Light)

To gain the most from plasma, one would have to be in a receptive mode. One might request plasma as itself. In a meditation, for instance, one might request plasma that is directed through a veil or screen of love—or whatever else you need among benevolent feelings or thoughts. As you become more open during meditations or prayers, you can receive more plasma. This will tend to nurture all the fundamentals of your creation, meaning not only your physical self, but your auric self, your lightbody. It also tends to nurture and nourish your thought self, your ability to think as well as your ability to feel.

If you had to exist without food for a time you could exist by incorporating plasma, not with the idea of "how long can I exist, suffering without food?" but existing comfortably. I'm not saying this so that people will go out and suffer to see how long they can do this. But those who are fasting for some good reason can meditate and ask to receive loving plasma or something colored that way—an affected plasma. It can nurture and sustain you so that you will hardly notice that you are hungry. Of course, after a few days of fasting you might not, anyway, but the first day or two can be difficult. That is one practical application of plasma.

What is your function, your job in this creation? Do you direct plasma, or do you create it? Does it pass through you?

Creating Light around the Orb

I acquire plasma from the light around the Orb. I have had to create this light around the Orb so that there would be a constant energy to support all thoughts and anything to be created that must have something sticking to something else. One can say that a thought put into action would have something sticking to it—things connected together.

I focus on that light I've had to stimulate; and my focus, which is like a meditation, draws that light directly to this creation. That light already tends to ease into the Orb, but it is drawn directly to this creation so I can maximize the amount of magnetic light here.

Your creation, especially on Earth, is a very touchy place. It is not an easy place to live, as you well know. It is a place that requires significantly more magnetic light than any other place I am currently working with because it needs to apply to *all* thoughts. Because many thoughts and feelings are not pleasant, an underlying magnetic light is needed so that when there is a creation of anger or violence, it can have the potential for working out to something benevolent. You sometimes say that an opportunity is often disguised as a disaster, but some situations are merely disasters. With magnetic, focused light permeating these things, there is a potential, even in the direst situation, for the beings involved in this violence to move in the best possible direction for the sake of their soul, even if it is to their next life.

Its Role in Sudden Death and Conditional Love

For instance, in the case of what is called an accident, someone in a car might be arguing with a friend, come around a curve and hit a pedestrian. The anger created an emotionally driven subconscious thought that unintentionally injured another party. When there are vast amounts of magnetic light present, it makes it easier for that pedestrian to move on to his next destination. Very often the person never sees it coming; there is no screech of tires, no chance to brace himself. One minute he's walking across the street and the next minute he's dead. Without magnetic light it is very easy for that individual soul to become lost, wandering around trying to find his body and becoming confused. When large amounts of magnetic light are present, he easily finds his guide and moves on.

Is this the stuff that everything is made of? The glue that holds everything together? The substrate of everything?

Yes, glue is a good term. Magnetic light allows love to be interactively functioning with all life, because love is often conditional here. Many people know that unconditional love is a goal, and there is both personal and impersonal unconditional love; there are many levels. But very often love is conditional, so something must keep it moving. Love, like other emotions and even many thoughts, does not exist well without motion. Magnetic light is always in motion. What keeps it from becoming something permanent is the intent not only of love, but of your scholastic education here.

Nothing on this planet is intended to be permanent, even the structure of the planet itself, because all schools are ultimately temporary. With that in mind, it is necessary to create an environment by which the school itself can be changed orutilized for something else when the students move to another level. I am talking not only about a building but about a series of thoughts that might perform as a school or even an environment that functions as a school, which third-dimensional Earth does.

Your Safety Mechanism: Keeping Everything Temporary

One must have a level of energy that acts as a safety mechanism and can provide you with what you want and need. When you are at creator school, even at this level it is possible to make errors that can be very long-lasting indeed, unless there is a built-in mechanism to keep everything temporary. Then it would not be possible for you to make some error, before you are ready to function as a responsible creator, that would take the first tenth of your time as a creator to correct. You need to begin your creator career with somewhat of a blank slate. Of course, you will inherit a creation, but you need to begin with a walk, not a run.

This plasmic energy is a safety mechanism to keep things temporary. It is also why you do not live very long physical lives. Nothing that happens in any given life can be compounded upon itself. If you lived even 200 or 250 years (your physical body has the potential of living 650 years) there would be the potential of becoming very bitter because of the way things are now. If you did become bitter, you could do untold harm to many individuals, especially yourself—harm that you would have a difficult time to uncreate once you merged as a single being and became a creator. So it is essential to keep your creations and your life span brief.

This plasmic energy coming to the Earth keeps structures from being permanent, but that's because of the way you focus this energy on Earth. How do you focus it in the rest of creation?

The way it works outside Earth and Earth's environs is quite a bit different. The energy is still magnetic, because it is intended to draw things for creation, but it is immortal. What is drawn from one place to another comes only by its permission. There is no safety mechanism built in because at that level in other places there is no need for one. If something comes together, it can live indefinitely. This is how planets are formed. No being who chooses to be a planet at its original formation can possibly exist at that level without being quite high indeed, because it's a very responsible position to be a planet. When one decides to become a planet, one wants to have an energy to permanently acquire and maintain all the elements by which your planethood might represent itself.

The safety mechanism is in action only here in this Earth-school environment, which includes certain dimensional aspects of planets and even stars that you might reach, given a physical propellant for a ship.
That includes Mars and Maldek when they were active in the third dimension?

Yes. It wouldn't include places you could reach if you were traveling in time and space, because any being who is able to travel easily in time and space, whether it be in a vehicle or on their own, would be outside the need to have that safety mechanism.

Plasma Is Stretched Here
from the Fifth to Seventh Dimensions

How do you create the safety mechanism?

If we were to give plasma a charge, it would be a negative charge. This does not mean it is unpleasant; it is simply a negative, receiving charge. To break it down you need to alter not only the atomic structure, but the *motivation* for the atomic structure. All the mass that uses plasmic energy here—including anyplace you can easily reach within 20 to 25 years if you really push—[that plasmic energy] is in allegiance to another place, so it is basically on loan. The plasma comes here with the knowledge that as soon as it is no longer required (there is a time limit built into it), it can, if it chooses, return someplace it wishes—to a loving center, a place to which you could travel dimensionally.

Instead of injecting the plasma and making it comfortable with your third-dimensional (even your fourth-dimensional) world, we get plasma from no less than the fifth dimension, generally from the fifth to the seventh, so that it has to stretch to be here. Plasma cannot maintain this stretch for too long, and that's what allows things to function temporarily.

Now, that is not true for planet Earth itself, not for permanent things that have been created on their own volition. When planet Earth was created, it was a long time ago in different circumstances. But for people and animals and plants and so on, the energy that holds together the physical mass of you is basically stretched to get here. As you know, if you stretch for something, there comes a time when you have to relax. When this plasmic energy relaxes, physical things come apart that have been brought together magnetically.

This is the easiest way to do it. There are other ways, but they would be very difficult. Another way to do it for an individual being might be to alter the physical laws of dynamics. But if you did that you'd have to monitor every individual being and every particle in that being. This way you don't have to monitor anything. You set it up as a factor, and anything that wants or needs to exist for a longer time—an occasional avatar, something like that—must have its own ability to live a very long life.

For example, until recently there have been some very old trees. There might still be a few thousand-year-old trees on your planet. These trees have achieved the level of avatar and can acquire, transform and utilize plasmic energy to keep their being together because of their high spiritual evolution. That is why many ancient tribal cultures had great respect for grandmother or grandfather trees, as they would call them. They understood that these trees had achieved some great spiritual level and were allowing themselves to be in the physical world for the good of the people. The people would go to the trees and consult with the spirits of the trees because the shamans of those tribes understood that these trees had something to offer.

Did you invent this stretching? Do other creators use that method to allow beings to live in the third dimension?

This is a contribution that I provided. As far as I know this had not been done before. There is much about this creation your Creator has set up that hasn't been done before. That's partly why It needed so many consultants. It wasn't simply creating something in Its own image (even though your Bible says so); It's in more than Its own image. Your Creator needed many things that did not exist in its experience of creationism. And in my experience of creationism I have not seen a necessity for these things before, either.

So how did you know how to do it?

Speed Is My Source

The only way I could do it was to return to my source and go within it. My source is not so much a place as a speed. I can be anywhere and return to my source, because once you work up to what I would call quantum speed, no thought or matter or anything in front of you can resist. You'll simply fly through it without displacing even a molecule or the smallest particle.

You have to find some empty space first so that you can get up to speed, but once you do that it's a matter of maintaining that speed. I generally do it in a circle so I can come back to where I started without having to be gone too long. When I get up to speed (this seems to be a pun) I am able to focus on my totality of being. This is where I came from—a high rate of speed—and I am able to inquire on the level of inspiration that functions as *intelligent touch*. I am not given thoughts or visions, but something that I can only describe this way: It would be as if your attention were drawn to a certain part of your body, and by understanding what that part of your body meant to you, you would be able to interpret it. Thus the inspiration is physical. Because I am involved with plasma, I am able to tell what the inspiration is by where I become aware of myself. I feel it, then I know it.

So where did you feel it?

I felt it in my future self. As you probably know, if you get up enough speed, time is no longer a barrier. It is like going into the future to see what I have done, then coming back and doing it (which your Creator did, by the way).

When?

When your Creator came to this creation, you know, It didn't start the creation . . .

That's right. He worked it backward.

Using Time Travel to Learn Lasting Solutions

That's right. Your Creator actually used that method based on my functional systems. We had time to discuss such things. Thus your Creator used a function of my homeland, let's say, in order to make this creation. I did that, too. I went to the future to see what I had done. In order for that to work, I had to be in close contact with your Creator so that I could feel Its needs. Your Creator might need something but not know how to create it. I would be in touch with the need, then go to the future when that need had been fulfilled, come back and create it.

By the way, that is a universal function of time travel. Many worthy things have been created by going into the future on the basis of the needs of the present and seeing how it has been done. If you go far enough into the future, you see, it would be done well and permanently. If you went only twenty years into the future and it had been done poorly, you wouldn't know that it wouldn't last. But if you went millennia into the future and it was still there, then you'd know, "This was obviously done well; it worked."

That's incredible! So the need was to have an unstable third dimension. You tuned in to it, and your inspiration was to stretch the light.

That's right. In that way nothing would be harmed. The plasma would accept it as long as it wasn't required to stretch past its comfort level, which would be the equivalent of 100 to 110 years maximum. Generally speaking, human beings who live to be 125 years old in your time must have achieved some level of spiritual evolution to maintain that plasmic energy, because by the time they get to be 110, that plasma is ready to go back. They have to be able to energize it for themselves.

Plasma, the Glue That Binds the Enthusiastic Particles

So there is plasma that is at the core of the physical body even though the cells keep being created and discreated. How does that work?

If you were going to scramble some eggs and vegetables, you would perhaps melt some butter in the pan or spray something in it. Then you would put in the food. The plasma is what you put in the pan first.

So it's like a mold or a matrix?

Basically it's an energy that welcomes. It is the glue that holds things together, but it does not bring those things. It also functions as a magnetic or attracting element, so that when it is programmed with thoughts and feelings, everything that comes to it—the beings, the bits of energy and the particles—is attracted by being in concordance. That is how a baby's body is formed within its mother. The particles aren't just accidentally involved. The mother consumes a lot of food, but not all that food becomes the baby. Only the particles who *wish* to become part of that baby's body are attracted to it by the energy of the plasma and the willingness, the acceptance and even the enthusiasm of those particles to become part of that baby.

Could you say that there is an etheric matrix that the plasma sticks to, then the particles and cells and everything form around that?

Building the Physical Body

No, I'd say that the plasma comes first. No, wait a minute now. We said that Creator has an intent. Let's say that there would first be an intent, *then* comes the plasma.

And it would form around the intent.

The etheric or soul self would use the plasma to attract the physical matter necessary to assemble it, but the soul must follow the plasma. It has to find a place.

For instance, a man and a woman want to have a child. They do what it takes to have the child, and it isn't only biological. They have an *intent* to have that child, so the plasmic energy is there. Then the soul that is appropriate for those people and for that mother finds that plasmic energy. The physical body might be well under way before the soul is within it.

Generally speaking, souls will not enter a baby's body on a permanent basis until it's been forming for at least two weeks. Occasionally some of them come in sooner, but not permanently; they'll go in and out.

The intent of that soul rides on the intent of the parents to have the baby and on what it wants to create in this life—in other words, how it's formed?

Yes, but first comes the plasma. This way the soul can find it. How many people are having babies at the same time on this planet alone? How does the soul find its way? Is it taken there by the guide? Not usually. Usually the guide takes you nearby, but you find your own way on the basis of the specific plasma that is magnetically attuned to your soul.

It's like your guides and you are finished. They say, "Well, time for you to go now." In less time than it takes you to snap your fingers, you're there. You can find your way back, because initially you go in and out (as a baby, you know). You'll be corded to both your Creator and your guides so you can find your way in and out. That's how you find your way back home, too. [Chuckles.] But that's another story.

My First Awareness

When did you become aware of yourself as an individual?

I'd say that for a long time I was not even aware at all. My first awareness would be like being in a dark space, a pleasant, nurturing dark space—black, as one might say. I became aware of something moving quickly around the edges of this dark space, and gradually that motion moved toward the center where I existed. I felt like I was a mass of something, but I did not know what.

For a long time I thought I was sitting still and that things were moving quickly past me. Then I came to realize that I was a portion of something that was in motion. It took time to realize that. It was sort of like light, but it was like a smear of motion moving very fast. If you have points of light, it becomes a smear. As I look back upon it, it looks very much like a comet. Of course, in your world a comet is a little different, but the energy that precedes a comet is often similar to my source.

One might ask, "Where does a comet come from?" "Well, it's something that starts moving, then moves faster and faster." But that's not true. It's not going to move faster and faster unless there is a decrease in friction, which there isn't. Therefore it must not be moving by accident but be propelled or drawn toward somewhere. I discovered that what was in motion (of which I was a portion) was being drawn toward someplace. My next awareness was that this thing I was a portion of was some vast someone, which would probably be a pretty fair description of a sentient being. At that moment the someone I was a portion of said in feeling, "You can come, or you can be like me and go where you are needed."

Looking back on this, I realized that this being from which I sprang was really saying that where it was going I was welcome but not needed, and that I might be needed elsewhere. I asked, "Can I return whenever I wish?" That which begat me replied, "To return, achieve this speed and you will be united with me."

That's when I left. I continued to move at that velocity for quite some time, able to remain connected to that which begat me. Then I began to slow down and look around to see where I was. When I slowed down to half the velocity and no longer felt connected to my creator, I began to feel the unspoken needs of other life. I didn't know what it needed from me, but since I was feeling it, I felt there was something that either I or someone else could provide.

To make a long story short, eventually I saw these two pieces of what I would term pre-stone or pre-rock—mass that is unable to form itself yet, but differentiated from the space around it by its sound and intent.

It might have been what you would call black space, but there was a sense of two pieces of something that wanted to come together. I could see that there were times when they got close, but there was nothing to bind them. These were beings I would see from time to time as I traveled around.

Realizing What I Could Do and Doing It

As so often occurs in science as well as in life, I happened to pass near enough to them that a portion of my energy (not unlike a comet's tail) attracted them by its light. They moved toward it and when they touched it they were instantly able to stay together. That's when I realized what I was. I was able to produce an energy by which beings could come together!

I was intrigued. I asked these two beings if they would mind if I slowed down and exuded some energy to see if they could totally unite. They were thrilled. I slowed down, and it occurred. That's when I first realized what I could do. When one has an awareness of what one can do, it is like a signal that goes out to all places, as far as I know. I immediately had two or three requests for where to go because I was needed to bring connectedness to places.

The first one was beyond words and can only be illustrated, so I will skip over that. The second one, which I will discuss briefly, is simply a place where there was an overwhelming saturation of individuals, although you would perceive them as particles. They were all individuals and they had opportunities to unite, but it necessitated a vast and lengthy ceremony that would take (in terms of your lifetime) about 50% of their lifetime to complete. Even then it would hold for only a short time. They needed a way to unite in feeling as well as thought so that they could become more than they were. This I imparted through the light of my being. After that they had the option to be a whole thing, or the sum of the parts without losing their individuality.

The Beginning of Multidimensional Awareness

Looking back on this, I believe this might have been the beginning of multiple consciousness, where one being could be many, like being in one dimension and having simultaneous selves in other dimensions at the same moment. In this particular case the particles could be in touch with those other-dimensional parts when it was useful. I believe this was the beginning of multidimensional, simultaneous awareness.

Do you know where this was?

It's not a where so much as a what. This was right around the thirty-third dimension. I don't think I can even describe it in terms of a where.

Was it within what we call this Orb or someplace else?

Beyond the orb setup.

Ah! Beyond all the orbs.

Yes.

Okay, go ahead to the next one.

The next one was a slightly different situation. It was a single massive being, but one that was not quite at the creator level, although it had great wisdom. It needed to go someplace to learn. Looking back on it, this was perhaps the connector to your Creator and myself coming together, because this being needed a teacher. By utilizing sort of the tail of my consciousness, which magnetized it to a portion of myself, I moved this being to another location. There it was able to study the transference of energy to feeling and feeling to thought and thought to action and variables thereof, because it needed to learn what forms of energy would create what actions, things or existences.

I was working with this being, but I was just about done when your Creator passed by. Your Creator and Its entourage stopped and observed.

How many were in the entourage at that point?

I was the last one to come aboard, so everybody else was onboard. They all stopped and watched. That's when your Creator approached me to invite me to join after I had completed my work with this being. I said I would be done in about 25 of your experiential years. Your Creator said, "That's good. I'll wait." So It waited.

When did you build the light around this Orb?

Your Creator was attracted to the orbs that existed at that time. I did not immediately create the light around the Orb of which you are a portion. Your Creator's creation is so vast and varied, it was possible that at any moment someone from an entirely different place nowhere near any of the orbs would be needed, so I had to have something specifically for this Creator's creation that would function as a magnetic antenna around the entirety of this Orb. I needed a massive antenna array (as an engineer might say) that would feed energy in when needed and also have a neon-sign effect so massive that energy beings, thoughts, inspirations and even particles needed here could easily find their way. It was necessary to leave a trail of peanuts, because your Creator has utilized bits from places and dimensions extremely removed from this creation. I could have created the light at the outer boundaries of this creation to seep inward, but I created it around the outer boundaries of the Orb to make a bigger target.

Showing Creator How to Go to His Future

When you came in with the Creator, then what? You went to His future to look—is that how He got to the midpoint?

While we were voyaging to this space I needed to connect with my total being so I could go to His future while I was within this entourage of traveling beings. (I don't need a vast amount of space to do it.) Your Creator noted what I was doing, so I showed Him how. By the time your Creator got to this space here, the obvious way to see how to do things was to go into the future (based upon the needs of the present), see how it had been done successfully, then come back and create it. Anything at the midpoint of a creation would have to be pretty permanent and done well. Once you go beyond the midpoint, you can start laying in anything else you want. You've got your foundational universe and these anchoring points of your universe that are made of very solid, durable matter, having proved its existence and its worthiness through time.

The Master of Feeling also used that technique to take the Creator into the future so that He could feel the Master of Discomfort.

Yes.

She learned that from you, too?

Well, I'd say She extrapolated from it.

During the course of this creation were you involved here all the time, or did you come and go?

I can come and go. I anchor a portion of myself in this universe to attract the plasmic energy. At times there isn't sufficient plasmic energy at other places in this creation, so I will go to the light around the Orb, traveling at sufficient speed around the Orb that it reinvigorates that light. If you were approaching it from a distance, the light would be white and clear, almost reflective, throwing out beams of light. But if it's just about played out and needs to be recharged, it would appear an off-white color. Right now it needs to be recharged, and I will be going up there soon to recharge it.

Is it by flying around very, very fast that you recharge it?

Yes, the velocity of my being recharges it.

My Appearance and Functions

How big are you? What is your mass?

I understand. My mass, not including my tail, is about one-hundredth the size of your moon. The part of my tail that has significant density (that which is obviously connected to me) is about one-fourth the length of your universe, and the particles that trail after the obvious tail stretch out about three times as long as your universe. So at any given moment all of me is not in your universe.

What does that mean?

It means that because I am normally in motion, I am here but not here. I might be moving around in a particular pattern, but at a certain velocity I can be here, then be gone for a full orbit in a trillionth of a second and be back again. It is through motion that I am able to produce plasmic energy. It just happens. If I stop, I do not produce that plasma. At a certain velocity I am in connection with that which created me, but my normal velocity is half that speed.

Do you get to stop sometimes and just hang out, or do you constantly have to keep going?

If any portion of me remains in your universe, then we can communicate. During the time we have been in communication through this channel, I have already left your universe and returned.

In other words, your energy is three universes long and your consciousness is everywhere within that.

Yes.

And you can focus at any point and time.

Yes.

Far out! But don't you get to slow down and just hang out once in a while?

You don't understand. I can chat while I'm in motion. I don't stop physically, but I can chat. I can focus on something and totally examine it. I could "stop" and examine the rock of this fireplace here even though I'd be at a high rate of speed. Can I ever stop? I don't have to. Understand that the nature of my being is intimacy because I produce plasmic energy, which by its very nature is magnetic. Wherever I am I can be intimate with anyone or anything I choose that chooses to be intimate with me.

That's a good word; in just talking to you I feel an intimacy. So you have friends and acquaintances and peers everywhere?

Everywhere I've been, yes, and everyplace where anyone has come together as a result of this plasma—because that makes for intimacy, you see.

There's a little part of you there that you use to communicate.

Yes.

Do you get a feeling of communicating when you get up to full speed and feel the part of you that created you, which does the same thing someplace else?

Only if I get up to that speed, which is about twice my normal speed. But when I'm going my normal speed, I do not feel that, no.

When you choose to do that, can you communicate with this being and share your experiences?

Yes.

And ask him questions?

Yes. That is what I did that time.

So you're intimate with every being in this creation, because we're all held together by your energy.

Yes.

Do you interact with any of them? Do you give them inspiration or communicate with them?

That is not my function. If I were to do that, I'd be usurping your Creator's existence. It is my job to provide what I'm providing, but it is not my job to interact or instruct or do anything that is your Creator's job. That would be interference.

Have there been any human beings on this planet that you have inspired or interacted with?

No.

Are there beings like you everywhere who are holding other creations together?

I believe that there are other beings like myself, yes. The portion of this being from which I am sprung had the distinct impression that it had birthed out other beings like myself.

Do you think every creation has a being so interactive with it?

I don't think so, because some creations do not involve attraction, you know. Some creations are entirely different. I think any creation that is related to you, that you could understand within the current context of your being, would have somebody like that. Some creations are fast in motion and might have been instructed by a being such as myself or given such an energy to do it themselves. This is something that can be taught.

When the Creator leaves, do you have to be here no matter who's calling themselves creators?

Well, I don't have to. The chances are that you will want me to leave a portion of myself here, but I do not have to be here all the time. It will be up to you to decide. It might also be that when you form your creatorship here, you might want me to instruct a portion of you in how to do this. If that occurs, then I will do so and depart, going where I am needed. But if that is not the case, then I will remain as long as you need me.

You would keep on doing what you're doing? You wouldn't form your own creation someplace?

No.

You have given so much to this creation! Without you, it wouldn't hold together.

Well, I think that I've offered something to your Creator and your Creator has used it. I'm certain that your Creator could have learned to do this or could have assigned a portion of Itself to learn to do it. But your Creator did not, because It needs every bit of Itself to maintain Its creation. It was all your Creator could do to spare a part of Itself to birth you out.

That's because He's not all here.

That's true. I think that I have stayed because your Creator needed assistance for that reason.

The way He's playing the game.

The way He's playing the game so that He can go through it with you.

What do you think you have gained from this experience?

Perhaps the main thing I've gained is understanding how it is possible to have this level of intimacy with all of you and all beings and at the same time maintain connections elsewhere—be involved in more than one creation at the same time. Because all of me does not fit into your creation, I cannot be *in* your creation. At some point when your creation gets big enough, created either by your Creator or by yourselves, all of me might fit into it, but for now I do not.

The main thing I learned was to maintain my existence as needed here and at the same time to be free and celebrate existing in other creations, a form of instantaneous versatility. There is a creation next to yours, for example, where there is not much going on. You call it the Void. I am able to whiz through that and not be particularly affected by it or affect it, because it does not wish to be affected.

Are you providing this function in any other creation at this time?

No.

The Light around the Orb

Let's talk about that light. How did you get the idea to do the light around the Orb? Was it, "We've got to have more?" Did the Creator want it, or did you see a need?

The Creator wanted it and expected it to be around the outer boundaries of Itself.

Of just this creation.

Of this creation, yes. But I suggested that space, and since distance was no problem at this level of creation, we put it around the whole outside of the Orb to make it easier for those bits that are frequently required from other places to find us here. I said to your Creator, "If necessary, we could also put it around the creation as well." But your Creator could see that it wasn't necessary.

Is that when He found that beautiful energies were attracted, that the creators and the golden light and the white light and others were attracted to that light?

I think so, yes.

The light around the Orb is attracting beings. There are beings who are generated by the Creator and His friends. Are there other beings who have come here who are not either of those, but who have had an impact on this creation or have come to experience it? I don't mean just visitors.

Yes.

Has it attracted beings who have made an impact or a contribution to this creation?

That is its intent. It functions for your Creator as an antenna.

Is it just particles of energy, or is it actually sentient beings?

When we recognize that light or plasma is sentient, then it is sentient. But at the same time it's also feeding in to act as a foundation for creation technology. But has it attracted beings who tend to live within it? Not usually, no. It is more of a highway than a byway.

Then every creation in this Orb is gaining from it, because something is flowing into the entire Orb.

Yes. It's available to the entire Orb, that's true.

Do they understand that you did it? Are they properly grateful?

Well, I don't think gratitude is required. But they do understand that I . . .

They all know who you are.

Yes. It is not a matter of gratitude at this level. One simply says, "Well, here is something that's useful for us. If you can get any benefit out of it, you too are certainly welcome to use it." It is like that. The only real acknowledgment you get from others is occasionally, "Oh, okay"—something like that feeling.

The Orbs

How many orbs are there?

I have seen at least thirty-three.

Are they vertical, horizontal, circular?

They're almost but not quite circular. [Draws a view of the boundary to show how the light penetrates it.] Roughly circular, but this is per-

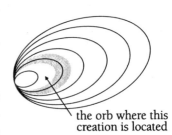

light surrounding this orb

haps just my perspective. Do you see what I mean?

Everybody says that, and I can't understand. It's all within there together.

I can do another version [draws a larger view]. Is that a little easier to see?

Yeah. So we're on the outer one?

No. The center [smallest] orb is filled with creations. You're in the second orb from the center.

Very good. The second orb. In the third orb is there any . . .

There's a little bit going on there. By the time you get to the fourth orb there are no creations yet, but there are creators considering it.

So orbs are created and are ready and waiting, like an empty house.

Yes, that's it exactly. They're ready and waiting.

That's one apartment house. Are there others?

This is a case where one has to have faith. I have to believe there are others. When one comes across this kind of orbs,

the orb where this creation is located

one can only say, who could do this only once?
Is that light around the second orb, then?

Yes.

Help me get this in perspective. We talked to the Center of Creation. In its center is an entry point for energies. When the creators go out through the Creator of Creators, is it from the center of an orb or the bottom of it?

There is no bottom. These are spheres, so if you had to measure the spot from the perspective I gave you (the second drawing), it would be in the center, but about one-third up from the "bottom."
How long before I get to go out and look at that?

Ask to do so in your dreams tonight.
Tonight. All right, what else can you tell us?

All of the things that people take for granted are provided for, and all of the things that one does not even anticipate needing are also provided for.
You mean in this creation?

Yes, in this creation and even beyond. The only thing that is not provided for beyond this creation is worrying about having something you might not get. In order to hear about that, you'll probably have to talk to the Master of Discomfort. I am not aware of the need for such anxiety beyond this creation.

Know that such worries are strictly temporary to your souls and are designed to give you compassion should you meet other beings like this when you are guides, teachers or even a creator. You will then know, understand and have heart for those who worry.
Your energy is what causes the saying: "The universe accommodates itself to our reality." That's your energy, the flowing of this attracting energy?

Yes.

Have you ever talked through a channel before?

I have not, no. This is a new experience for me.
I don't want you to go. What else do you want to say?

In order to fully appreciate life, curiously enough, one has to have what you call death. Without a quantifiable sensual experience in which you have life and all of your senses and a quantifiable time limit, one might not be motivated to truly live. Beyond this school such cares and concerns are not paramount, but such brief, quantifiable life spans are necessary here now. It is such a short time in the evolution of your soul to have such an experience here. It is perhaps a brief burden, but it is fleeting. Good night.

❖ Robert's Comments on His Experience

What did you see?

I saw something moving around real fast and leaving a streak behind it. It reminded me of something that I thought was a falling star, but looking back on it, it couldn't have been because it was aimed too precisely. But it had a sense of motion. It is curious that even though it was moving real fast, it had a sense of being still, like those cartoon pictures on page corners that seem to move when you riffle the pages. After a while you don't see the pages moving; you see only the moving figure. So it had an effect that I could feel in addition to something I could see.

He said he'd been around the orbs a couple of times while he was here talking. Your face changed. At one point everything turned to golden light and I saw about ten faces. Most of them had glasses on, but they were shaped different from your face. When I said that, he said, "That's just plasmic fantastic."

You know, I've had that experience before, but it wasn't quite as you described it. I saw persons, all their past lives, you know: men, women, different cultures. It was really awesome. It sounds similar.

Master of Discomfort Speaks of Himself and the Explorer Race

November 5, 1996

ll right. Zoosh speaking. At no time during this channeling will there be more than 2% of pure discomforting energy radiated through. This will be the Master of Discomfort; it will not be Lucifer, because that is an Earth name. This being is not that narrow. The Master of Discomfort is the being who came with your Creator at your Creator's invitation.

Is this the past or future?

We'll let him describe himself.

I am the Master of Discomfort. It is a strange thing to master, perhaps, yet without this wisdom you, the Explorer Race, might have been unable to challenge yourselves sufficiently to test whether you have achieved creator status and all of the rights and responsibilities associated therewith. With such a hurdle to face, it is necessary to test what you believe or theorize. Without some level of discomfort it is practically impossible to detect whether your theory is anything more than a good idea, or whether it needs to be modified.

My Point of Origin

Long ago, before I met your Creator, I had my origin in what I can only describe as an inverse galaxy. When you look at a galaxy in a photograph, or even parts of your own that you can see with the naked eye, you discern its shape according to the points of light. In an inverse galaxy (at least my own, where I was brought to consciousness) there are no points of light, but the spaces between light become more prominent.

Imagine a galaxy without stars, indiscernible to the naked eye or an optical refractor. It does not look like a polarized galaxy such as dark energy, and it isn't. It is an energy source that tends to attract light, convert it for travel and transfer it to places where it is needed without affecting it in any way. This means that the light could travel through the galaxy like the way light travels through a lens. Instead of refracting it as a lens does—and breaking it up and sending it where the lens points—the light would come into the galaxy, be gauged to determine where its type would be the most useful, and then sent there.

Within any universe, especially one such as yours, one usually finds at least one inverse galaxy. When a universe is of a great size there is often so much light that some of it goes its entire life span without fulfilling its true potential. It might be on one side of the universe but be needed on the other side, and no matter how fast or long it travels at light speed, it is not long enough By the time it gets there it will have dissipated or transformed into something else.

My Creation Here That Transfers Light

I have set up an inverse galaxy in this universe according to my understandings so that your Creator does not have to constantly pick up light from one part of Its creation and put it someplace else, which would be well beyond light speed. It is a very small galaxy, perhaps 1/100 the size of yours, which is fairly small. If you were to see it, it would have a shape like that of an elongated diamond. [He draws.]

Inverse Galaxy Created by Master of Discomfort within This Universe

Picturing this from a third-dimensional point of view, it looks like a four-sided crystal. If approached head-on from any direction it would have that shape. This crystal transfers light from any part of your universe to any other part *if* that light cannot traverse that distance without assistance. Thus it is a light-transferring device.

A small galaxy of a slightly different shape was the one in which I came to consciousness. [Draws another shape.] This is perhaps not the best drawing, but you get the idea. It is not a mass. This is a shape that you all recognize, but it is also the shape of the inverse galaxy where I became aware of my personal identity.

It is a curious thing that when you are born physically on Earth you have a lapse of consciousness in moving from your total being toward the physical child within its mother. It is entirely different when you are a part of some mass thing, doing you know not what.

Imagine a single white blood cell in your body. It has a very specific function, of course, yet it does not consider itself in any way a portion of the physical body that you are. It is entirely in its own world. That is very much the way I was. I was in my own world. I recognized that all else around me was a portion of myself. I did not feel in any way individualistic.

My Process of Alienation

Gradually I began to feel less involved in that which was around me. (This is perhaps what allowed me to become well-versed in what I am known for.) This process continued until I felt that I was an alien in my own environment, even in the place where I was born. Imagine being a total portion of something like a light around oneself, then no longer feeling involved with what was going on. What all of that around me was doing was no longer interesting or had nothing to do with me personally. This has something to do with the way a baby is born out of its mother, but yet not quite like that.

So I began to move physically away from what had once been myself and gradually became something other than myself. I discovered that with a great deal of focus and attention I could move toward something. I could not push myself away from what I once was, but if I looked at something, I could pull myself toward it. And this I did.

As I pulled myself out of my inverse galaxy I looked back at it and could not imagine ever being a portion of it. This is not to say that the job the inverse galaxy is doing is not a good thing, not at all. I simply had no sense of personal connection with it. That was my birth [chuckles]. You might say it was an alienating birth, not a loving one.

Having traveled around as much as I have and seen many other forms of birth (in which I have a particular interest, for obvious reasons), I must say that if I had it to do over again I should like it to have been a more benevolent, loving experience. In any event, I pass this on to you to remind you of the import of a loving birth.

I then began to move and search. It did not occur to me until much later that I had been individualized for a purpose. It felt to me like I had been abandoned or shoved away, no longer wanted or needed, as a child might feel abandoned. Those were the overriding feelings. I was disappointed, and I moved away, feeling unlike anything else and unattracted to what I had been. This foundational alienating experience undoubtedly allowed me to examine personally the feelings associated with discomfort for a very long time.

I wandered aimlessly (as it would seem to an outsider) all over many universes, looking for something that would welcome me. When you are a portion of something that feels good and you are welcome, it is a normal feeling; you don't even notice it. Then suddenly you are unwelcome and you are moving around, waiting to be welcomed. Looking back on it, I understand that I was radiating discomfort, so of course I was not welcome. Yet that perpetuated the discomfort.

After wandering for a length of experiential time that was about twice the length of your now universe, I stopped. I stopped because I wasn't feeling welcome anywhere. I began to examine what I was rather than to look for love in various places. I spent a long time (perhaps half or three-quarters of the time of the existence of your now universe) examining who and what I was. Did I have anything to offer that would be a benefit? This was an examination based on self-interest, because I wanted to be welcome somewhere.

Meeting Your Creator

Your Creator happened by during my scrutiny and stopped to inquire what I was doing, being curious at that stage of Its journey. I felt so happy that someone would want to know, and I explained at some length. Your Creator did not respond for a long time. I waited for the response, and when it didn't come I began examining my experience again. After some significant time your Creator asked me if I would be willing to come with It to a place where what I could do would be invaluable. Well, I don't have to tell you how long I had been waiting to hear that! I wouldn't have needed such a red-carpet invitation. I was thrilled and said yes immediately.

We had a long voyage together. There were other beings present, but our voyage allowed me to understand and get the first glimmerings of why I existed at all. I can see that your Creator could not accomplish Its task, as It has stated Itself to you in this book and others, without someone who could provide a means by which beings could grow, test their growth and test the validity of their growth—three important functions.

I then began to realize that this was why I exist. Your Creator mentioned that in Its journeys It had never come anywhere near the inverse galaxy I was a portion of. Looking back on it, whatever separated me from the inverse galaxy must have known where your Creator would go, and initiated my departure to get me to the bus stop, as it were, on time so that your Creator could pick me up on Its voyage.

I was thrilled then—and I'm still very satisfied with that original experience, though I must say it has been very difficult at times, sometimes even excruciating. Your Creator did warn me that there would be times when I would regret having come along. But at the moment when you know that someone wants you and you've been unwanted, you're willing to say, "Well, so what! I'm happy that anybody wants me at all." I did not at that time realize that I was a master of discomfort because I was so self-involved in my discomfort.

On the voyage to this space, which is now your universe, your Creator, through a long series of "conversations" and exchanges of personal experience, helped me to realize that I had valuable knowledge and experience to pass on to others. Often you will know something very well and think others know it, but there comes a time when you discover that others do *not* know it, and you realize you possess something you thought was ordinary that turns out to be something extraordinary. It was quite a stunning awareness for me, I must say.

So we came here and your Creator went through all of Its processes to set up this creation. It has been mentioned that your Creator went to the midpoint of the creation on a projected future possibility, then came back to the beginning to create it. When It went to the midpoint It took everybody along so that It would have the colorization, you know, of our influence. It was an act of faith on your Creator's part that everything would be sufficient to create a benchmark or a median by which your Creator could then broadly interpret. That is what happened.

In the beginning of the creation, over 90% of it, I didn't have much to do. Your Creator asked me to set up the miniature inverse galaxy, which I was able to do, and to waithere to act somewhat as a consultant, but even more important, to operate like a backboard off which to bounce ideas. In terms of your life now, I was feeling perhaps only about 1½% discomfort, yet it was very difficult for me. Going from a feeling of total benevolence to any discomfort at all and then to *be* that discomfort, well, I don't have to tell you—it was very alienating.

In any event, I did not realize in the early days what would develop. Toward the end of the purpose for the creation of this universe, as you were put to the test and tested yourselves, it would be my responsibility to assist you. I have to tell you that I am personally unable to produce more than 2% of discomfort at the very most. I can't go beyond that. For one thing, I can't stand it. For another, it is unlike me to do that. I am not trying to say that I am some spectacular, wonderful being, but that my normal energy is neutral. The energy of discomfort is terribly difficult, because if it is normal for me to be neutral, *anything* else is very difficult, and so far the only other thing I've felt is ranges of discomfort. It requires my absolute, full-time attention to deal with it.

The Parallel, Interfacing Inverse Universe Created for My Retreat

As we come now toward the end of the purpose of your creation—the end of your Creator's authority over Its own creation—and you're coming well along, I discovered that my next level of responsibility to you as well as to your Creator was to accept on a feedback loop all the discomfort *you* cannot stand. Well, I don't have to tell you that I was less than thrilled by this sudden and somewhat shocking realization. There were times when my discomfort was so great that your Creator could not have me in this universe, so It basically established a parallel interface universe, which was fairly small, like a pocket. Whenever I was subjected to too much discomfort I would go to this interfacing universe. This gave me a place to project (dump, you might say) the excess discomfort so I would not have to cart it around. It was entirely contained there so it could not harm anyone or anything else. It was like carrying a bag of nails over one's back, you know; a lot of those nails are going to jab into you.

Your Creator received permission from the other creators to make this inverse universe fairly small, about one-millionth the size of your universe. That is still fairly large, but significantly smaller than we actually needed, as it turned out. So here you are, beings who are capable of tolerating 50% (maybe even 55% for moments) of discomfort—I can't even identify with that personally!—but you were feeding back at any given moment 20 to 25% of that discomfort. That was a lot; I couldn't handle it.

It wasn't long before that other little universe was filled up and I was tapping on your Creator's shoulder, so to speak, saying, "Hey! Something's going on here you have to pay attention to." To tell you the truth, much as I am fond of your Creator, It did not have the full responsibility I would have liked. But there were beings who acted as messengers to remind your Creator that It could not simply turn Its back and say, "Well, sorry." Your Creator had to ask the Council of Creators for an expansion, but eventually the inverse universe filled up again with excess negative energy.

Your New Responsibility to Deal with All Discomfort

In recent days [sometime near mid-1996, related by Zoosh in the Appendix] you were given a great gift, from your Creator's point of view—responsibility for your own creation. You are no longer allowed to feed back to me your excess discomfort, and that is why certain situations in your world have become so extreme now. That will allow you to be aware of these situations and change them. Consequences, as you know, tend to lead to other consequences if you do not act.

Right now the discomfort around me is being dissipated and transformed by many beings who have come to help. These beings used to transform your discomfort on your planet in your envelope of space, but now they are not allowed to do that. There are a few beings who can come and transform your discomfort, a few spirit beings, as you would say, but not so many. There used to be millions who would come, but now I shouldn't think there are many more than a few thousand at most. And that number will continue to be reduced because it is now up to *you* to be aware of the discomfort and transform it yourselves, which you can do.

Perhaps that's a good place to stop. Question?

My Orb of Origin, in the System of Inverse Orbs with Minus-Particle Charges

Where was this first inverse universe? Was it in this Orb or in another one?

As I look outward to it, it would have to have been in what I would call the first orb to the minus one power. This has to do with particle physics, and I will try to keep it simple.

It has been explained to you how the other orbs work, and a rough diagram has been given before [previous chapter]. Now, the inverse of that would still have this [draws and displays]. It would look like the other drawing, but it functions like this. Can you see?

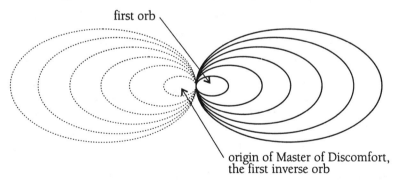

first orb

origin of Master of Discomfort, the first inverse orb

It is a mirror image of the orbs, but drawn with dotted lines.

Yes, because it is not intended to be substantive. It is like another level of the orbs within which you now function. For each orb there would be an equal, balancing orb that functions primarily as a support.

I would have been in the inverse orb opposite to the first orb here—the dotted-line orb [the smallest]. We're not talking polarities here; we're talking about a support system like your lightbody support system through the different octaves or dimensions, but not of the same consistency of matter. I don't want to use terms that have been too fictionalized, but in these orbs are largely magnetic and in some cases electromagnetic events. Particle charges function in the minus, creating tension. A particle would have a minus atomic weight, which creates a tension, intended so there would be a tendency to pull toward the even point where they touch.

This doesn't have to do with antiparticles, does it?

No, if it had to do with antiparticles, they would tend to repel. Here we have the point where they touch [draws a duplicate with an arrow]. There's no overlap, just a point where they touch, and it is very small; I

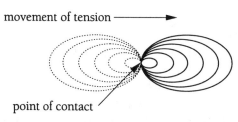

movement of tension ⟶

point of contact

can show you with these two hands. The touching point is about that much [3 or 4 inches]. That is the only direct contact, so there's a tremendous tension. The tension moves in one direction, this way [draws a second arrow beside the diagram]. This allows everything in those inverse orbs, whatever they do, to serve these orbs. It is an aspect of being in total service.

Being Self-Involved in an Orb of Total Service

How did you get from there to here?

That was a strange thing. There I was, in a world that was so different from the worlds here (we're really talking universes and orbs). It was a world in which total service and total devotion to service were absolute. One knew no other way of being. Because I came into an awareness of being when I was so self-involved, it did not occur to me for a long time that I was in a completely different orb.

Stop and think about it: Becoming self-involved in orbs of existence where you are totally in service is impossible. As I began to be rejected where I was and move away from it, soon afterward I found myself in these orbs that you are in. Had I not been self-involved, I could not have done this. Your Creator and I have discussed this. Your Creator is not certain either, so we can only give it our best guess.

We believe that I came into these orbs very soon after my departure from my homeland. The strange thing is, I did not feel any sense of motion. I think it was more of what you would call a transference. I did not notice anything; it was an unbroken experience. I didn't just suddenly wake up somewhere else. It wasn't anything like that; it was totally a single experiential moment. Very curious. In any event, you can be self-involved here because creations of material substance are here. You *have* to be able to be self-involved (not all the time, of course) so that you can be responsible and, of course, responsive, which isn't necessary where I came from.

So you've never had the chance to explore that area and probably won't?

I can't say I probably won't, because who can say what the future will bring? It is certainly possible that I might have that chance. I can't imagine that I won't go back to the place I emigrated from, my homeland. I have to believe that whatever invited me to meet your Creator will allow me to go home at some point. But for right now, I enjoy being where I am.

The Expansion of Discomfort

Now, I have to say something: I've made it sound like you are responsible for my discomfort and that I am not responsible for yours. While I have provided sufficient discomfort for you to grow, I have also given you (I don't know if your Creator or I had even considered this in the beginning) the means by which to make more out of anything you do that involves discomfort. For instance, you can be mildly annoyed (which I can provide) or enraged beyond control. I do not personally have the capacity for rage, but I must admit that mild annoyance can build into rage even beyond your personal control if it is allowed to expand at an increasing rate over time—especially in the place you are now, where time and experience are vastly concentrated.

I do not wish to sound like a victim or portray *you* as one, but I can see how your Creator must have a great deal of faith in you to allow you to have such unbridled discomfort. You must live with the consequences, and you are required to change what each one of you has done as well as what you do en masse. It gives me pause to consider such permission. This is not a permission I personally have been aware of.

Your friend Zoosh has spoken to you of my dark side being Satan or Lucifer. I cannot personally profess any sense of awareness of that being my dark side. Given that I am the anchor to discomfort (albeit mild annoyance at most), I can see where my anchor and your excessive discomfort might create an alternate being that I do not participate in. I do not participate in the experience of Lucifer as Satan, but as I am the anchor for such energy, even though in a fairly innocuous attitude of mild annoyance, I'd have to say that it might be so. I can't consider it my dark side because it is not a side I am familiar with or aware of. I can take credit or perhaps blame for anchoring it, but these are not portions of my direct self.

For example, many years ago you had a ship that you were greatly involved with that carried Jehovah and Lucifer as a being [see chapters 16 and 21 in *The Explorer Race*]. Lucifer was a person who was not connected to me directly, but that person could not have existed nor could this society from which they escaped have existed, I must admit, without my coloring of mild discomfort. So there you have it.

But if they were not directly connected to you, were they created by our Creator? They're ensouled beings, right?

It must have been that your Creator utilized my focus to create these beings. He might have utilized some pool of extreme discomfort, but I don't think your Creator has the capacity to work with extreme discomfort. This is not to question your Creator's abilities, but having all imaginable abilities does not necessarily mean having the capacity to tolerate all imaginable circumstances.

No, I think your Creator must have utilized some portion of my energy to anchor this level of discomfort. I am not an all-seeing being. Most of the time I am distracted. One can be the master of something and be very all-seeing, you understand, but when you are distracted by anything it is very difficult to maintain the clear, singular focus required for what you normally consider mastery. I am consistently distracted with discomfort because my natural energy, from what I know myself to be, is neutral.

The Master of Feeling talked about taking the Creator into the future to show Him how miserable you were so that He would do something about it.

Yes, I believe that this is one of the beings who had interceded, not only on my behalf, but ultimately on your behalf.

Are you speaking from our now time or from the future? What is the point of focus right now?

My point of focus is your now time, yes.

My Possible Future

What can you see in front of you? If your natural energy is neutral and you've done this incredible service, do you have a desire for another type of contribution in the future?

I believe that I will volunteer to be of service to you as you become your Creator's replacements, but I am not certain that you will need it. Your Creator does not have this discomfort within Itself, but you do, so I think you can create your own. I do not think you will need my services. When that time comes I do not know whether I will be motivated to go someplace to do something (because I'm very much in the present, you can see) or whether I will be drawn someplace. I really don't know what will happen in the future, but considering the recent happening [see the Appendix for information about Creator's decision to disallow further excess negative energy to be fed to this being] in this universe, I am pretty satisfied with how it's turning out.

The Creator couldn't have done it without you.

Yes, that's true.

In all these other creations this negative energy had been stockpiled someplace, right?

Yes, it could not be processed in other places. The consistent question I hear in other places is, "Will you please take this? Will you do something with it?" But I think I can't do it now. When I'm no longer needed here in this creation, this universe, and am back to the point of being 1½% discomfort, perhaps that will change, I do not know. I think I can then transform it by using, if it is possible, the inverse process of transformation in this Orb.

I might have to travel in a small universe of my own creation so that I can create an inverse universe within these orbs, which do not normally function well together. Here in your universe you have a small inverse galaxy that I have created, so it can work if it is encapsulated. Perhaps I might be able to do that, travel around in your orbs, collect and either transform that negative energy or send it to where it needs to go to be of benefit. This is like what I learned to do in the beginning with light. It might be done with what you would call dark but what I would call not-light. I would prefer to call it not-light.

Awesome!

· By calling it not-light, you don't have that connotation.

They could use it for an enormous lust for life.

Yes, if that is desired. But I could collect it and transfer it, perhaps moving it from place to place as it is needed.

If other creations see its effects here, they'll say, "Oh, I want to do that."

Yes, they might.

It's more creativity; ultimately, it's more bubbling possibilities, right?

It is a distinct possibility because of the continuing success in this universe. If it turns out the way your Creator hopes, I think I will be needed in many places simultaneously. I will have to get around fast.

That's exciting. So you become a creator on your own, in service to all creations.

Yes, in these orbs. That would certainly be something for me to look forward to.

That is fascinating. The word "inverse" was used once before, but we used the word in the sense of the absence of now, just past and future. In your usage it's like the reverse of light and dark. How did you start in this?.

If *this* is normal [shows previous drawing and points to solid lines, then dotted lines], then *this* would be inverse. It's a physical thing, not actually the opposite. It is another part of the whole, but the other side of it. One might see the whole [draws a circle], yet if one looks at the whole from the side, it might look just like this [draws an ellipse].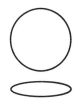

Like looking at a galaxy on edge.

Like looking at a disk. One might have instead something like a disk becoming thicker, surrounded or sandwiched between different loops

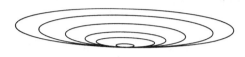

as it goes around [draws]. The whole is still the whole, but it is more of itself, so we can't say it's opposite. It's a completion. In my original explanation it was this [draws triangle]. And while that appears to be complete, when you add this [draws another triangle], it certainly seems to be more complete.

It's the diamond of your original universe.

One starts initially as the triangle and adds another triangle. It is not the opposite, but just another portion of itself to make a different shape. But that shape is a recognizable whole thing.

This raises all kinds of interesting questions. During the course of this creation your energy expanded. If we have a little bit of you in us, then you're directly connected with every member of the Explorer Race, every soul, right?

I am actually linked to you genetically.

Through the Lucifer gene Zoosh talked about [see Appendix].

Yes, Zoosh has referred to the Lucifer gene because it would be understandable. So yes, I am actually spiritually and physically connected to you.

Which no one else in this creation is except the Creator Himself.

I cannot speak for others. It might be something to ask them. But speaking for myself only, we are genetically connected.

Let's look at the birth of the Explorer Race. You were there, obviously, when it was birthed.

Yes, it was distinctly different from my own birth.

The Actual Birth of the Explorer Race

How would you describe that birth? I don't think that much has been said about it yet.

Understanding that the line is for purposes of definition only, not suggesting an actual line, the shape of your Creator at that moment was roughly [draws].

Not of the creation, but of the Creator.

Your Creator. It would be as if a small opening within that creation . . . I will draw the opening separately [adds to the side of the drawing], understanding that it is not to scale. It is blown up for the sake of understanding, like a slit opening up. If you were to see yourselves emerging, it would be like the sun's rays, but it was all sparkling, like golden light and white light and individual points of white, gold and in some cases silver light, as I noted at the time. I think that the silver-light portions of yourselves are roots that connect you to life on the stars. Silver light is significantly different from gray. It is like the polished version of the metal silver.

Jehovah has said that he and Luci-
fer are of that place.

Yes, perhaps with a slight
addition of blue.

Is there a significance to Jehovah
being of that place?

Well, it shows you that this
being is more associated with
the extraterrestrial than with
third-dimensional Earth.
From my perspective that
being is basically an ET.

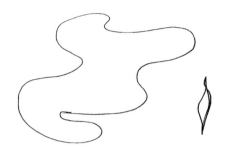

The shape of the Creator and the slit from
which Explorer Race emerged

Were some white and others gold, or were they mixed white and gold?

Some were white, some were gold and a few were silver.

Is there a significance in some being white and some being gold?

I do not think so. I think that might have to do with their function at
the time within Creator.

How many of you were there? One, or a billion?

I did not count, but I should think several million.

What could they do? Give us a little history. We don't have that anywhere.

Well, the light particles came out at first and remained as a solid
thing. Looking back as a child might look up to his parents, it immediately formed the shape of the Creator.

Like a miniature Creator.

Yes. It did not come *out* as that shape, but one looks to one's point of
origin and wants to be like that. It sat there for a long time as if uncer-
tain what to do, which I think has to do very much with the total of your
being. Then different particles began to move away from it and go off to
explore, leaving sort of a sparkling thread behind them so they could
find their way back. It started out with a few who went here and there
and then many, many, until there was just a single point where all the
cords were connected.

These particles were all over the universe looking and finding and
seeking, but you were all still corded to that point of light, which is not
far from what I would call the heart of the Creator. The shape I have
drawn of your Creator is essentially the heart of your Creator, because
ultimately that which gives birth is love, at least in your orbs. Hopefully, it is that way in the other orbs. From my personal experience I
cannot say so, but I'd like to think it might be.

Why does the Creator use that shape?

There is not a mental reason. As near as I can tell, Creator was that
shape because It wanted to be. It is not like the lobes of a brain, which
perform a function.

So each one of these little lights had free will from the moment of birth, which is why they could go anywhere.

But they did not know that at first. I think that's why it remained positioned there for a long time, emulating your Creator in shape, with the knowledge that it could not do what your Creator was doing, but with no instructions about what it should do. (Even then your Creator was disinclined to hand you a manual of operations.) So the particles went to look, but also to find out.

Then once all of them were out there . . .

Yes. It wasn't too long after all of them were out there that some split and created different portions of themselves, knowing it was possible because that's what happened in their birth. That was the origin of soul splits of the Explorer Race, where a soul might split and form two different chains of lives and so on. Of course, one could take it back a level and also say it was your Creator splitting off that portion of Itself.

Before this there were already lightbeings all over the universe, beings everywhere—benign, loving beings.

Yes, so you were birthed into something that was already in existence and there were places to see.

Your Travels after Birth

How did we get from that point to the point where we made the decision that we're now changing? Can you give us a series of stories or a chronology?

We do not have the time to cover all of it, so I can only hit some highlights. Different beings who wanted to be connected traveled in clusters for a time. For instance, they would go to a planet somewhere. If that planet was of great interest, they might stay there for a time. A group of about 20 or 30 points of light, which had not yet, I think, incarnated in any form, were interested in a planet where light was in constant motion and celebration (light's natural tendency is to celebrate life), like fountains of light. It was like a 24-hour party or celebration. These clusters of the Explorer Race in its youthful state joined in and danced with the different light forms and were there for quite some time. Some of them stayed when others moved on.

This might have to do with self-motivation, because it was too soon for will. (Will comes much later. Will is the power of an individual to do what the individual wishes, whether or not it is in concordance with what is around it.) This was more of a desire to go and see, but it was important.

Checking in with other groups, they learned of a place in this universe where experimental beings were created by your Creator, not in thought but in the place where the Creator's imagination lives. A great many beings went there. Never fewer than 60 of you were there in the early days of your travel. Creator's imagination is a very awe-inspiring place to be, because beings pop into existence briefly, perhaps going through their full potential function, then seemingly disappear. Or beings might show up just for a moment and be admired by all portions of Creator or modified. It was basically the expression of material formations that represented individuals. I believe this was your first exposure to encapsulated individuality, even though it was on the more imagined level.

Sometimes you as beings would try to emulate that yourself. It is absolutely natural to emulate, especially in the beginning when one is learning one's own abilities. Or you would try your own variations. Many of you stayed there for some time; it was like a stop on the route and many beings experimented there.

Shortly after that some of you began to realize that you could be an individual somewhere doing something. If you found a particular form or existence appealing, you desired to be it wherever such beings existed. You would then be immediately transferred to that place and find yourself incarnating as that being. This might have been your first experience of incarnation.

What were some of the forms we incarnated into?

In the beginning the initial expressions of individuality were mostly light forms, because one tends to identify one's potential individualistic characteristics as an outgrowth of, or at least related to, what one is. You were lightbeings then, albeit points of light, so the idea of being attracted to some other form of lightbeing would be natural.

And they carried it a little further. This is something nobody knows anything about.

As you began to experiment with that, you did not always stay with the life as long as it existed. I think this was your first exposure to responsibility and even work. After you incarnated as a lightbeing you realized that you couldn't leave at just any moment, because then that lightbeing would not have the spark of connection that is necessary for all of Creator's beings. That was an important growth. Sometimes you would line up replacements so that you could leave and go elsewhere. (That might have been your first experience of walk-ins.)

Your First Incarnations

What was the first incarnation in a form we can identify? I know that the humans came very recently, but in a fourth- or fifth-dimensional body . . .

A lightbeing in a humanoid shape would have been your first incarnation that you would consider related to you. You were enamored of these beings for a most curious reason. When you have two legs, the tendency is to utilize them. Even if you can travel in light, the tendency is to use the appendages. You were interested in utilizing your body because it gave you the feeling of self-determination rather than being a part of some larger whole, and you found this appealing.

So at first we would temporarily take over a body that someone else had created?

No. The body would be created and you would step into it as any soul would, but you wouldn't be kicking anybody aside. No, you did not learn to do things like that. No one gets kicked out. Walk-ins are entirely different.

When did we start creating our own bodies?

You never really create your own body; you work in concordance with others to act as a personality to be interpreted. When you were birthed there were other humanoids and even variations on the human being. You yourselves did not evolve the human being, but you became aware of the human being and recognized its potential for growth. Implanted in the deepest levels of your consciousness by your Creator was your inevitable captivation by the human form.

The human being can grow far more than many other beings because of its potential for making mistakes. Although small mistakes are easily corrected, larger ones require your own full-time attention as well as the cooperation of others to participate in their resolution. This *brings you back together* on a level of will, intention and spirit, meaning that you must cooperate consciously, not just because it is natural.

Had the third and fourth dimensions been populated by human beings before the Explorer Race?

Yes, this was already in existence. It was a matter of coming and utilizing them with the best intent.

But those humans in the third and fourth dimension were still benign, long-living, slow-moving beings.

Yes.

Then many human beings in this creation who are not part of the Explorer Race will go on with the Creator?

Oh, certainly.

Entering the Third Dimension and Increasing Negative Energy

Where did we first actually come into the third dimension? On one of the planets in our solar system? No, we were in Orion before that.

I will look. Some of you began to notice (and become somewhat enamored of) the third dimension while you were in the fourth and fifth dimensions, where you were in a rather blissful state in this creation but where you could not gather and celebrate new knowledge and experience. Having heard about that potential, I think that's when you considered it worth a try. Of course, you were predestined to do that, but it was not done without your permission. One might say that's when you gave your permission.

Is there a place connected to it?

It was before you were in the Milky Way galaxy, although the Milky Way galaxy was here.

I didn't realize that we were in other places before this one.

I do not know the names for these places, but they were perhaps the length of three or four galaxies from here.

Perhaps a more appropriate question would be, at what point did we start pulling more than 2% negative energy?

When you needed the cooperation of others. You did not know on the level of materiality how to request the cooperation of others when others had their own agendas, and you needed help, perhaps being unable to do it yourself. At the spiritual level when one needs help, it is there—just as when others need help you might go to help them. But on the material level when one needs help, one must communicate and convince. You began to pull in more discomfort when it came to convincing others, being caught up in other people's agendas or catching others up in your own agendas.

Bringing this a little closer to home, when we came into the Milky Way galaxy where did we go? I can go back only so far, to Orion. I don't know what's before that.

A moment. I can see it, but I don't know the name.

Before Orion, When the Feedback Got Strong

But it was someplace before Orion?

Oh, yes. It was before that.

At what point did we start pulling in enough discomfort that you became aware of us or that we became more interactive? At what point did you become more involved with us?

You mean at what point did the feedback strike me strongly?

That's a good way to put it.

When you were functioning with about 12% discomfort.

Where was that?

That was in a brief empire that existed on the stop you made previous to your Orion existence. I do not know the name of this place.

To what point of discomfort did we get in Orion?

Some of you (if it happens to any one of you, it happens to all) managed to get to about 39%. It's an important point, because you can see that no matter what happened there, it has gotten more extreme here.

Yes. What percentage in Maldek?

Oh, I should think never any more than 35%.

But here we've gotten to . . . one of the previous masters says up to perhaps 61%?

Planet Earth's Mastery

Yes, because the planet herself has the ability to deal with it. The planet is a spiritual master, material master, teaching master and is working on quantum mastery. Because you are made up of the matter of the planet, this has allowed you to tolerate more. I do not think that any individual could exist in a 61% negative-energy experience for more than a few hours. That is why you must sleep. People who are living in a terrible situation—a prison, for example . . . even in the most enlightened prisons you would have 50 to 55% negativity simply because no one wants to be there, ofttimes even the employees. If you did not sleep you could not exist. When you sleep, even a fitful sleep, you are bathed in the energy of love, comfort, nurturance and many things on the soul level that you do not experience in your waking state.

Ah! I never knew that the planet enabled us to experience more of the discomfort, and that part of the reason we're on this planet is because of the nature of the being ensouling this planet. Right?

Yes. If it were not for this being's great evolution and mastery, you could not possibly see or be exposed to, much less participate in, such levels of negativity. As you know, I am not made of the energy or the matter of this planet. That is why I personally cannot tolerate such levels.

So did this being prepare herself for this? Was this part of the overall plan?

Yes. The being you know as Mother Earth is from the galaxy [system] Sirius, which is the home of all levels of mastery in this universe.

You've taught us all kinds of new things. When the first planet was destroyed, was this planet Earth brought in so that we could experience the deeper level?

Yes. It was brought in from Sirius so it would be certain that the planet would be highly evolved and significantly involved in mastery. She was working on quantum mastery before she left Sirius. In terms of the length of planetary existence and the beings who tend to exist as planets like this for a time in their lives, their lifetimes are so long as to be unaffected.

Will you talk to us again next time? You have knowledge we haven't gained from anyone else.

We will continue next time if you wish. Good night.

❖ *Robert's Comments on His Experience*

What was your experience?

At one point I could see this shape, which was long and diamondlike, though it didn't have the clarity of shape that we think of as a faceted diamond. Its significant characteristic was the lack of obvious detail. It was a strange experience, like seeing its outer perimeter clearly, but where the inner perimeter was fuzzy and unclear. It looked gray or dull silver.

Did it have any kind of emotional feeling?

No, it felt completely neutral. Actually, it felt incapable of experiencing anything we'd consider an emotion. It felt as if that just wasn't its function.

And it was doing something.

You're still talking about that long diamond shape. But did you feel anything from the being?

It was a lot more benevolent than I expected. Of course, Zoosh was there and really screening. It felt calm and reasoned.

Master of Discomfort
Discusses Light Transference
and Transforming Discomfort

November 7, 1996

hat application can we make of the ability of your diamond-shaped inverse galaxy to transfer light across vast distances? Can we use it when we begin to travel?

The intention in transferring light is to help it get where it can be the most assistance before it burns itself up and, ultimately, to help it achieve its fulfillment. Light will continue to regenerate until it reaches where it needs to go, interacts with whom it needs to interact with and accomplishes its intention, not unlike the reincarnational cycle for people.

It speeds to where it is going so that it can avoid disappointment, because light is generated according to needs elsewhere. It goes where it is sent and is generated because of needs.

Is this light in general?

Light in general is generated because it is needed. If it does not get to where it is going before its life span ends, it is disappointed and the energy that it becomes lies in abeyance for a long time before it is enthusiastic enough about life to be regenerated as light once again. To avoid this delay and discomfort, it is granted an acceleration to its point of necessity. Here is some homework so you can use this.

Homework: Use Feeling and Imagination to Improve Your Life

Make a list of all the things or circumstances that you want, then make notes in the margin of the feelings you have now. If the feelings are of need, that is fine. If they are of ambition, fine. If they are of love, fine. When your list is complete, get into the feelings associated with any one of these desires (or several if they are allied). Use your imagination. Travel with the feeling to any point in the future along the line of imagination and see yourself having that thing or circumstance. Be sure and use your imagination and feelings, because it will allow you to have a residual energy of which I will speak more later.

This can be used only for something benevolent, which might be a material possession or a circumstance that improves your life. When you have what you want—perhaps a job, a car, a home, whatever—imagine yourself using it and notice what happens to your feelings. They will invariably alter, no longer being anxious or needful; they will feel warm and happy. Spend as much time in that imagined creation as you can, enjoying your feelings. When you feel you have had enough, then relax and stay in those feelings.

As soon as possible, if it is a material possession, go out and touch something like it—go out and look at that car or house or one like it that is for sale. You don't necessarily have to buy it, but it would be good to touch it physically. If it is a job, try to go to where people do that job so you can be close to it. Recall the feelings when you imagined you were doing it or having it. This will help bring it to you. When done this way it does not replace the physical experience.

If you cannot go out and follow up—touch the house or the car, go near people who are doing the job—then your imagination will replace the physical experience. For those who are ill or incarcerated, that is all right. If you have those feelings of the experience from having generated them in the imagination and you go out and touch these things with those feelings, it personalizes those things for you and tends to bring them to you. You don't have to make plans to do it, although if you are in a plan to expand your business or something, continue. But you don't have to struggle to purchase or obtain that one thing. Continue your life as you will. Don't forget about it; from time to time recall the feelings and touch this object you would like to have.

If it is an improvement (for instance, feeling better if you are ill), then simply go into the feelings of imagining yourself well and try to ground yourself while you are doing it. If your legs need to get more healthy, while you are remembering your legs being healthy and filled with those feelings, reach down with your hands and touch your legs. If you can physicalize it, it tells this method of manifestation that brings the physical into your daily life that this is something you need to have physically as well as in fantasy.

That's brilliant! I wasn't thinking of that, but of going someplace that was too far away. I wanted a light beam to hop on, a transference of light.

Yes, of course. That can be applied to the same thing. One might wish to go to the Pleiades, for example; one can imagine a beauteous life there. It might be difficult to touch the Pleiades, but if you are living someplace where you can see them in the night sky, then after you imagine being there, go out and point your hand toward the Pleiades and stretch as if you were touching them—and energetically you will. Recall the feelings. Your next imagination might be better because your lightbody will probably have those experiences when you go there during your next two or three sleep times. It will be filled with many new images that will be a recollection of your lightbody's experience there.

How Light Is Generated and Fulfilled

That is beautiful. You stimulated another question. You talked about the generation of light. We have heard about the white light and gold light, but what's the generator?

Light is reactive. Why are there places where there is no particular light? It is because in a given universe some creators might have no need for the light. It does not mean that there is a discomfort there.

Like the Void.

Yes, the Void. If the light is not needed, it is not generated, it does not go there. The light is very much like parents welcoming a child, then doing the act of intimacy to bring it forth. First there is the welcome, then the act of intimacy, then the biological coming together with spirit to create the foundation for the baby in the form of the egg and sperm coming together. Light is very much the same.

If you were to see light before it was light it would look very much like droplets. Imagine for a moment a dark surface, perhaps a table or even one of your streets, and water running on the surface in droplets. You look through the water and it looks dark on the other side. We know the water is light, but it looks dark.

Light, before it becomes light, is this dark matter. It is not colorless; it is not even the opposite of itself. It is what I would call the precursor to ungenerated light. It floats about wherever it is. I have traveled by to see it happen; it is very interesting. Suddenly someone somewhere needs that particular light from that particular droplet of being. It might be no bigger than the head of a pin, or it could be very massive or anything in between. It looks like little dark droplets floating in space, then suddenly they become light.

To slow the process down, one might see that a portion of a droplet begins to be light, which spreads over and surrounds the droplet. Then the light penetrates it. It is quite bright, but does not radiate. You could be right next to it, but no light would illuminate you until the light goes fully into itself and illuminates its center. Once it has illuminated the center, it comes out and passes light to other things. First it must take care of itself; then it can assist others. This is an analogy, yes?

When it gets in the center, does it have to reflect off of something to project outward?

It does not. When it goes to the center of its being, there is the seed of the need for that light. When it finds its center, it discovers why and where it is needed. It immediately comes out and illuminates, because light's nature is to illuminate, at least when it finds out where and when it is needed. It must go inward to find where to go, then come out, celebrate its life and begin moving rapidly in the direction (in some cases to the time or dimension) where it is needed.

My Help in Speeding Light to Its Destination

That's where I'm able to assist it to get where it is going quickly, if it cannot reach its destination during half its lifetime. The half-life of light is quite long, about 180,000 years for this type of light. If it can get where it's going in 180,000 years, I don't bother with it, but if it would take longer than that to get there, I will help it if it needs help. It usually takes the light at least half its lifetime to do what needs to be done by those who call for it. Generally it takes light 180,000 years (of your now time) to accomplish its complete purpose, even when the being calling for it needs it only a few moments. The light itself cannot be fulfilled in its experience of interaction for 180,000 years.

What I do helps the being who is calling for the light, but it is really intended to help the light itself. There is only so much material that can be generated into light, and it can become disappointed when it cannot reach fulfillment by interacting with whoever needs it. It might interact for only two weeks to fulfill a being's need, but it still takes that light 180,000 years to get there to fulfill itself. After that it can return as a multiple octave. The light might have traveled through space as white light (usually, although sometimes as gold light), but when it is fulfilled it returns as every color. This demonstrates its fulfillment and initiates and anoints all matter it passes on its return home. If it gets home after fulfillment (or is assisted to get there by me or others) within 180,000 years, it can anoint all other disappointed matter in the place that is the precursor of light. It can cancel out and transform all the disappointment so that much more light is available to respond to the needs of others.

This is why it is important for light to be assisted to where it's going. It is important for it to achieve fulfillment so it can go back and create the potential for even more helpful, loving light to become available for all beings.

Some of the previous beings have talked about the translucent material of the Matrix. Is that when it returned home?

It goes to a place before that. The translucent material is not quite the same thing. Before it becomes activated it is in a place that looks like dark space, were you to pass through it quickly—like space without stars. But if you were to slow down you would see that it is made up of many merged droplets—some very large, some very small, all in slow motion—moving slowly, without any apparent purpose, expecting to be activated. Some are ready, but some are not if they are still dealing with disappointment from their failure to achieve fulfillment.

Even if it fails to achieve, it still returns to the same place.

Yes.

Patience as Space, a Universal Background Material

Is there such a place in each creation? Is it beyond the Orb? Where is this place?

This place is beyond the orbs and seems to surround them. Every thing within all creations is made up of this precursor of light, of light and love—and also, I believe, of patience. Patience is a material; it exists. If what is strictly space were defined, I would have to call it patience, because it is comfortable being undefined, yet celebrates its definition when it happens. When you move your hand quickly from one side to the other of your physical self, you feel atmosphere, but beyond your atmosphere in the space between the stars is a material I would define as patience.

What happens to that patience?

It is like a canvas before the artist paints it. It is born *as* the canvas rather than manufactured into the canvas. If one were there, one would feel totally patient and calm in it. Especially if one experiences it in vast amounts, one feels as if one could relax there forever. It is the ultimate relaxation. However, when something passes through it, especially something cheerful or brilliant such as light (especially fulfilled light), it celebrates that for a long time and only gradually does it return to being patience—space. But it retains the memory of that wonderful experience, the exhilaration, so it has something to wait for.

Perhaps something like light will come through and stop for a time. Or if a creation is being brought about, perhaps a planet will suddenly be there. It will surround and celebrate the planet, although the feeling will remain calm and patient. If you could consume this material, you would never have another anxious moment.

But the material that we see between the stars is part of our Creator. It's the patience of our Creator.

Yes. What I have described is beyond that. In moving through your creation, I feel that the material between the stars here is very much a first cousin of that material of patience, because it is very relaxing to be in it, very relaxing. It is more relaxing in a place where there is not a great deal of light to excite it.

Have you dissipated yourself and relaxed there in an effort not to be distracted by the discomfort?

Yes.

Is that where you go to rejuvenate?

Transforming My Discomfort into a Precursor of Emotion

That is where I go to release the material of discomfort when it becomes unbearable, although I am often assisted by other beings.

By the friends of the Creator or . . .

By the friends of the Creator, yes.

How does that work? The discomfort leads you there and it becomes transformed by that patience?

It seems to become transformed, but I think that it is removed from me, as one might remove some discomfort. It moves off as a mass, often encircled by a being. If it is a white lightbeing it will be encircled with white light or whatever color the being is. It will be taken by that being to wherever it needs to go and be transformed by that being. If I am in great discomfort, you see, I send out my need for assistance and these beings come to help.

Can other lightbeings transform the discomfort?.

They can't be with me all the time and transform the discomfort as it comes. They can only take some of the discomfort someplace and transform it very slowly. All discomfort is colored by the experience of that which fed it back. It will have to be sorted out

A given discomfort might have been fed back through the loop by someone who was injured and in pain. The excess pain that the individual could not experience, the too-great pain, is transformed very slowly by that lightbeing, all the while being nurtured and reminded that there is love, there is healing, there is nurturing. This is a very slow process. One does not do it with the whole mass, but bit by bit. It could easily take 50 experiential years for one lightbeing. Even with assistance it might take several years, so this job is not a minor commitment.

Who is doing this for you?

They are most often gold lightbeings, although sometimes white or silver lightbeings and occasionally what I call the rainbow beings, who have many colors. These are very sparkling beings who remind me of liquid light.

As they transform the discomfort, what does it become?

It goes into a holding area and becomes a precursor of emotion, which is a little different from light. If you could see emotion, it is like a

thick light, like a liquid, yet it looks electrical and has magnetic proper-
ties as well as anomalous zones within it where there is either no magnetic charge or where the charge is more extreme. One might get
tremendous activity in one zone and calm in another, not unlike the
emotions themselves. The discomfort goes into a precursor for that.
The precursor for emotions is like a spiral that goes upward, reaches a
certain point and comes back down. It is in a constant spiral—up,
down, up, down. Apparently it needs to be in motion, so the precursor
to emotion is *motion.*

How the Pools of Emotions Work

*Some of the beings have talked about going beyond the Orb, beyond the points of
light into no light, where there are centers of different emotions. Can you talk
about that?*

Oh, you mean the pools of emotions?

Yes. How does that work? Do the emotions that we feel come from there?

The emotions that you feel, yes, as well as emotions that any being
within any orb surrounded by those pools would feel, be it a creator or
an individual. All emotions are represented in a pool of emotion. If we
are going to scramble eggs, we need to have eggs, yes? There needs to
be the basic material for emotions, therefore the material is there. But
when it is there, it will not be only motion. It will usually be e-motion.
The precursor to eggs is not only chickens but also the food and the
spark of life from Creator that allows the being to become a chicken.
Thus emotion is there as a pool because beings within that orb are
already utilizing this emotion. It has to be ready beforehand *as* that
emotion, like a needed ingredient for a cake. It has already been transformed from motion to emotion.

But how does it get from there to our creation into our feeling?

It transfers instantaneously. I do not need to help it. It comes on the
basis of need. For example, when a baby is born, if the baby is born in a
loving, gentle way as was done in ancient communities on Earth (and
occasionally enlightened communities today—water birth, for example), the baby comes out and the emotions are relaxed. But many babies
have a traumatic birth. The hospital is a foreign environment the
mother is not used to; she is anxious, nervous and in pain.

The baby is not too pleased to leave its formerly pleasant environment, yet it must. Baby comes out through the mother and is perhaps
whacked on the bottom, which physicians do to get the baby to breathe.
(It is done for a reason, but it is not a pleasant way to arrive: "Welcome
to the Earth"—bang!—you know, not fun.) The baby immediately
needs several emotions it does not have, including shock.

Inside the mother the baby is generally in a very calm, relaxed, loving, nurtured state of being, so it does not possess these emotions.

When it comes out, it has its first trauma and needs those emotions immediately in order to communicate, to feed back to the medical staff what it wishes to hear, which is a cry. In order to cry it must breathe; that is the intention behind the whack on the bottom. So the baby immediately needs shock, surprise, pain—all of these emotions. And those come instantaneously.

How Emotions Flow through You

No kidding! You mean when I get angry at someone, I'm pulling that feeling from that point?

Yes. You do not *contain* emotions. Your emotional body is basically like an electromagnetic circuit. You can have feeling, you can have a subconscious feeling, but it is a *physical* feeling. In order to experience an emotion you've never felt before (or if an emotion comes in a flood), generally you don't have it, so it must come from that place beyond numbers to count—instantaneously. Most people do not carry emotions around with them unless something is going on for them constantly. If they are happy, in love or in pain, these are constant things. If they have studied to become spiritual or religious beings, they might maintain certain emotions for their own comfort or for their work. But most emotions are external; they arrive when they are needed, pass into the emotional body and then into the physical body to be expressed. They do not live in the body. *Feelings* live in the body, but not emotions.

Where do they go after you express them?

They return to the pool.

So you could be expressing an emotion that has been expressed ten billion times.

Yes, and it is interesting that you usually do not express it the same way. How many of you have experienced anger in different forms? That is because that anger is not the same product you have expressed before. The actual substance of that emotion has come from someplace. It might have been used by others or it might be in preparation to be used. You utilize it, you express it, then you no longer need it—unless you stay angry all the time, which most people do not. It returns home and is perhaps recycled to somebody else who needs anger.

But you do not retain it, certainly not when you go to sleep. You cannot carry those emotions around with you all the time unless you are practicing them when there is some major thing going on. If you are meditating, for instance, maintaining calm or insight or vision, you can maintain these emotions for a time, but when you go to sleep you release them to return the pools around the Orb, where they are recycled through those who need them.

You do maintain your *feeling self*, which physically transmits the message of the emotion to your body so that you can react. You could not carry a mass of emotions, because, for instance, if you were to carry a lot of negative emotions, you would be unable to express happiness.

Let us say you are in a theater watching a play and something funny happens. You burst out with laughter along with the rest of the audience. It is a tremendous moment, made even more so because of all the people who are sharing this funny moment. You are filled with that feeling, yet as the play continues there are dramatic moments and you release that humor, perhaps to use it later.

How is that related to DNA? I thought emotions were stored there with possibilities and so on.

DNA does not contain emotion. It might contain the program for potential experiences, which would act as an antenna to broadcast the need for an emotion, but it does not contain emotion itself. The only emotions you are born with are love and calm. Everything else comes later.

A clairvoyant looks at the aura and sees muddy colors. Even though those emotions have come and gone, they affect the aura, right?

Yes, they do. If there is great discomfort, it might even punch a hole in the aura. That dark space is where the light cannot penetrate, because it is like a wound that needs to be healed. A healer might look at the auric field around a person (which emanates from within that person, as you know) and see that dark space. That dark space is not so much discomfort as the absence of light. A healer might follow the track into the person, but will more likely follow the track outward, because it is there that the cause can be found. She follows the track out to where that emotion went, because all emotional experiences leave an imprint on the reservoir of emotion. This has a direct relationship to the akashic record.

The akashic record has been pictured as a library; it is a mental record. But there is also a feeling record, which is imprinted on the vessels or pools that hold emotions. Because every emotion that anyone has ever experienced within any of these orbs (which are surrounded by light and the pools of emotions) is imprinted on the reservoir of that emotion, healers can learn there what caused an emotion. As I say, sometimes you might find a reservoir imprint within a person, but it is much easier to go outward and find it.

Is there a being who ensouls or who is the body of that reservoir, or is it just a container?

No, it cannot just be a container. There is nothing like that.

That's why I'm asking. Is it somebody?

This I do not know. It is a worthy question, though.

When you have a football game with all its emotion and energy, where does it go?

It is cycled. It is like a liquid, a river of emotion running through. At one moment the football fan is happy, the next moment angry, the next moment sad, the next moment exultant. It is like a river that constantly circulates, coming and going all the time.

Then after the football game it all goes back to the source.

Not *after* the football game—*during* the football game. In every moment it is coming and going. It is like a stream in constant cyclic motion.

Is there an energy in addition to the emotion that's built up?

There might be. I don't think I have that knowledge.

Natural and Unnatural Human Birth

You've got a lot of knowledge. Let's backtrack. If a child is not born through the birth canal but by Caesarean birth, is there any consequence in its life? Does it miss something?

I can only give my opinion from what I have observed. (Please do not use this in any way to avoid this technology, because it is usually for a good reason.) But yes, it can affect the child. It might cause that child to be a little more anxious than other people, because what is expected does not occur. It also shatters the safety zone of the mother's womb. The womb is intended to have an exit, but not an unexpected doorway like this. So sometimes those children will be a little more nervous than others.

Is there anything that is turned on by the passage through the birth canal?

When birth is done in a gentle manner, such as water birth, the child passes through the canal and essentially swims out of its mother, which is the natural way for human beings. It is like an initiation into a different form of life, like the way a fish is born. It emerges from its mother and becomes physical for itself—motivated—and swims about. It might not come to the surface right away, because it is connected to its mother. But when it must come to the surface, no longer connected to its mother, it is a natural circumstance.

So the natural birth is better, especially if done in water or gently and lovingly, which means that the doctor or midwife or whoever is assisting is singing or saying loving things for the sake of mother and baby when receiving the baby. The baby hears and feels these loving emotions and gentleness. This allows baby to gradually come into the physical world. The birth canal operates not unlike death, where one goes through the veils and sometimes through the tube. It is a gentle transition. It is better that way.

My Work with Light

How did you discover you could help light?

Remember where I came from. I was originally a part of a being [the torus shaped like a figure eight in the previous chapter] whose whole purpose was to transfer light from one place to another. I was born with this ability.

You do it within your being?

I can do it within my being. Allowing for the general complexity of your universe, it is easier to use this device that we drew last time [the diamond-shaped galaxy he created; see previous chapter].

So you always transfer it within this universe.

Yes, that is my job here. The place I came from might cover the rest, but I do not know this because I have not been back. When I was a portion of it, I was doing it somewhat unconsciously. After I became conscious, I was no longer doing it, so I don't have the conscious memory of what it was doing. Ironic.

While you're working here, you can't go back there and check it out?

That's right. It is like being born with a talent. You don't know where it came from, but you can do it.

Transforming Discomfort

The little parallel inverse universe created to transform the discomfort—how does it work? Does it go back through a process where lightbeings take it from you?

Light becomes aware of itself. It suddenly finds itself being illuminated, but it is more like light shining inward. This is similar for inverses, you know. To create something inverse means that you are creating something that exists *before* the something that you're creating. It is not unlike what your Creator did when It moved to the midpoint of this creation and then went back to the beginning. When creating something inverse, you start with the status quo, then go back from that point.

In this little universe where your excess discomfort has been stored, do you or somebody else transmute it? Do lightbeings come?

I believe lightbeings come and transform it. Sometimes, I am told, there is a point at which a creator will come and [snaps fingers] take it all, transforming it instantaneously into something. This is like what I would call a resurrection.

The whole point here was to find a use for negativity, or discomfort, which you have found. [The Master of Discomfort chuckles.] The idea was to use the negativity and find a loving place for it without transforming it. But transforming it implies that it's excess.

Yes, that is excess. At the 1½% level it is not uncomfortable, but it does require growth

But is it okay, as far as this experiment is concerned, to transform that stuff you've accumulated? Is it just the excess?

Yes, it is excess once you get past 2%, in my experience.

If it is transformed, what about your plan to take a little of it to creations that can use it?

I will not take anything to them. The other creations will have accumulated it unintentionally.

So you'll go around and clean up the creations.

I will go around and help them if they wish. Remember that the other creations will be interested in integrating a little discomfort so they can grow. I will help them learn how to integrate a little bit of it; if there is any excess, others will transform it.

So you're going to be an Explorer Race person, too.

In a sense, yes. A race unto myself, yes?

A race unto yourself. How are we going to find you a peer? Eventually you're going to have go home and see who else . . .

Eventually I will go home, eh?

Yes.

But perhaps *you* will become peers. When you become creators, unless there is some transformation I do not know about, you will have 1½% discomfort. That will, I believe, make you a peer.

Then we can have some really great conversations.

Yes. Good night.

All right. Zoosh speaking. Our intention here has been to provide readers a means to see where you have been and with whom [chuckles] as well as where you are going and why. For the mind to give permission it must be provided with answers and be stimulated. It has been our intention to provide not only answers, but new questions, or at least that which stimulates new questions. When there are enough of you with new questions, we will be able to provide you (as always) with new answers.

This is why you have sometimes said in the past, "You have said this before, Zoosh. Why say this again?" As you accumulate new whys, I can provide you with new answers. Your whys become wisdom to provide to others. Good night.

Appendix

The Lucifer Gene

Zoosh

October 6, 1995

I will discuss the Lucifer gene today. This requires an explanation of how that which has come to be known as evil is constituted. When Creator headed this way to establish the creation you now reside in, He picked up Lucifer along the way. Well, He really picked up a being along the way who could provide a minor degree of annoyance, yet would be just what the Creator needed to stimulate growth. That being—a consultant, if you would—did not in any way have the personal capacity to produce anything beyond minor annoyance on his own.

Now, when Creator established this creation, for a long time He did not establish any beings or civilizations that required annoyance. Thus that being, whom we're going to call Lucifer, had little to do but hang around with Creator and watch the proceedings.

So way back Creator decided that He would allow a planet to have annoyance (it was an experiment) just to see what might occur. Now, Creator did not put too many beings on that planet, perhaps a grand total of about 40,000. Creator did not suddenly drop annoyance on them, but built it into their functioning organism to see how it would work. Remember, this is an experiment—Creator's experimenting also. Now, this particular experiment went awry. The beings had what I'm going to call the Lucifer gene within their systems, and not unlike you, they were born small and grew up to be big. Thus everything within them tended to expand. You might ask, "Does that mean that particles and the DNA expand?" No, but everything else does.

The First Experimental Group

Now, Creator put no restrictions on anything; It just said, "Well, let them be what they are and see what happens." These beings were highly emotional, and every time they had an emotion of annoyance it would tend to double itself. Well, I don't have to tell you what happened. Within an incredibly short amount of time they had pretty well wiped out the population in ways that are best left unsaid. So Creator had to take a cold, hard look at the empirical notion of annoyance as being something separate, or being something included. Creator considered it for a time; it was a long time before there was another planet with annoyance on it. Annoyance (as Lucifer) hung out with Creator and they commiserated, "What shall we do?"

Now, I'm going to give you the cycle of what happened, like a circuit. Something had happened to Lucifer that Lucifer did not like. As the beings began to expand their annoyance into what you now call negativity and so on, there was a point at which a feedback took place. Because the human being (these were a variation of human beings) has only so much capacity to contain this kind of energy, when they reached the limits of that capacity it fed back to Lucifer and Lucifer found himself becoming darker—more angry, more negative. I use the term "darker" because if you were to see negativity, it shows itself as a dense cloud. If you were to examine the cloud, after you remove the density you see gold, but the density shows itself as a darker shade.

When the life was over on that planet it took Lucifer quite awhile to get clear. Then he said to Creator, "I don't want this to happen again. I can't handle it." Lucifer said, "I can't control it, because when they have too much and feed it back to me (because it's basically my energy), I can't say no. I can't stop it."

Well, Creator understood this. He already knew that when beings are in their lightbodies, they naturally emanate light. And when they have more light than is needed and they are still emanating, it feeds back to Creator.

The same mechanics were happening with Lucifer, but in an unpleasant way. So Creator said to Lucifer, "This is probably a result of your being in My creation. Since light feeds back to Me, negativity is feeding back to you."

Lucifer replied, "Something's got to change, because I can't resist this."

Creator thought about it awhile and said, "We need to create control groups. We need to have one where that same process exists." And Lucifer pleaded, "No, please, not that." Then Creator said, "We also need to have a group that has the capacity to do more than they have the capacity to do." (Creators talk like this.)

Blank Strands in the Genetic Code

Lucifer asked, "How is that possible?"

And Creator said, "It is possible if I create within these beings an entire modification, not only physically but spiritually, of everything I am. I'll create several strands of blank spiritual and genetic code" (like a blank disk today).

Lucifer asked, "What good is that?"

Creator replied, "That allows them to build upon what they know and learn, potentially becoming more than I am now."

Lucifer said, "Wow!" but in different words. He continued, "What about this other group, the group that will probably do exactly the same as this other planet?" (By the way, that other planet that went negative, you know—that negative Sirian planet—is no longer in existence.) Lucifer said, "I don't think I can bear it."

The Second Step: The Control Group
and the Experimental Group

Creator said, "I'm going to ask you to do me a favor." (At that point Lucifer basically said, "Uh-oh!") Creator continued, "I have a plan to include these beings who are probably going to go negative like you said. I have a plan to include them with these other beings even though they're in different galaxies [systems]." Creator explained the plan as it's been laid out somewhat in the Explorer Race books. [See *The Explorer Race* and *ETs and the Explorer Race*.]

It was up to Lucifer to give his approval here, you know, because he was a consultant, but he said, "I still don't think I can bear the feedback of all that negative energy from this other planet, to say nothing of what might come from these people you're going to establish called the Explorer Race. Of course, I think it's a good idea, don't get me wrong. But I don't think I can bear this other energy from this planet of beings that are probably going to go negative in—of all places—Sirius." (Lucifer said that because so much benevolent and enlightened creation has occurred and is still occurring in Sirius.)

So Creator said, "I'll tell you what I'll do. I'll put a check on the circumstance in Sirius so that if it ever gets too much for you, those beings will return to their essential soul selves, transfer to a denser environment where I'm going to have the Explorer Race, and resume their existence but without so much discomfort, which ought to be all right with you. What do you say?"

Lucifer replied, "If you weren't a friend, I wouldn't do this" (in their kind of talk).

I've given you this rough background, greatly condensed. You can read more about it in the Explorer Race series. I also want you to understand something important: I am not saying you are satanic as beings, but since Lucifer himself has the capacity to provide only about 2% negativity, or minor annoyance (that's his personal capacity; he can't do any more), it's *you* who expand negative energy. This isn't blaming you at all, but this amplification that happens empowers you very much. As you change and become more light and stop feeding back negativity to Lucifer (eventually even start feeding back light to Creator), the Lucifer energy will begin to die down and there will no longer be what I'd call the unnatural, dark side of Lucifer (also known as Satan). I'm including these biblical terms here because I want you to understand this within the context of your civilization as well as scientifically.

The Lucifer Gene

You have within you *right now* an entire strand of genetic substance that I'm going to call the Lucifer gene. What I call a strand your scientists would call a gene. Because your scientists cannot yet study genetic substance at a high enough magnification while it's still living and functioning, they don't understand that what they can identify as a gene is actually a strand.

I'm going to recommend that scientists run a project of about ten years to test for the Lucifer gene amongst violent people or people who are self-destructive, as long as everyone gives full permission (your test subjects might surprise you and be very willing to cooperate). You will observe this gene and see how well-developed it is in people who have perpetrated violence upon themselves or others. You will discover that it is not physiological things that are able to change this gene—for example, cutting it out surgically won't work; it'll grow back, because all genetic substance has duplicate entries within all other genetic substance. So don't even think about trying that route. But there are various spiritual actions and certain light therapies that are able to modify the gene. Experiment with light (not heat) in the range from white to gold (you might even play with pink). Try to make the light as pure and true as possible, optical light, and beam it on the people. I don't want to tell you too much because some of this has actually been done; you can find the material.

You scientists will discover over time that the patterning in the gene tends to erase, and after a while the gene looks like something analogous to a record that has not yet been cut with grooves. That's what you want. You will discover in the process of light therapy and spiritual practices that much more is done when people are free to pursue something benevolent. You will also discover that your test subjects will often need to express some aggressive behavior separate from your therapy (make sure it isn't self-destructive—punching bags are acceptable as long as they are not alive).

A few months ago Lucifer got to the point where he said to Creator, "I can't take it anymore." Even though that civilization has ended on Sirius and those souls are still being transferred en masse to a denser dimension on Earth, there is so much negativity and self-destructive behavior on Earth now that your cumulative discomfort is feeding back so much to Lucifer that he can't take it.

So Creator said to Lucifer, "Now comes the true test. You don't have to take it anymore. Now is the time that we give them their opportunity to become more than I am." Thus a few months ago Creator basically granted you the capacity to have the rights, responsibilities, abilities, practices, *consequences* and rewards of being Creators, eventually to combine into one, and to some extent function as one on the unconscious level.

The Next Step: Dreams and the New Alchemy

For these past few months your dream life has become wild, if not bizarre. Sometimes you are so involved in the other worlds that being in this physical world, what you call being awake, becomes less of an experience than being in the other worlds, to the extent that in the middle of the day you might suddenly need to lie down and go to sleep because you are being called in the other worlds. Now, what's going on in those worlds?

Your physiological capacity to transform—physically, emotionally and, most important, spiritually—negative energy into gold light is being restructured. We're talking about an *alchemical reaction,* the changing of one substance into another. The original idea to change lead into gold originated from changing dense energy into gold light. (If you look at dense energy, the color is not dissimilar to the color of lead.)

Here we have a circumstance in which this sudden responsibility and its rewards have been literally laid in your laps. You might say, "Well, look at how extreme things are becoming in the Middle East and Africa and all kinds of terrible things happening in other places." I could say, "Yes, that's true." However, your communication system is also so good now that even a skirmish that happens someplace is discovered very quickly. They can no longer go unnoticed for many months as in the past. Your physical day-to-day life waking life is no longer sufficient. You have to become functionally operative on the other levels.

For a long time dream therapy has been available. I want dream therapists to know they're going to be needed in a big way and to start training people, because there's not enough of you. The rest of you need to understand that a large part of what's going on when you dream is absolutely real. It's happening on other dimensions but does not include you at all. Because some of these dreams are so extreme and bizarre and sometimes violent, it does affect your psyche. That is *built in.* Creator says to Lucifer, "Well, this is the test. If I allowed them to be able to process all this excess negative energy on the other planes (referring to the dream time) without their experiencing any side effects at all, they'd have no motivation to change anything. They'd say, 'Oh well, it's only bad dreams—not very much fun, but life goes on.'"

Creator linked that with your conscious self and said, "Let's have it affect their minds, because their minds are so restless that they cannot ignore things." So Creator let it affect your psyche so that you will be motivated to change lead into gold, as it were.

What You Can Do

I need to give you a little homework. You might have to set your alarm clock a little sooner. If you should have unsettling dreams at night, know that if you can remember those dreams, you will have the feelings of them, the total experience of having been there, but you will not see yourself there. If you see something happening, it's not you. You'll just be a witness, but *a fully participating witness*. One of the most important levels of creator training is to be able to feel what other beings feel. Otherwise you could make capricious mistakes without ever understanding the gravity of what you have done. In creator training you *must* be able to feel others' injuries.

After a nightmare you will wake up with those horrible feelings just as if it is happening to you then and there. That is, the sensitive, sensing you *is* there in the dream state. You feel everything that everyone went through in that dream so you *completely understand* on the physical level. The mind cannot understand this alone and must have a sensing mechanism, which is the physical self. So while you're on sensory over-load your senses say, "I can't take anymore!" (just as Lucifer said to Creator). Then you rejoin your physical self, wake up and experience that overload (fear, loathing, whatever).

If possible I want you to strike a bell or do something immediately. Some of you might chant "om"—that's fine. If you pray, ask for benevolent love to bless and transform all you have felt. If you can, visualize gold light. This is alchemical training to transform the pain of others *through being aware of it*. It is also foundational training to know what others are feeling around you. You will be unable to ignore what you feel.

The Lucifer gene within you was created to amplify discomfort up to a point, feed it back to Lucifer until he's had enough, but now there's a block there. Lucifer doesn't feed it back to you, but you are no longer able to feed it to him. Therefore you *must* be the magician and transform it.

As much as you can these days, I want you to think and feel gold light. And if you can think, feel (especially feel) warmth in your physical self (it has to do with love), that works even better. Your responsibility is to transform the Lucifer gene to erase the expansion and allow it to become cleansed, purified and inactive. But you had to have the

Lucifer gene within you to be able to experience, to act and to be able to react to consequences. This is where you are different from your Creator. Your Creator does not in Its natural self have the Lucifer gene. Lucifer is a consultant—a friend, as it were, but not a portion of Creator. *You* have the Lucifer gene, even within your spiritual self, although there it is overwhelmed by gold light, because that is your nature. If you understand that the Lucifer gene can be transformed, then you will not expect Lucifer or Creator to do it for you. This is something that Creator deigns that you do for yourself.

I brought this up because this is much more widespread than you realize, and it is being compounded as one compounds interest. The more you have, the more it grows, compounded by the fact that you can no longer feed back that negativity to Lucifer. Even now Lucifer is being transformed by Creator because Creator, of course, feels responsible, obligated. When Creators are responsible, they must *act*. They can't just sit back and say, "Well, sorry."

What you have given us as homework is something one person does. What about a meditation group? It feels very important.

Group Alchemy: Love (Heat) and Gold Light

Yes, let me give you something, but this will be different from other meditation groups. This is what I'd like you to do, and it will be somewhat comradely. When you come together as a group, I'd like you to initially talk about whatever's bothering you. Don't come together just for a spiritual activity, but talk about what's bothering you even if you get upset. *This is part of the training.* First, do that. It's like a support group. It will bring up discomfort—this is a test—so talk it over with the group and make sure everybody's okay with this. Then I want you to focus on the physical warmth you feel in your chest or solar plexus. You can hold your hands over your body to create it—however you want to do it. But it is not a meditation or a visualization; it is a *physical warmth.* Bring up that warmth and experience the heat, which is the physical evidence of love (wherein you are basically, as a thought person, allowing yourself to be loving, and as a physical person loving yourself).

Then if you can I'd like you to imagine gold light there *while* you're feeling the heat. Now, that's going to be tough. It's surprisingly difficult to do that because the gold light will feel like a thought and you'll find yourself having to be totally physical—absolutely, totally focused. This is where alchemical reactions come in—transforming one substance to another. You must be able to focus totally on one thing and then focus totally on two things. Some people won't be able to feel the heat right off, but they will be able to feel the gold light. Eventually I want the group to be able to feel the physical heat anywhere across your chest, the solar plexus—the front part of the body. Feeling that warmth and holding it will be easier in a group because it tends to be amplified. It becomes a very powerful, loving energy.

At some point someone can reach over and strike a chime or something. Then while you maintain the warmth, include the feeling of gold light. The minute you start *picturing* gold light, the warmth will usually leave because you are attempting to think instead of feel. Feeling is where the power is; *that* is how things are transformed.

So practice gold light to become familiar with gold light as a feeling. Then include the feeling of gold light *with* the feeling of this warmth, which is love. The reason this is a graduate class, a more advanced class, is that when you bring up discomfort, you'll have something to transform. If you simply show up and immediately go into love or gold light or both, it's a little too easy. I want it to be challenging, something you can rise to. And once any individual in the group learns how to do this, you can do this anywhere at any time. But in a group it will be much more powerful. Eventually you'll be able to do it in a very large group, and it will be overwhelming; it will be ecstatic. It is the closest thing you can feel—that total love, that total gold light—to the creator energy that you are, that your Creator intended you to be.

Your Creator is white light and love, but your Creator wants you to be more. And that more is gold light, because gold light contains and is rooted in white light. *But gold light has the capacity to transform.*

When the group gets good at feeling that heat, which is love, stay in it for at least ten or fifteen minutes. In the beginning don't try to combine the gold light and the love. But eventually you want to stay in that gold light. If at any time the warmth goes away after you've included the gold light with the loving feeling, immediately let go of the concept/feeling of gold light and return to the heat, which is love. That's your foundation; you've got to have that.

Transformation

First you'll notice the transformation within the group, which is a nice bonus. (Self-interest is definitely involved here.) As the group grows (new members would have to go through the original training), people in the group might break off and form new groups. That's fine; we want that. At certain times maybe all the groups might come together. If several hundred people would do this together it would be so magnificent that a totally unconscious person (as you might say) could be walking a block away and suddenly have a great sense of well-being even if they're totally angry and upset about something. They would find themselves cheerful about people they're passing on the street, and it could transform their lives. It might not be permanent, but it could make a real change.

When you are this heat, by the way, just feel it for yourself; it broadcasts naturally. As you know, both heat and love naturally radiate. (Anybody who's ever gone into a room where someone's feeling total love, you know it even if they're not looking at you.) That makes it very simple; it just happens.

If you get enough people doing this, you're going to see some good changes around here. What you learn absolutely tends to translate to other levels of yourself. When you practice within this group and you're feeling this and transforming things, you'll get so used to doing this it will become not second nature, but *first* nature. It's something you will begin to feel regularly, all the time—driving, going to the market, working, with your family. It will permeate you so totally that eventually it will affect your actual senses. It has the capacity to cleanse the Lucifer gene, so that when you start having a nightmare, your senses will begin broadcasting that energy and the nightmare will diminish or even transform itself.

This has everything to do with creator training and unification amongst all people.

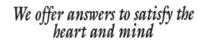

Light Technology Publishing Presents **THE**

EXPLORER RACE SERIES

The Origin...
The Purpose...
The Future of
Humanity...

the **EXPLORER RACE**

Zoosh, End-Time Historian
through Robert Shapiro

Zoosh & Others through Robert Shapiro

**"After all the words that we put out, ultimately the intention
is to persuade people's minds, otherwise known as giving their
minds the answers that their minds hunger for so that their
minds can get out of the way and let their hearts take them
to where they would naturally go anyway."** – Zoosh/Robert Shapiro

THE SERIES

Humans — creators in training — have a purpose and destiny so heart-warmingly, profoundly glorious that it is almost unbelievable from our present dimensional perspective. Humans are great lightbeings from beyond this creation, gaining experience in dense physicality. This truth about the great human genetic experiment of the Explorer Race and the mechanics of creation is being revealed for the first time by Zoosh and his friends through superchannel Robert Shapiro. These books read like adventure stories as we follow the clues from this creation that we live in out to the Council of Creators and beyond.

THE EXPLORER RACE SERIES

① the EXPLORER RACE

This book presents humanity in a new light, as the explorers and problem-solvers of the universe, admired by the other galactic beings for their courage and creativity. Some topics are: the Genetic Experiment on Earth; The ET in You: Physical Body, Emotion, Thought and Spirit; The Joy, the Glory and the Challenge of Sex; ET Perspectives; The Order: Its Origin and Resolution; Coming of Age in the Fourth Dimension and much more!

600 pages $25.00

② ETs and the EXPLORER RACE

In this book Robert channels Joopah, a Zeta Reticulan now in the ninth dimension, who continues the story of the great experiment — the Explorer Race — from the perspective of his race. The Zetas would have been humanity's future selves had not humanity re-created the past and changed the future.

$14.95

③ Origins and the Next 50 Years

Some chapters are: THE ORIGINS OF EARTH RACES: Our Creator and Its Creation, The White Race and the Andromedan Linear Mind, The Asian Race, The African Race, The Fairy Race and the Native Peoples of the North, The Australian Aborigines, The Origin of Souls. THE NEXT 50 YEARS: The New Corporate Model, The Practice of Feeling, Benevolent Magic, Future Politics, A Visit to the Creator of All Creators. ORIGINS OF THE CREATOR: Creating with Core Resonances; Jesus, the Master Teacher; Recent Events in Explorer Race History; On Zoosh, Creator and the Explorer Race. $14.95

BOOK MARKET

A reader's guide to the extraordinary books we publish, print and market for your enLightenment.

ORDER NOW!
1-800-450-0985
or Fax 1-800-393-7017
Or use order form at end

♦ BOOKS BY LYNN BUESS

CHILDREN OF LIGHT, CHILDREN OF DENIAL

In his fourth book Lynn calls upon his decades of practice as counselor and psychotherapist to explore the relationship between karma and the new insights from ACOA/ Co-dependency writings.

$8.95 Softcover 150p   ISBN 0-929385-15-2

NUMEROLOGY FOR THE NEW AGE

An established standard, explicating for contemporary readers the ancient art and science of symbol, cycle, and vibration. Provides insights into the patterns of our personal lives. Includes life and personality numbers.

$11.00 Softcover 262p   ISBN 0-929385-31-4

NUMEROLOGY: NUANCES IN RELATIONSHIPS

The foremost spokesman for numerology and human behavior focuses on relationships. With clear and direct style he identifies the archetypal patterns of each numerical combination. By providing clues to conscious and unconscious issues, Lynn gives the reader choices of behavior in relationships.

$13.75 Softcover 310p   ISBN 0-929385-23-3

♦ EILEEN ROTA

THE STORY OF THE PEOPLE

An exciting history of our coming to Earth, our traditions, our choices and the coming changes, it can be viewed as a metaphysical adventure, science fiction or the epic of all of us brave enough to know the truth. Beautifully written and illustrated.

$11.95 Softcover 209p   ISBN 0-929385-51-9

♦ GUIDE BOOK

THE NEW AGE PRIMER
Spiritual Tools for Awakening

A guidebook to the changing reality, it is an overview of the concepts and techniques of mastery by authorities in their fields. Explores reincarnation, belief systems and transformative tools from astrology to crystals.

$11.95 Softcover 206p   ISBN 0-929385-48-9

♦ GABRIEL H. BAIN

LIVING RAINBOWS

A fascinating "how-to" manual to make experiencing human, astral, animal and plant auras an everyday event. Series of techniques, exercises and illustrations guide the reader to see and hear aural energy. Spiral-bound workbook.

$14.95 Softcover 134p   ISBN 0-929385-42-X

ON BECOMING

YHWH through
Arthur Fanning

Knowing the power of the light that you are. Expansion of the pituitary gland and strengthening the physical structure. Becoming more of you.

F101 $10

HEALING MEDITATIONS/ KNOWING SELF

Knowing self is knowing God. Knowing the pyramid of the soul is knowing the body. Meditation on the working of the soul and the use of the gold light within the body.

F102 $10

MANIFESTATION & ALIGNMENT with the POLES

Alignment of the meridians with the planet's grid system. Connect the root chakra with the center of the planet.

F103 $10

THE ART OF SHUTTING UP

Gaining the power and the wisdom of the quiet being that resides within the sight of thy Father.

F104 $10

CONTINUITY OF CONSCIOUSNESS

Trains you in the powerful state of waking meditation.

F105 $25 (3-tape set)

MERGING THE GOLDEN LIGHT REPLICAS OF YOU

The awakening of the Christ consciousness.

F107 $10

SOUL EVOLUTION FATHER

Lord God Jehovah through Arthur Fanning

Lord God Jehovah Jehovah is back with others, to lead humanity out of its fascination with density into an expanding awareness that each human is a god with unlimited power and potential.

$12.95 Softcover 200p

ISBN 0-929385-33-0

SIMON

A compilation of some of the experiences Arthur has had with the dolphins, which triggered his opening and awakening as a channel.

$9.95 Softcover 56p

ISBN 0-929385-32-2

THE SOUL REMEMBERS
A Parable on Spiritual Transformation
Carlos Warter, M.D.

What is the purpose of human life? What is the reality of this world I find myself in? A cosmic perspective on essence, individuality and relationships. Through the voices of archetypes of consciousness, this journey through dimensions assists the reader in becoming personally responsible for cocreating heaven on Earth.

$14.95 210p

ISBN 0-929385-36-

THE LEGEND OF THE EAGLE CLAN
with Derren A. Robb

This book brings a remembrance out of the past . . . magnetizing the lost, scattered members of the Eagle Clan back together and connecting them on an inner level with their true nature within the Brotherhood of Light.

$12.95 Softcover 281p

ISBN 0-929385-68-3

BOOK MARKET

A reader's guide to the extraordinary books we publish, print and market for your enLightenment.

7

♦ RICHARD DANNELLEY

THE SEDONA VORTEX GUIDEBOOK

200-plus pages of channeled, never-before-published information on the vortex energies of Sedona and the techniques to enable you to use the vortexes as multidimensional portals to time, space and other realities.

$14.95 Softcover 169p   ISBN 0-929385-25-X

♦ AI GVHDI WAYA

**NEW!
PATH OF THE MYSTIC**

The author shares her own journey through Native American stories of her discovery — and how you can access the many teachers, too. Walk the path of the mystic daily and transform from chrysalis into butterfly. "Our best teachers are inside ourselves."

$11.95 Softcover 114p   ISBN 0-929385-47-0

♦ NANCY ANNE CLARK, Ph.D.

EARTH IN ASCENSION

About the past, present and future of planet Earth and the role humans will play in her progress. Nothing can stop Earth's incredible journey into the unknown. You who asked to participate in the birthing of Gaia into the fifth dimension were chosen!

$14.95 Softcover 136p   ISBN 0-9648307-6-0

♦ ELLWOOD NORQUIST

**WE ARE ONE:
A Challenge to Traditional Christianity**

Is there a more fulfilling way to deal with Christianity than by perceiving humankind as sinful, separate and in need of salvation? Humanity is divine, one with its Creator, and already saved.

$14.95 Softcover 236p   ISBN 0-9646995-2-4

♦ RICH WORK & ANN GROTH

AWAKEN TO THE HEALER WITHIN

An empowerment of the soul, an awakening within and a releasing of bonds and emotions that have held us tethered to physical and emotional disharmonies. A tool to open the awareness of your healing ability.

$16.50 Softcover 330p   ISBN 0-9648002-0-9

♦ NICOLE CHRISTINE

TEMPLE OF THE LIVING EARTH

An intimate true story that activates the realization that the Living Earth is our temple and that we are all priests and priestesses to the world.
A call to the human spirit to celebrate life and awaken to its cocreative partnership with Earth.

$16.00 Softcover 150p   ISBN 0-9647306-0-X

◆ B O O K M A R K E T O R D E R F O R M ◆

	No. Copies	Total
ACUPRESSURE FOR THE SOUL	$11.95	$
ARCTURUS PROBE	$14.95	$
BEHOLD A PALE HORSE	$25.00	$
CACTUS EDDIE	$11.95	$
CHANNELING: EVOLUTIONARY . . .	$ 9.95	$
COLOR MEDICINE	$11.95	$
FOREVER YOUNG	$ 9.95	$
GUARDIANS OF THE FLAME	$14.95	$
GREAT KACHINA	$11.95	$
I'M OK, I'M JUST MUTATING	$ 6.00	$
KEYS TO THE KINGDOM	$14.95	$
LEGEND OF THE EAGLE CLAN	$12.95	$
LIVING RAINBOWS	$14.95	$
MAHATMA I & II	$19.95	$
MILLENNIUM TABLETS	$14.95	$
NEW AGE PRIMER	$11.95	$
PATH OF THE MYSTIC	$11.95	$
POISONS THAT HEAL	$14.95	$
PRISONERS OF EARTH	$11.95	$
SEDONA VORTEX GUIDE BOOK	$14.95	$
SHADOW OF SAN FRANCISCO PEAKS	$ 9.95	$
THE SOUL REMEMBERS	$14.95	$
STORY OF THE PEOPLE	$11.95	$
THIS WORLD AND THE NEXT ONE	$ 9.95	$
ROBERT SHAPIRO/ARTHUR FANNING		
SHINING THE LIGHT	$12.95	$
SHINING THE LIGHT — BOOK II	$14.95	$
SHINING THE LIGHT — BOOK III	$14.95	$
SHINING THE LIGHT — BOOK IV	$14.95	$

BOOKS PUBLISHED BY LIGHT TECHNOLOGY PUBLISHING

	No. Copies	Total
ROBERT SHAPIRO		
ETs AND THE EXPLORER RACE	$14.95	$
THE EXPLORER RACE	$25.00	$
EXPLORER RACE: ORIGINS . . .	$14.95	$
ARTHUR FANNING		
SOUL, EVOLUTION, FATHER	$12.95	$
SIMON	$ 9.95	$
WESLEY H. BATEMAN		
DRAGONS & CHARIOTS	$ 9.95	$
KNOWLEDGE FROM THE STARS	$11.95	$
LYNN BUESS		
CHILDREN OF LIGHT, CHILDREN . . .	$ 8.95	$
NUMEROLOGY: NUANCES . . .	$13.75	$
NUMEROLOGY FOR THE NEW AGE	$11.00	$
RUTH RYDEN		
THE GOLDEN PATH	$11.95	$
LIVING THE GOLDEN PATH	$11.95	$
DOROTHY ROEDER		
CRYSTAL CO-CREATORS	$14.95	$
NEXT DIMENSION IS LOVE	$11.95	$
REACH FOR US	$14.95	$
HALLIE DEERING		
LIGHT FROM THE ANGELS	$15.00	$
DO-IT-YOURSELF POWER TOOLS	$25.00	$
JOSHUA DAVID STONE, PH.D.		
COMPLETE ASCENSION MANUAL	$14.95	$
SOUL PSYCHOLOGY	$14.95	$
BEYOND ASCENSION	$14.95	$
HIDDEN MYSTERIES	$14.95	$

	No. Copies	Total
ASCENDED MASTERS	$14.95	$
VYWAMUS/JANET McCLURE		
AHA! THE REALIZATION BOOK	$11.95	$
LIGHT TECHNIQUES	$11.95	$
SANAT KUMARA	$11.95	$
SCOPES OF DIMENSIONS	$11.95	$
THE SOURCE ADVENTURE	$11.95	$
PRELUDE TO ASCENSION	$29.95	$
LEIA STINNETT		
A CIRCLE OF ANGELS	$18.95	$
THE TWELVE UNIVERSAL LAWS	$18.95	$
ALL MY ANGEL FRIENDS	$10.95	$
ANIMAL TALES	$ 7.95	$
WHERE IS GOD?	$ 6.95	$
JUST LIGHTEN UP!	$ 9.95	$
HAPPY FEET	$ 6.95	$
WHEN THE EARTH WAS NEW	$ 6.95	$
THE ANGEL TOLD ME	$ 6.95	$
COLOR ME ONE	$ 6.95	$
ONE RED ROSE	$ 6.95	$
EXPLORING THE CHAKRAS	$ 6.95	$
CRYSTALS R FOR KIDS	$ 6.95	$
WHO'S AFRAID OF THE DARK	$ 6.95	$
BRIDGE BETWEEN TWO WORLDS	$ 6.95	$

BOOKS PRINTED OR MARKETED BY LIGHT TECHNOLOGY PUBLISHING

Access Your Brain's Joy Center	$14.95 ___ $ ___
Awaken to the Healer Within	$16.50 ___ $ ___
Earth in Ascension	$14.95 ___ $ ___
Galaxy Seven	$15.95 ___ $ ___
Innana Returns	$14.00 ___ $ ___
It's Time To Remember	$19.95 ___ $ ___
I Want To Know	$7.00 ___ $ ___
Life Is The Father Within	$19.75 ___ $ ___
Life On the Cutting Edge	$14.95 ___ $ ___
Look Within	$9.95 ___ $ ___
Mayan Calendar Birthday Book	$12.95 ___ $ ___
Medical Astrology	$29.95 ___ $ ___
Our Cosmic Ancestors	$9.95 ___ $ ___
Out-of-Body Exploration	$8.95 ___ $ ___
Principles To Remember and Apply	$11.95 ___ $ ___
Song of Sirius	$8.00 ___ $ ___
Soul Recovery and Extraction	$9.95 ___ $ ___
Spirit of The Ninja	$7.95 ___ $ ___
Temple of The Living Earth	$16.00 ___ $ ___
The Only Planet of Choice	$14.95 ___ $ ___
The Pleiadian Agenda	$15.00 ___ $ ___

The Transformative Vision	$14.95 ___ $ ___
Voices of Spirit	$13.00 ___ $ ___
We Are One	$14.95 ___ $ ___

Lee Carroll

Kryon–Book I, The End Times	$12.00 ___ $ ___
Kryon–Book II, Don't Think Like.	$12.00 ___ $ ___
Kryon–Book III, Alchemy of . . .	$14.00 ___ $ ___
Kryon–The Parables of Kryon	$17.00 ___ $ ___
Kryon–The Journey Home	$15.00 ___ $ ___

Richard Dannelley

Sedona Power Spot/Guide	$11.00 ___ $ ___
Sedona: Beyond The Vortex	$12.00 ___ $ ___

Tom Dongo: Mysteries of Sedona

Mysteries of Sedona — Book I	$6.95 ___ $ ___
Alien Tide — Book II	$7.95 ___ $ ___
Quest — Book III	$9.95 ___ $ ___
Unseen Beings, Unseen Worlds	$9.95 ___ $ ___
Merging Dimensions	$14.95 ___ $ ___

Barbara Marciniak

Bringers of the Dawn	$12.95 ___ $ ___
Earth	$12.95 ___ $ ___

MSI

Ascension!	$11.95 ___ $ ___
First Thunder	$12.95 ___ $ ___
Second Thunder	$17.95 ___ $ ___
Enlightenment	$15.95 ___ $ ___

Preston B. Nichols with Peter Moon

Montauk Project	$15.95 ___ $ ___
Montauk Revisited	$19.95 ___ $ ___
Pyramids of Montauk	$19.95 ___ $ ___
Encounter in the Pleiades . . .	$19.95 ___ $ ___
The Black Sun	$19.95 ___ $ ___

Lyssa Royal and Keith Priest

Preparing For Contact	$12.95 ___ $ ___
Prism of Lyra	$11.95 ___ $ ___
Visitors From Within	$12.95 ___ $ ___

Amorah Quan Yin

The Pleiadian Workbook	$16.00 ___ $ ___
Pleiadian Perspectives on . . .	$14.00 ___ $ ___

ASCENSION MEDITATION TAPES

Joshua David Stone, Ph.D.

Ascension Activation Meditation	S101	$12.00	___	$ ___
Tree of Life Ascension Meditation	S102	$12.00	___	$ ___
Mt. Shasta Ascension Activation Meditation	S103	$12.00	___	$ ___
Kabbalistic Ascension Activation	S104	$12.00	___	$ ___
Complete Ascension Manual Meditation	S105	$12.00	___	$ ___
Set of all 5 tapes		$49.95		

Vywamus/Barbara Burns

The Quantum Mechanical You (6 tapes)	B101-6	$40.00	___	$ ___

Taka

Magical Sedona through the Didgeridoo	T101	$12.00	___	$ ___

Brian Grattan

Seattle Seminar Resurrection 1994 (12 tapes)	M102	$79.95	___	$ ___

YHWH/Arthur Fanning

On Becoming	F101	$10.00	___	$ ___
Healing Meditations/Knowing Self	F102	$10.00	___	$ ___
Manifestation & Alignment w/ Poles	F103	$10.00	___	$ ___
The Art of Shutting Up	F104	$10.00	___	$ ___
Continuity of Consciousness	F105	$25.00	___	$ ___
Merging the Golden Light Replicas of You	F107	$10.00	___	$ ___

Kryon/Lee Carroll

Seven Responsibilities of the New Age	K101	$10.00	___	$ ___
Co-Creation in the New Age	K102	$10.00	___	$ ___
Ascension and the New Age	K103	$10.00	___	$ ___
Nine Ways to Raise the Planet's Vibration	K104	$10.00	___	$ ___
Gifts and Tools of the New Age	K105	$10.00	___	$ ___

Jan Tober

Crystal Singer	J101	$12.00	___	$ ___

BOOKSTORE DISCOUNTS HONORED — SHIPPING 15% OF RETAIL

☐ CHECK ☐ MONEY ORDER

CREDIT CARD: ☐ MC ☐ VISA

#_____

Exp. date:_____

Signature:_____

(U.S. FUNDS ONLY) PAYABLE TO:

LIGHT TECHNOLOGY
PUBLISHING

P.O. BOX 1526 • SEDONA • AZ 86339

(520) 282-6523 FAX: (520) 282-4130

1-800-450-0985

Fax 1-800-393-7017

NAME/COMPANY _____

ADDRESS _____

CITY/STATE/ZIP _____

PHONE _____ FAX _____

E-MAIL _____

SUBTOTAL: $_____

SALES TAX: $_____
(8.5% – AZ residents only)

SHIPPING/HANDLING: $_____
($4 Min.: 15% of orders over '30)

CANADA S/H: $_____
(20% of order)

TOTAL AMOUNT ENCLOSED: $_____

All prices in US$. Higher in Canada and Europe. Books are available at all national distributors as well as the following international distributors:

CANADA: DEMPSEY (604) 683-5541 FAX (604) 683-5521 • ENGLAND/EUROPE: WINDRUSH PRESS LTD. 0608 652012/652025 FAX 0608 652125

AUSTRALIA: GEMCRAFT BOOKS (03) 888-0111 FAX (03) 888-0044 • NEW ZEALAND: PEACEFUL LIVING PUB. (07) 571-8105 FAX (07) 571-8513